KW-110-830

The International Monetary System and the Less Developed Countries

Graham <u>Bird</u>

Senior Lecturer in Economics
University of Surrey

Second Edition

WITHDRAWN

© Graham Bird 1978, 1982

All rights reserved. No part of this publication may be
reproduced or transmitted, in any form or by any means,
without permission

First Edition 1978
Second Edition 1982

Published by
THE MACMILLAN PRESS LTD
London and Basingstoke
Companies and representatives
throughout the world

ISBN (hardcover) 0 333 33002 1
ISBN (paperback) 0 333 33004 8

Printed in Hong Kong

The paperback edition of this book is sold subject to the
condition that it shall not, by way of trade or otherwise, be lent,
resold, hired out, or otherwise circulated without the publisher's
prior consent, in any form of binding or cover other than that
in which it is published and without a similar condition including
this condition being imposed on the subsequent purchaser

To Mum, Dad, Heather, Alan and Anne

Contents

Preface   xi

1 INTRODUCTION   1
  Background   1
  Balance-of-Payments Problems and International Monetary
    Issues in LDCs   3
  Alternative Policy Approaches   5
  LDCs and the Reform of the International Monetary System   6

2 RELATIONS BETWEEN THE IMF AND LDCs   10
  The Relationship between Development and Stabilisation   12
  Relations between the IMF and LDCs: A Historical
    Perspective   15
  Concluding Remarks   23

3 PRIMARY-PRODUCT PRICE INSTABILITY AND
    EXPORT INSTABILITY IN LDCs   25
  The Causes of Export Instability: Theoretical Analysis   25
  Export Concentration   35
  The Causes of Export Instability: Empirical Evidence   36
  The Consequences of Export Instability: Theoretical
    Analysis   40
  Empirical Evidence and Interpretation   48
  Empirical Evidence of the Extent of Export Instability   51
  Concluding Remarks   61

4 TRENDS IN THE TERMS OF TRADE, EXPORT
    EARNINGS AND IMPORT PAYMENTS OF LDCs   63
  Theoretical Analysis   63
  Empirical Evidence on LDCs' Terms of Trade   67
  The Impact of Adverse Movements in the Terms of Trade   71
  Foreign Trade Elasticities   76
  Concluding Remarks   80

5 THE DEMAND FOR INTERNATIONAL RESERVES
   IN LDCs   82
   International Reserves and Liquidity: Demand and Need   82
   The Theory of the Demand for International Reserves   83
   LDCs' Demand for International Reserves   89
   Concluding Remarks   111

6 BALANCE-OF-PAYMENTS ADJUSTMENT IN LDCs   114
   The Causes of Balance-of-Payments Disequilibria   114
   Basic Policy Alternatives: Adjustment and Financing   117
   The Objectives of Adjustment   120
   Adjustment Policy in LDCs: Theoretical Analysis   124
   Optimal Adjustment Strategy in LDCs   130
   Adjustment Policy in LDCs: Empirical Evidence   133
   Devaluation and the Balance of Payments   138
   Concluding Remarks   139

7 THE IMF AS A SOURCE OF INTERNATIONAL
   LIQUIDITY FOR LDCs   142
   Normal Facilities   142
   Special Facilities   146
   Concluding Remarks   159

8 AN EVALUATION OF IMF-BASED SOURCES OF
   INTERNATIONAL LIQUIDITY FOR LDCs   160
   The Facilities in the General Account   160
   Evaluation of General Account Sources of International
      Finance   179
   The SDR Account   197
   The Trust Fund   207
   Concluding Remarks   208

9 PRIVATE SOURCES OF INTERNATIONAL FINANCE
   FOR LDCs   210
   Reasons for the Growth of Commercial Borrowing by LDCs   217
   Benefits Associated with Commercial Borrowing   218
   Problems Associated with Commercial Borrowing   219
   Concluding Remarks   222

10 THE COMMODITIES PROBLEM AND THE
    INTERNATIONAL MONETARY SYSTEM   224
    Compensatory Financing   226
    Buffer Stocks   226
    The Role of the International Monetary System   237
    The Commodity-Reserve Currency   237
    SDRs and the Financing of Commodity Stabilisation   239
    The Size of the Financing Problem   245
    Implications for World Economic Stability   248
    Concluding Remarks   249

11 THE LINK BETWEEN SDRs AND AID   251
    The Theory of Social Saving and Seigniorage   251
    SDRs and the Informal Aid Link   253
    Forerunners of the SDR–Aid Link   256
    Types of SDR–Aid Link   259
    Some other Considerations Relevant to the Choice of SDR–
        Aid Link   261
    The Burden-Sharing Implications of the Link   264
    Arguments For and Against the Link   266
    A Summary Assessment of the SDR–Aid Link   274

12 EXCHANGE-RATE POLICY AND LDCs   277
    LDCs' Attitude to Generalised Floating   277
    LDCs' Own Exchange-Rate Policy   281
    Exchange-Rate Behaviour in LDCs: Empirical Evidence   288
    Concluding Remarks   291

13 POSTSCRIPT TO THE SECOND EDITION   293

    Notes   304
    Chapter Bibliographies   331
    Index of Names   351

Preface

This book examines the relationship between the international monetary system and the less-developed countries (LDCs). Chapters 3, 4, 5 and 6 look at some of the international monetary problems faced by LDCs (as regards balance-of-payments instability, inadequacy of reserves, and choice of adjustment strategy); the middle section of the book (Chapters 7, 8 and 9) examines the major channels of balance-of-payments financing available to LDCs; and the final chapters (10, 11 and 12) investigate various policy alternatives.

The book assumes an elementary knowledge of basic economics but no mathematical expertise. It is primarily designed for undergraduates who are studying either international economics or development economics or both, but it is hoped that postgraduates will find certain chapters of interest.

In writing the book I have been helped by the following colleagues and friends, who have read and commented on various chapters or sections: Heather Bird, John Burton, Lorenzo Perez, Maxwell Stamp, Tony Thirlwall and John Williamson. In particular, however, I owe a debt to Geoffrey Maynard and Danny Leipziger, both of whom read a substantial proportion of the book in its early stages. Their observations caused me to make a number of changes which I feel have improved the text. Since all the above-named people assisted me out of the goodness of their hearts, it is only fair that they should be exonerated from any responsibility for errors which have passed unnoticed.

Finally, I should like to thank Sheila Brigenshaw, who, in her usual kind and efficient manner, typed and retyped most of the manuscript; and also Sally Greenland, who, as the publisher's deadline grew imminent, happily helped by typing the final draft of some chapters.

Department of Economics   Graham Bird
University of Surrey

September 1977

1 Introduction

Background

At the time of the Bretton Woods Conference in 1944, international monetary reform was fairly solidly the preserve of the developed countries of the world. The interests of less-developed countries (LDCs), if considered at all, were viewed as being in parallel with those of the developed countries, and not seen as warranting special treatment. Although, in the period between the establishment of the International Monetary Fund (IMF) in 1946 and the effective collapse of the par-value international monetary system in 1971, the activities of the Fund were constrained by its own Articles of Agreement, which define the IMF as a stabilisation rather than a development agency, a number of special facilities were introduced the prime objective of which was to assist less-developed member countries in dealing with particular aspects of their balance-of-payments problems. In 1963 the Compensatory Financing Facility (CFF) was introduced, to help members cope with the implications of a temporary shortfall in export receipts, whilst in 1969 the Buffer Stock Financing Facility (BSFF) was introduced, to help members cope with the implications of contributing to international commodity schemes. Other, ostensibly more minor, but in effect perhaps more significant, modifications were also beneficial to LDCs, such as the review of small quotas, and the softening of the IMF line on certain exchange practices.

Paradoxically, during the 1960s, when the IMF was demonstrating a growing awareness of the problems faced by developing countries, the Fund's influence with the developed countries seemed simultaneously to be declining. The developed countries were primarily concerned with two related international monetary issues: the supposed inadequacy of global international liquidity, and the deficiency of an international monetary system which heavily relied on the existence of a balance-of-payments deficit in the United States for the creation of international liquidity. Discussion about these two issues began under the auspices of the Group of Ten and culminated in the establishment of the Special

Drawing Rights (SDR) facility. LDCs were not involved in the discussions, and some developed countries saw no reason why LDCs should even participate in the SDR scheme once activated. Consistent with its previous attitude, however, the IMF argued that all member countries should be treated on equal terms, and when the SDR scheme was activated, in 1970, SDRs were allocated to LDCs and developed countries alike.

The SDR scheme, however, failed to prevent the breakdown of the Bretton Woods system, and it has been in the period since this collapse that international attention has become more sharply focused on the position of LDCs in the international monetary system.

After 1971, LDCs for the first time had the opportunity to participate fully in the reform of the international monetary system. At an institutional level, LDCs were well represented on the Committee of Twenty,[1] which established two technical working groups that specifically examined issues of direct relevance to LDCs: first, the idea of a link between the creation of SDRs and aid; and, second, alternative ways in which a transfer of real resources to LDCs could be engineered. The institutional momentum was maintained following the Committee's Final Report, with the setting up of a Joint Ministerial Committee of the Board of Governors of the Bank and the Fund on the Transfer of Real Resources to Developing Countries (the 'Development Committee').

The post-1971 era has, however, witnessed not only the inclusion of LDCs in the discussions relating to international monetary reform, but also the proliferation of measures specifically designed to assist them. Both the CFF and the BSFF have been liberalised, and the Extended Fund Facility (EFF), Oil Facility (OF), Subsidy Account, and Trust Fund have been introduced.

These modifications to the activities of the IMF in relation to its less-developed member countries are, in some ways, quite strategic. The EFF, for instance, marks a more overt involvement with developmental policies in LDCs than was previously the case, whilst the OF represents a departure from the previous emphasis on the balance-of-payments implications of a fall in export earnings, as opposed to a rise in import payments. The modifications have, however, in no way exhausted the scope for international monetary reform, which is biased towards solving the balance-of-payments problems faced by LDCs.

In Chapter 2 of this book the relationship between the IMF and its less-developed member countries is traced both analytically and historically. Chapter 7 presents a statement of the avenues through which the IMF makes financial assistance available to LDCs, and Chapter 8 evaluates these sources of finance. Attention is concentrated on the IMF because, until the 1970s, LDCs had little recourse to commercial borrowing. The significance of non-IMF sources of finance is, however, discussed in Chapter 9.

Balance-of-Payments Problems and International Monetary Issues in LDCs

Many of the balance-of-payments problems encountered by LDCs result from export instability, the causes and consequences of which are investigated in Chapter 3. Changes in the terms of trade of LDCs, as well as recent changes in LDCs' trading and balance-of-payments positions, are examined in Chapter 4. The commodities problem, of which export instability and declining terms of trade are two aspects, has in the 1970s become a central issue in discussions between the developed and less-developed countries about a new international economic order. Various aspects of the commodities problem are examined in Chapter 10, which in particular, looks at ways in which the international monetary system may be used to help solve the commodities problem, through the provision of compensatory finance, and the financing of buffer stocks.

When faced with a balance-of-payments deficit a country may either attempt to adjust its economy in a way which reduces or removes the deficit, or finance it. In most cases adjustment requires a reduction in real domestic expenditure, and thus it is often, understandably, a course of action which countries – especially, perhaps, developing countries – are reluctant to adopt. Alternatively, deficits may be financed through either the decumulation of international reserves or international borrowing. The choice of appropriate balance-of-payments policy in LDCs is discussed in Chapter 6.

Following the rise in the price of oil in 1974, oil-importing LDCs were confronted with balance-of-payments problems of much increased severity. The combined annual current-account balance-of-payments deficit for these LDCs was over $30,000 million in each of the years 1974, 1975 and 1976. Different LDCs have reacted to the deficit in different ways; although it should be noted that the different reactions can frequently be explained by differences in the range of policy options available. In many of the poorest LDCs, for instance, the option of commercial borrowing has simply not existed, and thus the countries concerned have been forced to reduce the volume of their imports, draw down their reserves, draw on the IMF under its various facilities, particularly the OF, and rely on inflows of official capital. Perhaps not surprisingly, these countries have been unable to achieve even a modest rate of economic growth over recent years. Better-off oil-importing LDCs have been able to maintain development only by resorting to private borrowing, especially through the Eurocurrency market. For oil-importing LDCs in general, the period since 1974 has brought with it an increase in international indebtedness, an increase in debt–service ratios, and a fall in the real value of reserves. These developments emphasize questions concerning the adequacy of multilateral concessionary financial assistance to LDCs; the adequacy of LDCs' access to IMF facilities; the wisdom, for LDCs, of using the Eurocurrency market; the adequacy of international reserves in LDCs; the optimal adjustment strategy in LDCs; and the homogeneity of LDCs in terms of their international monetary problems.

The question of concessionary aid lies outside the scope of this book, although, in a situation where countries possessing per capita incomes of below $200 per annum have had to accept zero growth for a number of years, and a reduction in imports to a level some 20 per cent below their level in the late 1960s, there would appear to be a *prima facie* argument that official concessionary aid to these countries is inadequate – especially since such LDCs cannot gain access to private loans, or afford to borrow on commercial terms. Certainly the Development Committee has reached this conclusion, and it is currently investigating ways in which the flow of concessionary aid to LDCs can be increased. The remaining questions mentioned above do fall inside the terms of reference of this book and all of them are examined in the chapters that follow.

The adequacy of IMF facilities (Chapter 8) is a matter that has both quantitative and qualitative aspects. Despite the expansion in LDCs' IMF quotas over recent years, the ratio of quotas to imports has fallen, and drawings on the Fund remain largely conditional and subject to relatively short repayment periods, which may be inappropriate where structural changes are required.

Considerable use of the Eurocurrency market (Chapter 9) has been made by a limited number of high- and middle-income LDCs. The long-term viability of this source of balance-of-payments financing is, however, open to debate, in part because of the risks of default and lack of confidence; and it would probably be better if, instead of being based on short-term Eurocurrency credits, commerical borrowing were based on long-term bond issues.

As to the adequacy of international reserves (Chapter 5), oil-importing LDCs have, over recent years, experienced both a decline in their percentage share of total world reserves, and zero growth in reserves; indeed, in 1975 their reserves actually fell by SDR 4 million. This, along with certain supplementary factors, such as the fall in the ratio of reserves to imports, the adoption and extension of import controls, the increase in the size of the balance-of-payments deficit, and reluctance to make proportionately greater use of adjustment, would seem to indicate that the adequacy of reserves in oil-importing LDCs has declined.

Given that LDCs have generally not, in recent years, taken much action to adjust their economies, the deterioration in their balance-of-payments position and the size of the associated financing problem is likely to force them in the future, to undertake a close examination of adjustment policy (Chapter 6). In particular, the exchange-rate policy of many LDCs (Chapter 12) would seem worthy of scrutiny, since evidence suggests that in a significant number of cases policies have been pursued which are not necessarily appropriate.

With regard to homogeneity, LDCs do not, except in a fairly narrow sense, constitute an homogeneous group in terms of their international monetary problems (this theme recurs in many of the following chapters). At any one time there are likely to be a number of dichotomies within the LDC group. For instance, following the oil-price rise the problems of oil-exporting and oil-importing countries became sharply contrasted, with oil-exporting countries having to decide what to do with their balance-of-payments surpluses and oil-importing countries having to find ways of financing or correcting their deficits. Within the oil-importing group of countries there also developed a sharp distinction between, on the one hand, those high- and middle-income LDCs which had access to unconditional commercial borrowing, and which were therefore able to maintain at least positive economic growth, and, on the other hand, the low-income LDCs which had to rely almost exclusively on the IMF as a source of balance-of-payments financing assistance, and which were therefore subject to the conditions imposed by the Fund: in these countries the rate of economic growth stagnated.

Alternative Policy Approaches

Although there is an undeniable relationship between the operation of the international monetary system and economic growth in LDCs, the proper nature of this relationship is a subject of some dispute. Which policies are advocated depends very much on which view is taken of the proper relationship between the international monetary system and development. One policy approach builds on the notion that there is no conflict of interest between developed and less-developed countries. This approach maintains that, from an international monetary point of view, what is best for developed countries is also best for LDCs. The policy implications of this approach are that national and international authorities should concentrate on establishing the most efficient international monetary system, irrespective of distributional or equity considerations. Policies which assist the growth of national incomes and trade in developed countries will, it is suggested, be of indirect, but significant, importance to LDCs.[2]

A second policy approach rejects this line of argument and maintains that the international monetary system should be constructed so as to yield direct, and in some cases exclusive, benefits to LDCs. The benefits derived by LDCs under such an approach would be achieved at a balance-of-payments or resource cost to developed countries, thereby specifically involving a degree of redistribution. Direct policies might be based on the existing international monetary framework, or they might involve substantial modification to this framework. Into the former category would fall plans designed to modify the quota formula in order to increase the size of LDCs' quotas, and also those to extend various facilities in the IMF, such as the CFF. Into the latter category would fall plans involving the introduction of an SDR—aid link (Chapter 11).

In any case, the heterogeneity of LDCs' international monetary problems suggests that grouping all LDCs together is inappropriate from the point of view of policy, which therefore has to take a more disaggregated approach. This indeed has already been recognised, inasmuch as international concern and, to some extent, international monetary reform have been focused on the least-developed countries, which have been the most seriously affected by world economic developments.

LDCs and the Reform of the International Monetary System

As international monetary reform is an exercise in political economy, LDCs should perhaps be prepared to forgo, for the time being, first-best reforms which may currently be politically infeasible, and instead settle for feasible second- or third-best reforms which generally improve their position in the international monetary system and which may act as stepping-stones to first-best reforms in the future. Clearly, changes which benefit LDCs at a visible cost to developed countries, are less likely to be accepted by the latter than are those which do not impose costs on them. Unfortunately, from the point of view of LDCs, it is frequently the reforms which impose the greatest costs on developed countries which yield the greatest benefits for LDCs. Thus, many of the most far-reaching reforms require from the richer countries in the world a genuine and actual commitment, rather than a merely verbal commitment, to the transfer of resources. The approach of LDCs to international monetary reform should perhaps represent a balance between endeavouring to introduce reforms specifically designed to assist them, and coming to terms with certain features of the existing system.

The SDR–aid link, which is discussed in Chapter 11, constitutes one LDC-specific reform. The version of the link which LDCs would find most beneficial, i.e. one involving a competitive interest rate for holders of SDRs and a subsidised concessionary rate for LDC users, is probably the one least likely to be accepted by developed countries, since it would involve them in the extra cost associated with interest-rate subsidisation. In current circumstances, and in the light of the IMF's Second Amendment, it may be to the advantage of LDCs to concentrate on that version of the link which does not rely on new SDR emissions but which ties the link to reserve-currency amortisation.[3] Also, at a time of world recession, the expansionary aspects of the link, which could be expected to lead to higher levels of employment, real output and exports in developed countries, could be used to strengthen the case for it. It is also true that the recycling of oil revenues, which has taken place both directly and, through the mediation of the Eurocurrency market, indirectly, has helped not only to protect development in LDCs but also to maintain employment and exports in developed countries. LDCs might further exploit areas of common interest with developed countries. Commodity stabilisation, for instance, might yield benefits not only for less-developed producing countries but also for developed consuming countries; and the international monetary system could be modified to assist in the financing of stabilisation schemes.

Whilst reform proposals such as the SDR–aid link, which purposefully adapts the international monetary system in order to expand the amount of aid going to LDCs, constitute fairly fundamental changes in the role of the international monetary system – or, more narrowly, the IMF – other, less fundamental reforms could be made which would, nonetheless, assist LDCs in coping with their balance-of-payments difficulties, or, indeed, reduce the incidence of such difficulties. LDCs would gain from any expansion of existing IMF facilities and any liberalisation of the conditions attached to these facilities, such as lengthening the repayment period on drawings. A further beneficial modification would be the orientation of financing assistance towards the protection of development plans. Such an idea has been discussed in the past under the proposal for Supplementary Financing Measures. A modification of this type would embody the closer co-operation between the IMF and the IBRD (International Bank for Reconstruction and Development, the World Bank) which some commentators feel would be appropriate.

Commercial borrowing by LDCs is currently hampered in a number of ways. On the borrowing side, many LDCs find it difficult to gain access to world capital markets, and are in any case reluctant to build up the related debt obligations. On the lending side, commercial lenders lack confidence in the ability of LDCs to repay their debts. One possible reform would be for richer countries to subsidise the commercial interest rates paid by LDCs, as is to some extent done under the Subsidy Account in relation to borrowing under the OF; another would be for those same countries to guarantee the repayment of long-term loans by LDCs. A possible advantage of the guarantee system from the point of view of developed countries is that guarantees would probably be activated only rarely. Thus, even though a guarantee system might yield LDCs relatively fewer benefits than a subsidy system would, it may have a better chance of acceptance.

With regard to flexible exchange rates, it is probable that the view of LDCs will remain ambivalent. For, whilst floating may enable developed countries to pursue more stable, expansion-oriented policies, it may also reduce the likelihood of future SDR allocations; to LDCs then, the opportunity cost of generalised floating could be high. It would, however, appear to be in the best interests of LDCs to adapt to the existing environment of flexible rates rather than to hanker after a fixed-rate system. They could minimise the costs and maximise the benefits associated with floating by developing adequate forward-exchange facilities, by choosing their currency peg carefully, and even by making more aggressive use of the exchange-rate instrument. In the circumstances in which many LDCs find themselves, however, universal exchange-rate variations may be inappropriate and the selectivity offered by some form of multiple exchange-rate system possibly warrants further investigation, even though such arrangements have never found favour with the IMF.

Many of the international monetary problems which face LDCs are merely monetary manifestations of more basic structural and trading problems.[4] The balance-of-payments positions of LDCs in general could no doubt be substantially improved through greater aid, which would permit industrial diversification, and through trade reforms, which would permit LDCs greater access to the markets of developed countries. What is needed first of all, however, is for the developed countries firmly to commit themselves to helping the poor countries of the world. A concerted and complementary programme of aid expansion and trade reform, along with international monetary reform, could then follow.

2 Relations between the IMF and LDCs

The principal economic objective of most LDCs is almost certainly that of stable development, or of development linked with stability. Development is·desirable because it permits an improvement in a nation's standard of living. It involves policies relating to the various factors of production: land, labour, capital and entrepreneurship. Stability means the minimisation of deviations around a certain trend. Aspects of stability include the eradication or dampening of cycles in economic activity, the control of inflation, and the avoidance of balance-of-payments disequilibria.

Although in many circumstances the objectives of development and stability are mutually reinforcing, occasions can and do arise when they conflict. Thus it may be that balance-of-trade or current-account balance-of-payments deficits have to be endured (and financed) in order to protect a particular development programme, or that inflation cannot be removed or reduced without pursuing a range of monetary and fiscal policies which would be injurious to economic growth at least in the short run. Where conflicts of this nature emerge, a choice has to be made concerning the extent to which the one objective will be sacrificed in favour of the other. Casual empirical observation would suggest that, when such a choice has to be made LDCs normally prefer to maintain development rather than stability. This is perhaps hardly surprising when one bears in mind the very low levels of per capita national income which exist in many LDCs.

The objectives of the IMF are clearly stated in its original Articles of Agreement. Article 1 states that the purposes of the Fund are:

(i) To promote international monetary co-operation through a permanent institution which provides the machinery for consultation and collaboration on international monetary problems.
(ii) To facilitate the expansion and balanced growth of international trade, and to contribute thereby to the promotion and maintenance of

high levels of employment and real income and to the development of the productive resources of all members as primary objectives of economic policy.

(iii) To promote exchange stability, to maintain orderly exchange arrangements among members, and to avoid competitive exchange depreciation.

(iv) To assist in the establishment of a multilateral system of payments in respect of current transactions between members and in the elimination of foreign exchange restrictions which hamper the growth of world trade.

(v) To give confidence to members by making the Fund's resources available to them under adequate safeguards, thus providing them with opportunity to correct maladjustments in their balance of payments without resorting to measures destructive of national or international prosperity.

(vi) In accordance with the above to shorten the duration and lessen the degree of disequilibrium in the international balances of payments of members.

Article 1 clearly presents the IMF as a balance-of-payments stabilisation agency the main function of which is to provide members, on terms precluding the adoption of extensive trade restrictions and/ or exchange-rate adjustment, with short-term financial assistance. This assistance is directly related to the state of the balance of payments. Basically, the IMF aims to provide its members with the time needed to take the internal measures necessary in order to correct balance-of-payments disequilibria. The Fund emphasises internal adjustment, as opposed to adjustment through alterations in the external value of any particular currency.[1]

Even though Article 1, Section (ii), of the Articles of Agreement of the IMF makes reference to the 'development of the productive resources of all members', the Fund is not a development agency. Development is instead the major concern of the IMF's sister institution, the International Bank for Reconstruction and Development (IBRD) and its affiliates. The Fund and its representatives have consistently denied any *responsibility* for aiding development. As early as 1946 the Executive Directors of the IMF interpreted the Articles of Agreement as meaning that the Fund's purpose was that of giving 'temporary assistance in financing balance of payments deficits on current account for monetary stabilization operations', while as recently as 1976 the Fund's Deputy Managing Director re-emphasised[2] that the activities of the IMF are

limited to the granting of credit, 'in support of internationally acceptable policies of payments adjustment', to those members who, on
account of their balance of payments, have a temporary need for
finance. The criterion for determining the availability of Fund assistance
remains the state of the balance of payments and not the level of
development.

Whilst reference to the Fund's Articles of Agreement clearly demonstrates the validity of the claim that the IMF has no defined
responsibility for development, it is true to say that, in pursuing its
defined purposes, the Fund does exert an incidental influence upon
development. Indeed, it does rather more than this, since, in the course
of its own development, it has gradually responded to certain economic
problems which LDCs tend to face and has introduced facilities
purposefully designed to help counter these problems.

The Relationship between Development and Stabilisation

As noted above, the finance provided by the IMF is specified as balance-
of-payments assistance. This specification has two dimensions. The first
is that assistance is made available only when the state of the balance-of-
payments requires it. The second dimension is that conditions are
attached to the provision of assistance, in an attempt to limit the
purposes for which it is used.[3] The conditions relate to policies and
performance with respect to the balance of payments. In some ways the
distinction between balance-of-payments assistance and development
assistance is difficult to draw. A development programme which
involves industrial diversification may in the long term have a very
tangible effect on the balance of payments; whilst balance-of-payments
assistance which enables internal adjustment to be undertaken less
rapidly than it would otherwise need to be may have definite implications for the pattern of development. Given, however, that the IMF
uses the state of the balance of payments in determining its response to
requests for finance, and specifies conditions relating to the balance of
payments, a question is posed concerning the precise impact that IMF
activity has on development. The precise impact in fact depends on a
complex set of relationships between economic development and
stability. This dependence may be illustrated by suggesting two
hypothetical scenarios.

In the first of these, excessive domestic money creation has resulted in
a rapid rate of inflation and a balance-of-payments deficit. The rapid

rate of inflation has, in turn, discouraged saving and investment and, as a result, the rate of economic growth is declining. In these circumstances monetary stabilisatiòn may simultaneously prove to be an appropriate balance-of-payments policy and an appropriate development strategy. This example shows that concentration on the balance of payments and on stabilisation need not necessarily result in the pursuit of policies harmful to growth and development.

Imagine, however, as a second scenario, a situation where an LDC with an undiversified export base encounters a decline in the world demand for its principal export goods. Imagine further that, at the same time, the prices of the LDC's imports rise. With an import-demand schedule which is inelastic in the short run the implications of these changes will almost certainly be a deterioration in the balance of payments and cost inflation. Where cost inflation is passed on in the form of higher export prices the demand for exports may fall further, and export receipts will fall if the elasticity of demand is greater than unity. Facing this situation, the most appropriate long-term policy for the LDC to follow is one of diversification of the export base and import substitution. Such a policy is simultaneously a development strategy and a long-term balance-of-payments strategy. Short-term stabilisation could, no doubt, be achieved through the use of alternative con-tractionary policies. In one positive sense contractionary policies are appropriate, since they merely reflect the equilibrating response to changes in world economic conditions. In a more normative sense they are inappropriate. The economic problems faced by the LDC are the result not of domestic excesses, but, rather, of factors outside the LDC's control. It is perhaps unreasonable to ask poor countries to pursue short-term policies which involve hardship, in terms of reductions in a domestic standard of living which is already low, when longer-term policies involving less hardship are available. Our second hypothetical example shows, then, how a conflict may arise between *short-term* stabilisation, the main objective of the Fund, and *long-term* development and stability, the main objective of the Fund's developing members. Thus, there may be a major difference between the wishes of the IMF and those of LDCs as regards the time period over which stability is to be achieved.

Given that the IMF is basically a short-term balance-of-payments stabilisation institution, it can be seen that the conditionality of financial assistance may either help or hinder development, depending on the causes of any particular balance-of-payments deficit. In many of its published statements, however, the IMF has maintained that monetary stability is always appropriate for development. The Fund's view[4] is that monetary and fiscal stability constitutes a necessary precondition for development. The conditions under which the Fund has made balance-of-payments assistance available to members wishing to use its resources reflect this philosophy. These conditions are difficult to discuss in any quantitative and informed manner, since the relevant details and data are confidential and largely unavailable. The published 'letters of intent' do, however, give some indication of the sorts of policies which the Fund has supported. They include measures to control some or all of the following: domestic credit expansion, government expenditure and taxation (this, of course, being related to the money supply), foreign indebtedness, prices and wages, trade practices and exchange rates.

Thus the IMF, whilst seeing it as its duty to provide financial assistance when a member country's balance-of-payments is temporarily in disequilibrium (deficit), expects, and in the case of drawings in the higher tranches of a member's total drawing rights, can insist, that the member pursue the monetary and fiscal policies that the Fund itself deems necessary for removing the deficit within a reasonable period of time. Under its original Articles, the Fund accedes to the use of exchange-rate adjustment only where the member has demonstrated the existence of 'fundamental disequilibrium'. Whether concentrating on internal adjustment, or using the exchange rate, however, the Fund has consistently sought to follow the Bretton Woods notion of eschewing controls over trade and current payments which would interfere with the free movement of goods and capital.

As the second scenario outlined above illustrates, a preoccupation with domestic monetary stability and a belief in the efficacy and appropriateness of internal adjustment as a means of ensuring it can result in a conflict with the objective of development. Critics of the Fund's philosophy have indeed adopted this theme as the essence of their case.[5] The critics' view is that the IMF has put too much emphasis on internal adjustment as a means of obtaining balance-of-payments equilibrium, and too little on development. Indeed, it is maintained that in many cases monetary restriction designed to temper inflation succeeds only at the cost of development. Critics argue that the balance-of-payments problems which LDCs encounter are more of a structural rather than a monetary nature. If LDCs export goods which have low price and income elasticities, but at the same time import goods for which the LDC's own income elasticities are high, then it is likely that economic growth at anything but a meagre rate will be inconsistent with balance-of-payments equilibrium. In this situation the balance-of-payments options are clear. One is to adjust imports to match exogenously determined export earnings by altering the rate of growth and the level of national income. The other is to change the structure of the balance of payments, including the structure of protection, in such a way that an acceptable rate of development is consistent with balance-of-payments equilibrium. Whereas the Fund has adopted the first approach, LDCs favour the second.[6] This difference in approach has been the source of some friction between LDCs and the IMF.[7]

Relations between the IMF and LDCs: A Historical Perspective

Although the IMF's view of its proper sphere of responsibility has remained unchanged, the Fund has responded to some of the problems which LDCs encounter by modifying the circumstances under which financial assistance will be provided. Since many structural problems, such as export instability, have monetary manifestations – in the form, for instance, of balance-of-payments difficulties – the Fund has, to some extent, relieved LDCs from the monetary implications of their structural problems.

The period since 1945 has witnessed a growing general international awareness of the problems faced by developing countries. This growing awareness has been reflected in the relations between the IMF and its developing member countries. These relations may be seen in an historical perspective.

The setting up of the IMF

The Bretton Woods Conference and the previous meetings which, taken together, resulted in the establishment of the IMF were dominated by a few industrial countries, and most significantly by the United States and the United Kingdom. European countries (other than the UK) and the LDCs exerted only a minimal influence. It is not true to say, however, that LDCs were completely excluded from the discussions. Indeed, it appears that there was some debate concerning the problems of development.

For instance, in drafting the Articles of Agreement of the IMF, India, in particular, pushed hard for some appropriate reference to LDCs. To some extent the final version of Article 1, Section (ii), was a compromise between the United States, which was particularly opposed to any direct reference to LDCs, and India. The Articles of Agreement did not make any distinction between developed and less-developed countries, but there was a direct reference to development. It is difficult to know whether the wording of the Articles of Agreement has made any difference to the Fund's attitude towards LDCs. Certainly the uniform legal position of all member countries under the Articles has not prevented the Fund from adopting policies which have primarily favoured LDCs. Even so, a feeling remains that a more specific and direct commitment to development in the Articles of Agreement would have encouraged a rather more active approach to dealing with the problems which face LDCs.[8]

The IMF in operation: late 1940s to late 1950s

During the first few years of its existence, the Fund showed relatively little concern with the problems of LDCs. This was partly because it viewed development as lying outside its terms of reference, but also because it regarded development as a relatively unimportant issue. It is interesting to note that between 1947 and 1949 Western Europe accounted for three-quarters of total drawings from the IMF and LDCs for well under a quarter, and this at a time when the problem of post-war reconstruction in Europe was being met through Marshall Aid, the conditions of which precluded the use of IMF resources in anything other than 'exceptional and unforeseen circumstances'.

Even so, certain policy changes and other innovations that occurred in the early 1950s were beneficial to LDCs. Amongst these were the proliferation of technical and advisory missions to LDCs, and the introduction by the IMF of a limited range of educational courses. Also in the early 1950s, steps were taken to make drawings on the gold tranche virtually automatic, and drawings on the first credit tranche more easily available. Furthermore, in 1952 the stand-by arrangement was concluded.[9] Under certain conditions, this provided member countries with an assured line of credit. In the same year it was also announced by the then Managing Director of the IMF that an agreed par value would no longer necessarily constitute a precondition for Fund assistance. In retrospect it appears that these modifications did act to the advantage of LDCs.[10]

Annual Reports of the IMF during the early and middle 1950s, however, confirm that the Fund had little specific interest in the particular problems of LDCs as such. LDCs were treated as if their problems were no different from those of developed countries. Fund policy continued to rest on the notion that the encouragement of monetary stabilisation and free trade was the main purpose of the IMF and that such policies were in the interests of *all* members.

To the extent that IMF assistance under the stand-by arrangement was made conditional upon the acceptance of a certain package of economic policies, and to the extent that recommended policies were pursued, the IMF's commitment to the efficacy of monetary and fiscal policy in LDCs became effective. In a comparative sense, the IMF in the 1950s was more actively involved with the formulation of policy in LDCs than it was with policy in developed countries. This involvement resulted not only from the negotiations, alluded to above, over stand-by arrangements, but also from the fact that Article 14, Section (iv), of the Articles of Agreement of the IMF required that all members retaining restrictions on non-capital international payments should consult annually with the IMF.

Commentators on the activities of the Fund at this time, such as Seers (1964) and Kenen (1963), have also suggested that the IMF was apparently not thoroughly aware of the significance of political factors in international economic policy. Related to this, perhaps one particularly relevant factor in the early years of the Fund's existence was the dominance of the United States. Indeed, there is some evidence to support the view that the Fund's policies, at least during the first twelve years of its existence, reflected the economic foreign policy of the United States.[11]

Although, over the period of the 1940s and 1950s, IMF policies assisted LDCs in certain ways, the policies were not designed with this specific intention. The IMF view of the world economy was essentially static and little consideration was given to the dynamic potentialities for assisting development.

The IMF in operation: late 1950s and 1960s

It would appear that in the late 1950s and through the 1960s the Fund's attitude towards development shifted significantly. This apparent shift, the tangible aspect of which was the introduction of a number of innovations explicitly intended to help alleviate the monetary implications of the economic problems faced by LDCs, may be put down to a number of factors, including, first, the deteriorating terms of trade of primary-product exporting countries; second, a growing awareness of the instability of the export receipts of LDCs; third, the increasing representation of LDCs in international councils; fourth, the gradual thaw in the Cold War, and the related reduction in the United

States' preoccupation with international stability, which had previously been pursued even at the cost of development; and, finally, the appointment of Per Jacobsson in place of Ivar Rooth as Managing Director of the Fund, to which this brought 'more imaginative leadership and a somewhat more flexible outlook'.

The innovations that serve to illustrate this apparent change in attitude include: first, action to increase the size of quotas; second, a considerable shift in the direction in which the Fund made its resources available, away from industrial countries and towards LDCs; and, third, the fact that in 1960 Jacobsson went on record as recognising that the IMF did have a positive role to play in promoting development – not, admittedly, by the provision of development capital, but, rather, by protecting development plans through the provision of short-term finance to countries experiencing temporary balance-of-payments difficulties. Monetary stability was still viewed as being the main objective of Fund policy, but it now became specifically related to development, being seen as a precondition for stable growth. A fourth change was that, after some initial resistance, in 1963 the IMF reached a decision to introduce a scheme to compensate members against shortfalls in export receipts. This facility, although officially open to all members alike, was of greatest benefit to primary-product exporting countries, and represented the first formal institutional response to the demands of LDCs. At first, compensation was available only on relatively restrictive terms, but in 1966, following a substantial degree of lobbying by LDCs, amendments were introduced that served to make the Compensatory Financing Facility (CFF) more attractive. The Fund continued, however, to resist demands to make the facility automatically available. A fifth change was that in 1969 the Fund took action to assist members who faced balance-of-payments difficulties as a result of their participation in international buffer-stock schemes. This Buffer Stock Financing Facility (BSFF) was again of direct help to LDCs. Finally, the adoption of measures designed to expand the educational and the advisory activities of the Fund also benefited LDCs.

Writing in 1967, Scott felt sufficiently confident to conclude that 'the overwhelming evidence is that the Fund is currently doing all it possibly can to assist developing nations within its traditional sphere of operations, but that it is resisting with equal vigor any substantial modification of this very limited sphere'. The shift in attitude, then, occurred only within the constraints imposed by what the Fund considered to be its terms of reference. Financial assistance provided by the IMF to LDCs remained constrained by quotas, the short-term nature of agreements, and the balance-of-payments orientation of the assistance. Such assistance clearly may help LDCs, but the help remains essentially indirect and may be misdirected.[12]

The period of the 1960s was very actively filled with discussions at both an academic and an official level about international monetary reform. LDCs were regarded as irrelevant to this particular debate and were virtually ignored during its course. The reasons for this relative neglect were, first, that the interests of LDCs were not seen as conflicting with those of developed countries; second, that development issues were not of such general interest as was the issue of maintaining full employment; and, third, that development tended to be regarded as concerned mainly with the long term and outside the scope of the international monetary system.

Certainly the discussions, which culminated in the introduction of the Special Drawing Rights (SDR) scheme in 1969, appeared to concentrate on the global adequacy of international liquidity, rather than on the distributional aspects of the liquidity problem. Whilst the global adequacy of international liquidity is clearly of considerable importance to LDCs, there is some evidence to suggest that LDCs had particularly inadequate reserves and required special treatment.[13] Not all the plans for the reform of the international monetary system ignored the problems of LDCs, but it is probably fair to argue that the majority of plans related to LDCs only in a very tangential way.[14]

At an official level, much of the discussion of international monetary reform was not centred on the IMF. This was consistent with international monetary developments in the 1960s. This period witnessed the establishment of the General Arrangement to Borrow, the Basle Agreements, and the evolution of a system of bilateral swap agreements. With little if any exception, these modifications were introduced by industrial countries primarily, at least, to act to their own advantage. There was therefore some cause, during this period, for LDCs to feel that international monetary reform was the preserve of the relatively rich countries in the world. A certain degree of counterbalance was provided by the United Nations Conference on Trade and Development (UNCTAD), which was first convened in 1964; but initially this body spent much of its time examining the issues of compensatory and supplementary financing rather than more aggregative reforms.

In a report it published in 1965, however, the UNCTAD did state that LDCs had a pressing need for international liquidity, and did put forward, as a general suggestion, the Hart–Kaldor–Tinbergen plan for international monetary reform based on a commodity-backed reserve currency. Though this plan did not at the time become a serious candidate for activation, its existence showed that economists were beginning to consider the specific problems of LDCs in relation to the international monetary system.

The plan that was in fact activated was, as has already been noted, the SDR scheme. Few would deny that this scheme is of benefit to LDCs, but initially there was considerable discussion and disagreement as to whether or not LDCs should be included within the scheme. The IMF argued that they should be included in it on an equal basis with industrial countries. This attitude might be interpreted as showing that in the late 1960s the IMF began more actively to represent the interests of LDCs.[15]

It is interesting and perhaps not coincidental that it was at a time when it was exerting less influence than before over the developed countries that the IMF began to show more concern over the problems of LDCs.

The IMF in operation: 1970s

The 1970s have represented a particularly significant period for relations between the IMF and the LDCs. From an international monetary point of view, the period has been dominated by two developments: first, the breakdown in the Bretton Woods system; and, second, the large increases in the price of oil. These developments have presented LDCs with additional problems but also with opportunities. Certainly it has been this most recent phase which has been the most active in the history of relations between the IMF and the LDCs.

The virtual collapse of the Bretton Woods system in 1972 resulted in the establishment of the Committee on Reform of the International Monetary System and Issues.[16] This so-called Committee of Twenty was given the task of advising and reporting on all aspects of international monetary reform. The membership of the committee was such that the interests of LDCs (nine members) were well represented; indeed, two of the technical groups set up by the committee looked at issues of specific concern to LDCs: the SDR–aid link and related proposals, and the transfer of real resources. The Committee's report and 'Outline of Reform'. published in June 1974, gave an explicit commitment to organise future international monetary arrangements in a way which would serve 'to give positive encouragement to economic development and to promote an increasing net flow of real resources to developing countries'. To this end the 'Outline' stressed the importance of complementary and supporting arrangements for trade and development assistance, including the access of LDCs to both financial and goods markets in developed countries.

More specifically, the 'Outline' suggested that the reformed international monetary system should serve to dissuade developed countries from adjusting their economies in a way injurious to LDCs – for instance, by limiting the access of LDCs or development-finance institutions to their financial markets, or reducing the volume or hardening the terms of official development assistance. It was suggested that the Executive Board of the IMF should, at regular intervals, 'review the aggregate net flow of real resources to developing countries and its financing, and the consistency of countries' balance-of-payments aims and policies with any internationally agreed resource transfer targets that they have adopted'. With regard to adjustment in LDCs, the 'Outline' argued that explicit account should be taken of the fact that, 'the special characteristics of developing countries . . . make it difficult for them to achieve prompt adjustment without seriously damaging their long term development programmes'. Furthermore, it was stated that 'wherever possible developing countries will be exempted from controls imposed by other countries, particularly from import controls and control over long term investment. The special circumstances of developing countries will be taken into account by the Fund in assessing controls which these countries feel it necessary to apply.' With regard to liquidity, the Committee discussed the 'special concerns' of LDCs, and their need both for liquid assets to spend and – essentially a question of balance-of-payments financing – for liquid assets to hold.

In the light of the 'agreed objective to promote economic development', the 'Outline' maintained that any reformed international monetary system should contain arrangements which make this commitment effective; an annex was devoted to a discussion of such arrangements.[17] The arrangements proposed in the 'Outline' included the establishment of an SDR–aid link, and an extended facility in the Fund under which LDCs would receive longer-term balance-of-payments finance than had previously been available. The 'Outline' also maintained that immediate steps should be taken to increase, on appropriate terms, the flow of financial resources to LDCs (particularly those in greatest need). One method by which it was suggested that this could be done was by recycling financial surpluses at concessionary rates.

Clearly, the Committee, its report and its 'Outline of Reform' are significant landmarks in the evolving relations between the IMF and LDCs. For the first time LDCs were able to participate fully in the remaking of the international monetary system. Furthermore, the report and 'Outline of Reform' clearly reflect the notion that the international monetary system should be organised in a manner which specifically caters for the problems of development.

The momentum generated by the Committee of Twenty has to some extent been maintained subsequently. Indeed, concern with the problems facing LDCs has been enhanced as the implications of the energy crisis and oil-price rise for oil-importing and oil-reliant LDCs have become more fully and more generally realised. At both the 1974 and the 1975 annual meeting of the IMF, a, if not the, dominant theme was the economic situation of the developing countries; and there was wide-ranging discussion about ways in which economic growth in LDCs could be protected from the effects of world inflation and recession.

Although expressions of a commitment to the fostering of economic development are significant, actions are more important. Certain modifications to the international monetary system that have actually been made or have been very specifically proposed in the early 1970s have been or would appear to be of benefit to LDCs, although other opportunities for amending the international monetary system in favour of LDCs have been neglected, and certain proposals, such as the SDR–aid link, have in effect been shelved.

Following a suggestion of the Committee of Twenty a Joint Ministerial Committee of the Boards of Governors of the Bank and the Fund on the Transfer of Real Resources to Developing Countries was set up. In this way, international monetary reform and the economic development of poor countries became institutionally linked. The 'Development Committee' (as the Joint Ministerial Committee is commonly called) has been concerning itself with all aspects of the transfer of real resources to LDCs, paying particular attention to the problems of the least-developed countries and those LDCs most seriously affected by balance-of-payments difficulties. Areas of study by the Development Committee include: access by LDCs to the financial and goods markets of developed countries; capital requirements of LDCs and the adequacy of current development assistance; and the organisation of primary markets and the question of commodity-price instability.

Further suggestions made by the Committee of Twenty resulted in the establishment of the Oil Facility (OF), designed to assist members in withstanding the impact of the increase in oil prices, and the Extended Financing Facility (EFF), designed to provide members in difficulties over their balance-of-payments with longer-term assistance than had been available under stand-by arragements. In addition, a 'Third

Window' has been established in the World Bank, to provide the poorer LDCs with a lending facility on terms intermediate between those of standard World Bank loans and International Development Association (IDA) loans. The LDCs most seriously affected by the rise in the price of oil, world inflation and recession also benefit from the Subsidy Account, which was designed to reduce the interest burden arising from drawings on the OF. Further benefits result from the Trust Fund, which provides highly concessionary resources to assist the lower-income LDCs in meeting their balance-of-payments needs. Additionally, the CFF has been further liberalised.

There can be little doubt, then, that in the 1970s the LDCs have made a major breakthrough in their relations with the IMF. The reasons for the increased influence of LDCs and the increased recognition by other countries of the problems of development are not difficult to find. First, this reflects the continuation of a trend that was apparent some time before the creation of the Comittee of Twenty. Second, it reflects the growing power of the influential group of oil-exporting LDCs, and the willingness of LDCs to exploit any monopoly power which they might possess individually or as a group. Third, and related to this second point, it reflects the increasing importance to the IMF of the petroleum producers, as a source of funds. Paradoxically, the increasing concern with development also reflects the stark and extremely tangible impact that increases in the price of oil have had on the oil-importing LDCs in terms of their balance-of-payments financing problems. As the IMF has come to take greater cognisance of the problems of LDCs, the oil-price rise has made the maintenance of development in LDCs more reliant on the provision of finance through the IMF. Finally, the increasing influence of LDCs reflects the success with which they have been able to organise themselves into a relatively coherent pressure group, in the form of the Group of Twenty-Four.

Concluding Remarks

Relations between the IMF and the LDCs have changed markedly since the IMF was established at Bretton Woods. Although, throughout the period of its existence, the IMF has viewed development as being not at all or only to a small degree its responsibility, in the 1950s and 1960s it made available certain special facilities that proved of importance to LDCs. The reform of the international monetary system, however, remained until the late 1960s the preserve of the developed countries.

Circumstances changed in the 1970s. The energy crisis served to concentrate international attention on the problems facing the oil-importing LDCs, and to increase the influence of the oil-exporting LDCs; indeed, with the advent of the 'oil crisis' the parameters of power in the international monetary system changed.[18] At the same time, the collapse of the Bretton Woods international monetary system provided LDCs with the opportunity to press their case for its replacement by a system with a more direct and formal responsibility for encouraging economic development. A reformed international monetary system represents to LDCs one component of the 'new international economic order'. It is perhaps rather too early to assess the success of LDCs in pursuit of this goal, but current evidence seems to indicate that some progress has been made in this direction, and the signs appear to suggest that this progress will continue, though not at a rapid rate and not without reversals.

3 Primary-Product Price Instability and Export Instability in LDCs

It is often suggested that one of the main economic problems with which LDCs have to cope is instability in their export earnings. Export instability is felt to constitute a problem since it can affect a country's domestic income, consumption, savings, investment, tax revenues, balance of payments, and, perhaps most significantly from the point of view of developing countries, capacity to import. Since imports are largely financed from export receipts, an export shortfall will have a direct impact on an LDC's ability to finance imports. Where imports are of a developmental nature, such as capital goods and fertilisers, and are not domestically substitutable, a shortfall in export earnings will tend to exert an adverse influence on development and growth. To the extent that export instability is unpredictable, at least to any precise degree, the uncertainties generated by it will impede efficient development planning.

In this chapter we first of all investigate the causes of instability in both commodity prices and export earnings; then move on to examine the implications of export instability for LDCs; and, finally, discuss the empirical evidence on the extent of export instability.

The Causes of Export Instability: Theoretical Analysis

It might be helpful to begin this section by explaining briefly the concept of instability. For many economic phenomena, including prices and export earnings, there exists a time trend.[1] Over a lengthy period of time there may be a tendency for export prices or earnings to rise or fall by an average annual or monthly percentage amount. This long-term trend is affected by secular movements in certain determining variables.[2] In any particular month or year, however, there may be short-term factors at work which cause prices or earnings to deviate from the value that might have been expected on the basis of the trend. The greater the propensity of a time series to deviate from trend, the more unstable that series is said to be.

Instability may, however, be seen as comprising two elements. The first is the incidence, frequency or sporadicity of deviations from trend, whilst the second is the mean amplitude of deviations. Although, under either criterion, the central notion of instability remains that of deviations from trend, most instability indices fail to differentiate between the amplitude and sporadicity elements of instability.[3]

The deviations which constitute instability will be both positive and negative; and, in the long term will have to cancel each other out if the trend is to remain unchanged. A preponderance of deviations in either direction would eventually influence the trend in that direction.[4]

In this section we shall be examining the short-term factors which cause a country's export earnings to deviate from their trend value, whilst in the next chapter we shall examine factors which influence the trend. Let us begin our examination by isolating those factors which might cause the price of any particular commodity to change.

In theory, the equilibrium or market-clearing price of a commodity is determined by the interaction of forces of demand and supply. The equilibrium price is that price at which demand equals supply. Any equilibrium price may be disturbed by autonomous changes in either demand or supply or non-offsetting changes in both demand and supply. A change in any of the determining variables will cause price to change and carry on changing until a new market clearing price is established. Thus, for example, an autonomous increase in demand will, *ceteris paribus*, create excess demand at the old equilibrium price. In order to eradicate this excess demand, market forces will encourage the price to rise. The rise in price will tend to have two effects. First, it will tend to reduce demand, the extent of the reduction depending on the price elasticity of demand. The higher the price elasticity of demand the greater will be the reducing impact of the rise in price on demand. The second effect of the rise in price will be to encourage profit-maximising, and indeed growth-maximising, producers to increase their supply. The extent to which a rise in price brings forth an increase in supply depends positively on the price elasticity of supply.

In a free market, price variations occur in such a way that equality between demand and supply is maintained. An autonomous increase in demand or fall in supply creates excess demand and causes price to rise, whilst an autonomous fall in demand or increase in supply creates excess supply and causes price to fall. The size of the price variations is inversely related to the price elasticities of demand and supply. Where these elasticities are low, the size of the price variations which occur in response to autonomous shifts in demand and supply schedules will tend to be large.

In principle, then, fluctuations in the price of a commodity may be explained in terms of autonomous variations in either the demand for, or the supply of, that commodity. Short-run shifts in the demand curve for a product may occur as a result of a number of factors. Perhaps the most important influence on short-term demand variations is changes in the level or distribution of world income. The extent to which variations in world income induce variations in the demand for particular commodities depends on the income elasticity of demand for these goods. Where the income elasticity of demand for a good is high, a given change in world income will, other things being equal, exert a more marked impact on the price of this commodity than where income elasticity is low. It might be assumed, for instance, that the demand for raw materials would be influenced by the level of industrial activity and income in the world to a much greater extent than would the demand for basic foodstuffs, and that, therefore, fluctuations in the level of world income would have a much greater influence over the price movements of raw materials than of foodstuffs. This need not necessarily be the case, since the impact on price of any given shift in a demand curve depends on the price elasticity of the supply curve (see Figure 3.1). It is frequently

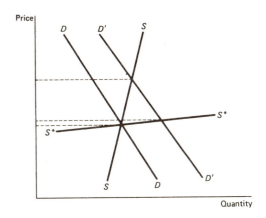

FIGURE 3.1 Shows how the effect on price of a given rightward shift in the demand curve from *DD* to *D'D'*, depends on the price elasticity of the supply curve. Compare the size of the change in price when the supply curve is price elastic (*S*S**) with the size of the change in price when it is inelastic (*SS*)

assumed, however, that the short-run price elasticity of supply of most primary products is low. If this assumption is valid, autonomous variations in demand will cause relatively large fluctuations in commodity prices. Furthermore, and in the case of primary commodities in particular, price movements may be exacerbated or cushioned by changes in the price expectations of speculators. Thus, if, for example, speculators take a rise in the price of a commodity as an indication that the price will rise further, demand will increase and the price will indeed rise.

Short-run fluctuations in the supply of commodities such as food and agricultural raw materials may be caused by variations in weather and the incidence of disease. Again, the impact of such phenomena on the price of a commodity will depend on the price elasticity of demand (see Figure 3.2). The lower this is, the greater will be the change in price.[5] It is

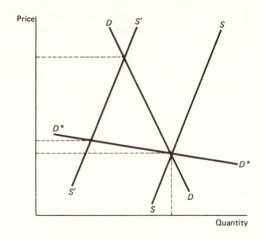

FIGURE 3.2   Shows how the effect on price of a given leftward shift in the supply curve from *SS* to *S'S'* depends on the price elasticity of the demand curve. The increase in price is larger where the price elasticity is low (*DD*) than where it is high (*D*D**)

characteristically assumed that the price elasticity of demand for many of the world's primary commodities is low, largely because of the absence of substitutes. In these circumstances, short-run fluctuations in world supply will exert a relatively large impact on the prices of these commodities.

It clearly emerges from our analysis that, where variations in the demand for, or the supply of, particular commodities are induced not by changes in the price of the commodities but by other factors, they will themselves exert an influence over the prices of the commodities. If, as is usually assumed, neither the demand for primary products nor the supply of primary products is very responsive to changes in price, at least in the short run, then it would appear to be quite valid, theoretically, to anticipate that autonomous fluctuations in the demand for and the supply of such commodities would cause significant variations in the prices of those commodities.

Another potential factor in the explanation of commodity-price instability is the operation of cobweb-type adjustment systems. In some kinds of production there is a considerable lag between production decisions being made and the resultant output coming onto the market. Production decisions may be taken on the basis of prices which do not prevail when the output actually comes to be sold. Let us suppose that from an intial situation of equilibrium the demand curve for a certain agricultural commodity shifts to the right. In the short term, supply cannot respond to this increase in demand, because of the assumed and technically determined gestation period for production. As a result of this, and in order to ration the unchanged supply, the short-term price rises above its long-term equilibrium level as determined by the intersection of the long-term demand and supply curves; producers may respond to this temporarily high price by planning their future supply on the basis of this price rather than the lower long-term equilibrium price. When these supply plans come to fruition, the price of the good will fall below the long-term equilibrium price, because of excess supply. Again, producers may respond to this short-term fall in price by cutting back supply to a level less than that associated with the long-term equilibrium price. The short-run inelasticity of supply serves to generate a series of prices which lie above and below the long-term equilibrium price. The price cycle may be stable or unstable depending on the relative slopes of the demand and supply curves. Where the slope of the supply curve is greater than the slope of the demand curve, the system is dynamically stable and the price will eventually gravitate towards its long-term equilibrium. But, where the slope of the supply curve is less steep than the slope of the demand curve, the system is dynamically unstable and the market price will move progressively further away from equilibrium. The basic notion behind the cobweb model is that, from a long-term point of view, producers over-respond to short-term price movements. They may, by their actions, actually cause further price instability.

We have clearly established that price instability may result from autonomous variations in either demand or supply. The question now emerges of whether supply changes are more or less important than demand changes in explaining commodity-price instability. In theory it might be expected that the relative importance of demand and supply factors will vary according to time period and commodity. During the period of world boom around 1973, for example, demand factors were clearly significant in explaining the rise in primary-product prices[6], as indeed they were during the Korean War, when anticipated supply bottlenecks resulted in the stockpiling of commodities on a world-wide scale. During a period of world recession such as 1975, demand factors again may be seen as contributing significantly to the price reductions witnessed. More broadly (and assuming that the income elasticity of demand for food is positive), it might be anticipated that a period of generally rising (falling) primary-product prices, typified by raw-material prices rising (falling) more rapidly than those of foodstuffs, could, in the main, be explained in terms of world-demand factors, and that reasonably isolated fluctuations in the prices of certain foodstuffs could, perhaps, be explained more appropriately by short-term supply variations. The problem of identifying the countribution made by demand and supply forces to price instability is, of course, more complicated than the above explanation might suggest. For example, the significance of demand influences will vary between different commodities, depending on factors such as income elasticities of demand, and technological advances in the use of materials. Even so, since supply forces are perhaps more likely to be commodity-specific than are demand forces, some indication as to the cause of commodity-price instability may be gleaned from the general pattern and universality of the instability.[7]

Developing countries will be less directly concerned about commodity-price instability as such than about the instability in export earnings to which it may give rise. Commodity-price instability need not necessarily be accompanied by export instability; in fact, price instability is neither a necessary nor a sufficient condition for export instability. Let us investigate the factors other than price instability which are relevant to the determination of export instability.

The first of these is the volume or quantity of a commodity which is sold at particular prices. In considering export receipts we are interested not only in the unit price of exported goods but also in the number of units of the goods that are sold at each price. Revenue is, after all, equal to price multiplied by quantity. Given an autonomous variation in demand, the extent to which instability in export receipts is divided between changes in price and changes in quantity will depend on the price elasticity of supply. Whereas, with an inelastic supply curve, price and not quantity will tend to fluctuate as a result of shifts in the demand curve, with an elastic supply curve it will be the change in quantity which contributes most to the change in export receipts. In either case, however, where it is a variation in demand which is the predominant case of instability, price and quantity will move in the same direction and therefore the impact on export earnings will be intensified. The movement in quantity will endorse the movement in price (see Figure 3.3).

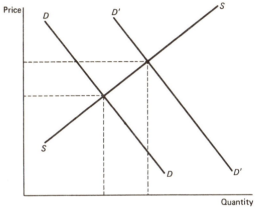

FIGURE 3.3 Export earnings rise as the demand curve shifts from *DD* to *D′D′*, since both price and quantity rise

Autonomous fluctuations in supply may also cause instability in export earnings, although, in this case, the movements in price and volume are in opposite directions and thus tend to offset or neutralise one another as far as export receipts are concerned (see Figure 3.4). The degree of neutralisation depends on the price elasticity of the demand curve. Where this is unity, price variations will have absolutely no effect on receipts, and changes in quantity will perfectly compensate for changes in price. Where the price elasticity of demand is greater than one, a fall in price, caused by a rightward shift in the supply curve, will result in an increase in receipts; and a rise in price, caused by a leftward shift in the supply curve, will result in a fall in receipts. Where the price elasticity of demand is less than one, a fall in price will result in a fall in receipts and a rise in price will result in a rise in receipts.

The price elasticity of a demand curve may, of course, and indeed probably will, vary along its length. From an initial equilibrium price,

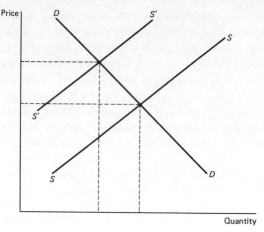

FIGURE 3.4   Export earnings may rise or fall as the supply curve shifts from *SS* to *S'S'*, depending on the price elasticity of the demand curve. In the case of a demand curve with elasticity equal to one, export earnings will remain unchanged as the supply curve shifts

for instance, demand may be relatively inelastic in an upward direction but relatively elastic in a downward direction. In this case a leftward shift in the supply curve will cause a relatively large increase in both price and earnings. A rightward shift in the supply curve would serve to produce quite a small fall in price, but would still serve to increase earnings as compared with the initial equilibrium (see Figure 3.5).

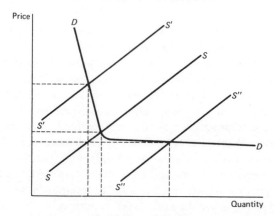

FIGURE 3.5   Shows that, with varying price elasticity of demand about a point, both a leftward and rightward shift in the supply curve may cause export earnings to rise

Earnings instability from a particular commodity may then be either greater or less than the degree of commodity-price instability, depending on whether the dominant cause of instability is demand- or supply-oriented, and depending further on the elasticities of the demand and supply schedules for the commodity. The price elasticity of foreign demand for a particular commodity which a producing/exporting country encounters will depend on the importance of the exporting country as a supplier of that commodity. Where the country's share of the export market is relatively small, the foreign-demand curve will tend to be relatively elastic, since substitute sources of supply will be available. The elasticity of the foreign-demand schedule that faces an exporting country will, indeed, tend to be inversely related to the significance of that country as a world supplier of the commodity. It follows that for many LDCs which supply only a small fraction of the total world supply of a commodity, autonomous domestic variations in the supply of the commodity will directly result in proportionately greater fluctuations in the export earnings derived from that commodity than in the price of the commodity. In the extreme, the quantity of a commodity supplied and exported by a small LDC will have no influence at all over the world price of the commodity; the LDC will be a price taker. In these circumstances a shift in the supply schedule of the LDC will simply mean that more or less of the commodity is sold at a given price. Where the demand schedule is infinitely elastic, then, domestic supply variations will affect quantity and total revenue but not price (see Figure 3.6).

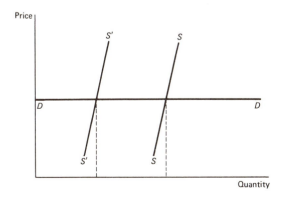

FIGURE 3.6 Shows that, with an infinitely elastic demand schedule, autonomous supply variations influence quantity (Q) and total revenue (PQ) but not price (P)

On the other hand, domestic supply variations in an LDC which supplies a large fraction of the world output of a commodity may serve to vary the price of that commodity at the world market level. For such a major producer, then, a shift in its supply curve will induce a change in price and a change in its export earnings (unless the demand curve exhibits unit-price elasticity). Where, in a particular market, there coexist major and minor producing countries, it is quite possible that supply variations in a major producing country will induce price and earnings instability in the minor producing countries, since these major supply variations will cause the demand curve facing the small producers to shift vertically.

It emerges from the preceding analysis that we should be able to derive something about the actual causes of export instability from information concerning the directional relationship between changes in the prices and volumes of particular exports. Furthermore, it should be possible to derive some indication of price elasticities from the relative stability of the price and volume series.

The nature of the relationship between price and quantity will tell us whether instability has been predominantly caused by shifts in the demand schedule or by shifts in the supply schedule. Where price and quantity move in the same direction (are positively correlated), the dominant cause of instability is shifts in the demand curve. Where price and quantity move in the opposite direction (are negatively correlated), the dominant cause of instability is shifts in the supply curve. Let us assume that in a particular instance price and volume are positively correlated. The dominant cause of instability is in this case a shift in the demand schedule. Assuming that the supply curve does not shift at all, evidence that the proportionate change in volume is greater than the proportionate change in price will tell us that the supply schedule is elastic. On the other hand, greater proportionate price instability than volume instability would be consistent with a price-inelastic supply curve.[8]

Export receipts earned from any one commodity may further depend on the income elasticity of domestic demand. This will be a particularly important factor where a substantial proportion of production is consumed domestically, since in these circumstances shifts in the domestic demand schedule encouraged by, for example, internal-demand management policies will influence the amount of the good that is available for export and thus the level of export earnings.

Export Concentration

So far we have explained price instability in terms of shifts in demand and supply; and the degree of price instability, and the effect of shifts in demand and supply on export earnings, in terms of the price elasticities of demand and supply. We have so far, however, been talking about factors which will influence the stability of export earnings made from one particular commodity. The factors which we have discussed are relevant to any producer of a primary product. We may now move on to examine an additional factor which influences the stability of a country's *total* export earnings. The additional factor is export concentration and it is perhaps this factor which is of particular relevance to less-developed primary-product producing countries.

On the basis of the simple notion that it is possible to spread risks by means of diversification, it may be hypothesised that countries which specialise in the production and export of one commodity are more likely to encounter export instability than are countries which produce a range of exports or, whilst still selling one or a few commodities, sell them in a range of different markets. Export instability will tend to be inversely related to the degree of export diversification. Thus it might be anticipated that export instability would be more marked for countries which have an undiversified export mix, and which, therefore, have export receipts reflecting, more precisely, instabilities in the prices of particular commodities. For countries with a diversified export mix, the closeness of the relationship between export receipts and the prices of individual export commodities will be reduced if individual export prices are not positively and linearly related. Differential export-price movements will in these circumstances tend to offset one another to some extent. Although export concentration is neither a necessary nor a sufficient condition for export instability, it will, as we have seen, tend to result in export instability where the demand for or supply of the commodity exported fluctuates. Similarly, whilst diversification is neither a necessary nor sufficient condition for export stability, it will tend to reduce export instability where the various commodities exported are negatively interrelated. Since the theory of comparative advantage and, perhaps more especially, the pursuit of economies of scale may encourage small developing countries with limited domestic demand and limited natural resources to specialise fairly narrowly in the production of one or a few commodities, it might also be anticipated that small countries will tend to experience more export instability than larger and more developed countries. Whilst the presentation of the relationship between export diversification and export instability given above seems intuitively quite plausible, care has to be exercised inasmuch as the notion of instability incorporates both the average amplitude of deviations and their sporadicity. Diversification may simultaneously lower the average amplitude of deviations but also make deviations more sporadic and uncertain.[9] If it is the uncertainty aspect of export instability that is deemed undesirable, diversification may enhance the problem of export instability rather than mitigate it.

It emerges from our discussion that, in essence, the factors which might account, or help to account, for instability of export earnings in a particular country reduce to the nature, type and range of commodities exported, and certain structural characteristics of the individual country under examination.

The Causes of Export Instability: Empirical Evidence

In the foregoing section we have managed to identify a number of factors which are theoretically relevant to the explanation of export instability. A certain amount of empirical research is available which provides evidence on the causes of export instability. The usual approach adopted in the empirical studies has been to regress export instability on a number of independent explanatory variables.[10]

Unfortunately, no clear picture emerges from the empirical evidence; indeed, much of the evidence is conflicting. Early work by Coppock (1962) and Massell (1964) failed to find very much association between export instability and either the commodity concentration of exports or, more specifically, the concentration of exports on primary products. This finding has recently found substantiation in the research of Askari and Weil (1974) and Khalaf (1976). Furthermore, Kingston (1976) maintains that geographic export concentration has little discernible effect on the stability of export earnings. Somewhat surprisingly, Coppock discovered that over the period 1946–58 the export proceeds from primary products were more stable than those from manufactured goods. This finding is confirmed by Askari and Weil for the period 1954–68. However, Massell (1970) did find evidence to support the belief that the degree of export instability is positively related to the degree of export concentration. It would appear from this piece of research that dependence on a limited number of export commodities is a factor in explaining export instability. The IMF and IBRD in a Joint

Staff Study (1969) found that the degree of coincidence between fluctuations in earnings from different commodities was such that diversification did reduce the mean amplitude of fluctuations in total export earnings. Considering all LDCs together, the IMF–IBRD observed that a weighted average of fluctuation indices for earnings from individual commodities was greater than the fluctuation index for total export earnings. Indeed, it was discovered that the existence of offsetting fluctuations in the earnings derived from different commodities served to reduce fluctuations in the total export earnings of LDCs as a group to less than a third of what they would have been in the absence of any offsetting effects. The existence of a large amount of residual instability which remains unexplained by concentration does, however, suggest that export concentration is not the sole cause of instability.

There is some empirical evidence available (see Massell, 1970) which suggests the existence of a positive relationship between export instability and the ratio of domestic consumption to exports, and a negative relationship between export instability and the ratio of food exports to total exports. These findings may, in theory, be interpreted quite satisfactorily. First, as has been noted, where a substantial proportion of production is consumed domestically, instabilities in domestic demand may be reflected in export-earnings instability. Second, if the price of foodstuffs is more stable than the price of raw materials, it might be expected that a country's export instability would decline as exports of food assume a greater importance relative to exports of raw materials. The relative stability of food prices as compared with raw-material prices, implied by the empirical relationship mentioned above, in turn implies certain things about the basic causes of export instability. Assuming that variations in demand from abroad are the principal cause of fluctuations in the prices of raw materials, whilst shifts in supply are the main cause of fluctuations in the prices of foodstuffs,[11] it follows that fluctuations in demand may be relatively more important than fluctuations in supply when explaining overall export instability. Unfortunately, this inference conflicts with the conclusion reached by Porter (1969) concerning the causes of commodity-price instability. Porter found that, although fluctuations in both demand and supply exert a significant influence over price variations, for about half the commodities studied, supply fluctuations tended to dominate. The suggestion that fluctuations in demand may be more important than supply fluctuations in explaining export instability also conflicts with an inference which may be drawn from Glezakos's finding that LDCs experience greater volume instability than price instability (see Glezakos, 1973). Relatively larger volume than price instability is consistent with the view that fluctuations in the export earnings derived from any particular commodity are caused by the fact that the commodity's supply schedule is both price-inelastic and unstable, whilst its demand schedule is price-elastic. Larger volume than price instability would be consistent with a demand model of export instability only if it were simultaneously hypothesised that the short-run supply curve for raw materials is price-elastic – a hypothesis which theoretically would appear to be rather untenable.

It may, of course, be rather misleading to take an aggregative approach to the causes of export instability in LDCs. As was noted in the first section of this chapter, in theory, the causes of observed export instability in any particular LDC depend very much on the significance of the country as a supplier of individual commodities, and the nature of its commodity exports. Given snippets of information concerning the sign of the correlation between price and quantity, relative price volume and earnings instability, the proportion of world output supplied by individual LDCs, and even direct information on price and income elasticities of demand and supply,[12] it may be possible to suggest the particular configuration of demand and supply forces which individual LDCs face. Thus, instability in the export earnings of a raw-material exporting country are perhaps more likely to be caused by shifts in the demand schedule than by shifts in the supply schedule, whilst shifts in the supply schedule are likely to be more significant in explaining instability in a food-exporting country. Where an LDC is a major producer of a food product, shifts in the supply curve will tend to influence the market price, though, where quantity and price are closely and negatively correlated, export earnings may be relatively constant. For small food-exporting LDCs the existence of greater volume and earnings instability than price instability would suggest that earnings instability is caused by domestic supply variations, whilst in bigger exporting countries a relatively high degree of price instability might suggest that supply variations are a major cause of instability. Unfortunately, comparison of proportionate changes in price and quantity do not allow us to draw firm conclusions concerning price elasticities, since it is quite likely that demand and supply schedules will both be shifting at the same time.

The theoretical appraisal of empirical evidence may, then, allow us to group developing countries, as producers of particular commodities, into a range of categories as suggested by Figure 3.7. We have already

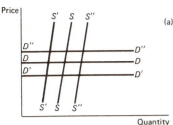

(a) Small food-producing countries; e.g. Mauritius (sugar).
Domestic supply variations are the dominant cause of
export instability, and volume and earnings instability
will be greater than price instability.

(b) Small raw-material producing countries; e.g. Cyprus (copper).
Price and earnings instability will tend to be greater
than volume instability.

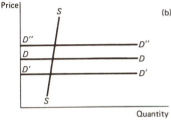

(c) Large food-producing countries; e.g. Ghana (cocoa),
Brazil (coffee), Burma (rice).
Export earnings will tend to be more stable than either
price or volume. Price and volume are negatively
correlated.

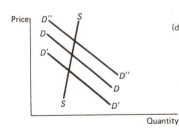

(d) Large raw-material producing countries; e.g. Chile (copper)
and Malaysia (rubber).
Relative price, volume, and earnings instability will
depend on the elasticity of the supply curve. Price
and volume are non-negatively correlated. The diagram
shows a case where, because of the inelasticity of the
supply curve, the degree of price and earnings
instability exceeds the degree of volume instability.

FIGURE 3.7

established that, in theory, export instability depends, in part, on the
degree of export concentration. For all the countries cited in Figure 3.7,
heavy concentration on one commodity means that price, volume and
earnings instabilities for that commodity get transmitted through to
total export earnings and the balance of payments. It might be expected

that, as countries diversify their export base, so instability in export earnings as measured by the average amplitude of deviations from trend will tend to decline. Empirical evidence exists that is consistent with this expectation. Diversification is one element of economic development. This being so, it might further be expected that the level of development would be negatively associated with instability; direct evidence to support this expectation exists. Lawson (1974), for instance, discovered an inverse relationship between export instability and the absolute size of the export sector.[13] Over a period running from 1954 to 1966, Erb and Schiavo-Campo (1969) found that export instability was significantly and inversely related to the size of an economy, as measured by gross domestic product (GDP). Confirming this, in the eight LDCs in their study with GDP greater than $4000 million they observed that the degree of export instability was not very different from that common amongst developed countries. Khalaf (1976), however, finds no relationship between country size and either export instability or income instability.

Although, because of the absence of uniformity amongst empirical studies, it is difficult to generalise about the causes of export instability, a number of conclusions do appear to emerge from the theoretical analysis and the available empirical evidence. LDCs in general do seem to possess fairly undiversified export mixes.[14] The commodities upon which LDCs tend to concentrate their export production do tend to be those sorts of commodities which are susceptible to short-run shifts in demand and supply and price variability. Such shifts in demand and supply, given the lack of diversification, tend to have rather a direct impact on export earnings and therefore the balance of payments. Largely then, it does seem reasonable to explain export instability in LDCs in terms of the nature of the exported commodities and the structural characteristics of LDCs. However, the fact that some LDCs do experience less export instability than developed countries[15] endorses the idea that the explanation of export instability is to be found in the structural characteristics of economies rather than in the low level of per capita national income itself. Even so, it perhaps remains true that the circumstances most likely to result in export instability are more likely to be found in developing than in developed countries.

The Consequences of Export Instability: Theoretical Analysis

In order to isolate the economic implications of export instability, we theoretically need to be able to make a comparison between the actual values of certain key economic variables in a situation where export instability exists and the values that these variables would assume were exports to behave according to trend. For such a comparison to be meaningful, it would, furthermore, be necessary for all other economic influences to be the same for both situations; otherwise, observed differences in the key variables could not legitimately be attributed solely to export instability. In assessing the influence of export instability on any particular country, we are forced to compare a known state of affairs with an unknown one. All that can be done is to make an informed estimate of what the situation would have been in other circumstances. Similarly, in the case of a cross-sectional comparison between countries which is designed to calculate the influence of export instability, it is theoretically necessary to find two countries which are identical in all aspects other than the degree of export instability which they experience.

In assessing the consequences of export instability it is important clearly to establish that we are not concerned only with the implications of an export shortfall or excess. Rather, we are concerned with the implications of instability about a trend, instability which, by definition, over the long run incorporates equivalent positive and negative deviations.

In Figure 3.8, *AB* represents the time trend in the export earnings of a particular country, whilst *CD* represents the actual time path of export earnings. The shaded areas *E* and *G* represent export excesses, whilst the shaded areas *F* and *H* represent export shortfalls. Given that the areas *E*, *F*, *G* and *H* are by assumption exactly equivalent, it may not be clear at

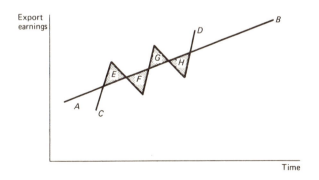

FIGURE 3.8

first sight why export instability should be undesirable, since export shortfalls are, in this case, matched precisely by export excesses. Instability in export earnings will constitute a problem only if any costs associated with export shortfalls exceed any benefits associated with export excesses, or if export excesses themselves involve costs, or if instability as such involves costs. Let us examine each of these possibilities.

The costs of an export shortfall may outweigh the benefits of an export excess

An export shortfall will tend to have a number of macroeconomic consequences for the country experiencing it. These consequences may be conveniently analysed on the basis of a simple income-expenditure model,

$$Y = C + I + G + X - M$$

where Y represents the level of national income, C represents consumption, I represents investment, G represents government expenditure, X represents exports and M represents imports. The model suggests that an autonomous fall in exports will induce a multiplied reduction in income, the size of the reduction depending positively on the size of the multiplier. Since the marginal propensity to consume in developing countries might, theoretically, be expected to be larger than in developed countries, it might be anticipated that the size of the multiplier will be larger in LDCs than in developed countries, and that, therefore, a given fall in exports will have a greater reducing impact on national income in LDCs than in developed countries.[16]

A change in income will influence the value of those variables that depend, at least partially, on it. Thus a fall in income will tend to cause a decline in domestic consumption, personal saving, government tax receipts, and private investment. These changes will, in turn, tend to exert an adverse influence on the rate of economic growth,[17] the level of employment, domestic living standards and the fiscal balance. The fall in the rate of economic growth will tend to result from the fall in investment. The fall in the standard of living will result from the fall in consumption and national income. The fall in the level of employment will result from the fall in consumption, investment and output. The deterioration in the fiscal balance will result from the fact that the level of tax receipts is likely to be more dependent on the level of national income than is government expenditure. If the fall in tax receipts creates or worsens a fiscal deficit, the authorities will become faced with the problem of financing this deficit. A fiscal deficit may be financed through borrowing and/or the creation of money; a policy of domestic money-creation will, however, cause inflation in circumstances where the rate of growth of the money supply exceeds the rate of growth of real domestic resources.

Although, in theory, a fall in income brought about by an autonomous fall in exports will tend to reduce the demand for imports, the balance of trade will still tend to deteriorate following an autonomous fall in exports. The extent of the deterioration in the balance of trade will, however, tend to be less than the export shortfall, because, as just explained, imports will also tend to fall, thereby offsetting to a degree the impact of the export shortfall on the trade balance. The effect of an export shortfall on the balance of trade depends on the size of the multiplier, the size of the income elasticity of demand for imports, and the relative price implications of the export shortfall. The lower the value of the multiplier, and the lower the value of the income elasticity of demand for imports associated with a fall in income, the greater will be the deterioration in the balance of trade, relative to any given fall in exports.

It might be assumed that in LDCs the demand for imports is income-inelastic in a downward direction, since many LDCs will import only the minimum of non-essential goods. To the extent that imports of a developmental nature are reduced, economic growth will be inhibited. Perhaps in LDCs particularly, a balance-of-trade deficit which has been caused through an export shortfall is likely to be dealt with by means of the imposition or strengthening of import controls. Again, where these controls limit or reduce the import of not only luxury, or non-essential, goods, but also strategic developmental goods, the impact on output, growth and development can hardly be anything but deleterious. The conservation of foreign exchange in such cases may, indeed, involve a high opportunity cost.

A final 'cost' associated with an export shortfall relates to its distributional implications. For any country, a fall in export earnings will tend to disturb the existing distribution of income. There is likely to be a relative fall in export-sector incomes. To the extent that re-distribution is resented and resisted internally, problems of economic management may be created.

It might be supposed that the consequences of export earnings rising above their trend value would be the exact opposite of those associated with an export shortfall. Certainly, on the basis of a simple income-expenditure model, a rise in exports would be expected to bring about a multiplied expansion in national income; an increase in consumption, saving and investment; and an increase in the fiscal surplus and balance-of-trade surplus (or, in the case of an initial deficit, a movement towards surplus). An export excess would, in theory, serve to weaken the foreign-exchange constraint on development and permit an increase in imports, since a higher level of imports would now be associated with balance-of-trade equilibrium. In the specific case of LDCs, however, there is some reason to doubt whether these consequences would necessarily follow an export excess. LDCs will, rather more than developed countries perhaps, tend to lack the domestic resources that are required to combine with extra imported resources in order to generate economic growth. Even where the domestic resources exist, LDCs may have low levels of structural mobility and flexibility, which effectively prevent the immediate realisation of the potential developmental gains which an increase in export earnings makes possible. It may be, then, that domestic supply bottlenecks and low absorptive capacity will hinder growth.

It is basically for this sort of reason that some commentators have suggested that, on balance, export instability exerts an adverse affect on LDCs.[18] The argument runs as follows: whilst LDCs cannot take immediate advantage of an increase in export earnings, an export shortfall immediately reduces an LDC's ability to finance imports. If LDCs had large international reserves, it would be possible to finance the short-term decline in export receipts without reducing imports; and, if a sufficient proportion of LDCs' imports were 'non-essential', it would be possible to reduce these without affecting the fundamental basis of development. Where, however, reserves are low and access to international borrowing is limited, and, furthermore, where non-essential imports have already been reduced to the minimum, the implication of a shortfall in export receipts is a reduction in strategic 'developmental' imports. A reduction in such imports is likely to have a fairly direct impact on economic growth, since it is unlikely that it will be possible to substitute domestic production for importation at zero opportunity cost.

The argument just presented possesses one important flaw. This is that, even though an LDC may not be able immediately to derive full developmental gains from an export excess, because it is not in a position to use all the extra export receipts, there is nothing to prevent the LDC in question from storing up the gains in the form of additional, precautionary foreign-exchange reserves. Subsequently, when faced with an export shortfall, the LDC may use its accumulated reserves to maintain imports and thus avoid the developmental costs of an export shortfall. Theoretically, then, there is nothing to stop LDCs from taking the gains associated with an export excess and using them to avoid the costs associated with an export shortfall; but in practice such a policy might be difficult to operate.

Export excesses may involve costs

In the previous sub-section, export excesses were presented as potentially providing real gains. This need not necessarily be the case. If, for instance, an increase in a country's international reserves, generated by an export excess, is, in turn, translated into an increase in the domestic money supply, then, where aggregate monetary demand expands at a faster rate than real supply, the result is likely to be inflation and an increase in imports.

Not only might the monetary implications of an export excess be directly inflationary, but inflation may also result from the operation of a spillover mechanism. An increase in the level of profits in the export sector may encourage an increase in money wages in the export sector, which, at the sectoral level, is non-inflationary. The increase in money wages in the export sector may, however, through parity awards spill over into the rest of the economy, where, if the increase in money wages is greater than the increase in productivity, it will be inflationary.

In addition to the fact that an export excess may be inflationary as an automatic result of its monetary and spillover consequences, governments in LDCs may find themselves, following an excess in export earnings, under considerable pressure to pursue discretionary expansionary policies. Such policies may be inappropriate in terms of the productive potential of the economy, and may generate inflation, which is difficult to control. Indeed, where the inflation becomes expected, the costs of correction may easily outweigh any short-run benefits, in terms of additional real output and higher levels of employment, deriving from the expansionary policies.

Export instability as such may involve costs

In addition to examining the costs of export shortfalls and export excesses separately, it is necessary to see whether export instability as such might involve costs to the exporting country. There are, in theory, various ways in which costs may be generated. To begin with, short-run instability in export earnings may lead to a net fall in export earnings in the long run, both because consumers switch away from commodities with unstable prices to those with more stable prices, and because suppliers may be risk-averters and may prefer to produce goods the returns on which are more predictable. Furthermore, for a natural material, the existence of an albeit temporarily high price may induce the innovation of a synthetic substitute. The production and marketing of a synthetic substitute will probably exert a fairly permanent reducing impact on the demand for, and the export earnings to be had from, the natural product. Demand irreversibility may also serve to exert a ratchet effect on export earnings. Customers may switch out of a product when its price is relatively high, but may fail to switch back into it when the price is relatively low. This effect is likely to be most marked for those primary products where synthetic substitutes are available, and where the customer's cost of switching between inputs is high.

The effect of export instability on long-term supply is likely to be greatest in the agricultural sector, where uncertainty about the future price of agricultural commodities may deter the transition from subsistence agriculture to the production of cash crops. However, the main problem associated with the uncertainty surrounding export instability relates to development planning. An important strand of planning in LDCs is that of formulating a view on the future foreign-exchange position. This depends on projected imports payments, debt servicing, capital flows and, of course, export receipts. Since export instability usually means that it is difficult to forecast export earnings with any precision, risk-averting planners may be tempted to opt for 'robust' and flexible development plans, which need not be optimal from the point of view of any specific and actual set of circumstances, but may be near-optimal in most eventualities. Wrong prediction, uncertainty and risk-aversion may then bring about a misallocation of resources. Furthermore, uncertainty, which directly applies to the export sector, but which indirectly, and through the export sector, applies to the entire economy, may deter investment, and, thereby, slow down the rate at which output expands. [19]

The degree of uncertainty generated by export instability may itself depend on the nature of the instability. Less uncertainty will be associated with export instability which takes the form of fairly frequent, small and even, perhaps, predictable cyclical deviations from trend than with export instability which takes the form of large, random and therefore unpredictable deviations from trend. Furthermore, in theory, the existence of diminishing marginal utility of income would suggest that the welfare losses following a fall in income induced by an export shortfall would fail to be compensated by the welfare gains that would be derived from a similarly sized increase in income induced by an export excess. If the notion of diminishing marginal utility of income is accepted, then it is fairly clear that, given a similar trend in export earnings, social welfare will be higher the greater the degree of export stability about that trend; or, given a certain degree of export instability, measured by the percentage deviation from trend, the smaller and more regular are the deviations.

So far we have concentrated on the consequences of export instability for exporting countries. As events in the early 1970s clearly demonstrated when there was an unanticipated and substantial increase in the prices of many important primary commodities, export instability in the exporting countries may, since the exports of one country, or one group of countries, simultaneously constitute the imports of other countries, have implications for importing countries as well. Export instability is, indeed, another way of looking at import instability. Although the implications of export instability in one foreign country or group of countries may be dissipated for importing countries by the diversification of imports, importing countries may, if the instability relates to a strategic primary import, experience definite and definable consequences as a direct result of export instability elsewhere in the international economy. Where import instability causes short-term fluctuations in the terms of trade, these fluctuations will have macroeconomic consequences for the standard of living, the level of employment and/or the balance of payments in the importing country.[20] For primary-product importing LDCs, relatively low levels of access to international liquidity will serve to lessen the degree of flexibility which they enjoy in the formulation of their domestic economic policy following a sudden rise in import prices as compared with developed countries.[21]

LDCs may, furthermore, be more vulnerable to, and more effected by, import instability than are developed countries, since they are more likely to be heavily reliant on individual imports such as oil. From a microeconomic viewpoint, LDCs may again find it less easy than do developed countries to adjust their economies to short-term (or, indeed, long-term) relative price changes, either by shifting to and from alternative imported substitutes or by shifting to and from domestically produced substitutes. In the case of the sudden rise in the price of oil that occurred in 1973, LDCs which depended heavily on oil imports and related oil-based goods experienced a very substantial deterioration in their balance of trade. The economic structure of many of these LDCs proved to be such that they found it extremely difficult to adjust their economies to this relative price change in the short run.

Although, again, import instability may be defined so that in the long run it is biased neither in terms of import price increases nor in terms of import price falls, the uncertainty to which instability gives rise and the short-term structural inflexibility which is likely to exist in many LDCs will still serve to create problems for those LDCs experiencing instability. The problems may be felt in the form of development planning, growth, employment, living standards and the balance of payments. The problems will perhaps be especially accentuated, however, where the instability takes the immediate form of a large, sudden and unforeseen increase in import prices.

It transpires that export instability will have short-term and perhaps even long-term international redistributional consequences.[22] An upward movement in the export prices and, perhaps, earnings of primary-product exporting countries and the related benefits or gains, will coincide with a rise in the import prices and, perhaps, payments[23] of primary-product importing countries and the related costs or losses. LDCs may, of course, be at one and the same time both exporters and importers of primary products.

Empirical Evidence and Interpretation

Most empirical studies which have set out quantitatively to estimate the consequences of export instability have attempted to do this by cross-sectionally regressing an index of export instability on the values of certain key economic variables such as national income. The commonly held belief that export instability exerts an adverse influence over development was challenged by results achieved in a study by MacBean (1966). Examining eleven LDCs over the period 1950–60, MacBean found little evidence to support the hypothesis that export instability is detrimental to growth. As with any finding which calls into question a commonly held belief, MacBean's conclusion that export instability did not necessarily impede development was not immediately and universally accepted, even though, as we have seen, there is some theoretical reason to believe that on balance the gains from export excesses might compensate for the losses from export shortfalls. As a consequence of this, MacBean's methodology was closely scrutinised and the relationship between export instability and development retested using different measures of export instability, different methodologies and different time periods. Unfortunately, the interest and research which MacBean's seminal study generated has failed to produce a clear picture as to the implications of export instability. Thus, although MacBean's results have been confirmed by Kenen and Voivodas (1972) and Lim (1976), Maizels (1968) found that export instability did have a significant adverse impact on GNP in about half of the LDCs in MacBean's study when the investigation was carried out on a country-by-country basis rather than on a cross-sectional one. Glezakos (1973) also doubted MacBean's results, and in his own investigation found a significant negative relationship between export instability and real per capita income growth in thirty-six LDCs. Naya (1973) also concludes that LDCs have suffered as a result of export instability. However, Rangarajan and Sundararajan (1976) find that, although the impact of export instability on income growth is significant, the direction of the relationship varies among LDCs. Whilst Kenen and Voivodas (1972), rather surprisingly in the light of their other finding, found evidence of a strong inverse connection between export instability and the level of investment in LDCs, Massell, Pearson and Fitch (1972) found that export receipts had only a negligible impact on investment. They did find, however, that annual changes in foreign-exchange receipts from all sources, and not merely exports, did have significant short-run effects on imports, investment and GNP.

The empirical evidence currently available does not permit a firm conclusion to be reached concerning either the quantitative or indeed the qualitative consequences of export instability. Whilst there are theoretical reasons, and some data, which suggest that many developing countries could suffer as a result of export instability, there is also enough evidence to suggest that not all countries which experience export instability do necessarily or automatically suffer as a direct result of it.

The question arises as to why certain LDCs appear to suffer rather more than others as a result of similar amounts of export instability. Theory provides us with a number of potential answers to this question. In theory, the extent to which a change in export earnings will effect national income will depend on the value of the expenditure multiplier. The lower the value of the multiplier, the less will be the size of the fluctuations in national income caused by variations in exports. On the basis of a multiplier formula

$$\Delta Y = \frac{\Delta X}{1 - c(1 - t) + m}$$

and assuming similar degrees of export instability, national income will be relatively more stable in countries where the marginal propensity to consume (c) is low and therefore the marginal propensity to save is high, where the marginal tax rate (t) is high, and where the marginal propensity to import (m) is high. In these circumstances export instability will exert relatively little impact on national income. The smaller are the variations in national income, the smaller will be the fluctuations in those variables (such as consumption, saving, investment, tax receipts and imports) which depend on national income.[24]

The simple income-expenditure model also predicts that export instability will have a less marked impact on the level of national income in economies where the authorities effectively pursue offsetting domestic-demand management policies. The effects of variations in exports may be offset by countervailing changes in some other component of autonomous expenditure. Basically, and for most purposes, these other components will constitute private investment and government expenditure. Investment may of course itself respond directly to export instability. The extent to which investment changes as a result of export instability will depend both on the nature of the investment function and on the government's policies towards investment. Where the determinants of investment vary as between LDCs, or the values of the response elasticities to similar determinants vary, then it is likely that the effects of export instability will, in turn, vary. More generally, it is likely that export instability will exert less of an adverse effect on growth where government control of the economy is relatively sophisticated and flexible, and where governments are able to counteract the uncertainty stemming from export instability.

Furthermore, exchange-rate policy, as conducted by the authorities, could influence the extent to which export instability exerts an impact on the domestic economy. For example, a fall in the dollar price of a primary commodity in an environment of fixed exchange rates will imply a fall in the earnings of the export sector, in terms of both foreign and domestic currency. Depreciation of the exchange rate could be used in these circumstances to maintain the value of export earnings expressed in domestic currency, although of course the value of export earnings expressed in foreign currency would still fall. Through use of the exchange rate, then, the impact of export instability on the value of exports expressed in domestic currency could be neutralised.[25]

In developing countries the supply repercussions of export instability may be as important as the demand repercussions. Variations in export receipts affect an LDC's capacity to import. From the point of view of development, there might be a vital need for imports. In serving to limit imports, an export shortfall may therefore exert a direct and significant influence over the domestic supply of commodities which have a high or strategic import content. The easier that countries find it to reduce imports without harming development, or to maintain imports in the face of an export shortfall through international borrowing, the less the detrimental affect of export instability on development will tend to be. Since different LDCs are likely to have different ratios of essential to total imports, and different degrees of access to international liquidity (even though to some extent access is positively related to the degree of export instability[26]), it is probable that LDCs will differ in terms of the effects that export instability will have on them.

Empirical Evidence on the Extent of Export Instability

As we have seen from our analysis, export instability comprises a number of determinants. A first determinant is variations in the prices of certain primary commodities, whilst a second is export concentration on these primary products.

Fairly extensive evidence on primary-product price instability has recently been presented by Stern (1976). Having assembled individual price series for thirty-three commodities over the period 1948–75, Stern first of all identifies the time trend of individual price movements, and then moves on to isolate the degree of instability about this trend. His findings with regard to both the time trend and the incidence and size of deviations from this trend are presented in Table 3.1, where a footnote explains the methodology used. It emerges from Table 3.1 that, over the period 1948–75, price instability was greatest for sugar, linseed oil, sisal, zinc, petroleum and cocoa, and least for bananas, aluminium, iron ore, butter, lamb, tea, meat and woodpulp. Rankings derived by using slightly different methodologies and different time periods do tend to show slight differences. Thus the UNCTAD, by constructing an instability index based on the average percentage deviation of monthly commodity prices from their linear trend over the period 1965–70, found that, in terms of price instability, commodities ranked as follows

TABLE 3.1
Results Derived by Stern (1976) of Logarithmic Trend Functions Fitted
to Annual Commodity-Price Series, 1948–75

	Trend coefficient[a]	Instability index[b]
Tropical products		
Coffee	0·001	0·060
Cocoa	0·033	0·085
Tea	0·006	0·044
Sugar	0·087[c]	0·137
Bananas	0·001	0·016
Food grains and feedstuffs		
Rice	0·050[d]	0·069
Wheat	0·072[e]	0·065
Corn	0·008	0·075
Fishmeal	0·076[e]	0·075
Meat and dairy products		
Meat	0·036[d]	0·046
Lamb	0·042[e]	0·041
Butter	0·023[d]	0·040
Tobacco [f]	0·037	0·078
Oilseeds and oils		
Soybeans	0·039[d]	0·054
Copra	0·012	0·064
Palmnut oil	0·023	0·068
Groundnut oil	0·088[e]	0·079
Linseed oil	0·071[d]	0·101
Fibres		
Cotton[g]	0·090[e]	0·078
Wool	0·001	0·058
Jute	0·021[e]	0·039
Sisal	0·065	0·099
Rubber	0·014	0·060
Forest products		
Woodpulp	0·028[d]	0·046
Lumber	0·085[e]	0·049
Metals		
Zinc	0·055[c]	0·090
Tin	0·053[e]	0·050
Copper	0·042[e]	0·056
Lead	0·033	0·072
Aluminium	0·037[e]	0·030
Iron Ore	0·000	0·031
Phosphates[j]	0·039	0·066
Petroleum	0·099[d]	0·089

(in descending order): sugar (21·8), copper (15·3), pepper (14·7), rice (14·6), palm oil (14·3), cocoa (13·1), tungsten (12·5), lead metal (12·4), bananas (12·0), rubber (10·6), copra (10·4), coffee (9·6), groundnut oil (9·0), palm kernels (8·9), coconut oil (8·9), groundnuts (8·9), sisal (8·0), tea (7·8) and tin (7·3). Although the different empirical studies tend to give different instability rankings, what does emerge from the studies is which commodities are particularly vulnerable to price instability. It might be anticipated that it will be those countries which concentrate on the production of these commodities that will tend to be the ones that encounter problems of export instability.

That LDCs do tend to concentrate on the export of a few commodities was stressed by the Pearson Committee (1969). Using data collected by the IMF–IBRD Joint Staff Study and reproduced here as Table 3.2, the Committee concluded that, 'almost 90 per cent of the export earnings of the developing countries derive from primary products. Moreover nearly half of these countries earn more than 50 per cent of their export receipts from a single primary product. As many as three-quarters of them earn more than 60 per cent from three primary products.' Although a very substantial proportion of the world output of many primary products comes from non-LDCs, a peculiar feature of LDCs does seem to be their relatively high degree of export concentration on primary products. A further indication of this is provided by Table 3.3, which is derived from *International Financial Statistics*. It emerges from

Table 3.1 contd.

[a] To obtain these values, a trend function of the form, $\log P_t = a + bt + e$, was fitted where P_t is the price index (1970 = 100) for year t, t is time, and e is the residual. Since, in this formulation, there was evidence of high positive correlation in the residuals, a single-stage, semidifference formulation was applied to remove the autocorrelation. This took the form $\log P_t - \hat{p} \log P_{t-1} = a_1(1 - \hat{p}) + b_1[t - \hat{p}(t-1)] + e_1$, where $\hat{p}$ is the coefficient of autocorrelation, calculated as $1 - DW/2$, and DW refers to the Durbin-Watson statistic. The corrected trend values reported in the table are the coefficients, b_1.

[b] The instability index has been calculated as the standard error of estimate of the fitted (uncorrected) trend function divided by the mean value of the dependent variable.

[c] Significant at 0.10 level.
[d] Significant at 0.05 level.
[e] Significant at 0.01 level.
[f] Series covers 1948–74.
[g] Series covers 1951–75.
[h] Series covers 1954–74.
[i] Series covers 1950–75.

Sources. Based upon data published in IBRD, *Commodity Trade and Price Trends*, 1974 edition, EC166 174 (Aug 1974); and IMF, *International Financial Statistics*, 1972 supplement and July 1975 issue.

this table that in 1970, of thirty LDCs, eighteen produced at least one primary commodity which alone accounted for over 30 per cent of that LDC's total export value.

TABLE 3.2

Commodity Concentration in the Export Trade of Developing Countries, 1965

	Percentage share of commodities in total export earnings	Three commodities as percentage share of total export earnings
Saudi Arabia	Petroleum 100	100
Libya	Petroleum 99, oilseeds 1	100
Mauritania	Iron ore 99, fish 1	100
Venezuela	Petroleum 93, iron ore 5, coffee 1	99
Gambia	Oilseeds and vegetable oils 83, fodder 14, fish 1	98
Mauritius	Sugar 96, tea 2	98
Iraq	Petroleum 94, dates 2, barley 1	97
Cuba	Sugar 86, nickel and oxide 6, tobacco 5	97
Liberia	Iron ore 73, rubber 22, coffee 1	96
Iran	Petroleum 90, cotton 4, hides and skins 1	95
Zambia	Copper 92, tobacco 1, corn 1	94
Sierra Leone	Diamonds 64, iron ore 19, oilseeds 10	93
Ceylon	Tea 63, rubber 16, coconut products 14	93
Senegal	Oilseeds and vegetable oils 79, phosphate 8, fish 4	91
Panama	Bananas 51, petroleum 30, fish 10	91
Rwanda	Coffee 52, tin 36, pyrethrum 2	90
Gabon	Timber and products 47, manganese ore 28, petroleum 15	90
Congo, People's Rep.	Timber 44, diamonds 43, oilseeds and vegetable oils 3	90
Trinidad and Tobago	Petroleum 82, sugar 6, fruits 1	89
Chad	Cotton 77, livestock 8, petroleum 4	89
Central African Rep	Diamonds 54, cotton 20, coffee 15	89
Uganda	Coffee 48, cotton 27, copper 13	88
Cambodia	Rice 49, rubber 33, corn 5	87
Uruguay	Wool 47, meat 32, hides 8	87
Sudan	Cotton 46, oilseeds and vegetable oils 30, gum arabic 11	87
Dahomey	Oilseeds and vegetable oils 78, cotton 5, coffee 3	86
Chile	Copper 70, iron ore 11, nitrates 4	85
Ghana	Cocoa beans 66, timber 12, diamonds 7	85
Columbia	Coffee 64, petroleum 18, bananas 3	85

Table 3.2 contd.

	Percentage share of commodities in total export earnings	Three commodities as percentage share of total export earnings
Niger	Oilseeds and vegetable oils 64, livestock 16, pulses 5	85
Ethiopia	Coffee 67, oilseeds 8, hides and skins 8	83
Guinea	Alumina and bauxite 65, coffee 10, bananas 8	83
Guyana	Bauxite and alumina 41, sugar 27, rice 14	82
Vietnam	Rubber 73, tea 6, oilseeds and vegetable oils 2	81
Ivory Coast	Coffee 38, timber 27, cocoa beans 16	81
Malawi	Tobacco 38, tea 28, oilseeds and vegetable oils 15	81
Surinam	Bauxite 74, rice 4, fish 2	80
Bolivia	Tin 72, lead 4, silver 4	80
Burma	Rice 62, teak 13, oilseeds 5	80
Somalia	Bananas 46, livestock 28, hides and skins 6	80
Ecuador	Bananas 53, coffee 15, cocoa 11	79
Nigeria	Oilseeds and vegetable oils 37, petroleum 26, cocoa beans 16	79
Algeria	Petroleum 52, wine 17, citrus 9	78
Jamaica	Alumina and bauxite 47, sugar 23, bananas 8	78
Togo	Phosphates 33, cocoa beans 25, coffee 20	78
Upper Volta	Livestock 58, oilseeds and vegetable oils 12, cotton 7	77
Malaya	Rubber 44, tin 28, iron ore 5	77
Indonesia	Rubber 30, petr. 38, oilseeds and vegetable oils 7	75
El Salvador	Coffee 51, cotton 20, oilseeds and vegetable oils 3	74
Dominican Rep.	Sugar 49, bauxite and conc 9, coffee 6	74
Philippines	Coconut products 35, timber 21, sugar 17	73
Afghanistan	Fruits and nuts 34, karakul skins 23, cotton 16	73
Nicaragua	Cotton 46, coffee 18, oilseeds and vegetable oils 8	72
Laos	Tin 61, coffee 5, teak 5	71
United Arab Rep.	Cotton 56, rice 8, petroleum 7	71
Costa Rica	Coffee 42, bananas 25, sugar 4	71
Guatemala	Coffee 49, cotton 18, sugar 3	70
Mali	Livestock 33, fish 20, oilseeds and vegetable oils 17	70
Haiti	Coffee 55, sugar 7, sisal 6	68
Pakistan	Jute and products 51, cotton 12, rice 5	68

Table 3.2 contd.

	Percentage share of commodities in total export earnings	Three commodities as percentage share of total export earnings
Angola	Coffee 47, diamonds 16, sisal 5	68
Honduras	Bananas 42, coffee 18, timber 8	68
Congo. Dem.		
Rep. of	Copper 52, vegetable oils 7, diamonds 7	66
Cameroon	Cocoa beans 23, coffee 23, aluminium 17	63
Tunisia	Phosphates 34, olive oil 21, iron ore 5	60
Syrian Arab		
Rep.	Cotton 44, barley 8, livestock 7	59
Thailand	Rice 34, rubber 16, tin 9	59
Paraguay	Meat 33, timber 17, cotton 8	58
Brazil	Coffee 44, iron ore 7, cotton 6	57
Argentina	Wheat 25, meat 22, corn 10	57
Malagasy		
Rep.	Coffee 32, spices 16, meat 7	55
Tanzania	Sisal 22, cotton 19, coffee 13	54
Peru	Fishmeal 22, copper 18, cotton 13	53
Morocco	Phosphates 25, citrus 14, fresh vegetables 14	53
Cyprus	Copper 24, citrus 18, potatoes 10	52
Kenya	Coffee 30, tea 13, sisal 8	51
Rhodesia	Tobacco 34, asbestos 8, copper 5	47
Mozambique	Cotton 18, cashew nuts 16, sugar 9	43
India	Jute and products 23, tea 14, iron ore 5	42
China,		
Rep. of	Sugar 13, bananas 11, rice 9	33
Mexico	Cotton 19, sugar 7, coffee 5	33
Lebanon	Citrus 8, other fresh fruit 8, pulses 8	24
Korea,		
Rep. of	Fish 9, iron ore 4, tungston ore 4	17

Note. Where a country's name is given in italics, this indicates that more than 50 per cent of total exports is derived from one commodities or commodity group.

Source. United Nations, *International Trade Yearbook*, 1965; IMF, *International Financial Statistics*; and IBRD economic reports.

TABLE 3.3
Concentration of Production of Certain Primary Products

	Country's exports of commodity as a percentage of world export of commodity		Country's export of commodity as a percentage of its total exports	
	1963	*1970*	*1963*	*1970*
Beef				
Argentina	46	13	24	14
Cacao				
Ghana	39	35	70	68
Nigeria	18	22	17	15
Cameroon	7	—	28	—
Coconut Oil				
Philippines	57	62	6	9
Sri Lanka	26	9	6	6
Coffee				
Brazil	40	32	53	34
Colombia	16	16	68	64
Ivory Coast	5	5	43	33
Uganda	4	3	50	51
Guatemala	4	3	51	34
El Salvador	4	4	49	50
Ethiopia	—	6	50	59
Copper				
Chile	29	21	69	73
Zambia	25	24	91	95
Zaire	15	15	60	67
Copra				
Philippines	85	60	23	7
Cotton				
Egypt	13	14	53	45
Mexico	9	5	20	9
Sudan	6	8	58	61
Groundnuts				
Nigeria	50	29	23	5
Senegal	34	5	74	7
Jute				
Pakistan	62	50	47	18
Lead				
Mexico	16	8	3	2

TABLE 3.3 *contd.*

	Country's exports of commodity as a percentage of world export of commodity		Country's export of commodity as a percentage of its total exports	
	1963	*1970*	*1963*	*1970*
Rice				
Burma	24	5	63	37
Thailand	23	11	36	17
Rubber				
Malaysia	36	38	48	38
Sri Lanka	5	6	15	22
Thailand	8	8	20	15
Sisal				
Tanzania	38	33	36	10
Sugar				
Philippines	12	10	20	17
Dominican Rep.	8	4	58	49
Tea				
India	48	31	17	10
Ceylon	41	20	66	55
Tin				
Malaysia	43	50	18	20
Bolivia	15	16	71	39

Source. IMF, *International Financial Statistics.*

In principle, then, it might be expected that it will be countries such as the Dominican Republic, Chile, Zambia, Zaire, Egypt, Sudan and Burma which will experience the greatest degree of export instability. This expectation may be tested, since a large amount of empirical work has been carried out which measures export instability directly. Much of this empirical work has been oriented towards discovering whether LDCs as a group experience more export instability than do developed countries. Various methodologies have been employed in the estimation of export instability.[27]

Whilst not denying that the problem of export instability might be very serious for some countries, MacBean (1966) suggested that the magnitude of fluctuations in the export earnings of LDCs was not significantly larger than that of developed countries. In examining export instability over the period 1946–58, he reached the conclusion that LDCs' export instability tended to be 'only' about 30 per cent greater than that of developed countries. Similar conclusions had previously been reached by Coppock (1962) and Massell (1964), and were subsequently reaffirmed, again for the period 1946–58, by Erb and Schiavo-Campo (1969) and, more recently, by Askari and Weil (1974). Erb and Schiavo-Campo discovered, however, that during the period 1954–66 export instability for both LDCs and developed countries was less than during the period 1946–58, but that a sharper decline had occurred for developed countries. The implication of this, namely that the inter-group variation in export instability had increased, was confirmed by their finding that the percentage difference between the mean instabilities of the two groups had widened from 31 per cent in 1946–58 to 118 per cent in 1954–66. This finding has, in turn, been confirmed by Glezakos (1973), who, studying a slightly more recent period, found that export instability was, on average, about twice as high in LDCs as in developed countries. Naya (1973) also finds that LDCs experience greater export instability than do developed countries.

Further confirmation of the decline in export instability has been provided by Lawson (1974), who examined the periods 1950–9 and 1960–9. However, Lawson maintains that the size of the decline, and whether it has been more marked for developed countries than for LDCs, depends on the particular instability index used. Where deviations from an exponential time trend are used, Lawson also discovers that over the period 1960–9 export instability was about twice as great in LDCs as in developed countries.

Examination of more recent evidence (see Hambolu, 1976) as presented in Tables 3.4 and 3.5 reveals two things of particular interest. The first finding relates to inter-group variations in export instability. Although over the period 1955–64 export instability was only moderately greater in LDCs than in developed countries, over the period 1965–74 export instability was at least twice as great in LDCs as it was in developed countries.[28] The second finding relates to inter-temporal change. Table 3.5 shows that, for both developing and developed countries, the degree of export instability was greater in 1965–74 than in 1955–64. Consistent with the first finding concerning inter-group variation, however, it may be observed that the increase was very much more marked for LDCs than for developed countries. Instead of falling, as it appeared to do in the 1950s and 1960s, over recent'years world export instability has, it seems, been increasing quite dramatically. The explanation of this increase probably lies in the rather exceptional

TABLE 3.4
Export Instability Indices for LDCs, 1955—64
and 1965—74

Country	Instability Index[a]	
	1955—64	*1965—74*
Argentina	0·096	0·252
Algeria	0·183	0·383
Bolivia	0·189	0·254
Brazil	0·062	0·302
Burma	0·088	0·206
Egypt	0·087	0·191
Ghana	0·062	0·219
Honduras	0·093	0·082
India	0·080	0·182
Iraq	0·158	0·501
Iran	0·065	0·515
Kenya	0·078	0·205
Malaysia	0·104	0·263
Mauritius	0·097	0·394
Mexico	0·108	0·235
Morocco	0·062	0·318
Nigeria	0·086	0·570
Philippines	0·101	0·259
Saudi Arabia	0·086	0·629
Singapore	0·065	0·320
Sudan	0·148	0·116
Tunisia	0·120	0·378
Venezuela	0·028	0·356
Zambia	0·171	0·189
Mean	0·105	0·305
Weighted mean[b]	0·086	0·432

[a] Standard deviation of residuals from log-linear export-earnings trend.
[b] Weighted by export share.

Source. IMF, *International Financial Statistics.*

demand and supply variations that occurred in the first half of the 1970s. Not only was there an increase in the export earnings of certain primary-product (particularly oil) exporting LDCs, but, in addition, there was a reduction in the export earnings of many oil-importing LDCs, as the recession amongst industrial countries served to reduce the demand for many of these LDCs' exports. Further examination of the statistical evidence for the periods 1955—64 and 1965—74 reveals that most of the

TABLE 3.5

Export Instability Indices for Less-Developed and Developed Countries as Groups, 1955—64 and 1965—74

	Weighted[ac]	Unweighted	Weighted[bc]	Unweighted
1955—64				
LDCs	0·105	0·086	0·091	0·074
Developed countries	0·089	0·083	0·057	0·057
Non-oil exporting LDCs	0·106	0·091	0·091	0·074
1965—74				
LDCs	0·305	0·432	0·409	0·581
Developed countries	0·217	0·202	0·203	0·207
Non-oil exporting LDCs	0·243	0·254	0·271	0·268

[a]Standard deviation of residuals from log-linear trend.
[b]Standard deviation of residuals from linear trend.
[c]Weighted by export share.

Source. IMF, *International Financial Statistics.*

increase in the export instability of LDCs relative to that of developed countries is accounted for by the export excesses of the oil-exporting LDCs. The degree of export instability in non-oil exporting LDCs did rise – indeed, more than doubled – but the increase was if anything only slightly greater for oil-importing LDCs than it was for developed countries.[29] Our conclusions with regard to the inter-group and inter-temporal variations in export instability would therefore seem to depend on whether oil-exporting LDCs are included in or excluded from the LDC category.

Although the precise details of the export-instability picture depend upon the particular instability index used and the time period studied, it clearly emerges from all the available empirical work that LDCs, as a group, do encounter greater instability in their export earnings than do developed countries. Although LDCs differ widely in their experience, the empirical evidence endorses the *a priori* belief that in general the degree of export instability will be greater in LDCs than in developed countries.

Concluding Remarks

Generalisations concerning the degree, causes and consequences of export instability amongst LDCs as a group are difficult to make, since there is a great deal of intra-group variation. However, empirical evidence exists to support the view that substantial numbers of LDCs have witnessed considerable instability in their export earnings. Unstable export earnings have a number of ramifications, not least for the balance of payments. Although the cause and implications of export instability are not always clearly defined, the degree of export instability in a country does seem largely to depend on the nature of that country's exports, defined to incorporate the relevant elasticities, and the country's industrial structure, defined to incorporate the concentration of exports. Even though, from the point of view of individual LDCs, some measure of progress is being made in reducing the degree of reliance on particular export commodities, and such diversification of the export mix might be expected to reduce export instability over time, the amount of diversification achieved has as yet, in the case of many LDCs, proved insufficient to remove the problem of export instability. It may be anticipated that export instability and the balance-of-payments problems to which it gives rise will remain a significant issue for a large number of LDCs for many years to come. The international monetary system may be used to help LDCs cope with the balance-of-payments problems that are associated with export instability. What has been done in this context, and what might be done, are questions which are examined in later chapters.

4 Trends in the Terms of Trade, Export Earnings and Import Payments of LDCs

Theoretical Analysis

In some respects rather more important than the degree of instability about a particular trend in export prices and earnings is the nature of the trend itself. It may even be that the nature of the instability problem as such depends on the trend. Thus, where the trend in export earnings is upwards,. instability may be less of a problem than where the export trend is downwards. Long-term and short-term relative price movements may be related in other, rather more direct ways. The long-run demand for a primary product may, for instance, be adversely affected by short-run price instability, especially where consumers have the option of substituting a synthetic commodity which is more stable in price. Again, long-run supply may be adversely affected by the vagaries of price and the implied difficulties of forecasting returns.

LDCs are not, of course, exclusively interested in the trend in export prices, but are rather more concerned about the trends in their export earnings and import payments, since these trends in turn determine the long-term trend in the balance of payments on current account and indicate whether future balance-of-payments difficulties are likely to arise. More generally, they are concerned about developmental problems, such as those of diversification and industrial structure. LDCs will, then, be concerned about the trend in their export and import prices to the extent that these price movements contribute to movements in export earnings and import payments.

Before moving on to discuss trends in LDCs' export earnings and import payments, it may be beneficial to examine the price component of earnings and payments in isolation. We shall begin, therefore, by examining not the trend in export price alone, since in itself this is not of central significance, but the trend in the price of exports relative to the price of imports; or, in other words, the terms of trade.

There exists a commonly held belief that LDCs have, in fact, experienced a long-run deterioration in their terms of trade such that the prices of their exports have fallen in relation to those of imports. Whilst a short-term cyclical export shortfall will tend to be compensated by a cyclical export excess, a long-run secular downward movement in the terms of trade will not be so compensated. For this reason alone, the problem of deteriorating terms of trade may be viewed as being more fundamental than that of instability.

A number of factors exert pressure on the terms of trade that face developing countries. Most important amongst these are the forces of demand and supply as applied to the particular commodities which LDCs export and import. Relative prices will tend to change where there are relative changes in the demand for and/or supply of individual imports and exports. Thus an autonomous increase in the demand for those goods which LDCs import will tend to cause the prices of these goods to rise and the terms of trade of LDCs to deteriorate, whilst an autonomous decrease in the demand for those commodities which LDCs export will cause the prices of these goods to fall and, again, the LDCs' terms of trade to deteriorate. Autonomous supply variations could similarly influence the prices of particular imported or exported goods and thus the overall terms of trade; a long-term increase in the relative supply of LDC exports would tend to bring about a deterioration in the terms of trade of LDCs.

LDCs are frequently characterised as being exporters of primary products and importers of manufactured final goods. If this characterisation is accurate, a fall in the prices of primary commodities relative to the prices of manufactured goods will bring about a decline in the terms of trade of LDCs. Such a relative price fall could be generated by differential income elasticities of demand for primary and manufactured goods. By assuming that the income elasticity of demand for manufactures is greater than the income elasticity of demand for primary products, it might be anticipated that, other things being constant, the prices of manufactured goods would rise faster than the prices of primary commodities in the wake of world income growth. Indeed, if the income elasticity of demand for primary commodities is negative, making these goods, by definition, inferior, whilst the income elasticity of demand for manufactures is positive, then world income growth will, other things remaining constant, result in an absolute fall in primary-product prices and an absolute rise in the prices of manufactured goods over the long term. To some extent, of course, the differential effects of world income growth on the prices of primary commodities and manufactured goods may be tempered by differential elasticities. Where the price elasticity of supply of primary commodities is lower than the price elasticity of supply of manufactured goods, then, even though the income elasticity of demand for primary goods may be less than the income elasticity of demand for manufactured goods, world income growth may still cause the prices of primary products to rise as much as, or even more than, the prices of manufactured goods.[1]

Inasmuch as individual LDCs generally exert little influence over the growth of world income or the relative price of the synthetic substitutes for the primary commodities which they export, it follows that LDCs will have little control over the demand determinants of their terms of trade.

On the supply side, the influence which any individual LDC has over the price of its exports and thus its terms of trade will depend, as we have seen, on its supply of particular commodities as a proportion of the world supply of these commodities. Where the proportion is very small it is unlikely that variations in the supply emanating from any one LDC will exert a significant influence over the world price of the commodity. These LDCs will, in effect, be price takers. In these circumstances, and bearing in mind that LDCs generally are not able to affect the price of the goods which they import, most LDCs are not in a position to influence their terms of trade.[2] The terms of trade of LDCs instead mirror changes in world demand and supply over which, in general, they have no control. Thus, differential movements in the terms of trade amongst LDCs to some extent reflect the different commodity composition of their exports and imports and the differential price movements of these commodities. Recent evidence has, however, clearly demonstrated that differential terms-of-trade movements amongst LDCs may also reflect the fact that LDCs have differing amounts of control over their own terms of trade. Control will tend to be at its greatest when individual LDCs supply a large proportion of the world supply of a commodity or when LDCs as an exporting group can form effective commodity cartels. Even here, however, the LDCs involved can directly influence only one element in their terms of trade: namely, the price of their exports. Their ability to bring about a permanent improvement in their terms of trade therefore largely depends on the long-term price elasticity of world demand for their exports, and the long-term price elasticity of their demand for imports. The more price-inelastic the world demand for their exports and the more price-elastic their demand for imports, the greater will be their ability to bring about a long-term improvement in their terms of trade.

The above discussion suggests that the terms of trade of LDCs will tend to decline if LDCs concentrate on the export of primary commodities and the import of manufactured goods; if the income elasticity of demand for primary commodities is lower than that for manufactured goods; if technological advance permits the production of synthetic materials at a relatively low unit cost as compared with the production of the natural material; and if the demand for primary commodities tends to be elastic in response to upward price movements, whilst the demand schedule for manufactured goods is price-inelastic. [3]

The view that the terms of trade of LDCs will show a tendency to decline is most commonly associated with Prebisch (1964). In addition to the points made above, Prebisch supported his case by arguing that, whilst primary commodities are produced in world-wide competitive markets, manufactured goods tend to be produced in oligopolistic or monopolistic markets. Imperfect market structure tends, in theory, to result in lower output and a higher price. Furthermore, Prebisch argued that, whilst productivity gains in countries producing manufactures take the form of higher incomes rather than of lower prices, productivity gains in the production of primary materials in LDCs tend to be passed on to the consumer in the form of lower prices.

As they stand, these additional points are rather simplistic and not necessarily accurate, but, instead of critically appraising the case for expecting a decline in the terms of trade of LDCs, we may note that there are also theoretical reasons, again rather simplistic, why one might expect a secular improvement in LDCs' terms of trade. The first of these reasons is that the kind of industries upon which LDCs tend to concentrate, such as agriculture and extraction, are those which are most likely to be subject to increasing unit costs, whilst those industries upon which developed countries tend to concentrate are those which are most likely to be subject to decreasing unit costs. The second reason is that world economic development might be expected to accentuate the relative scarcity of primary products. Recent concern over prospective shortages of natural resources [4] has re-emphasised this expectation. It emerges as being theoretically unclear whether the terms of trade will move in favour of or against LDCs. Let us therefore turn to the empirical evidence.

Empirical Evidence on LDCs' Terms of Trade

We have noted that LDCs are frequently characterised as being primary-product producers, whilst developed countries are characterised as being producers of manufactured goods. It is often further argued that a decline in the price of primary commodities relative to manufactures will result in a decline in the terms of trade of LDCs. In fact, excluding oil, LDCs account for only just under half of the world exports of primary commodities; but they do tend to have undiversified export mixes and to concentrate on the export of primary products. However, even concentration on primary-product exports does not necessarily imply deteriorating terms of trade, since the prices of various primary commodities show divergent trends over similar time periods. For example, over the period ranging from the early 1960s to the early 1970s, the prices of agricultural raw materials fell quite substantially in relation to the prices of manufactured goods, whilst the relative prices of food and metals showed a slight increase. If, as it would seem, the prices of primary products are not perfectly positively correlated, then it follows that different LDCs may experience different movements in their terms of trade, depending upon the particular commodities which they export.[5]

Perhaps the most balanced empirical study to date on the terms of trade of LDCs is that carried out by Wilson, Sinha, and Castree (1969). In their study they examine movements in both the commodity, or net-barter, terms of trade ($N = Px/Pm$ where Px is the price of exports and Pm the price of imports) and the income terms of trade ($I = Px/Pm \times Qx$, where Qx is the quantity of exports). The commodity terms of trade on their own tell us only about prices and not about the trade gains and losses which result from relative price changes. Before these gains and losses can be evaluated, something needs to be known about the price elasticities of demand for exports and imports. The income terms of trade, on the other hand, by multiplying the commodity terms of trade by the quantity of exports, do reveal something about the interaction between the commodity terms of trade and the price and income elasticities of demand for exports.

Wilson, Sinha and Castree discovered that between 1950–3 and 1962–5 LDCs experienced a deterioration in their net-barter terms of trade of about 9 per cent, whilst developed countries witnessed an improvement in theirs of about 10 per cent. They found that over the same period the income terms of trade for both less-developed and developed countries improved. The improvement was 57 per cent for LDCs and 136 per cent for developed countries. Thus, whilst, as a group, LDCs experienced substantial improvement in their income terms of trade over the period studied, they did considerably less well than developed countries.

As Table 4.1 illustrates, within the group of LDCs there are considerable variations. For Peru, I more than doubled whilst N fell by nearly 20 per cent. For Argentina, I increased by 76 per cent whilst N fell by 9 per cent. For Brazil, I showed a 20 per cent improvement whilst N did not improve at all. Meanwhile, for Colombia, I fell by 2 per cent and N by 17 per cent. The fact that, on average, the income terms of trade of LDCs improved over the period studied whilst the net-barter terms of trade deteriorated serves to indicate the significance of Qx, the volume of exports.

Depending on the price elasticity of demand, a fall in the price of exports may, of course, itself generate an increase in Qx. Within the LDC group, certain LDCs may face relatively price-elastic demand curves for their exports, but for LDCs as a group the price elasticity of demand for exports is usually thought to be low. Assuming, in general, that the exports of LDCs are not substitutable for those of developed countries, so that an increase in Qx cannot be explained by a relative change in group export prices, it would appear that the growth in Qx for LDCs as identified by Wilson, Sinha and Castree resulted mainly from the growth of national income in those countries which import LDCs' exports. The broad conclusion seems to be that, over the period from the mid 1950s to the mid 1960s, LDCs managed to improve their income terms of trade in spite (rather than because) of a deterioration in their commodity terms of trade. That they could do so was thanks largely to the existence of economic growth amongst developed countries, and also because in developed countries the ratio of the rate of growth of imports from LDCs to the rate of growth of GDP fell relatively little (see Balassa, 1968).

The apparently satisfactory improvement in the income terms of trade of LDCs has, however, to be qualified in a number of ways. First, the observed growth of Qx for developed countries was considerably more than that for LDCs. Comparatively, then, LDCs did less well than developed countries. Second, it was basically only because industrial countries experienced a period of rapid growth that LDCs' exports expanded. It might be anticipated that in a time of recession a deterioration in N would be positively associated with I. Third, the more-than-expected expansion in LDCs' exports in the early 1960s

TABLE 4.1
Commodity and Income Terms of Trade in LDCs, Four-Year Averages
1950—65

		1950–3	*1954–7*	*1958–61*	*1962–5*
Panama	N	100	123	105	106[a]
	I	100	147	148	309[a]
Cameroon	N	100	115	110	96[b]
	I	100	140	194	198[b]
Pakistan	N	–	100[c]	101	109
	I	–	100[c]	99	155
Jamaica	N	100	104	94	87
	I	100	170	208	233
Peru	N	100	91	75	81[a]
	I	100	126	154	221[a]
Malaysia	N	100[d]	123	130	117
	I	100[d]	135	165	188
Argentina	N	100[e]	88	89	91
	I	100[e]	110	127	176
El Salvador	N	100[d]	113	78	69
	I	100[d]	129	130	177
Philippines	N	100	92	90	81
	I	100	118	134	161
Chile	N	100	113	101	111
	I	100	137	129	166
Morocco	N	100	110	111	106
	I	100	138	146	153
India	N	100[d]	102	109	111
	I	100[d]	111	118	143
Nigeria	N	100	106	104	93[a]
	I	100	126	149	179[a]
Tunisia	N	100	100	108	100[a]
	I	100	107	139	129[a]
Cyprus	N	100	119	104	112
	I	100	180	119	146
Ghana	N	100	121	108	80[a]
	I	100	121	134	136[a]
Brazil	N	100	128	113	102
	I	100	125	128	121
Sri Lanka	N	100	110	106	91
	I	100	121	121	118
Colombia	N	100	117	85	83
	I	100	119	91	98
Ethiopia	N	100[f]	105	89	75[b]
	I	100[f]	99	97	88[b]

Notes
[a] 1962–4.   [d] 1952–3.
[b] 1962 only.   [e] 1951–3.
[c] 1955–7.   [f] 1953 only.

Source. Wilson, Sinha and Castree (1969).

tended to be concentrated on fuels and manufactures. This fact implies problems for those LDCs whose exports consist primarily of foodstuffs and raw materials. Fourth, and finally, tariff reductions have tended to be concentrated amongst, and have worked mainly to the benefit of, developed countries.

So far we have focused our attention on the terms of trade of LDCs till the mid 1960s. Evidence appears to show that, although there exists considerable diversity of experience, the commodity terms of trade of LDCs deteriorated in the 1950s and early 1960s. Subsequent evidence drawn from the later 1960s and the early 1970s suggests that the deterioration in the LDCs' terms of trade has been arrested. Indeed, after a period in the mid to late 1960s when the commodity terms of trade of LDCs were, in general, fairly static, the period 1969–74 showed a marked improvement in them, except for in 1971, when the relative price of imports rose. However, the general picture, which is illustrated in Table 4.2, hides the intra-group variation, which has become even more marked over recent years than it was in the 1950s and 1960s. As Table 4.2 reveals, in the first part of the 1970s there occurred major price increases in both the exports and imports of LDCs. These price increases had a differential impact amongst LDCs, depending on their individual trade structures. Most notoriously, the terms of trade of oil-exporting LDCs improved, whilst the terms of trade of oil-importing LDCs worsened. More generally, of course, an individual LDC's terms of trade are positively associated with the proportion of exports accounted for by those primary products that have increased most in price, and negatively associated with the proportion of imports accounted for by such products. After the rise in primary-product prices which occurred in the early 1970s, the United Nations set out to identify those countries which had been most seriously affected by adverse world price movements. It turned out that most of these countries were African, although in terms of population the Asian countries predominated. For example, India, Pakistan and Bangladesh all experienced quite severe adverse movements in their terms of trade. In contrast, Morocco, which experienced broadly equivalent increases in the prices of its imports between 1970 and 1974, was able, in 1974, to show a significant improvement in its terms of trade, because of the very large increase in the world price of phosphates in that year.

Generalisations with regard to the terms of trade of LDCs have, then, over recent years, as the dispersion of experience has widened, become increasingly difficult and meaningless. Group means may now give a very misleading guide to the experience of LDCs; indeed, they may

TABLE 4.2
(a) Commodity Terms of Trade of LDCs 1964–74 (1963 = 100)

	1963	1964	1965	1966	1967	1968	1969	1970	1971	1972	1973	1974
Index of LDCs' export prices	100	103	103	104	103	103	106	110	112	122	164	341
Index of LDCs' import prices	100	102	103	103	103	102	105	109	116	122	149	211
Terms of trade, N	100	101	100	101	100	101	101	101	97	99	110	162

(b) Commodity Terms of Trade Disaggregated between LDC Sub-Groups 1971–4 (1970 = 100)

	1970	1971	1972	1973	1974
Oil exporters	100	106	115	124	268
Other Western Hemisphere	108	88	93	108	102
Other Asian	100	93	90	100	99
Other African	100	89	91	100	–

(c) Commodity Terms of Trade Disaggregated between Individual LDCs 1971–4 (1970 = 100)

	1970	1971	1972	1973	1974
Colombia	100	90	98	106	111
Costa Rica	100	84	84	83	76
El Salvador	100	94	97	101	90
Korea	100	99	99	94	76
Morocco	100	98	89	90	107
Panama	100	97	101	99	107
Philippines	100	85	71	90	97
India	100	103	111	103	80
Sri Lanka	100	93	88	78	69
Thailand	100	91	94	115	101
Tunisia	100	105	108	126	201

Source. IMF, *International Financial Statistics.*

reflect the experience of no single LDC. An LDC group mean that shows the terms of trade to be static may be concealing the fact that one sub-group of LDCs are experiencing major improvements in their terms of trade and that another sub-group are experiencing a major deterioration in theirs. Certainly the group-mean improvement that has occurred in the LDCs' terms of trade in the late 1960s and the 1970s fails to draw attention to the severe terms-of-trade problems which face many developing countries.

The Impact of Adverse Movements in the Terms of Trade

The common belief that LDCs have in the post-war period *suffered* from a deterioration in their terms of trade comprises two elements. The first element, which we have just examined, is that empirically the terms of trade of LDCs have deteriorated. The second element, to which we now turn, is that, for certain reasons, such a deterioration is undesirable.

A given deterioration in the terms of trade may have different impacts on different economies, depending on, first, the configuration of the deterioration in the terms of trade; second, the nature and pattern of foreign trade; and, third, other features of the particular economy, such as its industrial structure.

A country's terms of trade will deteriorate if the price of exports falls or the price of imports rises, or, more generally, if the price of exports falls relative to the price of imports. As we have seen, such relative price changes may themselves be caused by a number of factors, but, although these factors may influence the terms of trade equivalently, equivalent changes in the terms of trade may not have equally deleterious effects on the economy, depending on the causes of the change. A fall in the price of exports the demand for which is inelastic may, for instance, be caused by an expansion in the output of foreign producers; or by an improvement in domestic efficiency, which is passed in the form of lower prices, to consumers. Although both changes serve to worsen the terms of trade, they are not equally undesirable to the LDC concerned, since an export price fall induced by an increase in world supply is likely to be associated with lower output and lower export earnings, whilst an export price fall induced by an improvement in efficiency is likely to be associated with rising output and, quite possibly, rising export earnings.[6]

Whatever the cause, an adverse movement in the terms of trade of a particular country may have implications in that country for the balance of payments, real income and living standards, development, the level of employment and the rate of inflation.

The effect that a deterioration in the terms of trade has on the balance of payments basically depends on the foreign-trade price elasticities. Where import and export price elasticities of demand are high, a deterioration in the terms of trade will tend to bring about an improvement in the balance of trade, since export earnings will tend to rise and import payments tend to fall. The efficacy of exchange depreciation in improving the balance of payments relies, after all, on the price-induced increase in demand outweighing the adverse terms of trade effect. If, however, both imports and exports are subject to inelastic demand, an adverse movement in the terms of trade will tend to be associated with a worsening balance-of-trade situation. If, then, as is often suggested, LDCs face relatively inelastic demand curves,[7] a deterioration in their commodity terms of trade will, other things remaining constant, result in a deterioration in their balance of payments.

The often-voiced opinion that deteriorating terms of trade are undesirable from the viewpoint of LDCs implies therefore, a belief either that demand schedules are price-inelastic, and therefore that a fall in export prices and a rise in import prices will result in a deterioration in the balance-of-payments and foreign-exchange position of LDCs, or that the developmental costs of reducing imports, and the short-term standard-of-living costs of increasing, relative to domestic consumption, the foreign consumption of domestically produced commodities outweigh the balance-of-payments benefits.[8]

Of course, 'the other things' may not remain constant: the demand curve for exports may, for instance, shift to the right over time, thus serving to improve the balance of payments.

The effect that a deterioration in the terms of trade has on real income and living standards depends, again, on the initial causes of the deterioration. A fall in export prices brought about by an increase in efficiency will tend to induce an expansion in demand for exports and thus an increase in real income.[9] A rise in import prices will tend to have a rather different effect. Where the value of exports cannot be increased by increasing export prices, a rise in import prices will effectively reduce the real purchasing power of exports in terms of imports and will reduce the country's capacity to import. Where the demand for imports is price inelastic, the volume of exports will have to be increased in order to pay for the more highly priced imports, if a deterioration in the balance of trade is to be avoided. Domestic consumption of exportables, and therefore the standard of living, will have to fall. Thus, deteriorating terms of trade imply a worsening balance-of-trade situation, or falling living standards, or both.

Rising import prices may have additional implications for the level of employment and the rate of inflation. Other things remaining constant, unemployment will tend to rise if the increasing price of imports shifts expenditure away from domestic goods and towards imported goods. At the same time as exerting a domestically demand-deflationary impact, however, rising import prices may have cost-inflationary repercussions.

World price changes in the early 1970s, and, in particular, increases in the price of oil, demonstrated that the problems created by adverse movements in the terms of trade are not solely the preserve of developing countries. LDCs, however, do tend to face particular problems in adjusting to adverse movements in their terms of trade. Imports are likely to be vital to development, and LDCs may be unable, in the short run at least, to supplant them by domestic production. Furthermore, factors of production may be relatively immobile, so that LDCs find it difficult to shift resources away from production for the home market into the production of exports and/or import substitutes.[10]

Apart from structural inflexibility and low price elasticities of demand, the income elasticity of demand for exports may be low, with the result that rightward shifts in the demand curve for exports compensate little for adverse price changes. In the early 1970s, those developed countries affected by the rise in the price of oil tended to grow only slowly, if at all, and attempted to reallocate expenditure away from imports. For oil-importing LDCs, this meant that there were two factors causing their income terms of trade to deteriorate: the rise in import prices, and a tendency for demand for their exports to stagnate or fall.

Export Earnings and Import Payments: The Balance of Trade

As we noted earlier, the trends likely to be of most concern to LDCs are not those in their terms of trade, but those in their export earnings and import payments, and thus their balance of trade. We have now seen that deteriorating commodity terms of trade will tend to be negatively associated with export earnings and positively associated with import payments where the demand schedules for both exports and imports are price-inelastic. Empirical evidence on the foreign-trade elasticities which face LDCs is available, and we examine some of this evidence in the next section. Table 4.3, however, provides a picture of what has happened to export earnings and import payments of LDCs over recent years. The general pattern is that, for LDCs as a group, both export earnings and import payments have risen.

In 1975, however, and as a result of the world economic recession, the value of non oil-exporting LDCs' exports fell by 35 per cent as compared with 1974. Particularly affected were countries such as Zambia and Zaire, which produce a commodity the demand for which is particularly sensitive to the level of industrial activity in the world economy. Again, a good deal of intra-group variation in LDC export performance may be observed. In 1976, for instance, whilst LDC food producers (and especially coffee producers other than Brazil) experienced a significant increase in export earnings, mineral-producing LDCs experienced little improvement. Partly in response to the stagnation in LDC exports, which encouraged LDCs to introduce import restrictions,

TABLE 4.3
Index of Export Earnings and Import Payments of LDCs

	Index of export earnings	Index of import payments
1951	100·0[a]	100·0[b]
1952	86·8	100·9
1953	88·1	90·2
1954	91·9	93·6
1955	98·3	101·3
1956	105·1	108·5
1957	107·2	123·9
1958	103·4	113·7
1959	107·6	114·5
1960	114·5	126·5
1961	113·7	129·1
1962	117·9	129·9
1963	130·6	135·9
1964	141·3	149·6
1965	149·4	158·1
1966	161·3	171·8
1967	166·0	177·4
1968	182·6	191·8
1969	205·5	213·2
1970	230·6	241·9
1971	260·9	274·4
1972	312·8	306·9
1973	467·2	425·2
1974	922·1	692·7
1975	856·2	820·8
1976	1060·8	908·0

[a] 100 = US$23,500 million.
[b] 100 = US$23,400 million.

Source. IMF, *International Financial Statistics*

the rate of growth of LDC import payments fell in the mid 1970s; indeed, in the first half of 1976 even the value of LDC imports fell.

Over the period from 1950 to 1972 import payments normally exceeded export earnings, thus implying the balance-of-trade deficit for LDCs that is revealed in Table 4.4. The balance-of-trade surplus for LDCs as a group in 1972, 1973, 1974 and 1975 simply reflects the fact that the trade surplus of oil-exporting LDCs in these years outweighed the trade deficit of oil-importing LDCs. Although, as shown by Table 4.5, the general trend amongst oil-importing LDCs in the mid 1970s has

TABLE 4.4
Balance of Trade of LDCs, 1951–74

	All LDCs[a]
1951	+100
1952	−3,200
1953	−400
1954	−300
1955	−600
1956	−700
1957	−3,800
1958	−2,300
1959	−1,500
1960	−2,700
1961	−3,500
1962	−2,700
1963	−1,100
1964	−1,800
1965	−1,900
1966	−2,300
1967	−2,500
1968	−2,000
1969	−1,600
1970	−2,450
1971	−3,570
1972	−580
1973	+7,430
1974	+51,980
1975	+10,640
1976	+36,830

[a]Exports minus imports, expressed in US$ millions.

Source. IMF, *International Financial Statistics.*

been into balance-of-payments deficit, certain exceptions may be found in particular years; balance-of-payments performance depends significantly on the commodities traded by LDCs. In 1975, for example, the coffee-producing LDCs of Colombia, Ivory Coast and Liberia all ran trade surpluses,[11] as did India, which, following good harvests in 1975 and 1976, was able to expand exports and contract food imports.

Foreign Trade Elasticities

It has emerged from the foregoing analysis that, in explaining the trade

TABLE 4.5

Export Earnings, Import Payments and the Balance of Trade of Oil-exporting and Oil-importing LDCs, 1970–6

	Oil-exporting LDCs			Oil-importing LDCs		
	Export earnings	Import payments	Balance of trade[a]	Export earnings	Import payments	Balance of trade[a]
1970	17,400	9,700	+7,700	36,940	47,090	−10,150
1971	22,100	11,400	+10,700	38,970	53,240	−14,270
1972	24,900	13,800	+11,100	46,270	57,950	−11,680
1973	39,300	19,900	+19,400	67,380	79,350	−11,970
1974	118,100	33,700	+84,400	97,740	130,160	−32,420
1975	109,300	53,700	+55,600	93,410	138,370	−44,960
1976	131,100	68,300	+62,800	118,200	144,170	−25,970

[a] Exports minus imports expressed in US$ millions.

Source. IMF, *International Financial Statistics.*

experience of LDCs, the values of certain foreign-trade elasticities are very significant. These elasticities are: the price elasticity of demand for LDCs' exports, the price elasticity of LDCs' demand for imports, the price elasticity of supply of LDCs' exports, the income elasticity of demand for LDCs' exports, and the income elasticity of LDCs' demand for imports.

Where synthetic substitutes do not exist, it might be anticipated that the price elasticity of demand for the exports of LDCs would be low. For individual small LDCs, of course, the demand curve which they face may be relatively elastic, even though the world-market demand curve for the product or products which they export may be price-inelastic. The price elasticity of demand for imports might be expected to depend very much on the nature of particular imports. In principle, the price elasticity of demand for essential developmental imports will be lower than the price elasticity of demand for non-essential imports. Given that a large proportion of total imports into many LDCs might be classified as being of a developmental nature, it might be anticipated that the price elasticity of demand for imports would be low. Again, the income elasticity of demand for imports, and also that for exports depend, in theory, on the nature of the goods traded. In the case of some commodities which are exported by LDCs, world demand may have reached its saturation level, and an increase in world income will exert little positive influence over the level of demand. The demand for basic foodstuffs, for instance, may rise following an expansion in world population, but is perhaps less likely to rise following an expansion in world income. Indeed, the income elasticity of demand for some LDC exports may be negative, (i.e. the exports are inferior goods). On the other hand, the demand for minerals and raw materials may have a high income elasticity. Meanwhile, given the low standards of living in LDCs, it would seem likely that the income elasticity of demand for imports would be high – either because of the importation of capital goods needed for the domestic production of manufactures, or because of the direct importation of manufactured consumer goods, which are likely to have fairly high income elasticities of demand. It is generally assumed that, because of the low levels of mobility of resources in many LDCs, and the length of the gestation period of production for many of the commodities produced by LDCs, the short-run price elasticity of supply will be low. Against this, the existence of excess capacity, and/or substantial domestic consumption of exportables, might lead one to expect that even the short-run price elasticity of supply could be relatively high.

Empirical investigation of some of these foreign-trade elasticities has been conducted at various levels of disaggregation, and a summary of the findings has been presented by Stern, Francis and Schumacher (1976). At the most aggregated level, attempts have been made to estimate general export and import elasticities by country, whilst, at a rather more disaggregated level, researchers have examined the price and income elasticities pertaining to the particular commodities imported and exported by individual LDCs. One such disaggregated study has been carried out by Andic, Andic and Dosser (1971). They estimated the price and income elasticities for a series of commodities traded by Caribbean LDCs. Their methodology, which is similar to that used in most other investigations into trade elasticities, was to fit import functions, using the estimated price and income coefficients thereby derived, to indicate price and income elasticities. Using the Standard International Trade Classification, a good deal of variety in import elasticities was found, both between commodities and between countries, and no clear conclusions for LDCs as a group emerged, except in terms of the variety witnessed. Export elasticities are usually interpreted to mean the import elasticities of customer countries. Empirical research into the export price elasticities which face LDCs again suggests that the elasticity depends very much on the particular commodity studied. Andic, Andic and Dosser form compromise figures for export price elasticities on the basis of available empirical evidence.[12] For individual commodities the compromise figures are as follows; sugar (-0.4), paper

$(-1\cdot0)$, tobacco $(-1\cdot0)$ cocoa $(-0\cdot4)$, coffee $(-0\cdot4)$, bauxite $(-0\cdot3)$, bananas $(-0\cdot7)$, timber $(-0\cdot3)$, rum $(-1\cdot5)$, rice $(-0\cdot4)$, lard and margarine $(-1\cdot5)$, textiles $(-1\cdot0)$. Using rather broader categories of goods, empirical investigation shows quite unanimously that the price elasticity of demand for imports into developed countries becomes greater the less 'crude' and more processed are the imports. Ball and Marwah (1972), for instance, estimate that the price elasticity of demand for imports into the United States is, for crude materials, in the range $-0\cdot53$ to $-0\cdot65$; for semi-manufactured goods, between $-1\cdot89$ and $-2\cdot15$; and, for manufactured goods, between $-4\cdot74$ and $-5\cdot28$. Given that the exports of LDCs are largely made up of 'crude' commodities, it might be expected that the export price elasticities which LDCs face would be relatively low. This expectation is confirmed by Houthakker and Magee (1969) in a study of trade elasticities covering the period 1951–66. Houthakker and Magee find that the income elasticity of demand for the exports of LDCs is generally less than one. Indeed, out of the seven LDCs which they examine, only Peru and Venezuela face income elasticities in excess of one for their exports. Building on the work of Houthakker and Magee, Khan (1975) estimates import and export functions for fifteen LDCs over the period 1951–69. In some ways Khan's analysis is rather more sophisticated than that of Houthakker and Magee. In particular, Khan endeavours to make allowance for the fact that, first, supply as well as demand may respond to price changes; second, the import function of LDCs may be misspecified if allowance is not made for the existence of various forms of import control; and, third, demand may respond to changes in price after a time-lag, rather than immediately. Khan's results suggest that, as far as imports into LDCs are concerned, the existence of a price-inelastic demand schedule is not universal; nor does it appear that the income elasticity of demand is high. On the export side, however, price-inelastic demand exists in the case of ten LDCs, whilst for the other five LDCs in the study the price elasticity of demand for exports is greater than one. With only two exceptions, Khan finds that the income elasticity of demand for the exports of individual LDCs is less, often considerably less, than one.

Few clear conclusions emerge from the empirical work that has been done on the foreign-trade elasticities which LDCs encounter. This may be partly explained by the problems involved with statistical estimation, but it probably also reflects the fact that very much depends on the particular commodities traded, and that clear conclusions are not there to be discovered.

Concluding Remarks

Generalisations concerning movements in the terms of trade experienced by LDCs as a group are difficult to make, since there is a great deal of intra-group variation amongst LDCs. It would appear, however, that a substantial number of LDCs have experienced adverse movements in their commodity terms of trade, and have, partly as a result of the implied relative price changes as between their exports and imports, witnessed a deterioration in their balance of payments on current account. In addition to adverse price movements, however, the demand

TABLE 4.6
LDCs' Share of World Trade,
1951—75

	Share of world exports	*Share of world imports*
1951	30·6	28·7
1952	27·6	29·4
1953	27·6	27·5
1954	27·9	27·5
1955	27·5	26·6
1956	26·3	25·9
1957	25·0	26·8
1958	25·3	26·4
1959	24·8	25·0
1960	23·6	24·7
1961	22·4	24·1
1962	22·2	22·9
1963	22·5	22·0
1964	21·7	21·6
1965	21·2	21·0
1966	20·8	20·8
1967	20·4	20·4
1968	20·0	19·9
1969	19·7	19·4
1970	19·2	19·1
1971	19·4	19·4
1972	19·5	18·5
1973	20·9	18·6
1974	28·2	20·7
1975	25·5	23·5

Source. IMF, *International Financial Statistics.*

for many of the exports of LDCs, has been adversely affected by both technological progress in the supply of synthetic materials, and the low income elasticities of demand that exist. For some years researchers such as Balassa (1964) have been pointing to the secular deterioration in the balance of trade of LDCs.[13] During the 1950s and 1960s, LDCs accounted for a falling share of both world exports and imports (see Table 4.6) and experienced a generally deteriorating balance-of-trade position. During the early to mid 1970s the picture changed somewhat. The LDCs' share of exports, as a group, increased quite markedly, and their combined balance-of-trade moved into surplus. From the point of view of the 'typical' LDC, however, this picture was largely spurious. Although the balance-of-trade position of oil-exporting LDCs did indeed show a major improvement, the balance-of-trade position of oil-importing LDCs showed a very substantial deterioration. Indeed, since there are more oil-importing than oil-exporting LDCs, the balance-of-trade position of most LDCs deteriorated over this period. A balance-of-payments deficit may be corrected[14] or it may be financed. Financing requires access to the international means of settlement. Access to such international liquidity may come from owned reserves or international borrowing. It is to the questions of the LDCs' demand for international reserves, and of optimal reserve holding in LDCs that we turn next.

5 The Demand for International Reserves in LDCs

International Reserves and Liquidity: Demand and Need

International reserves may be defined as 'those assets of [a country's] monetary authorities that can be used, directly or through assured convertibility into other assets, to support its rate of exchange when its external payments are in deficit' (Group of Ten, 1964). The precise classification of reserves is, in fact, rather arbitrary, although reserves are conventionally defined to incorporate gold, convertible foreign exchange, Reserve Positions in the IMF and Special Drawing Rights (SDRs). International *liquidity* is a rather wider concept than reserves and may theoretically be defined as access to the means of international settlement. From a functional point of view the liquidity available to a country is, in principle, measured by its ability to finance a balance-of-payments deficit without having to resort to adjustment. Operationally, therefore, a country's liquidity position should perhaps include not only the customary forms of reserve assets, but also items such as its ability to borrow, the foreign-exchange holdings of its commercial banks, the willingness of foreigners to hold its currency in the event of a payments deficit, and the extent to which increases in interest rates or changes in the term structure of interest rates would encourage a capital inflow without also having undesired domestic repercussions. International liquidity will therefore tend to exceed international reserves. Assuming that a country's access to the international means of settlement will in part be free of conditions, and in part not, it would seem sensible to distinguish between conditional and unconditional international liquidity. For LDCs in particular, the conditionality of liquidity may be very significant.

Empirically it is less easy to deal with the rather intangible concept of liquidity than it is to deal with the concept of reserves. Whilst LDCs do, of course, hold reserves, their ability to finance balance-of-payments deficits may be more limited than that of developed countries. Unlike many developed countries, LDCs may find the possibilities for borrowing reserves severely limited: commercial banks in LDCs may have negligible holdings of foreign exchange, foreigners may not be keen to hold the currencies of LDCs, and capital inflows to LDCs may be relatively insensitive to minor (or even perhaps major) increases in interest rates.[1] For these reasons the theoretically more relevant concept of liquidity is more nearly approximated for LDCs than for developed countries by referring solely to those assets traditionally defined as reserves. On the other hand, LDCs do have access, though not unconditional access, to supplementary sources of international finance through the IMF, and these have to be taken into account when assessing the overall international liquidity position of LDCs.

Although, from an analytical as well as from a semantic point of view, the distinction between reserves and liquidity is valid, we, in line with most of the literature on the subject, shall tend to regard the terms as broadly interchangeable.

Similar problems arise in discussing the *demand* for reserves and the *need* for reserves. Clearly, demand and need are not equivalent words. Needs can be expressed quite objectively in terms of certain structural parameters, whilst demand is influenced by individual preferences. A situation of disequilibrium may exist where, even though reserves are adequate in the sense of meeting needs, the demand for reserves exceeds the supply.[2]

The Theory of the Demand for International Reserves

Reserves are held because they yield certain benefits. In principle, reserves act as a buffer stock against any undesirable and immediate adjustment which might be forced upon a country as a result of running a deficit in its balance of payments, owing to a drop in export earnings or a rise in import payments. The benefit of holding reserves is, then, equal to the cost of the forced adjustment which is thereby avoided. If reserves yield a benefit and are without cost, it may be assumed that the demand for reserves will be infinite. Reserves are, however, not held without cost. Holding reserves involves an opportunity cost in terms of the sacrifice of the real resources which could otherwise be purchased.

In theory, then, the demand for reserves is functionally related to the benefits and costs of holding reserves. More specifically, the demand for reserves will be a positive function of both the cost of adjustment and the probability that adjustment will be required; and it will be a negative function of the opportunity cost of holding reserves. Again, in theory, a country may be adjudged to be holding optimal reserves when the benefit provided by holding the marginal unit of reserves is equal to the marginal opportunity cost incurred.

The cost–benefit approach to reserve holding implies that the demand for reserves results from a rational optimising calculation. Such a calculation may be expressed as juxtaposing reserve holding and the speed of adjustment. In theory, reserve holding and the speed of adjustment are inversely related. There are a number of combinations of different reserve levels and adjustment speeds which generate a given and constant probability of reserve depletion. Monetary authorities then choose the optimal combination of reserve level and adjustment speed. A high level of reserves and a low speed of adjustment involves the economy in a relatively low but stable level of national income. National income is low since reserves are relatively unproductive in terms of real resources, but it is stable because imbalances may be financed without the need for demand deflation. A combination which involves a lower level of reserve holding and a faster speed of adjustment implies a higher but less stable level of national income. The optimising decision may, then, be reinterpreted in terms of choosing the most desirable location on a trade-off between the level of income, to which utility is positively related, and the variability of income, to which utility is negatively related. Optimum reserves will be held at a point where the marginal rate of substitution between income level and income variability equals their marginal rate of transformation. Given that reserves yield utility in the form of income stability or security, but disutility in the form of a lower level of current income than would be possible if the reserves were used to purchase real resources, the level of reserves which is optimal for a country depends on the shape of the monetary authorities' indifference curves between the stability of income and the level of income.

The optimising decision just outlined may be illustrated schematically by concentrating on four determinants of the optimal level of international reserves: first, the opportunity cost of holding reserves; second, the speed of adjustment to balance-of-payments disequilibria;[3] third, the openness of the economy and the instability of the balance of payments; and, fourth, the trade-off between the level and variability of domestic income. In the south-east quadrant of Figure 5.1 is shown the locus of combinations of reserve levels and adjustment speeds that are

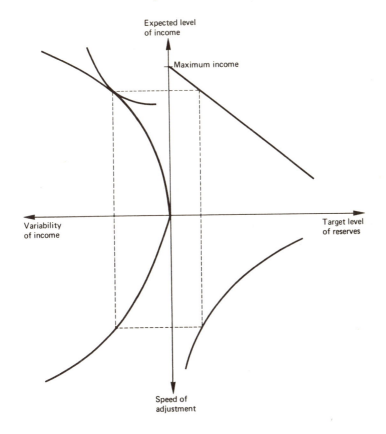

FIGURE 5.1

consistent with maintaining a constant probability of reserve depletion over a specific period of time. The problem of choosing the optimum level of reserves, and simultaneously the optimum speed of adjustment, entails determining the best point on this curve, bearing in mind the implications of this decision for the level and variability of income. Assuming that adjustment takes the form of demand-management policy, the south-west quadrant reflects the costs of adjustment in terms of the variability of domestic income: the faster the speed of adjustment, the greater is the variance in income. The costs of adjustment viewed in this way will depend on both the openness of the economy measured by the marginal propensity to import, and the size of the random component in the balance of payments. The less open the economy, and the more variable the balance of payments, the larger will be the costs associated with any given adjustment speed. The choice of a low adjustment speed and a correspondingly high target level of reserves will involve a sacrifice in the form of the expected level of income, since reserves are relatively inefficient at creating income. The opportunity cost of holding reserves is illustrated in the north-east quadrant of Figure 5.1 by the slope of the trade-off. The three relationships shown in the north-east, south-east and south-west quadrants of Figure 5.1 combine to trace out the relationship between the expected level of income and its variability that is shown in the north-west guadrant. On the basis of their preferences between income level and variability, the monetary authorities of a country will choose the best location on this trade-off; and this choice will, in turn, dictate the target level of reserves. The model illustrated in Figure 5.1 predicts that average reserves will vary positively with wealth and the inherent instability of the balance of payments, and negatively with the marginal propensity to import and the opportunity cost of holding reserves. Furthermore, the greater the monetary authorities' relative preference for stable income, the greater will be the demand for reserves.[4]

Although there does appear to be a broad degree of consensus that theoretically the demand for reserves may be approached in terms of the benefits and costs associated with holding reserves, difficulties tend to be encountered in finding suitable empirical proxies for these benefits and costs. As noted, the benefits which reserves yield basically depend on both the probability that balance-of-payments deficits will occur, and the real cost of adjusting to such deficits. Although observed changes in countries' reserves may give some indication of the degree of balance-of-payments instability and therefore of the likely incidence of deficits, observed reserve changes may also incorporate an economy's response to previous balance-of-payments disturbances. Thus, reserve changes do not necessarily reflect purely exogenous instabilities in the balance of payments, but may also reflect policy responses to previous instabilities. At the extreme, zero reserve instability might reflect either perfect balance-of-payments stability or instantaneous adjustment. Furthermore, in estimating the demand for reserves and optimal reserves, some allowance needs to be made for the probability that each and every unit of reserves will be required: this depends not only on the incidence of deficits but also on the size and duration of these deficits.

The other aspect of the benefits of holding reserves – namely, the cost of adjustment – is difficult to estimate, since it is crucially dependent on the method of adjustment adopted: whether, for example, adjustment takes the form of expenditure switching or expenditure reduction. If expenditure reduction is assumed, the problem of measurement evaporates, since it is then legitimate to represent the cost of adjustment by the extent to which domestic income will have to be reduced in order to reduce imports sufficiently to restore balance-of-payments equilibrium. The cost of adjustment may, in these circumstances, be measured by the reciprocal of the marginal propensity to import. But, where expenditure-switching policies are used, the marginal propensity to import will tend to overstate the associated costs of adjustment.

Moving to the cost side of things, the opportunity cost of holding reserves may, in theory, be calculated simply as the difference between the social rate of return on capital and the return, if any, on reserves. Although it may be relatively straightforward to measure the return on reserves, it is notoriously difficult to estimate social rates of return.

Acknowledging these various problems, but following the general cost–benefit line of approach, most empirical estimations of the demand for international reserves and the optimality of individual countries' actual reserve holdings have included as independent variables some measure of the variability of the balance of payments, some measure of the cost of adjustment, and some measure of the opportunity cost of holding reserves.[5]

Let us take each of these determining variables in turn and see what the empirical evidence suggests.

Balance-of-payments variables

The majority of empirical studies which have included some measure of balance-of-payments instability in cross-country regressions have found that this variable makes a significant contribution to explaining average reserve holdings: the more unstable the balance-of-payments is, the higher is the level of reserve holdings.

The propensity to import

From a theoretical point of view, we have already seen that the optimal level of reserves will tend to be positively related to the cost of adjustment. The larger is the marginal propensity to import, the smaller will be the fall in income required to bring about a given absolute fall in imports, and therefore the lower will be the real cost of adjustment. It may be anticipated, then, that reserve holdings will vary inversely with the size of the marginal propensity to import. In fact, the empirical evidence uniformly reveals a positive relationship between reserve holdings and the import propensity. Various suggestions may be put forward in an attempt to reconcile theory and evidence over this issue. First, it may be that too much weight has been put on expenditure-changing policies and not enough on expenditure-switching policies. The theoretically negative relationship between reserves and the propensity to import emerges from the assumption of expenditure-reducing adjustment policies. Second, the more open a country is, the more susceptible it is likely to be to external disturbances, and therefore the larger it may wish its reserves to be. If the propensity to import is used as a proxy for openness, then a positive relationship between reserves and the propensity to import may be anticipated. Finally, the theoretical rationale of a negative relationship between reserves and the propensity to import rests on the assumption that it is a fall in exports which generates the need to engineer a fall in imports and, in order to induce this, a fall in income. If, instead, the payments imbalance is caused by domestic income expansion and an induced expansion in imports with no change in exports, then the imbalance will be larger, and the need for reserves will be larger, the larger is the marginal propensity to import. This hypothesis would *a priori* lend support to a positive association between reserve holding and the propensity to import.

The opportunity cost of holding reserves

Empirical evidence on the opportunity cost of reserve holding generally suggests that this has a negligible influence on the demand for reserves. This finding, however, may reflect a number of things other than that the opportunity cost of reserves is actually insignificant in explaining the demand for reserves. It may reflect the inappropriateness of the proxies chosen, the insufficiency, in statistical terms, of the variation in the opportunity-cost series, and/or a low interest elasticity of demand for reserves. Indeed, Iyoha (1976) discovered, in the case of LDCs, a significant negative relationship between reserve holdings and opportunity cost, such that, other things remaining constant, a 10 per cent increase in the opportunity cost of holding reserves resulted in a 9 per cent reduction in the level of reserves held.

Having established in outline a general theory of the demand for international reserves, in the next section we move on to discuss potential differences between developed and less-developed countries in the demand for reserves.

LDCs' Demand for International Reserves

The theory

In theory there are few reasons why the structure of the demand function for reserves in LDCs should be any different from that in developed countries. If the demand functions are in fact similar in structure, it follows that any inter-country group differences in the demand for reserves may be accounted for by differences in the values of similar explanatory variables or differences in the demand response of countries to given changes in these explanatory variables. Abstracting from the influence of size, LDCs will tend to demand larger reserves than developed countries if their balances of payments are subject to greater instability, implying a greater incidence of deficits; if the cost of adjustment in LDCs is higher than in developed countries; and if the opportunity cost of holding reserves is lower in LDCs. Whilst it seems legitimate to argue that LDCs as a group experience greater balance-of-payments instability, and also that the cost of adjustment is higher in LDCs than in developed countries, because of the developmental nature of imports and their strategic role in fostering economic growth,[6] the opportunity cost of holding reserves is probably higher for LDCs because of the higher marginal productivity of reserves. Thus, although the benefits of holding reserves would appear to be higher for LDCs, thereby encouraging them to hold relatively larger reserves, the costs would also seem to be higher, thereby encouraging them to hold smaller reserves than developed countries. In theory, whether LDCs demand larger or smaller reserves than developed countries depends on the balance of these two factors.

Differences between LDCs and developed countries in their demand for reserves might further be explained through the existence of a wealth effect, and/or by the fact that monetary authorities in LDCs may possess different preferences from those of monetary authorities in developed countries. Taking the wealth effect first, if the security provided by holding reserves can be regarded as a luxury good, it might be anticipated that there would exist a positive relationship between the demand for reserves and the level of per capita national income, and possibly even a positive relationship between the income elasticity of demand for reserves and income. This notion would be supported by the view that per capita national income is subject to diminishing marginal utility. An LDC might then be expected to demand smaller reserves than a developed country, not only because of the higher marginal product in the LDC, as reflected by the higher opportunity cost of reserves, but also because of the higher level of utility associated with the marginal unit of production.

Moving on to the preferences of monetary authorities, these may be crucial in endeavouring to explain the demand for reserves in different countries. Some monetary authorities may be satisficers rather than optimisers with respect to reserves. Reserve holdings may, in these circumstances, be determined residually as the outcome of the pursuit of other policies. Except when reserves fall below a critical minimum satisfactory level, the authorities may not worry about the level of them at all. Even if authorities do set out to hold optimal reserves, the demand for reserves will still be influenced by expectational variables such as the likelihood of deficits and the estimated potential ease with which alternative adjustment strategies might be applied. Different estimations and expectations as well as different preferences could then account for differences in the demand for reserves.[7] Furthermore, if monetary authorities in LDCs possess a relatively strong preference for income level as opposed to income stability, their demand for reserves to hold may, theoretically, be lower than the demand for reserves in developed countries.

Comparing LDCs with developed countries, it would in theory seem that developed countries are more likely to be satisficers with respect to reserves – their main concern being that reserves should not fall below a critical level. LDCs, on the other hand, might be expected to be optimisers – concern that their reserves are too small being matched by concern that reserves should not rise above an optimal level. Monetary authorities in LDCs are probably more acutely conscious of the high opportunity cost, in terms of real resources, which is associated with holding reserves.

A final theoretical factor which may differentiate LDCs from developed countries in their demand for international reserves brings us back to the definitional distinction that was made at the beginning of this chapter between reserves and liquidity. If LDCs find it less easy and/or more expensive than developed countries do to borrow through channels other than the IMF, the monetary authorities of LDCs may tend to demand larger owned reserves. Assume that there are two countries, one developed and the other developing; assume further that these countries are similar in respect of the incidence of balance-of-payments deficits, the cost of adjustment, the opportunity cost of holding reserves, and policy priorities; abstracting from size, it is theoretically likely that the two countries will demand similar quantities of international *liquidity*. They may, however, demand a dissimilar composition of this common liquidity total. Scepticism concerning access to the more informal sources of financial assistance may encourage the LDC to demand a higher proportion of the liquidity total in the form of reserves. An LDC may therefore have to hold *larger reserves* than a developed country in order to acquire the same degree of security.

It may be interesting to re-examine Figure 5.1 in the context of a comparison between the reserve policy of LDCs and that of developed countries. Figure 5.2 presents Figure 5.1 adapted to depict the hypothetical situation of LDCs and developed countries.[8] In the north-east quadrant, because of the lower levels of national income in LDCs, the opportunity cost of holding reserves is shown as being higher than in developed countries. In the south-east quadrant it is hypothesised that, because of smaller monetised sectors and less effective monetary and fiscal policies, LDCs exhibit greater uncertainty with regard to the effectiveness and timing of their macroeconomic policies. It follows on from this that LDCs will have to hold larger reserves and adjust more rapidly than developed countries in order to achieve the same pro-bability of reserve depletion. Alternatively, given the greater difficulties that LDCs encounter in borrowing short-term capital, they may need to maintain a *lower* probability of reserve depletion than developed countries.

The relative position of LDCs' contours in the south-west quadrant, as compared with those of developed countries, is more ambiguous. Contour *A* might result if the balances of payments of LDCs are particularly volatile, as some evidence seems to suggest;[9] while contour *B* might be more appropriate if the economies of LDCs are relatively more open, with the result that domestic adjustments have less effect on domestic income variations.

As in Figure 5.1, interaction between the relationships in the north-east, south-east and south-west quadrants serve to trace out the trade-off between income level and variability that is depicted in the north-west quadrant. It may be seen that the trade-off for LDCs is rather different from that for developed countries. Just as the transformation curve relating income levels and the degree of stability for LDCs is likely to be different from that for developed countries, so the indifference

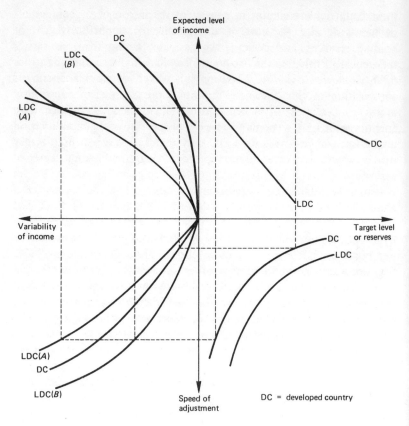

FIGURE 5.2

curves between income level and stability which illustrate the preferences of the monetary authorities may differ, since authorities in LDCs are likely to have a relatively stronger preference for income level than for stable income.

The significance of the preferences of monetary authorities emerges again when the authorities are interpreted as choosing the optimum combination of current consumption sacrifice (adjustment), and future consumption sacrifice (financing). If there exist differences between LDCs and developed countries with regard to which of various intertemporal consumption patterns their monetary authorities prefer, there will also tend to be differences in the extent to which adjustment or financing is used. Assuming that deficits are financed solely by means of decumulating reserves, then, as a direct result of differences in the proportion of any given deficit that is financed, there will be further differences in the demand for reserves.[10]

Whether or not LDCs will demand to hold average reserve levels greater than those of developed countries emerges from the theoretical analysis as being rather ambiguous. While some features, such as a higher opportunity cost of reserve holding, a stronger preference for current income level as opposed to stability, a greater degree of openness and a faster speed of adjustment might encourage LDCs to demand relatively low levels of reserves, other features, such as a greater degree of export instability, limited access to international borrowing and a slower speed of adjustment, would encourage them to demand and hold relatively high levels of reserves. Let us therefore turn to the empirical evidence.

The empirical evidence

A number of key issues relating to the LDCs' demand-for-reserves function have been implied by the theoretical analysis carried out in the previous section. The first issue relates to the structure of the demand function: is it similar for both developed and developing countries? The second issue relates to the elasticity of response to changes in determining variables: are these similar for both developed countries and LDCs? The third issue relates to the optimality of LDCs' holdings of reserves: do LDCs possess sub-optimal, optimal, or excess reserves? The fourth issue relates to the homogeneity of LDCs in terms of their demand for reserves and the optimality of their reserve holdings: can LDCs legitimately be treated as a group from the point of view of the demand for reserves? Empirical evidence is available on each of these issues.

(a) *The structure of the demand function.* Some empirical evidence exists which supports the *a priori* hypothesis that the structure of the demand function for reserves is basically similar for both LDCs and developed countries. Fitting an equation which relates the reserve holdings/size of trade ratio to the marginal propensity to import, per capita GDP at factor cost, and the standard deviation of the 'true disturbance' in the balance of payments adjusted for trade size, Clark (1970b) certainly concludes that the evidence which he examines supports this contention, even though the values, significance, and even the signs of the coefficients differ as between developed and developing countries.[11] A notable feature of Clark's results, however, is the large amount of variation in reserve holding which is unexplained by his demand function. We shall return to this point in a moment.

Kelly (1970), in testing a model of the demand for reserves that is similar to Clark's, also disaggregates between developed countries and LDCs. He finds that changes in the independent variables (the standard deviation of exports, the average propensity to import and per capita income) explain changes in the level of reserves less well in LDCs than in developed countries.[12] From the point of view of LDCs, then, certain explanatory variables appear to be missing from Kelly's equation.

An attempt to provide a more comprehensive statement of the LDCs' demand-for-reserves function has been made by Flanders (1971). In setting up this function, Flanders uses the reserves–imports (R/M) ratio as the dependent variable. She does not, however, provide a very convincing case for so doing. Indeed, the implied assumption that the direct relationship between reserve holdings and the level of imports is constant appears to be without foundation. Fortunately she does test a model in which she removes imports from the left-hand side of the equation and includes them as an independent variable on the right-hand side. The other independent, explanatory variables which Flanders investigates may be listed as follows, with the reasons for their inclusion briefly stated.

(i)   The instability of export earnings. This is an important determinant of the frequency and size of autonomous imbalances.

(ii)   The existence of near monies. This is assumed to indicate the existence of an efficient private market in foreign exchange and foreign credit. With large foreign-exchange holdings in the private sector, the authorities may be called upon to do less financing of deficits than would otherwise be the case. With the ability to mobilise private holdings, the authorities may demand a lower level of official reserves. Against this, the existence of large private holdings of foreign exchange may enhance the likelihood of destabilising capital movements.

(iii)   The opportunity cost of holding reserves. This may be represented by the marginal utility of imports forgone. The rate of return on investing foreign resources may be higher than the rate of return on domestic resources, since not only are foreign inputs relatively scarce, but also, with an exchange rate above its equilibrium, the correct shadow price of foreign exchange may be higher than its nominal price.

(iv)   The rate of return on reserves. That part of reserves held as foreign exchange and in the form of Eurocurrency deposits or government securities yields a financial return. The higher the proportion of reserves held in this fashion, the larger will be the level of reserves that a country will be willing to hold.

(v)   The variability of reserves. This variable is designed to catch any relationship between the variability of reserves and the R/M ratio. The relationship is hypothesised to be positive. Given the volatility of export earnings, the smaller the fluctuations in reserves, the greater is the implied extent of borrowing and/or adjustment. A high incidence of adjustment may reflect a need for more reserves.

(vi)   Willingness to change the exchange rate. The more willing to change its exchange rate are the authorities of a country, the less, it may be assumed, is the need for reserves.

(vii) The cost of adjustment. The welfare cost of adjusting the economy or of borrowing is critically dependent on the type of adjustment policy pursued. In the case of LDCs, where adjustment often takes the form of direct controls over trade, the cost of adjustment is basically equivalent to the cost of holding reserves.

(viii) The level, or change in the level, of inventories of traded goods. Inventories of traded goods may be regarded as a substitute for holding reserves. The more inventories that are held, the less is the need to hold reserves.

(ix)   The cost of borrowing. Since international borrowing is one option which faces authorities in financing a deficit, the demand for reserves may be seen as a function of the cost of borrowing. The cost of borrowing may be interpreted as having many dimensions – not only the direct financial cost, but also the ease with which funds may be raised, and the conditions laid down by creditors. Borrowing may be somewhat less costly where a sophisticated private sector financial market exists. In these circumstances the authorities may be able to borrow from the private sector or, through the money markets, induce a capital inflow. The less costly is borrowing, the lower is likely to be the demand for reserves.

(x)   Income. This may reflect a wealth effect, which will be measured by the income elasticity of demand for reserves. Reserves will tend to be a luxury good.

In terms of the current literature on the LDCs' demand for international reserves, Flanders's treatment of possible explanatory variables is probably the most thorough available. Unfortunately, none of these variables is particularly easy to measure. Indeed, the difficulties in making them operational are so great in some instances that Flanders omits certain variables altogether in her final estimating equations. The generally poor results which Flanders obtains may of course merely reflect the inappropriate measurement of determining variables, rather than the insignificance of the variables as such in the demand-for-reserves function.

In fact, Flanders refers to her results as being a 'dismal failure', and does not even bother to present the majority of them. One of the equations which Flanders attempts to fit to the data takes the following form:

$$\frac{L}{M} = a_0 + a_1 \frac{F}{L} + a_2 \sigma L + a_3 GR + a_4 D + a_5 Y + a_6 V$$

Where L/M is the average ratio of total official liquidity to commodity imports, F/L is the average ratio of official foreign exchange holdings to liquidity, σL is the coefficient of variation of L (the ratio of the standard deviation to the mean), GR is the annual percentage real rate of growth of GNP, D is an index of exchange-rate changes, Y represents per capita GNP expressed as a percentage of the per capita GNP of the United States, and V is an index of export variability. This equation is fitted cross-sectionally to the data of various groups of countries and over various periods of time. Other equations – incorporating the average ratio of the amount of foreign exchange held by private banks to total liquidity; using different measures of export instability; and dispensing with the Y variable and including M as an independent variable – are also tried.

Representative of the results is the following estimated equation, which was fitted for all thirty-two LDCs in the study over the period 1955–65.

$$\frac{L}{M} = \underset{(3\cdot0)}{0\cdot67} + \underset{(0\cdot49)}{0\cdot120} \frac{F}{L} - \underset{(0\cdot88)}{0\cdot094\,\sigma L} - \underset{(0\cdot95)}{2\cdot41\ GR}$$

$$+ \underset{(1\cdot9)}{0\cdot021D} - \underset{(0\cdot04)}{0\cdot000Y} - \underset{(0\cdot26)}{0\cdot082V}$$

$$R^2 = 0\cdot060$$
(t ratios in brackets)

Where imports are included as an independent variable, the results show some improvement and the R^2 rises to about 0·5. The coefficient on imports is highly significant. The coefficients on the other independent variables are, however, found to be insignificant, irrespective of whether L/M or L is used as the dependent variable. Few t ratios rise above 1, let alone 2. Indeed, the constant term and the import variable are the only exceptions to this general lack of significance. The results for all LDCs studied are summarised in Table 5.1.

TABLE 5.1

The LDCs' Demand for Reserves: A Summary of the Results Obtained by Flanders (1971)

Independent variable	Estimated sign of coefficient	Expected sign of coefficient	Significance of coefficient
B/L[a]	−	−	n.s.
F/L	+	+	n.s.
σL	−	+	n.s.
GR	−	−	n.s.
D	+	−	n.s.
Y	inconsistent	+	n.s.
V	inconsistent	−	n.s.

n.s. = not significant

[a] B represents the amount of foreign exchange held by private banks and B/L is the average of the annual ratios of B to L (the total amount of liquidity)

The signs of some of the coefficients do appear to vary as between LDCs and developed countries, but Flanders concludes that, although demand functions may differ from country to country, the differences are not correlated with the level of development.[13] More recently, Iyoha (1976) has tested a less complex demand-for-reserves function specifically for LDCs and has derived good results. He finds that the demand for reserves in LDCs is positively and significantly related to expected export receipts, the variability of export earnings, the interest rate on foreign-exchange holdings and the degree of openness of the economy. Overall, Iyoha's estimating equation explains about 93 per cent of the cross-country differences in the reserve-holding behaviour of LDCs.

(b) *The elasticity of response to changes in determining variables.* We have already noted that the work of Clark and Kelly suggests that the demand for reserves may be related to similar determining factors in both developing and developed countries, but that the precise nature of these relationships as reflected by the regression coefficients tends to vary. The extent to which the demand for reserves changes in response to changes in the independent variables has, however, been examined more specifically by Frenkel (1974). Testing a cross-sectional model which relates the demand for reserves to the variability of the balance of payments, the size of international transactions and the average propensity to import, Frenkel directly estimates response *elasticities*. It emerges that, as a group, whilst the LDCs' demand for reserves is more (positively) responsive to increases in the level of trade than is the demand for reserves by developed countries, it is less (positively) responsive than that of developed countries to greater instability in the balance of payments. With respect to the sensitivity of the demand for reserves to changes in the average propensity to import, it appears that LDCs and developed countries do not differ.

Frenkel attempts to provide a theoretical explanation of the different behavioural response elasticities which he derives. First, he suggests that developed countries may be more efficient in their use of reserves for transactions purposes than are LDCs and that they will therefore increase their demand for reserves less than LDCs as trade expands. Second, he suggests that the different behavioural responses may reflect the different activities and attitudes of governments, with governments in LDCs being less reluctant than those in developed countries to impose import restrictions. Third, he suggests that developed countries have wider access to means of finance other than reserves, and therefore do not need to 'cover' increases in imports with increased reserves to as great as extent as do LDCs. Unfortunately, none of these points is particularly convincing. Official reserves are primarily held not for transactions purposes, but rather to meet the residual demand for foreign exchange following payments deficits. Furthermore, if reserves are held as a buffer stock against imbalances, rather than in order to cover imports, it might be assumed that LDCs, which find it less easy and/or more expensive to borrow from abroad, would be more responsive than developed countries to payments variability, and not less.

On the basis of his study, Iyoha finds that the elasticity of demand for reserves with respect to expected export earnings is 0·76; that with respect to export instability it is 0·21; and that with respect to openness it is 0·77. The interest-rate elasticity of demand for reserves Iyoha estimates to be 0·86. From this piece of evidence it would seem that in LDCs the degree of responsiveness to changes in the opportunity cost of holding reserves is quite high, and that the monetary authorities in LDCs behave in a theoretically rational way.

(c) *The adequacy and optimality of reserve holdings.* This issue has generally been approached in one of two ways. The first way has been to assess the adequacy of reserves by reference to some supposed fairly direct relationship between the level of reserves and a proxy for reserve need.

Early efforts to judge the adequacy of international reserves tended to rely on the relationship between the level of reserves and the volume or value of trade. Imports constituted the most usual proxy for trade, and so the reserves–imports (R/M) ratio became the conventional guide to reserve adequacy at all levels of aggregation. Imports provided a useful scale variable which permitted cross-sectional inter-country comparisons of the adequacy of reserve holding, whilst at the same time also providing some evidence on the adequacy of reserve over time, since it was suggested that, if the value of the R/M ratio fell, this implied a *prima facie* case of reserve inadequacy. In none of this early literature, however, was there a rigorous explanation of why the level of reserves should be strictly linked with the level of imports, or why the demand for reserves should grow in line with trade. Usually a vindication was attempted by reference to the supposed domestic relationship between the transactions demand for cash and the level of national income. This analogy is unfortunate for a number of reasons, of which the most significant is that official reserves constitute a buffer stock against deficits rather than an active transactions balance which is used to finance trade.[14] Unless deficits grow in proportion to trade, it is not correct to argue that the demand for reserves will grow in proportion to trade. The relationship between the demand for reserves and the volume of trade is probably positive, but it may not be proportional. Clower and Lipsey (1968), for instance, conclude that although the casual empirical answer to the question 'Do we need larger reserves as the volume of trade increases?' should be in the affirmative, it is by no means clear whether 'the distribution of estimated disturbances shows a pattern of homoscedasticity or of heteroscedasticity when plotted against the volume of trade.'

From the point of view of time-series data, a fall in the R/M ratio could, then, reflect the fact that imbalances increase at a slower rate than the level of international transactions. Particularly where reserves are held for precautionary motives, a fall in the R/M ratio may merely illustrate the existence of economies of scale in reserve holding. (See Olivera, 1969.)

Some, not thoroughly successful, attempts have been made, particularly by the IMF (1970), to salvage the R/M measure of reserve adequacy, and a good deal more sophistication has been introduced by taking into account trend movements in the R/M ratio. Also the idea has been put forward that a reduction in the rate of decline in the ratio may be explained in terms of a stock-adjustment factor and a target R/M ratio, with the rate of decline in the R/M ratio falling as the discrepancy between actual and target values diminishes (Salant, 1970). Generally, however, the R/M ratio approach to the demand for reserves has been rejected as being too simplistic and theoretically inadequate.

Further attempts have been made to find an acceptable, direct, and constant theoretical and empirical relationship between reserves and some other variable representing need. Candidates for use as the denominator in such a reserve ratio have included the domestic money supply, and liquid liabilities held by foreigners (Johnson, 1958; Scitovsky, 1958; and Lamfalussy, 1968). The theoretical justification for their inclusion is that these variables reflect the potential vulnerability of the reserves to withdrawal. Brown (1964) has suggested that some measure reflecting the instability of the balance of payments might be related to reserves. He criticises the use of imports in the R/M ratio, arguing that imports represent only one component of the balance of payments. He argues instead that reserve adequacy should be evaluated against net external balance. Unfortunately, this measure still says nothing concerning the optimal reserves/net external balance ratio, and the measure can be thoroughly misleading, since it neglects the fact that external balances themselves tend to adjust to available reserves.

Perhaps the most devastating attack on the use of any ratios in the analysis of the demand for reserves has been undertaken by Machlup (1966). He argues that at both a theoretical and an empirical level there is little or no evidence to support the existence of a straightforward relationship between reserves and any other suggested explanatory variable. As an alternative he suggests an approach to the question of reserve adequacy that has become known as the 'Mrs Machlup's Theory of Monetary Reserves'. In this analogy Machlup compares the ambitions of monetary authorities to add to their reserves with those of his wife to add to her wardrobe. He concludes, basically, that year upon year monetary authorities wish to see their reserves grow in size. The demand for reserves in any period is then simply a function of the level of reserves in the previous period. The level of reserves demanded in period $t + 1$ is merely equal to the level of reserves in period t, plus a growth factor. Machlup, in fact, fails to specify the demand function for reserves with much precision, suggesting that this critically depends upon the rather nebulous preferences of monetary authorities.

The significance of the growth of reserves as opposed to the level of reserves has emerged elsewhere in the literature. The existence of an irreversible utility function with respect to reserves will tend to make any level of reserves inadequate over time (Bird, 1973). A general criticism of all ratio approaches to the analysis of reserve adequacy is that they make no reference to the optimal quantity of reserves. A fall in the R/M ratio, for instance, might simply imply that, judged on the basis of some optimality criterion, excess reserve holdings existed in the base year.

Although there are clearly many theoretical problems associated with assessing reserve adequacy by the use of ratios, considerable use has been made of them in empirical studies. Before moving on to examine the theoretically superior optimality approach, let us briefly review some of the empirical findings on the R/M ratio.

According to Kafka (1968), over the period 1951–66 the R/M ratio of LDCs as a group behaved not very differently from that of developed countries. Kafka uses this finding to support the conclusion that the need for liquidity is no greater or less in LDCs than in developed countries.

We have already examined the weaknesses of the R/M ratio as an indicator of reserve need. But, even if we accept this ratio as an approximate indicator, a similar trend in the ratio may still imply that LDCs' reserve holdings are less adequate than those of developed countries. This would be so if it could be shown that the import elasticity of demand for reserves is greater for LDCs than it is for developed countries. As we have already seen, this is one conclusion reached by Frenkel. If both groups of countries have optimal reserves in the base year in relation to trade (or they are 'on' their demand curves) and it is accepted that by the end of the period of study developed countries' reserves have become inadequate, then it is *a fortiori* the case that LDCs are short of reserves. If, on the other hand, both groups of countries are 'on' their demand curves at the end of the period, it follows that LDCs had larger excess reserve holdings at the beginning of the period than did developed countries.

More recent information on R/M ratios is contained in Table 5.2, which shows that group average R/M ratios hide a good deal of intra-group variation. Furthermore, examination of the available IMF evidence suggests that, whilst some LDCs hold relatively large reserves in relation to trade (for example, Thailand, Cyprus and Uruguay), others hold relatively small reserves (for example, Honduras, Peru, Indonesia and the Philippines). It would therefore seem that no single conclusion relating to LDCs as a group and regarding the adequacy of their reserve holdings based on R/M ratios can be regarded as legitimate.[15] In any case, as already mentioned, the evidence of R/M

TABLE 5.2
Reserve—Import Ratios by LDC Sub-Groups
(1970–6)

	1970	1971	1972	1973	1974	1975	1976
Oil-exporting	0·52	0·68	0·73	0·61	1·14	0·90	0·82
Other Western Hemisphere	0·28	0·26	0·38	0·38	0·20	0·17	0·27
Other Middle East	0·34	0·37	0·45	0·42	0·28	0·26	0·29
Other Asia	0·30	0·30	0·33	0·26	0·20	0·21	0·27
Other Africa	0·26	0·19	0·22	0·19	0·15	0·13	0·13

Source. IMF, *International Financial Statistics.*

studies has to be consulted with the shortcomings of the methodology firmly in mind.

Fewer theoretical shortcomings are to be found in the optimality approach to reserve holdings. The relevant factors determining a country's optimal level of reserves are, remember, the probability that reserves will be needed, the cost of the adjustment which a lack of reserves would necessitate, and the opportunity cost of holding reserves.

Heller's 1966 study is the path-finding work on optimal reserves. On the basis of his optimality formula [16] Heller concludes that LDCs as a group hold sub-optimal reserves. This finding may be explained, and indeed challenged, in a number of ways. The social rate of return is probably higher in LDCs than in developed countries, and this serves to raise the opportunity cost of holding reserves and to reduce the demand for reserves. Heller argues, in a fairly arbitrary fashion, that the opportunity cost of reserves is similar for both LDCs and developed countries, since the higher social rate of return in LDCs is perfectly offset by the fact that LDCs tend to hold a relatively larger proportion of their reserves in interest-yielding balances. If the higher interest on reserves fails to offset the higher opportunity cost, however, the reserve holdings which Heller identifies as being sub-optimal may, in fact, be optimal. Again, as we have already seen, Heller's optimality criterion rests on the assumption that expenditure reduction is the only means of adjustment. This will tend to bias estimated optimal reserve levels in an upward direction. Another reason why optimal reserve holdings in LDCs may in fact stand at a lower level than Heller estimated is that switching policies, such as devaluation or the imposition of tariffs, may be employed to correct deficits. Furthermore, Heller's estimates of optimality rest on the implicit assumption that LDCs and developed countries have similar response elasticities. If this is not the case, as subsequent work has suggested, inaccurate conclusions concerning optimal reserve holdings may be reached. Evidence seems to suggest that LDCs are less sensitive to the variability of reserves than are developed countries. The assumption that both LDCs and developed countries are equally sensitive to variability will, then, tend to lead to an over-estimation of what constitutes an optimal reserve level in LDCs relative to developed countries. Finally, even if Heller's conclusion, that LDCs as a group hold sub-optimal reserves, is accepted, this may reflect either of two things. First, it may reflect that the LDCs' demand function has been inappropriately specified. Monetary authorities in LDCs may lack probabilistic sophistication and may demand reserves on the basis of alternative criteria. LDCs, even though objectively holding sub-optimal reserves may, even so, be 'on' their own subjective demand curves. Second, and alternatively, LDCs may judge optimality in a theoretically acceptable fashion and their sub-optimal reserves may simply imply an inability to bring actual reserves into line with desired reserves. LDCs may, in these circumstances, be 'off' their demand curves.

The points raised in the preceding paragraph suggest that some caution should be exercised before accepting Heller's proclamation that LDCs *as a group* hold sub-optimal reserves. The phrase 'as a group' needs to be emphasised, since, in line with evidence on the R/M ratio, Heller's analysis suggests a good deal of intra-group variation. Unfortunately, this intra-LDC variation may not be fully explained in terms of one single characteristic. Table 5.3 illustrates this: it shows whether in one particular year, namely 1963, LDCs had optimal ($= 1$), deficient (< 1) or excess (> 1) holding of reserves.

Unlike Heller, Agarwal (1971), who estimates the optimal reserves holdings of seven Asian LDCs in 1971, attempts to formulate a model which specifically reflects the structural and institutional differences between developed and less-developed countries.

In illustration of these differences, he argues that LDCs are subject to a foreign-exchange constraint which forces them to indulge in exchange budgeting designed both to match exchange receipts with exchange payments and to channel scarce foreign resources into productive uses. Reserves are held by LDCs to finance temporary anticipated deficits which it is assumed will disappear during the course of the planning period as a whole, and also to cover any unanticipated shortfall in export receipts, or increase in import prices. The optimum level of reserves is defined quite conventionally by Agarwal as 'that amount which will enable a developing country to finance, at a given fixed rate

TABLE 5.3
Optimal International Reserves

	R actual/R optimal
Latin America	0·64
Argentina	0·29
Brazil	0·56
Chile	0·55
Colombia	0·40
Costa Rica	0·57
Dominican Rep.	0·78
Ecuador	1·33
El Salvador	1·19
Guatemala	1·14
Honduras	0·60
Jamaica	2·28
Mexico	0·98
Nicaragua	1·39
Panama	0·90
Paraguay	0·19
Peru	1·65
Venezuela	0·64
Asia	0·95
Burma	0·91
Ceylon	0·41
India	0·48
Indonesia	0·19
Korea	0·92
Malaysia	3·95
Pakistan	0·70
Philippines	0·56
Thailand	2·26
Middle East	1·51
Israel	1·99
Jordan	3·90
Lebanon	4·68
Syria	0·56
UAR	0·73
Africa	0·81
Ghana	0·60
Sudan	0·46
Tunisia	0·83

Source. Heller (1966).

of exchange, its temporary and unanticipated balance of payments deficits arising in a planning period and at the same time confer on the country a benefit equal to the opportunity cost of holding the reserve'. Both the benefit and the cost of holding reserves Agarwal expresses in terms of output. Opportunity cost is 'that part of gross domestic product which could be produced if the available foreign exchange were used for importing necessary inputs for production instead of being kept as monetary reserve', whilst the benefit conferred by reserve holding is 'related with that amount of gross domestic product which is saved with the help of the monetary reserves by avoiding an unnecessary adjustment in the event of a temporary and unanticipated deficit in the balance of payments'.

Being more precise, the opportunity cost of holding reserves depends on the import content of potential capital investments, the productivity of such investments and the availability of idle domestic resources. Agarwal argues that domestic resources remain idle in LDCs partly because of the scarcity of required foreign inputs. These domestic resources might be brought into productive use by employing reserves to purchase the required foreign inputs. The extent to which output rises as a result of extra investment depends, according to Agarwal, on the size of the incremental capital−output ratio. Using Agarwal's notation, the opportunity cost of reserves may be summarised by the formula

$$OCR = Y_1 = R.\frac{m}{q^1}$$

where R represents the amount of foreign exchange which could be used to import production goods, m is the reciprocal of the incremental capital output ratio, q^1 is the import content of additional employable capital, and y_1 is the amount of output which could be produced by using reserves to buy production good imports, otherwise the opportunity cost of reserves (OCR). The impact of economic growth on the importation of consumer goods is assumed away in Agarwal's analysis by the argument that LDCs impose direct restrictions on the import of consumption goods. The income generated by absorbing reserves, or, in other words, the opportunity cost of holding reserves, is likely to be higher in LDCs than in developed countries because of higher marginal productivity of imports. An increase in the importation of production goods into LDCs activates idle resources by a multiple equal to the reciprocal of the import content of new investments. These new investments, in turn, have a multiplier impact on national income. In developed, and fully employed, economies the opportunity cost of holding reserves equals only the value of the real resources which may be imported as a result of the reduction in reserve holdings. The multiplier effect is perhaps less likely to operate or will at least be smaller, since imports will probably in the nature of consumer goods. In any case, the multiplier effect of any new investment may occur more in monetary than in real terms.

Having examined the cost of holding reserves, the benefits may be analysed in similar vein. The benefit of holding reserves results from the fact that imports may be maintained even though a deficit has been incurred. The maintenance of imports avoids what would be a multiple contraction in income. Agarwal's approach, we may again note, is specific to LDCs inasmuch as it is implicitly assumed that income is a function of imports rather than the other way about. Adjustment to a deficit in an LDC is assumed to take the form of further import restrictions and foreign-exchange controls, which have the effect of lowering domestic income, rather than general deflation, which has the effect of lowering income and, thus, imports.

The benefit of holding reserves (RB) is summarised by the formula

$$RB = Y_2 = \frac{R}{q^2} \qquad (R = D)^{17}$$

where R is the amount of reserves, D is the size of the deficit, q^2 represents the ratio of imported production goods to total production in the economy, and y_2, which equals the benefit of holding reserves, represents the amount of domestic output which would have been lost had imports been reduced in order to correct the deficit.

This reserve-benefit formula rests on certain assumptions concerning the behaviour of LDCs. Most notably, the assumption is made, that, when faced with a deficit, LDCs attempt to reduce imports by granting fewer import licences. With the importation of consumer goods probably already at a minimum, the decline in imports occurs mostly in production goods which produces a multiple contraction in income. To the extent that the importation of consumption goods may be reduced, the multiple contraction is lowered and the benefit or reserve holding is reduced. Where the whole range of imports is affected equally, q^2 becomes the ratio of total imports to GDP.

Agarwal moves on to point out that y^2 is only equivalent to the benefit of reserves if the reserves are in fact used. As is conventional in the literature, optimal reserves are more accurately determined on the basis of the probability that reserves will be required, and this probability is not likely to be equal to unity. The reserve-benefit formula thus becomes

$$RB = R \cdot \frac{P}{q^2}, \qquad \text{with } P = (\pi)\frac{R}{D}$$

where P represents the probability that reserves will be used to finance deficits in the planning period, and π represents the chances of a deficit occurring. This formula illustrates the expectational nature of optimal reserves, since both D and π are expectational variables, the values of which may depend on a number of factors, such as the willingness of the authorities to change the exchange rate, the past behaviour of the balance of payments, or anticipated future changes in import payments or export receipts.

Optimal reserves may be determined by bringing into equality the costs and benefits of holding reserves.

$$R \text{ opt.} \frac{m}{q^1} = R \text{ opt.} \frac{(\pi)R \text{ opt}/D}{q^2}$$

or

$$R \text{ opt} = \frac{D}{\log \pi} \cdot (\log m + \log q^2 - \log q^1)$$

The marginal interpretation of optimality is rejected by Agarwal for statistical reasons, although he maintains that, for the above equation, 'the total as well as the marginal opportunity cost and benefit of the optimal monetary reserves are equal since the value of m and q^1 are assumed to remain constant in relation to changes in monetary reserves. In practice this assumption is quite realistic.'

Having constructed this optimality model, Agarwal proceeds to calculate optimal reserves for seven Asian LDCs in 1971. The results are presented in Table 5.4. Perhaps the main feature of these results is the wide discrepancy between these LDCs with regard to the optimality of their reserve holdings. Again the non-homogeneity of LDCs with respect to international reserves is illustrated.

As development takes place, Agarwal suggests, though with little empirical support, that the marginal productivity of capital rises and that the marginal import content falls. The impact of such trends will be to increase the marginal opportunity cost of holding reserves and lower the optimal level of reserves, since a corresponding increase in marginal reserve benefit is unlikely.

Agarwal's main contribution is in drawing attention to the fact that the optimality of reserves in LDCs may have to be judged on slightly

TABLE 5.4
Optimal Monetary Reserves of Selected Asian Developing Countries

Country	m	q^1	q^2	D^a	Monetary reserves at beginning of planning period $(R)^a$	Optimal reserves $(R\ opt)^a$	Excess reserves $(R-R\ opt)^a$
Ceylon	0.70	0·35	0·07	50	42	141	−99
India	0·50	0·43	0·05	158	1006	648	358
Pakistan	0·65	0·40	0·07	151	199	474	−275
Philippines	0·26	0·60	0·14	73	251	295	−44
Korea	0·78	0·85	0·24	75	610	163	447
Taiwan	0·38	0·77	0·21	35	624	114	510
Thailand	0·33	0·62	0·20	105	916	339	577

^{a} US $ millions.

R opt $= D/\log\pi\ (\log m + \log q^2 - \log q^1)$, where m is the reciprocal of the incremental capital output ratio, q^1 and q^2 indicate the relation of imported production goods to capital formation and GDP respectively, and π is the probability of a deficit occurring (assumed to equal 0·5).

D gives the highest consecutive cumulative deficit since 1960.

The value of m, q^1 and q^2 for 1971 were obtained mainly by trend extrapolation.

Source. Agarwal (1971).

different criteria from the optimality of reserves in developed countries. His analysis does not necessarily provide much information on the LDCs' demand function for reserves, and his statistical findings are sensitive to changes in estimated parameters. It is comforting, however, that at least some of Agarwal's results are consistent with those of earlier studies, such as those by Heller (1966) and Frenkel (1974).

The disaggregated studies by Heller and Agarwal reveal that, whereas some LDCs possess sub-optimal reserves, a significant number of LDCs hold reserves that are more than optimal. These examinations are, however, based on data drawn from 1971 at the latest. There is some reason to believe that the situation may have changed subsequently.

Between 1970 and 1976, world monetary reserves rose by about 120 per cent. The increase in reserves was, however, not evenly distributed among countries (see Table 5.5), and it is the distribution of changes in the level of world reserves that rekindles concern over the adequacy of reserves in LDCs.[18] Let us examine some of the indicators of inadequacy.

First, whilst the reserves of non oil-exporting LDCs rose by 5·8 per cent over the period 1973–75, the average trade deficit in these countries

TABLE 5.5

Distribution of Reserves, at Year's End 1950, 1960 and 1970–5 and at End of April 1976
(SDR thousand millions)

	1950	1960	1970	1971	1972	1973	1974	1975	April 1976
Industrial countries	36·8	48·5	65·8	88·8	97·5	96·0	97·9	104·1	108·0
More developed primary producing countries	3·7	3·6	8·5	12·1	19·4	19·9	17·2	15·4	15·5
LDCs (total)	9·8	9·0	18·9	22·3	29·7	36·6	65·2	75·2	79·3
Major oil-exporting countries	1·3	2·4	5·2	8·0	10·3	12·4	39·2	49·6	50·8
Other Western Hemisphere	2·4	2·2	4·3	4·4	7·3	9·7	9·1	7·7	8·4
Other Middle East	1·1	0·7	1·6	2·0	2·6	3·6	4·0	4·5	4·8
Other Asia	3·7	2·7	5·8	6·3	7·6	8·8	10·5	11·2	13·0
Other Africa	0·6	0·9	1·9	1·6	1·9	2·1	2·4	2·2	2·2

Source. IMF, *Annual Report, 1976.*

increased, in the same time, by almost 300 per cent. Since the main purpose of holding reserves is to finance temporary balance-of-payments deficits, the adequacy of reserves for this purpose would, *ceteris paribus*, appear to have declined.

Second, but in relation to this first point, the ratio between reserves and the value of imports fell for non oil-exporting LDCs from 34 per cent in 1973 to 23 per cent in 1975. As already noted, the reserves–imports ratio provides, at best, a very imperfect guide to the adequacy of reserves, but, even so, the fall remains suggestive of inadequacy. Third, the greater use of Eurocurrency borrowing by non oil-exporting LDCs, almost trebling over the period 1973–76, and the proliferation of import controls in these countries are both consistent with reserve inadequacy.[19]

Finally, whilst the greater use of exchange-rate adjustment which has characterised the period since 1973 will tend to reduce the developing countries' need for reserves, if they themselves make use of exchange-rate variations, it may increase an LDC's need for reserves if the value of its currency is pegged to that of a major foreign currency which, in turn, is floating against other foreign currencies. In these circumstances a variation in the value of the pegged foreign currency in terms of other foreign currencies may be inappropriate for the LDC involved. The LDC's external-payments position may then deteriorate and its need for reserves increase. It emerges that in a system where LDCs peg the value of their currencies to other currencies which are floating, the need for reserves in LDCs can, in theory, quite easily rise.[20] Pegging their exchange rates is precisely what the majority of LDCs have done in recent years.[21]

It would appear from the evidence presented above that during the early and middle 1970s the reserves of non oil-exporting LDCs have become less adequate, since, whilst their reserves have risen hardly at all, circumstances have caused their optimal level of reserves to rise considerably. The implications of reserve inadequacy are both short term and long term. In the short term, inadequate reserves imply higher levels of international borrowing and/or more adjustment. The majority of LDCs have severely limited access to international liquidity other than their owned reserves, and are therefore likely to be forced to adjust to their balance-of-payments deficits. At full employment, adjustment will entail a fall in current domestic living standards; but it will also involve an opportunity cost in terms of future living standards, since adjustment will probably preclude the importation of crucial developmental goods. The sacrifice of development may, furthermore, have undesirable long-term implications for the balance of payments, and thereby increase the need for reserves in the future. Development encompasses diversification, and in the case of many LDCs it is export concentration which is a major contributory factor to balance-of-payments instability. A short-term adjustment strategy which is forced upon an LDC because of inadequate ability to finance balance-of-payments deficits may then be both inappropriate from a long-term point of view, and costly from a short-term point of view.

Costs need not exclusively apply to LDCs. Where developing countries conserve foreign exchange by means of controlling and reducing imports, developed countries may suffer through the contraction of their export markets, which will in turn impose a deflationary impact on their economies.

(*d*) *The homogeneity of LDCs with respect to their demand for international reserves, and the optimality of their reserve holdings.* This issue has already been covered in the foregoing discussion. There appears to be no great or even discernible measure of uniformity amongst LDCs. In estimating individual LDCs' demand functions, some LDCs were found to have fairly persistent positive residuals (for example, Ecuador and Thailand), whilst others were found to have equally persistent negative residuals (for example, Costa Rica and Sri Lanka). With regard to the adequacy of reserves, R/M ratios show that there is considerable intra-group variation among LDCs; and, in terms of the optimality of reserve holdings, there is similar diversity. There would, furthermore, appear to be no obvious explanation for the pattern of reserve holding amongst LDCs, apart from the recent dichotomisation of LDCs into oil-exporters and non oil-exporters.

Concluding Remarks

The idea that every single LDC has deficient reserves appears to be inaccurate. It remains valid to argue, however, that, because of the instability of their balances of payments, as well as the high cost of adjustment in terms of real resources, which applies irrespective of the way in which the economy is adjusted, many LDCs need substantial international liquidity if stable development is to be maintained. Given that the opportunity cost of holding owned reserves will tend to be relatively high, developing countries may not wish to hold large reserves but do require a system which gives them adequate access to financial assistance as and when wanted. Furthermore, to the extent that the export instability which creates the need for liquidity is associated with the low level of development, LDCs require not only short-term liquidity but also long-term aid.

Most simple models do not fully explain the demand for international reserves either in LDCs or in developed countries. Even sophisticated demand functions which include a wide range of independent variables have failed to provide significant results. On reflection this is, perhaps, not surprising. After all, the demand for reserves may depend *inter alia* on the preferences of individual monetary authorities, on expectations concerning the likelihood that reserves will be needed, on the uncertainty of future capital and aid flows, and on the need to maintain the confidence of lenders and potential lenders. Such factors are not easily quantified. Indeed, it is difficult to make even the objective criteria empirically operational. Bearing in mind these limitations, a number of conclusions regarding the LDCs' demand for reserves do seem to emerge from a study of the empirical evidence. Perhaps the most important one is that LDCs do not form an homogeneous group with respect to their demand for international reserves and the optimality of their reserve holdings. There is some evidence to support the view that monetary authorities are roughly of two types. One type possesses relatively high levels of reserves and endeavours to maintain reserves at these high levels by means of adjusting quite rapidly to balance-of-payments deficits; the other type has lower reserve holdings and is generally less concerned with keeping reserves at a steady level.

Unfortunately, from the viewpoint of neatness, the monetary authorities of LDCs do not appear to fit exclusively into either category.

In terms of the adequacy of reserves, the rise in the price of oil served to widen the gap between the least and the most well-off LDCs. Oil-exporting LDCs have been faced with the problem of what to do with their excess reserves, whilst oil-importing LDCs have had to use their perhaps already inadequate reserves in order to finance payments deficits.

The problem of reserve inadequacy in such countries might be tackled in a number of ways through modifications to the international monetary system. One approach would be to redistribute world reserves through some form of recycling, so that reserves would be transferred from those countries with an excess to those with a deficiency. Some degree of recycling has been achieved through the operation of the Eurocurrency market, but the mechanism could be made more formal. The recycling could of course be achieved by means of trade expansion, involving an increase in exports from countries with inadequate reserves to countries with excess reserves.

A second approach would be to increase discriminatorily the reserves of LDCs. This could be achieved by increasing the quotas of LDCs in the IMF. Such an increase in quotas would serve to expand LDCs' access to all IMF facilities, since these are, at least in part, based on quotas. Alternatively, the proportion of quota which may be drawn under various facilities could be increased for LDCs; this modification would allow a more selective treatment to be made of particular facilities in the Fund than would the universal increase in the quotas of LDCs.

A third, and rather different, approach would not attempt to increase the quantity of reserves in LDCs, but would instead attempt to reduce the need for reserves, and improve the efficiency with which reserves are used. A reduction in the need for reserves might be achieved by encouraging LDCs to make greater use of their exchange rates as an instrument of adjustment. LDCs might also consider restructuring their trade in such a way that a greater proportion of it would be with each other. They could then introduce their own reserve asset, to be acceptable between them.[22] Alternatively, LDCs might simply expand on the various kinds of payments arrangements, such as clearing unions and reserve pooling systems, with which they already have experience.[23]

That the pursuit of stable development creates a need in many LDCs for amounts of liquidity in excess of their owned reserves basically implies one of two things. It implies either that these LDCs will be forced to follow adjustment strategies that at least in the short run impair growth, or that the international monetary system has to provide them with the required financial assistance. An equitable international economic order might dictate that relatively poor countries should not be called upon to make developmental sacrifices, especially in circumstances where balance-of-payments deficits result from factors beyond their control. A low level of development in itself often seems to be associated with both a high welfare cost of adjustment and a high probability that adjustment will become necessary, if reserve holdings are low. The IMF in its dealings with LDCs has exerted some influence over adjustment strategy, and has also given some degree of financial assistance. In later chapters we move on to examine IMF activity in the area of liquidity creation as it applies to LDCs, and more particularly the special facilities which are available to LDCs.[24]

6 Balance-of-payments Adjustment in LDCs

In this chapter we examine a number of questions relating to the balance of payments of LDCs. These concern the major causes of balance-of-payments problems; the basic policy alternatives, adjustment and financing , which are available to countries experiencing balance-of-payments problems; and the ways in which balance-of-payments adjustment may be achieved. Most attention will be focused on the appropriateness of exchange-rate variation as a tool of adjustment in LDCs.

The Causes of Balance-of-Payments Disequilibria

Although balance-of-payments disequilibria may take the form of either deficits or surpluses, and although durable balance-of-payments surpluses in LDCs may constitute a problem in terms of the high opportunity cost associated with reserve accumulation, we shall concentrate on balance-of-payments deficits, i.e. situations where there exists a net outflow of payments. Balance-of-payments deficits, although basically monetary phenomena, may be generated by a range of factors. These factors may be classified into two groups: structural or real causes; and monetary causes.

Structural causes

Structural causes normally are to do with the type and nature of traded goods, and the efficiency with which these goods are produced. One important structural characteristic relates to the income elasticity of demand for imports and exports. The exports of LDCs are predominantly primary products, and for many of these products the income elasticity of demand is rather low. Meanwhile, the income elasticity of demand for imports into LDCs tends to be relatively high.[1]

It might be anticipated, therefore, that, other things remaining constant, uniform growth in world income would tend to be associated with a deterioration in the balance-of-payments position of LDCs. Additionally, where the trading pattern of LDCs is such that trade is geographically concentrated on relatively slow-growing countries, the growth of the LDCs' exports is likely to be further restrained. Attempts to alter the industrial structure of LDCs so as to remedy the secular deterioration in the balance-of-payments situation are likely to be hampered by the low degree of structural mobility in many developing countries; added to which trading patterns may reflect well-defined historical and political ties which are difficult to break, and which, in any case, may yield other benefits (and, of course, costs) for the countries concerned.

Another structural characteristic of LDCs concerns the price elasticity of demand for imports and exports. Where export demand is price-elastic and import demand is price-inelastic, then, in a situation where import prices rise somewhat faster than export prices, the deterioration in the commodity terms of trade will tend to be translated into a deterioration in the balance of payments.

It transpires that both price and income elasticities may create balance-of-payments difficulties for LDCs. From the point of view of the balance of payments, then, LDCs may be producing the wrong goods. The right goods would, for instance, be those which possess relatively high income elasticities of demand. It is frequently assumed that, whereas the income elasticity of demand for primary goods is low, the income elasticity of demand for manufactures is high. If this assumption is valid, it might be thought that a transition from the production of primary products to that of manufactured products would serve to improve the balance of payments of LDCs. This need not be so, for, even if LDCs were producing the right goods, they might be producing them inefficiently as compared with the producers of similar commodities in industrial countries.[2]

Monetary causes

Inappropriate monetary policy in one country can have undesirable consequences for that country's balance of payments. Creation of money at a rate faster than the rate at which real domestic output is increasing will tend to cause inflation, and will tend to generate a balance-of-payments deficit. Starting from a situation of monetary equilibrium, in which the demand for money equals the supply of money, an increase in the supply of money will have the immediate effect of creating excess money holdings or excess real balances; attempts by individuals and firms to dispose of these excess real balances by spending them on domestic and foreign real and financial assets will cause some combination of domestic real income growth, inflation, and extra import demand relative to export demand. Growth, inflation and balance-of-payments deficits will continue to be generated until monetary equilibrium has been restored. Growth will serve to increase the real demand for money. Inflation will serve to increase the nominal demand for money or, by the same token, reduce the real supply of money, whilst balance-of-payments deficits will, similarly, serve to reduce the real supply of money. A further, at least short-run, effect of excessive growth in the money supply is that the rate of interest will tend to fall. In the case of major financial centres, a relative fall in interest rates will tend to cause an outflow of capital, which would have further implications for the balance of payments. It is, however, perhaps less likely that capital flows will be significantly influenced by interest-rate changes in LDCs.

Under a fixed exchange-rate system the deterioration in the balance of payments which follows excessive growth in the money supply is caused by two factors. The first of these is the real balance effect on the demand for imports. In addition to the real balance effect, however, there is a relative price effect, which results from the fact that domestic inflation will bring about a rise in the relative price of exports and a fall in the relative price of imports. Which of these two effects is initially the more significant will depend on the respective income elasticities of demand for domestic and foreign output. Where the income elasticity of demand for foreign output exceeds the income elasticity of demand for domestic output, the real balance effect will, initially, be more significant than the price effect.

Since, in monetary terms, a balance-of-payments deficit may be seen as an indication of an excessive real supply of money relative to demand, and as a reflection of an attempt by transactors to deplete and dispose of this excess supply of money it follows that, if it could be maintained that LDCs lack monetary sophistication and are more likely than developed countries to permit their money supplies to rise ahead of real output, LDCs will be more likely than developed countries to experience balance-of-payments deficits. In support of such a claim it can be said that the existence of money illusion in LDCs would allow governments to reconcile, in money terms, claims on resources which are irreconcilable in real terms. Furthermore, it is generally believed that governments in LDCs make relatively greater recourse to inflationary financing, whereby inflation is used as a means of increasing saving. The increase in saving may be achieved either as individuals attempt to restore the real value of their cash balances, or as the combination of inflation and a progressive tax structure raises forced saving through increased tax revenue.

Events in the early 1970s clearly demonstrated that neither domestic monetary mismanagement nor, indeed, more general internal factors can be identified as the sole cause of balance-of-payments difficulties. Two main factors accounted for the severe balance-of-payments problems which faced non oil-producing LDCs at this time. These were, first, the rise in the price of oil, which exerted an adverse terms-of-trade effect on oil-importing LDCs, and second, the recession in industrial countries, which brought about a decline in the demand for the exports of LDCs.[3]

Basic Policy Alternatives: Adjustment and Financing

When faced with a balance-of-payments deficit, countries have basically two alternative courses of action open to them. The first is to take no action at all and finance the deficit. A balance-of-payments deficit may be financed either by running down domestically held international reserves or by international borrowing. The second is to correct the deficit through the pursuit of appropriate balance-of-payments adjustment policies. As will be explained later, adjustment involves a reduction in domestic expenditure relative to domestic output.

Whilst the financing of a balance-of-payments deficit is quite appropriate where the deficit is of a transitory nature, it is different where the deficit is non-transitory, and reflects fundamental disequilibrium: in such a case, financing on its own will constitute only a short-term palliative and adjustment will be required.[4] Financing and adjustment are, of course, by no means mutually exclusive, and it is likely that a combination of financing and adjustment policies will be pursued. The greater the degree of financing, the less rapid need be the rate of adjustment. There thus tends to be a negative trade-off between financing and the rate of adjustment.

When faced with a balance-of-payments deficit, countries may pursue a range of combinations of adjustment and financing. Choice is bounded, on the one hand, by complete adjustment, which involves an opportunity cost in terms of the sacrifice of current spending and living standards, and, on the other, by complete financing, which involves an opportunity cost in terms of the sacrifice of future spending and living standards, either because interest on reserves is forgone or because loans have to be repaid. The financing of a balance-of-payments deficit does, however, permit the maintenance of current expenditure. Indeed, inasmuch as financing permits stable economic growth to be established, it will serve to increase future living standards. Economic growth which is facilitated by means of financing will reduce the long-term net costs associated with financing and may in fact make them negative. Even so, since a balance-of-payments deficit is financed by decumulating reserves or by borrowing, the real cost of financing, which is viewed as the sacrifice of consumption, may still exceed the real cost of adjustment.

As already noted, the choice facing authorities is not simply that between exclusive adjustment or exclusive financing. Adjustment and financing may be combined. As a greater proportion of the deficit is financed and a smaller proportion corrected, the marginal cost of financing, as represented by the rate of interest on borrowing, is likely to rise. Thus, the marginal cost of transforming adjustment into financing, as reflected by the size of the future reduction in living standards, will tend to increase as less adjustment is undertaken.

The question now arises of where on the trade-off between adjustment and financing a country will choose to locate itself. Its choice will depend both on preferences with regard to current and future expenditure and on the distribution of the costs and benefits of alternative strategies.[5] Given the choice between a certain amount of real expenditure now and the identical amount of real expenditure later, it may be assumed that expenditure now will always be preferred. The prospect of *greater* real expenditure in the future will be necessary to induce the sacrifice of a certain amount of current expenditure. Diminishing marginal utility of consumption will, in addition, imply a diminishing marginal rate of substitution between current and future consumption, since intra-marginal units of consumption will be valued more highly than extra-marginal units. Where the community's marginal rate of substitution between current and future expenditure equals the marginal rate of transformation between the sacrifice of current expenditure (adjustment) and the sacrifice of future expenditure (financing) the country will be using its optimal combination of adjustment and financing.

This equilibrium combination will be disturbed, first, if preferences change, or, second, if the relative costs of adjustment and financing change. Thus, a strengthening of any preference for current expenditure will tend to increase the degree of financing and reduce the degree of adjustment, whilst an increase in the cost of financing relative to that of adjustment will, other things remaining constant, encourage the substitution of adjustment for financing.

A further interesting question from our point of view is whether, given current-account deficits of similar size, LDCs would differ from developed countries in the combination of adjustment and financing that they would use. The foregoing analysis identifies the relevant factors. If, as seems likely, LDCs encounter relatively high financing costs as compared with developed countries, then, other things being equal, they will be encouraged to make relatively greater use of adjustment. But other things may not be equal: it is quite probable that the social marginal productivity of resources will be higher in LDCs than in developed countries, and this will act to reduce the net costs associated with financing and will in turn encourage LDCs to make relatively greater use of financing than would a developed country in otherwise similar circumstances. Furthermore, if LDCs, in comparison with developed countries, possess a relatively strong preference for current expenditure, they will, other things being equal, tend to make relatively greater use of financing. In practice, LDCs have, in fact, often tended to come up against an availability constraint on financing and have therefore been precluded from using that combination of adjustment and financing which they would have chosen had no such constraint existed. Where this financing constraint has been effective, LDCs have been forced to make greater use of adjustment and less use of financing than they would have preferred. On the other hand, through certain facilities at the IMF, LDCs have access, albeit limited, to sources of relatively low-cost financing; this developed countries may not have. Up to a certain point, then, the opportunity cost of failing to adjust, expressed in terms of the sacrifice of future real spending, may be comparatively low for LDCs, and, up to such a point, LDCs may therefore make relatively greater use of financing. Thus, for LDCs as compared with developed countries, the cost of the financing which they use may be lower, but they may, because of the financing constraint which they tend to encounter, be forced to make relatively greater use of adjustment than they would like.[6] A hypothetical comparison between a 'typical LDC' and a 'typical developed country' is made in Figure 6.1. The LDC may be distinguished from the developed country by the stronger preference for current expenditure, the lower initial cost of financing, and the existence of a financing constraint.

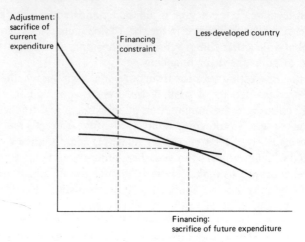

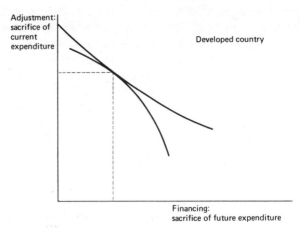

FIGURE 6.1

The Objectives of Adjustment

The objective of balance-of-payments adjustment is to bring into equality autonomous payments (P) and autonomous receipts (R). Where inequality between payments and receipts exists, the balance of payments (B) will reflect this inequality in the form of either a deficit ($R < P$), or a surplus ($R > P$). Since transactions between residents (r) give rise to identical receipts and payments ($Rr = Pr$), it is not necessary, when studying the balance of payments, to focus purely on transactions between residents and foreigners (f), but it is quite legitimate to examine aggregate receipts and aggregate payments. Thus,

$$B = Rf + Rr - Pf - Pr = R - P = Rf - Pf$$

A balance-of-payments deficit will exist where

$$Rf + Rr - Pr - Pf < 0$$

This presentation of a balance-of-payments deficit shows that balance-of-payments adjustment in a deficit situation requires an increase in receipts, or a reduction in payments, or, more generally, an increase in receipts relative to payments. Since transactions involve money flowing in exchange for, and in the opposite direction to, goods, a relative reduction in payments implies a reduction in the domestic absorption of goods relative to the production of goods. If real production cannot be increased during the relevant time period, adjustment will involve an absolute reduction in real domestic expenditure on domestic and foreign output.

It is crucial to underline that, in a situation where real domestic output cannot be increased, the correction of a balance-of-payments deficit entails a reduction in domestic expenditure. This will be the case even if the demand by foreigners for domestic output rises, since this demand may be met, in conditions of full employment, only if the resources demanded by foreigners are freed by residents. Greater absorption of domestic and foreign output by foreigners fairly clearly involves lower absorption of domestic and foreign output by residents. Irrespective of whether the initial impact of any balance-of-payments policy is to reduce domestic expenditure or switch expenditure from abroad, correction of the deficit will, in conditions of full employment, be achieved only if there is a reduction in real domestic expenditure. If this reduction in domestic expenditure is not achieved, the deficit will not be corrected.

A reduction in domestic expenditure may be achieved by means of pursuing a range of 'expenditure reducing' policies, such as contractionary monetary and fiscal policy, which, by lowering domestic income, serve to reduce expenditure on all goods, both traded and non-traded. The greater the income elasticity of demand for traded goods, the smaller will be the fall in income that is needed in order to bring about the required fall in payments to foreigners. Expenditure-reducing policies, inasmuch as they reduce the demand for imports, will be sufficient on their own to correct a deficit. In addition, and to the extent that expenditure-reducing policies also induce a fall in the price of domestically produced goods, they will encourage a switch in domestic and foreign expenditure away from foreign output and towards domestic output. The resources necessary to meet this extra demand for domestic output will have been freed by the reduction in domestic expenditure, provided only that the expenditure reduction occurred in terms of traded goods and not exclusively non-traded goods.

A transfer of expenditure from residents to foreigners is more conventionally engineered by means of other 'expenditure-switching' policies designed to lower the incentive for residents to buy foreign goods and raise the incentive for both residents and foreigners to buy domestic goods. Such a switch in real expenditure may, in theory, be encouraged by changing the price of domestic output relative to that of foreign output. Unlike expenditure-reducing policies, however, expenditure-switching policies on their own may be insufficient to correct a deficit. Although, in conditions where there are unemployed resources, the additional demand for exports and import substitutes induced by a fall in the relative price of domestic output may be met in real terms by means of utilising unemployed resources, in conditions of full employment the extra demand created by the expenditure-switching policies will simply generate inflation, unless action is simultaneously taken to free the resources needed to meet the extra demand. Expenditure-switching policies, however, may themselves be demand-deflationary in circumstances where the nominal money supply fails to adjust to the rise in prices which the policies tend to generate.

The above analysis of balance-of-payments policy rests on the implicit assumption that the basic determinants of a trade imbalance are to be found by examining import and export functions. Attention is focused on the relative price of domestic and foreign output, and on the level of national income as the major determinants of import and export demand.

A different emphasis to the analysis of the balance of payments is provided when it is remembered that excessive payments have to be financed in some way. Since changes in reserve levels reflect the overall state of the balance of payments, the balance of payments as a whole may be viewed as a monetary phenomenon. The monetary approach to the balance of payments[7] concentrates on the notion that changes in a country's balance of payments as reflected by changes in its international reserves, are directly associated with monetary disequilibria at the national level; changes in reserves being equal to the difference between the flow demand for money, and the domestic flow supply of money. The transmission mechanism through which monetary variables influence the balance of payments has not been clearly established, but, in theory, it would seem likely to operate either directly, via the effect of changes in real cash balances on domestic expenditure, or indirectly, via the effect of induced interest-rate changes on domestic expenditure and international capital flows. Balance-of-payments disequilibria may then be viewed as reflecting an attempt by transactors to establish a desired level of real balances, and the value of real balances may therefore be included as an argument in the import function. An excess real supply of money relative to the real demand for money will induce transactors to reduce real balances. Depending on the elasticity of substitution between money and other assets, transactors will move into goods (both traded or untraded), and financial assets, and this rearrangement of wealth portfolios will cause some combination of real income growth, domestic inflation, import expansion, and falling interest rates. Changes in these variables will, in turn, have implications for the balance of payments. Clearly, it is through an examination of the ways in which exogenous changes in monetary variables may influence income and expenditure in both the short and long run, and cause and correct divergences between them, that the monetary and absorption approaches to the balance of payments may be integrated. In as much as an excess demand for goods reflects an excess supply of money, the absorption approach, which focuses on the excess of claims on resources over the domestic production of these resources, may be given a monetary foundation.

On the basis of the monetary approach to the balance of payments, a deficit will be corrected only if the monetary disequilibrium associated with it is also corrected. Correction of a monetary disequilibrium where there exists an excess real supply of money necessitates either a reduction in the real supply of money or a rise in the real demand for money. A fall in the real supply of money may be brought about either by a fall in the nominal supply of money, or by a rise in the general price level, or, more generally, by an increase in the price level relative to the nominal supply of money; in this last case, the nominal demand will rise towards equality with the nominal supply as the real supply falls towards equality with the real demand.[8] A rise in the real demand for money may be brought about through a rise in the level of real national income, or through a strengthening in any preference for money as opposed to other assets.[9]

It emerges from our analysis of what adjustment policy has to achieve in order to improve the balance of payments that the elasticity of supply of real domestic output, as reflected by the level of employment, is crucial. In conditions of unemployment, policies which effectively encourage a switching of domestic and foreign expenditure away from foreign output and towards domestic output will be sufficient. In conditions of full employment and inelastic supply, however, expenditure-switching policies will not be sufficient on their own and will have to be accompanied by expenditure-reducing policies. In order to achieve the reduction in real domestic expenditure which is necessary in conditions of full employment, the appropriate monetary policy is required.

Having identified what it is that balance-of-payments adjustment has to achieve, we can now move on to examine in more detail the range of policies available which might rectify or help to rectify a deficit. We shall orient our discussion towards the question of which policies are most appropriate from the point of view of LDCs.

Adjustment Policy in LDCs: Theoretical Analysis

Adjustment policy endeavours to exert its effect by influencing a number of key variables. These are: relative prices, national income, output and expenditure, and the supply of money. In this section we isolate one particular adjustment policy – namely, exchange-rate depreciation or devaluation – and examine how, in the circumstances of LDCs, it will effect each of these key variables. Where it seems as though devaluation might fail to generate the necessary changes, we examine alternative adjustment strategies.

Devaluation and relative prices

Theoretically devaluation is usually defined as falling into the category of expenditure-switching policies. It operates in a way which increases the domestic price and/or reduces the foreign price of exports. De-valuation generates price incentives, which tend to lower the domestic consumption of imports, raise the domestic consumption and pro-duction of import substitutes, increase the foreign consumption of exports, and/or lower the domestic consumption of exports and increase the production of exports. The responses to these price changes depend on a range of demand and supply elasticities.

A prime issue of interest is whether devaluation in LDCs will cause the theoretically anticipated price changes. With regard to imports it is highly improbable that any individual LDC will be able to influence the foreign price of its imports, since its demand for any particular import will represent only a small fraction of the total world demand for the product. Even so, the domestic price of imports may not rise to the full extent of the devaluation, or may even fall if devaluation is accompanied by the removal of import controls, such as quotas, tariffs and multiple-exchange practices, that prior to devaluation served to maintain import prices at an artificially high level. Such controls are common amongst LDCs.[10]

With regard to exports, much depends on the significance of the LDC as a supplier of the particular export. Where the LDC accounts for only a small proportion of the total world supply of a product, it is unlikely that the foreign-currency export price will alter as a result of devaluation, since this price will be largely determined by the interplay of supply and demand in the world market. In these circumstances devaluation will instead tend to raise the price of exports in terms of the relevant domestic currency. Again, however, a rise in the domestic-currency price of an export which is also consumed domestically is not automatically implied by the constancy of the foreign-currency price. For instance, the exchange authorities may allow export producers a less beneficial exchange rate, thus effectively taxing the windfall increase in profits that would otherwise have been associated with devaluation, or the authorities may directly impose an export tax.[11]

Where the world supply of a particular product is concentrated in a particular LDC, the world foreign-currency price of the commodity may fall following devaluation in that country. Producers' pricing policies will, however, be influenced by the estimated size of demand and supply elasticities, as well as by institutional arrangements, such as the existence of international commodity agreements which discourage signatories from expanding their market share through price competition.

If relative price changes do result from devaluation, such that domestic output becomes cheaper in relation to foreign output, the success of the devaluation in improving the balance of payments depends on the responses to these price changes. In the case of imports, the demand in LDCs may tend to be price-inelastic. This reflects the developmental nature of imports in LDCs. The demand for foodstuffs, raw materials and capital goods may not be compressible. To some extent import substitution may permit a price-induced reduction in import demand, but in many LDCs the boundaries of import substitution may already have been reached.

On the export side, the foreign-currency price of exports may most commonly not fall as a result of devaluation. Where it does, however, the price elasticity of demand may prove to be low, since it might be anticipated that both the substitution effect away from other goods and the income effect associated with the fall in price will be small.[12] Where the foreign-currency price of exports remains constant and the domestic-currency equivalent rises, the issue of crucial significance in assessing the relevance of devaluation becomes the elasticity of supply of exports.[13] This elasticity, which is of course likely to vary with the time period studied, will depend on a number of factors: it will tend to be higher the shorter the gestation period of production, the greater the domestic consumption of the good, the greater the degree of unutilised capacity, the greater the availability of investment finance, and the greater the mobility of resources. Circumstances vary as between individual LDCs, but theoretically there is some reason to believe that, at least in the short run, the elasticity of supply in response to devaluation may be fairly low in LDCs, because of lengthy gestation periods, factor immobilities and inadequacies of investment and development finance. Supply inelasticity almost certainly constitutes a major impediment to the efficacy of devaluation, and, indeed, any form of expenditure-switching policy, as a method of balance-of-payments adjustment in LDCs. Such supply inelasticity need not necessarily imply full employment, and may merely indicate a general difficulty in expanding the output of exports and import substitutes which might arise from structural inflexibility.

Even though the success of all expenditure-switching policies, including devaluation, depends on the same basic factors, a significant distinction may be made with respect to the selectivity of various such policies. In most LDCs, devaluation will initially exert a fairly universal influence over the domestic-currency price of all traded goods. The impact of devaluation on the demand for foreign exchange depends, then, on the domestic-price elasticity of demand for imports. The impact on the supply of foreign exchange depends in the first instance on the foreign-price elasticity of demand for exports if the devaluation causes a change in the foreign price, and on the elasticity of supply with respect to increased profits in the export sector if it is only domestic prices that change. For commodities subject to price-inelastic demand and/or supply, devaluation will do little to improve the foreign-exchange position.

Tariffs and multiple exchange rates, which also count as expenditure-switching policies, can be applied very much more selectively than devaluation, and may, in certain circumstances, have advantages over it.

Let us concentrate on multiple exchange rates. This, as the name implies, means that instead of there being one exchange rate between domestic and foreign currency there are many. Which exchange rate applies to a particular transaction depends on the nature of the goods involved. In the context of our analysis, it would in theory be possible to apply different rates of exchange to different transactions, depending on the price elasticity of demand and supply of the commodities involved. As compared with overall devaluation, a system of multiple exchange rates could be used to increase the supply of, and reduce the demand for, foreign exchange. In theory, multiple exchange rates might work in the following manner.

In circumstances where the price elasticity of demand for a particular import is low, a relatively high exchange rate would be applied to transactions involving this import. For transactions involving an import for which the price elasticity of demand is high, the exchange rate would be relatively low and fewer units of foreign currency would be acquired by sacrificing one unit of domestic currency. In circumstances where the foreign price elasticity of demand for an LDC's export is high, and the LDC is in a position to influence the world price, a lower exchange rate would be used than in transactions involving a commodity which possesses a low price elasticity of demand. Where the foreign price of a commodity is fixed from the point of view of any individual LDC supplier, then a relatively high exchange rate would be applied to transactions involving commodities which possess low supply elasticities with respect to the domestic currency price, and a relatively low exchange rate would be applied to transactions involving commodities which possess high supply elasticities.

For the reason that a system of multiple exchange rates permits greater selectivity in the limitation of imports and in the fostering of exports and import substitutes, such a system may be viewed as representing a more efficient method of adjustment than the uniform depreciation of a single exchange rate.[14] Demand and supply price elasticities may not be of the value required to ensure that the relative price changes which a devaluation causes would prove an effective means of correcting balance-of-payments deficits in LDCs.

Although administrative difficulties would almost certainly preclude having a plethora of exchange rates, it might be possible to establish a system of dual exchange rates. Under this system, one relatively high exchange rate might be established for trade in traditional primary exports and essential imports, both of which are subject to inelastic demand; and a lower rate would be used for trade in manufactured, infant-industry exports, and for inessential imports, where the price elasticity of demand is high.[15]

Devaluation, domestic expenditure and the supply of money

In the circumstances in which many LDCs find themselves, the scope for expenditure-switching may be limited. Foreign expenditure on the exports of LDCs may fail to rise even with devaluation, since the foreign price of exports may be determined by world market forces and LDCs may be world price takers;[16] trade barriers may exist in developed countries and may be adjusted to neutralise any impact which devaluation might have on price; or it may be found that inelasticities in domestic supply preclude the meeting of any extra foreign demand which is generated by devaluation. If there is some doubt whether devaluation in LDCs will serve to increase domestic output by means of switching expenditure towards domestic output and away from foreign output, attention shifts to the influence that devaluation may exert on the *level* of real expenditure.

Holding other influences constant, there is some reason to believe that devaluation will tend to reduce real expenditure. First, it is possible that a domestically demand-deflationary influence will emanate from the trading sector. Where export demand does not respond to devaluation, even though the foreign-currency price of exports falls, but, at the same time and because of inelastic demand, expenditure on imports expressed in terms of domestic currency increases, there will be a net reduction in aggregate demand for domestic output. Where, on the other hand, it is the domestic-currency price of exports which rises, and not the foreign-currency price which falls, then, given equivalent propensities to spend on domestic output, the increase in domestic-currency export receipts will offset the increase in domestic-currency import payments and there will be no net demand-deflationary effect.

Second, devaluation tends to have a redistributive effect on income. The precise nature of the redistribution, which, incidentally, may occur both between trading and non-trading sectors and between the rewards of factors of production (in particular, profits and wages), depends on a range of issues and may differ as between the short run and the long run. These issues include: the response of money wages in the trading and non-trading sectors to the extra profitability which devaluation induces in the trading sector; the import content of traded and non-traded goods; the response in the non-trading sector to higher wage and import costs; the factor intensities of various sectors; and the degree of factor mobility. A number of scenarios may be imagined. Since wage receivers may differ from profit receivers as regards their marginal propensity to spend, different scenarios will tend to have different impacts on domestic expenditure. As one example, let us take a hypothetical case where devaluation raises the domestic-currency price of exports and imports (traded goods). In response to this rise in price, money wages in the traded-goods sector rise, because of demand-pull and/or cost-push pressures, but rise insufficiently to erode the extra profitability now associated with the trading sector. The increase in the domestic-currency price of imports pushes up the prices of those non-traded goods with an import content, and, indeed, reduces the extra profitability associated with the traded-goods sector. The general rise in the domestic price level is, however, not as great as the rise in the price of traded goods, but greater than the rise in the price of non-traded goods. Money wages in the non-traded good sector rise, partly as a spillover response to increased money wages in the export sector, and partly in response to the higher cost of living. The higher money wages in the non-trading sector may further push up prices in that sector. Assuming that money wages in both the trading and non-trading sectors rise less than the general price level, perhaps because of the existence of money illusion, real wages fall. Assuming further that there is a lower propensity to spend out of profits than out of wages, domestic expenditure will also fall. Alternatively, where money wages in both trading and non-trading sectors rise in line with the general price level, whilst the prices of traded goods rise more rapidly than the general price level and the price of non-traded goods rise less rapidly than the general price level, real wages will be maintained, and all that will happen is a redistribution of profits from the non-trading sector to the trading sector.

Whilst, in theory, devaluation may cause a change in relative factor rewards, depending on the factor intensities of different sectors, and may thus generate a movement of factors between sectors, in the case of LDCs, where factors tend to be rather immobile, and some factor markets may not even exist, the initial redistribution of income towards profits in the export sector may persevere. The permanence of the redistribution will crucially depend on whether those adversely affected by it recognise what has happened, and on what power they have to resist it.[17] If, following a devalution, all factor rewards are maintained at their pre-devaluation real levels, then devaluation will fail to exert an impact on expenditure.

A third potential source of demand deflation which might be induced by devaluation arises from debt-servicing. Devaluation will tend to raise the domestic costs of servicing any given external obligation expressed in foreign currency, and, other things remaining constant, will exert a reducing effect on domestic expenditure.

Although, for the reasons that we have just identified, devaluation might be expected to have an expenditure-reducing impact, real-expenditure reduction will, as we noted earlier, be achieved only if the appropriate monetary policy is simultaneously pursued. Indeed, from one point of view, it is the monetary implications of devaluation which are crucial to the success of devaluation in terms of improving the balance of payments. Devaluation may be interpreted as a monetary instrument inasmuch as, at full employment, it causes the general price level to rise and the real supply of money to fall, whilst in conditions of unemployment it causes real income and thus the real demand for money to rise. In fact, even in conditions of unemployment where it might be expected that devaluation would no longer be demand-inflationary, it may still be cost-inflationary, through its impact on import prices. Devaluation may therefore serve to reduce the real supply of money even in a situation of unemployment.

Optimal Adjustment Strategy in LDCs

The presentation of devaluation as an instrument of monetary policy which, at full employment, operates by means of reducing the real supply of money encourages us to examine the question of whether similar results could be achieved by alternative forms of monetary policy. In theory, either a reduction in the nominal money supply or an increase in the real demand for money could serve as an alternative to devaluation. In choosing an appropriate adjustment strategy, however, countries are guided not purely by considerations of whether a particular policy will or will not correct a balance-of-payments dis-equilibrium, but rather by considerations of whether the particular policy represents the best method of adjustment from a welfare point of view, and indeed, whether the policy is practicable. Devaluation, then, even though it might work in the narrow sense of improving the balance of payments, may not be the most efficient adjustment tool; direct, domestic monetary management, or a combination of monetary management and devaluation may be chosen in its place. Let us examine some of the factors involved in such a choice.

Basically, in circumstances where the marginal social cost of reducing the nominal money supply is greater than the marginal social cost of increasing the nominal demand for money by means of devaluation, devaluation will be the preferred policy. Building on from this: although, in theory, devaluation and a reduction in the nominal supply of money provide alternative mechanisms for reducing the real supply of money, countries are unlikely to be indifferent about which policy they use. One reason for this relates to the structural and distributional consequences of devaluation as compared with those associated with a reduction in the nominal supply of money. Devaluation increases the profitability of the trading sector and, as a result of the relative price effect which it induces, encourages resources to move into this sector. Furthermore, devaluation may bring about a reduction in real wages as measured by the ratio of money wages to absolute prices, and therefore involves a redistribution of income away from wages and towards profits. Devaluation may, then, encourage export-led growth. A reduction in the nominal supply of money, on the other hand, is less likely to induce a relative price effect and is therefore less likely to bring about structural changes in this way. Structural changes may still occur, however, inasmuch as certain firms may rely heavily on bank credit; an increase in the cost of such credit will create problems for these firms, especially if no alternative sources of finance exist. If the firms which rely heavily on bank credit are domestic as opposed to international and are concentrated in infant manufacturing industry, contractionary monetary policy may have marked consequences for the structural development of the economy. As far as distribution is concerned, and assuming downward price and wage rigidity, the ratio of money wages to prices may not fall following a reduction in the nominal supply of money, and whether domestic absorption is lowered will rest on whether the decline in real balances causes the propensity to spend to be reduced.

A second reason for lack of indifference between devaluation and a reduction in the nominal money supply relates to the effects of each policy on output, employment and inflation. Whilst devaluation attempts to switch expenditure towards domestic output, and is therefore likely to raise employment in conditions of unemployment, or to maintain employment in conditions of full employment (even though the domestic absorption of this full employment output has to fall if devaluation is to be successful), monetary contraction tends to reduce aggregate demand for output, and causes output to fall and unemployment to rise. On the other hand, whilst at full employment and from a monetary point of view devaluation works by means of creating inflation and reducing real balances, monetary contraction tends to lower the rate of inflation. It emerges that the choice between devaluation and monetary contraction will depend on the current level of unemployment and the current rate of inflation, and the community's preferences relative to these two factors.[18] In conditions of unemployment, devaluation is likely to be preferred, because of its expansionary influence on employment. In conditions of full employment the choice may not be so clear cut. Where the balance-of-payments deficit has been caused by monetary excesses rather than by structural factors, then monetary contraction might be appropriate; whereas, if the deficit reflects structural factors, devaluation, possibily accompanied by a measure of monetary restriction, might represent the most efficient policy.

The most efficient policy from an economic point of view may of course not be the one that is chosen. A third influence on the choice of policy relates to the political and technical feasibility of devaluation as opposed to monetary contraction. If the internal consequences of devaluation are not well understood, it may prove more acceptable politically. Monetary contraction may be politically unpopular, and may be technically difficult in LDCs, either because of the low level of central control over the rate of domestic credit expansion, or because of the government's additional objectives, such as that of financing a fiscal deficit. For these reasons devaluation may again be preferred.[19]

Monetary contraction is, of course, not the only alternative monetary policy to devaluation, since, in order to correct the deficit, all that is required is that the excess real supply of money is reduced, and this may be achieved equally well by holding the money supply at a given level and allowing the demand for money to rise, or by allowing the demand for money to rise more rapidly than the money supply. Since economic growth will, in theory, cause an increase in the demand for money, the faster the economy is growing the less likely it is that monetary contraction or devaluation will be required. Even where the rate of economic growth is slow, the demand for money may still be increased by means of, say, increasing any administered rate of interest on money holdings,[20] or changing the pattern of expenditure and payment so that a larger fraction of income needs to be held in the form of money to cover transactions.

Of course, even where the demand for money would eventually rise to equality with the supply of it, or where the supply of money could, over a certain period of time, be reduced to equality with the demand for it, for as long as the supply of money exceeds the demand a balance-of-payments deficit will exist, and this deficit will have to be financed. The choice of adjustment policy may then be related to the time-scale of adjustment. If international reserves are low, or the cost of borrowing is high, in terms of either the rate of interest on borrowing or the conditions stipulated by lenders, or both, devaluation may be used in the short run, even though over the longer run it would not have been required.

It emerges from the discussion undertaken so far in this chapter that theory allows us to predict the circumstances under which devaluation is likely to improve the balance of payments, and the circumstances under which devaluation will represent the best policy. It is therefore highly relevant to ask whether these circumstances exist in LDCs; and it is to an empirical investigation of this question that we turn in the next section.

To recapitulate, devaluation of the exchange rate will tend to improve the balance of payments if the elasticity of demand for exports is high; if the elasticity of demand for imports is high; if the elasticity of supply of both exports and import substitutes is high; and if, following a devaluation, real expenditure and the real supply of money fall. Devaluation will tend to be the most appropriate method of adjustment if the rate of economic growth is low; if monetary contraction is politically or technically infeasible; and if holdings of international reserves are low. In many LDCs the elasticity of demand for exports will be irrelevant, since LDCs are often effectively world price takers. Given the nature of imports it might be anticipated that the demand for imports will be price-inelastic,[21] whilst it might be further expected that the elasticity of supply of exports and import substitutes will be low, at least in the short run. Assuming that at least some groups of workers in LDCs are subject to money illusion such that they do not recognise, or, at least, do not fully recognise, a fall in their real wages provided only that their money wage does not fall, and/or are poorly organised, it might again be anticipated that real expenditure would fall following devaluation; such a reduction in domestic absorption would be sufficient to improve the balance of payments. Given that growth rates tend to be relatively low in many LDCs, that monetary policy tends to be relatively difficult to conduct, and that reserve holdings are relatively low, it might also be anticipated that LDCs would make relatively frequent use of devaluation. We now move on to examine these theoretical expectations against the available empirical evidence.

Adjustment Policy in LDCs: Empirical Evidence

As reference to IMF data reveals, LDCs have made considerable use of devaluation.[22] The success of devaluation in LDCs may be evaluated empirically at two levels. At the first level, the *potential* success of devaluation may be investigated by examining whether the conditions required for successful devaluation exist. At the second level, and more directly, the *actual* impact of devaluation on the balance of payments of those LDCs which have made use of it may be examined. Various methodological problems are, however, involved with empirical studies of devaluation. A central problem is that of correctly allocating effects to causes. This difficulty arises from the fact that studies of devaluation often involve a comparison between a known and an unknown situation. Since other influences are unlikely to remain constant, it is difficult to identify the extent to which prices, incomes, money supplies and trade flows change in response to devaluation, and the extent to which they change in response to other influences.

The intermediate determinants of the success of devaluation were identified in the theoretical section of this chapter. These determinants included: the values of a range of price elasticities; the effect of devaluation on prices and wages; and the effect of devaluation on the real supply of money and aggregate demand. Let us examine the empirical evidence relating to each of these in turn.

Price elasticities

Only a very limited amount of rather unsatisfactory empirical evidence is available on LDC price elasticities. This evidence does, however, tend to suggest that elasticity pessimism may be misplaced. In a study of fifteen LDCs over the period of 1951–69, Khan (1974) observes that both import and export demand is responsive to price changes, such that changes in the relative prices of traded and non-traded goods do exert a significant influence on the trade flows of LDCs. This conclusion does not, of course, necessarily mean that devaluation will be successful in improving the trade balance of LDCs, since success in these terms rests on the assumption that devaluation will in the first instance generate changes in the relative prices of traded and non-traded goods. Evidence on this matter is provided by Cooper (1971a and b) and Connolly and Taylor (1976b). In a study of twenty-four devaluations in LDCs over the period 1959–66, Cooper notes that in twenty cases devaluation was accompanied by some substantial measure of exchange reform or trade liberalisation, with the result that the effective devaluation differed from, and was usually less than, the nominal devaluation. Even though the effective devaluation usually varied as between imports and exports, with the impact on import prices being more marked, devaluation practically always generated a relative rise in the domestic price of traded goods as a whole, at least initially. Connolly and Taylor confirm this finding. Whilst devaluation appears to bring about a moderate acceleration in the overall rate of inflation, the rise it brings about in the price of traded goods is substantial. For the eight devaluations studied by Connolly and Taylor, over the two-year post-devaluation period the prices of traded goods rose by an amount approaching the extent of devaluation, whilst prices in general rose less than half as much.

The improvement in the profitability of exports which is associated with devaluation will, of course, result in extra exportation only if supply is not infinitely inelastic. Indeed, the success of devaluation in improving the trade balance and in increasing earnings of foreign exchange is crucially dependent on the elasticity of export supply. Unfortunately, there is little precise empirical evidence relating to export supply elasticities in LDCs. In a study, carried out by Bhagwat and Onitsuka (1974), of post-devaluation export performance in a number of non-industrial countries, it emerges that in the majority of cases export earnings and export volume did grow following devaluation. Where little or no expansion in exports resulted, or, indeed, where a decline occurred, special circumstances were usually found to exist. The response of exports to devaluation appears, however, to depend very much on the level of development, the type of export, and the concentration and structure of trade. For the small, least-developed countries which export little other than tree crops, the export-supply response to devaluation is not very apparent, and export earnings seem to be more responsive to variations in weather and extraneous fluctuations in world demand. For the more developed LDCs which export agricultural goods with shorter gestation periods, minerals, or manufactured goods, the supply response of exports to devaluation appears to be somewhat greater.

The observation that exports generally do rise following devaluation is consistent with an export-supply elasticity which is greater than zero; such evidence, however, cannot be conveniently used to calculate the exact size of the supply response to devaluation, since factors other than the currency devaluation may have exerted an influence over export performance. It seems probable, in any case, that the elasticity of export supply will vary markedly between LDCs, for reasons mentioned in the theoretical section of this chapter.

Price and wage inflation

For a combination of cost and demand reasons, devaluation is liable to be inflationary; this may be especially true where wage-earners are able to maintain the real wage level, and the elasticity of supply of import substitutes and exports is low. Import prices will tend to rise with devaluation, and such price increases will be reflected in rising costs where imported goods constitute inputs into the production of other goods. Furthermore, the price of domestically consumed export goods will also rise in response to devaluation.[23] A rise in the cost of living may lead to wage demands, and rising money wages may in turn result in higher prices (if wage increases are passed on to consumers) and/or in unemployment. On the demand side, increased profits may encourage exporters to expand output. As a result, wages throughout the economy may tend to rise and prices in slow productivity-growth industries producing non-tradable goods may be marked up.

The relevant empirical question, however, relates not to whether devaluation will generate inflation, since in isolation there is little doubt that it will; but, rather, to the size of inflation as compared with the size of devaluation. Provided that price and wage increases do not completely eliminate the greater profitability that devaluation initially brings to the foreign-trade sector, and provided that money wages do not rise sufficiently to maintain real wages,[24] devaluation is still likely to be successful in improving the balance of payments. The issue is primarily a quantitative one, although qualitatively it might be assumed that devaluation would be less successful in LDCs subject to wage-push inflation, inelastic output supply and expansionary monetary policy. Furthermore, use of indexation in LDCs will, of course, tend to ensure downward rigidity in real wages, and this will in turn reduce the effectiveness of devaluation.

It is difficult to isolate the quantitative influence of devaluation on prices and wages. Evidence presented by Cooper (1971a and b) does, however, appear to substantiate the claim that, for the first twelve months after a devaluation, the rise in prices and wages is considerably less than the size of the devaluation. As noted in the previous sub section, this finding is confirmed by Connolly and Taylor (1976b). From the evidence it seems that, following a devaluation in LDCs, money wages usually rise less than prices, i.e. real wages fall. Taking sixteen devaluations in LDCs for which data on consumer prices and wages are available, it transpires that, on average, in the year after devaluation, consumer prices rose by 22.9 per cent whilst manufacturing wages rose by 17.9 per cent. On the assumption that, following devaluation, money wages in the manufacturing sector rise rather faster than money wages in other sectors, in part because of the superior organisation of workers in manufacturing, it would seem fair to conclude that devaluation is frequently associated with a fall in real wages.

Aggregate demand

If the propensity to spend out of profits is lower than the propensity to spend out of wages, the redistribution of income implied by a decline in real wages may have a deflationary influence on aggregate demand. This deflationary, redistributive effect of devaluation seems to have operated to a particularly marked degree in the case of the Argentine devaluation of 1959, where the shift of real income to landowners, who had a lower propensity to spend than the urban workers, from whom the real income was diverted, served to generate a decline in import demand additional to the price-induced decline.[25] There is little doubt that the deflationary redistributive effect has also operated in other devaluations, although investment stimulated by higher profits in the traded-goods sector may tend to neutralise it. Of course, the increase in profits may be transferred to the government, and the effect on aggregate demand will then depend on how governments use their increased revenue. Redistribution apart, and holding other things constant, the higher the average propensity to import and the lower the price elasticity of demand for imports, the greater will tend to be the deflationary impact of devaluation. Higher import prices may act rather like an efficient, excise tax, since, although they are cost-inflationary in the narrow sense of increasing the price of certain goods, they may, at the same time, be demand-deflationary in terms of reducing domestic expenditure. If expenditure reduction is necessary in order for devaluation to be successful, the extent to which higher import prices are deflationary will be significant. In the case of most small LDCs, devaluation will fail to generate any extra foreign claims on domestic resources through a price-induced expansion in the demand for exports, since the foreign-currency price of exports will not fall. Increased expenditure may, on the other hand, result from attempts by exporters to expand their capacity in order to produce more exports, and this may to a certain extent, offset the deflationary impact of higher import prices.

A major factor influencing the effect of devaluation on aggregate demand is the response of the domestic money supply. It would seem that, for the nominal supply of money to fall following devaluation in

LDCs is almost unknown (see Cooper, 1971a and b). It does appear, however, that in certain cases the real supply of money falls after devaluation, and certainly in about half the cases investigated by Connolly and Taylor decreases in the rate of growth of domestic credit expressed as a percentage of the money stock occurred in the year after devlaution. Indeed, in a clear majority of devaluations in LDCs there occurred, over the two years following devaluation, decreases in the rate of growth of domestic credit.

Devaluation and the Balance of Payments

Since the principal objective of devaluation is to improve the balance of payments, let us now review the direct evidence relating to the effect of devaluation in LDCs on their balances of payments. Cooper (1971a and b) discovers that in about 75 per cent of cases the balance-of-payments on current account, measured in foreign currency, improves in the year following devaluation; and that in 90 per cent of cases either the current account or the capital account,[26] or both accounts, improve. In the few instances where devaluation fails to bring about an improvement in the balance of payments, special features such as extensive import liberalisation seem to be significant.

Merely to observe that in most cases the balances of payments improves *after* a devaluation does not of course necessarily imply that the payments position improves *because* of the devaluation; other factors may be at work. The balance of payments in the period preceding devaluation might, for instance, have been particularly poor because of a bad harvest in a key cash crop, a temporary phenomenon; or even because of anticipated devaluation. Again, the balance of payments might have improved as a result of the pursuit of deflationary domestic policies rather than devaluation, or because of an expansion in world demand, or, indeed, because of revaluations elsewhere. On the other hand, in the absence of certain other changes, such as import liberalisation, the imposition of export taxes, a decline in world demand, and devaluations elsewhere, the improvement caused to the balance of payments by devaluation on its own, might have been considerably more marked than is apparent from casual reference to balance-of-payments data.

An estimate of the influence of devaluation on the balance of payments may be made by trying to form an opinion on what the balance-of-payments position would have been in the absence of devaluation. If it is right to assume that LDCs would have maintained their pre-devaluation market shares in the world markets for their exports, and would have experienced an expansion in imports as determined by the interaction between the growth in real income and the income elasticity of demand for imports, it would appear that in most cases devaluation resulted in higher exports and lower imports (Cooper, 1971a and b).

An alternative approach to evaluating the impact of devaluation on the balance of payments is to regress changes in the balance of payments on the rate of devaluation. Such regressions suggest that devaluation does cause a significant improvement in the balance of payments of LDCs,[27] but that the balance of payments fails to improve by an amount even approaching the nominal amount of the devaluation over a one- or two-year post-devaluation period. Regression analysis further suggests that devaluation will be considerably more effective in improving the balance of payments if accompanied by 'contractionary' monetary policy. Indeed, Connolly and Taylor argue that the evidence strongly supports the notion that, with very few exceptions, a reduction in the rate of growth of domestic credit is, on its own, sufficient to guarantee an improvement in the balance of payments.[28] Viewing the issue from the opposite angle, Khan (1976, 1977) and Aghevli and Khan (1977) muster considerable empirical evidence from amongst LDCs in support of the monetary approach to the balance of payments, finding that changes in monetary variables work through a number of channels, such as the rate of inflation, the rate of interest, and the level of expenditure, to explain a large fraction of fluctuations in the balances of payments of LDCs. Such a finding could, of course, be consistent with a number of causal relationships and not just the simple one between money and the balance of payments. The issue is complicated by the fact that reverse causation is theoretically quite possible: exogenous changes in the balance of payments may, under a fixed exchange-rate system, induce changes in the domestic supply of money.[29] Furthermore, for the relatively large number of LDCs that employ some degree of exchange-rate flexibility, or make extensive use of trade and exchange controls, the apparent simplicity of the monetary model tends, in any case, to evaporate.

Concluding Remarks

In any country the appropriate balance-of-payments policy depends on the causes of balance-of-payments difficulties and the circumstances in which the country finds itself. There are some theoretical reasons to believe that, in the case of LDCs, devaluation will fail to improve the balance of payments. These reasons include the absence of a foreign-price terms-of-trade effect and the assumed inelasticity of supply. Empirical evidence is, however, almost unanimous that devaluation does in fact serve to improve the balance of payments in LDCs. This does not necessarily mean that devaluation will always be tangibly associated with such an improvement, since, particularly in the case of LDCs, devaluation may form only one part of a policy package which also incorporates trade liberalisation and exchange reform. These contemporaneous changes in other policies may negate or overwhelm the impact of devaluation on the balance of payments, so that no effect on the balance of payments is apparent or there is an apparent effect which is the opposite of the one expected. The policy-package approach to adjustment in LDCs, and the support which has often been given by the IMF to devaluation in LDCs can no doubt be partially explained by the IMF's dislike of trade controls and multiple exchange-rate systems Whilst the IMF would like its members to possess balance-of-payments equilibrium, to partake in a free system of multilateral payments and to use fixed exchange rates, it seems that of these objectives the IMF regards fixed exchange rates as having the lowest priority, and it is the pegging of exchange rates which tends to be sacrificed in order to help achieve the other two objectives. In instances where exchange-rate adjustments have been condoned by the IMF, the acquiescence of the Fund may well have been motivated by a desire to avoid the introduction or proliferation of trade and/or exchange controls by the countries concerned. Indeed, the Fund's financial support of stabilisation programmes which have incorporated devaluation may have depended on the acceptance, by the LDCs involved, of a substantial measure of trade liberalisation and exchange reform.

The success of devaluation in improving the balance of payments seems crucially to depend on the nature of the monetary policy which accompanies it. Indeed, it would seem to be the stance of monetary policy which is the really relevant factor in balance-of-payments adjustment in LDCs. As a general rule, devaluation does not seem to work if accompanied by expansionary monetary policy, whilst it does not seem to be required if contractionary monetary policy is pursued. In certain circumstances, such as where spare capacity exists, devaluation may be more appropriate than exclusive reliance on contractionary monetary policy. In perhaps most cases, however, it remains true that the success of devaluation rests on inducing the same effects as would be induced by contractionary monetary policy; if these effects, primarily the reduction in real living standards, are unacceptable, no adjustment mechanism is likely to work.[30] If the international community decides that poor countries should not be asked to undergo a reduction in their living standards, then, in the short term, balance-of-payments deficits will have to be financed, and adjustment will have to be of a longer-term structural type. The international reaction to the prospect of the long-term financing of LDCs' balance of payments deficits is liable to depend on the proximate causes of them. It is concern over the causes of deficits in LDCs which, in large measure, has dictated the IMFs conditional case-by-case approach to financing.[31]

7 The IMF as a Source of International Liquidity for LDCs

It has already been established that many developing countries experience balance-of-payments difficulties. These difficulties are caused in part at least by export instability. Furthermore, it would appear that, judged on the basis of certain reasonably objective criteria, such as the degree of export instability, a large number of LDCs have inadequate international reserves. Mainly and perhaps exclusively in order to avoid or defer the imposition of restrictionary trade and/or exchange-rate policies, the IMF has stood ready to provide relatively short-term financial help to members experiencing balance-of-payments difficulties. Although the significance of the IMF as a source of short-term financing varies amongst LDCs, it is true that LDCs as a group have relied very heavily on drawings from the IMF. These drawings are basically of two types: first, drawings within the ordinary facilities provided by the Fund; and, second, drawings made under certain special facilities which have been established during the lifetime of the IMF.

In this chapter a summary will be made of the various IMF-based sources of international liquidity, and in the next chapter an appraisal of these sources will be undertaken from the point of view of LDCs.

Normal Facilities

Ordinary drawings and stand-by arrangements

It is an oversimplification to say that members borrow from the IMF. In fact, they purchase the currencies which they require with their own currency. They then buy back their own currency from the Fund at a later date, normally within three years, with foreign currency which is acceptable to the Fund. Ordinary drawing rights are composed of two elements. The first element is the gold tranche. This represents 25 per cent of the member's quota, and since the early 1950s has *de facto* been automatically available. Indeed, if drawings by other members reduce the amount of one member's currency held in the Fund to less than 75 per cent of that member's quota, the automatic drawing right of this member is enlarged by the extent of the difference; this is known as the super gold tranche.

The second element of a member's drawing rights is the credit tranche, or, more accurately, the credit tranches. The total amount of the credit tranche before 1976 was equal to 100 per cent of the relevant quota. The tranche is divided into four equal sub-tranches, access to each of these becoming progressively less easy and more expensive.[1] The credit tranche thus provides 'conditional' international finance. On the first credit tranche, the Fund's policy is usually fairly liberal and access to it merely requires a demonstration that the member is making reasonable efforts to solve its problems. Requests for higher credit tranches 'require substantial justification' but 'are likely to be favourably received' when the transactions 'are intended to support a sound programme aimed at establishing or maintaining the enduring stability of the member's currency at a realistic rate of exchange'. For the higher credit tranches, however, the criterion is quite exacting and requires a member to make a specially convincing demonstration of the adequacy of the policies it is pursuing or intending to pursue.

The overall constraint on a member's drawing from the IMF is that the Fund's holding of that member's currency should not exceed 200 per cent of the member's quota. These constraints have not always been binding, however, since Article 5 Section (iv), of the Articles of Agreement allows for the waiver of the drawing conditions at the discretion of the Fund. Section (iv) states that, 'in making a waiver it [the Fund] shall take into consideration periodic or exceptional requirements of the member requesting the waiver'.[2] In its dealings with LDCs, the Fund has made fairly frequent use of waivers, particularly with regard to the 25-per-cent-of-quota limit on annual drawings.

Since 1952, ordinary drawings on the IMF have conventionally been made under stand-by arrangements which serve to guarantee a borrowing member an assured line of credit for a certain period of time, usually twelve months. The assured credit is over and above the gold tranche drawing and is renewable. Although a characteristic of the stand-by arrangement is that a member is given the assurance that it will be able to use the Fund's resources without any further review of its position and policies, the granting of a stand-by arrangement depends in the first instance on agreement between the Fund and the borrowing member with regard to appropriate domestic policies.

Following consultation with a mission from the Fund, the member country publishes a 'letter of intent', which sets out the objectives of its economic programme and the policies which it intends to pursue in order to realise these objectives. If the stated intentions meet the conditions of the credit tranches, the member is assured by the stand-by arrangement that it will be able to make purchases of foreign currency totalling a specified absolute amount during the life of the arrangement. The stand-by guarantees that the first credit tranche will be available in full, and will not depend on the *actual* economic performance of the member. The availability of subsequent credit tranches, however, depends on the observance of 'performance criteria'. These criteria have been defined as 'aspects of a member's policies, formulated in the letter of intent in quantified and other objective terms, that are of crucial importance for the success of the programme, so that if any of them is not observed there is a signal that the member of the Fund should consult on any necessary adaptation of the programme before the member resumes purchases under the stand-by arrangement'. Assurance of credit therefore relates, in some respects, to the definition of the circumstances under which credit will be unconditionally available. The 'performance criteria' incorporated into the stand-by arrangement by inclusion in the letter of intent usually refer to some aspect of monetary policy, fiscal policy and/or balance-of-payments policy.

There can be little doubt that LDCs have been considerably influenced by the operation of stand-by arrangements, both as regards the assured access to credit, which assists development planning, and as regards the technical advice provided by the IMF. Furthermore, early experience with stand-by arrangements suggested that the approval of a stand-by arrangement by the Fund encourages the inflow of assistance from elsewhere.[3]

Special Drawing Rights

Another significant source of international liquidity for LDCs has come through the introduction and operation of Special Drawing Rights (SDRs). The aim of the SDR scheme, which was first activated in 1970, is to provide the international monetary system with a method of creating liquidity which is independent of both the unregulated outcome of the United States balance of payments and the production of gold. There is a fairly extensive literature available on SDRs.[4]

The main features of the SDR scheme are as follows. First, SDRs constitute a purposefully created reserve asset. Second, they are allocated to 'participants' in the scheme in relation to the participant's quota. Third, they are not backed by debt: they are an 'outside' asset. Fourth, they are internationally acceptable in exchange for foreign currency. Fifth, the use of them is unconditional, although there is a provision for reconstitution which states that over five years a participant's average holding of them should not drop below 30 per cent of its average cumulative allocation. Sixth, the transfer of SDRs between participants in return for foreign exchange takes the form of a book-keeping entry in the Special Account of the IMF, and transfers do not serve to reduce the total amount of SDRs in existence; the SDR system is a giro system. Seventh, SDRs originally had a gold-value guarantee, the unit value for expressing them being equal to 0.888671 grams of fine gold. Since July 1974 the value of SDRs has ceased to be expressed in terms of gold, but is instead expressed in terms of a 'standard' basket of currencies.[5] Eighth, SDRs yield interest in the form of additional SDR allocations. Ninth, SDRs may be used to repay previous purchases from the General Account at the IMF.

SDRs are primarily designed to be used in order to meet balance-of-payments needs, but, with particular application to the United States, they may also be employed, in certain circumstances, to buy back currency liabilities created by the past running of deficits. SDRs are not, however, supposed to be used 'for the sole purpose of changing the composition of . . . reserves'.

The use of SDRs is unconditional inasmuch as the purposes of particular transfers are not subject to prior challenge. Improper use of SDRs is, however, discouraged by the fact that offending participants may be passed over in future SDR allocations, or may be forced to reaccept the SDRs improperly used. Apart from the qualitative constraints on the use of SDRs, quantitative limits are imposed through the reconstitution clause.

When an SDR transfer is activated, the IMF selects the participant or participants from which currencies will be drawn by reference to certain criteria. The Fund will normally call upon countries with strong balance-of-payments positions or strong reserve positions, or countries which are endeavouring to reconstitute their SDR holdings. A 'primary criterion' of the Fund in the operation of the SDR scheme is to maintain over time equality between participants in the scheme in terms of the ratios of SDR holdings (or of excess SDR holdings) to total reserves. Indeed, no participant is obliged to accept SDRs over and above three times its cumulative allocation, although it may decide to accumulate such 'super-excess holdings' of SDRs.

The amendment to the Fund's Articles of Agreement establishing the SDR facility came into force in July 1969 following its acceptance by three-fifths of the Fund's membership, representing four-fifths of the total voting power. SDRs were allocated to participants over the first basic period of three years, beginning on 1 January 1970, with allocations being made on the first day of 1970, 1971 and 1972. Allocations are expressed as a percentage of the quota of participants on the day before the allocation in question. The first basic period allocation was such as to yield allocations of about $3500 million in 1970, and about $3000 million in both 1971 and 1972.

Special Facilities

The compensatory financing facility

The establishment of the Compensatory Financing Facility (CFF) has been much discussed in the literature (see, for instance, Horsefield, 1969b; Horsefield and Lovasy, 1969; Lovasy, 1965; Krasner, 1968; Thornton, 1969; Scott, 1967; Corea, 1971; Schiavo-Campo and Singer, 1970; and Gold, 1971).

Before 1963 the IMF had always been prepared to accept shortfalls in the export receipts of primary producing countries as part of the justification for drawings by such countries. But the Fund had rejected the idea of establishing a specific facility to compensate for short-term export fluctuations. The IMF view was spelt out clearly in a report, *Fund Policies and Procedures in Relation to the Compensatory Financing of Commodity Fluctuations*. This report, which was prepared in response to an invitation by the UN Commission on International Commodity Trade (CICT) was submitted to the Commission in 1960. The report did indeed show that the export proceeds of primary producing countries tended to fluctuate somewhat more than those of industrial countries, but it argued that automatic compensation for export fluctuations would be inappropriate. It rejected the idea of any special form of Fund financing, other than ordinary drawings, to compensate for commodity fluctuations.

The report was subjected to a number of criticisms. Broadly speaking, ordinary drawings were seen by some as being inadequate to cope with the problem. In the wake of this discussion, certain specific proposals were put forward from various sources to deal with the issue of export shortfalls. These proposals included greater automation on the credit tranches, freer use of waivers, and the provision of additional drawings to compensate for export shortfalls.

The Fund itself undertook an exhaustive examination of the problem of finding a formula which measured the intensity of a shortfall in export receipts. Indeed Fund staff examined 137 variants of a scheme for compensating export shortfalls.[6] The schemes examined varied in terms of the weights given to the data for current and past years, in terms of the proportion which each country's cumulative indebtedness bore to its average amount of exports over preceding years, and in terms of the provisions for repayment of the debts acquired under the scheme.

In response to a further invitation by the UN Commission on International Commodity Trade in 1962, the Fund prepared a draft report on ways in which the IMF might play a larger part in providing compensatory finance. The report stressed a number of points. It emphasised the difficulties which might arise from complete reliance on some mathematical formula for estimating an export shortfall, and it pointed to the need to examine the whole balance-of-payments situation of a member in order to put the export shortfall into perspective. It then expressed qualms over an automatic financing facility, as well as over a facility which related exclusively to export shortfalls.

The outcome of discussions based on this draft report was the establishment of the IMF's Compensatory Financing Facility (CFF) in February 1963.[7]

The CFF permitted a member to make a drawing of up to 25 per cent of its quota (and beyond in exceptional circumstances) in order to cover a shortfall in export receipts. Two conditions were, however, made. First, the shortfall had to be short-term in nature and 'largely attributable to circumstances beyond the control of the member'. Second, the member concerned had to be prepared to co-operate with the IMF in endeavouring 'to find, where required, appropriate solutions for its balance of payments difficulties'. Granting of CFF assistance depends initially on whether an export shortfall has actually occurred. This is judged partly on past export performance and partly on anticipated performance. A shortfall exists to the extent that actual export earnings in a particular year are lower than might have been expected if price and output had both been normal in terms of the medium-term trend. This trend is determined by considering a five-year period centred on the shortfall year. Actual export data are used for the shortfall year and the two previous years, whilst forecasts are made for the two future years. To begin with, these forecasts assume that export earnings in the two post-shortfall years will equal earnings in the two pre-shortfall years multiplied by a growth factor.[8] The Fund, however, retains a considerable amount of discretion in evaluating export shortfalls and is not bound by mathematical formulae.[9]

The extent of any drawing on the CFF is limited such that it cannot exceed the export shortfall or 25 per cent of the member's quota, whichever of these is the smaller.

In the period between 1963 and 1966, CFF drawings were very few. One reason for this relative lack of use was that in 1963–4 primary-product prices tended to rise; the downturn in price which occurred in 1965 failed to erode completely the gain of the previous two years. In any case, LDCs seemed reluctant to compromise their future position with the Fund by making drawings which they considered might subsequently have pushed them into the higher credit tranches.

A complementary modification which occurred alongside the introduction of the CFF and was in some respects more immediately effective was the statement by the IMF that it would give sympathetic consideration to requests for adjustments in quotas where such adjustments would be appropriate in order to make the quotas more adequate to deal with fluctuations in export proceeds. In fact, sixteen countries applied for quota increases on these grounds and all of them had their applications approved.

As might have been anticipated, the CFF attracted a number of comments, criticisms and counter-suggestions. The CICT, which in 1960 had been involved with putting forward a scheme for automatic compensation through a Development Insurance Fund, viewed the CFF as a significant contribution to alleviating the problem of the short-term instability of export earnings; and the Organisation of American States (OAS), which in 1962 had put forward proposals for a scheme of automatic compensation in the form of loans, gave guarded support to the CFF, while suggesting that it might be liberalised. Perhaps the most vociferous reaction to the CFF came from the UN Conference on Trade and Development (UNCTAD) in 1964. At the UNCTAD it was suggested first that the drawing available to cover export shortfalls should be expanded to 50 per cent of the relevant quota; second, that the CFF should be placed entirely outside the structure of gold and credit tranches and be made clearly additional to them; third, that ways of refinancing drawings, where export receipts continued to decline for reasons beyond the control of the member, should be investigated; and, fourth, that, when determining the export shortfall, more weight should be placed on the applicant's actual export record. Support for a number of these suggestions was found at the Annual Meeting of the IMF in 1965.

Also during 1965, Fund staff undertook an extensive review of the CFF. This review centred on the nature of the CFF as an *additional* facility, and on the extension of that facility. As regards the first of these matters, the Fund had already stated that, in the case of CFF drawings, it would waive the 200-per-cent-of-quota limit on drawings. Drawings on the basis of the CFF were, however, to be taken into account by the Fund when reviewing requests for higher credit-tranche drawings, and it was this feature which became regarded as undesirable. It was suggested that the CFF should be made additional to ordinary tranche drawings in both a qualitative and a quantitative sense. As far as the extension of the size of the CFF was concerned, the evidence of the drawings between 1963 and 1965 suggested that the 25 per cent limit might be rather low, and it was suggested that the limit be extended to 50 per cent of quota, subject to the qualification that the net expansion of compensatory drawings should not normally exceed 25 per cent of the quota in any twelve-month period, and that compensatory drawings beyond 25 per cent of the quota would be granted only where the member was pursuing policies, 'reasonably conducive to the development of its exports'.

These suggestions were adopted and incorporated into Fund policy in 1966.[10] Another modification was that a member could, if its export position warranted it, reclassify an ordinary drawing, within six months of making it, as a drawing under the CFF. The reclassification provision was useful to members who found themselves unable, at the particular time when they required assistance, to provide full data in support of their claim of an export shortfall.

It was anticipated by the Fund that repurchases under the CFF would take place within the customary three to five years, and would thus be in line with the repurchase of ordinary drawings on the IMF. The Fund also recommended, however, that a member's currency should be gradually repurchased where export receipts moved above their trend value (an export excess), or, more generally, where after a year or two the balance of payments or reserve position of the drawing member improved. Repurchase of CFF credits automatically restores the member's drawing rights to the extent of the size of the repurchase.

Special arrangements have been made by the Fund to deal with the problem of 'double compensation', which arises where a previous drawing on ordinary tranches may have already partially compensated for an export shortfall at a time when a CFF drawing is requested. This problem will not arise where the member reclassifies the ordinary drawing as a CFF drawing, but it will if the member does not wish to reclassify. Since ordinary drawings are not specifically related to export shortfalls, but rather to the balance of payments as a whole, some method had to be introduced by which it was possible to estimate the extent to which the existing ordinary drawing had already compensated for the export shortfall. The rule adopted by the IMF assumes, to use the Fund's own language, that 'the earlier drawing will have covered one half of the shortfall for the part of the year ending at the date of the previous drawing which falls within 12 months of the date when the new drawing is sought'. The CFF drawing granted by the IMF will be either the value of this calculated export shortfall or 25 per cent of the quota, whichever is the lesser.

A further liberalisation of the CFF was announced in December 1975, the stated aim being to give members, and in particular primary-product exporters encountering balance-of-payments difficulties as a result of temporary export shortfalls, greater access to the Fund's resources. The decision of the Executive Directors of the Fund to liberalise the CFF followed a period during which many LDCs had faced considerable balance-of-payments difficulties, owing to the slackness in the demand for their exports amongst industrial countries and the related decline in primary-product prices. The decision also reflected the substantial support that had mustered behind the idea of reforming the CFF; support had been expressed at Annual Meetings of the Fund by a growing number of Governors, by the Group of Twenty-Four, by the Interim Committee and by the Development Committee. Indeed, the liberalisation of the CFF was preceded by a number of specific reform proposals. One of these was outlined fairly vaguely at the Seventh Special Session of the UN General Assembly by the United States. The US proposal was that the CFF as then constituted should be replaced by a Development Security Facility (DSF), which would provide both protection against disruptions caused by reductions in earnings and loans designed to sustain development programmes. The facility would not be available to industrial countries, and of the developing countries the least developed would be allowed to convert into grants the loans which they received under the facility. The grants would then be financed by means of the sale of gold by the Fund. The size of the DSF would be rather larger than the CFF 1966-version. Access to the DSF would be in part automatic, in part conditional and in part 'reserved for cases of particularly violent swings in commodity earnings'.

In fact, the modifications made to the CFF at the end of 1975 were by no means as adventurous as this and really only represented a fairly straightforward increase in the size of the existing compensatory facility. The details of the 1975 liberalisation are as follows. First, the limit on CFF drawings was raised from 50 per cent of quota to 75 per cent of quota. Second, the net amount by which outstanding drawings on the CFF may be increased in any twelve-month period was raised from 25 per cent to 50 per cent of quota and even to 75 per cent in the event of a 'disaster'. And, third, the period of time during which ordinary drawings may be reclassified as compensatory drawings was lengthened from six months after the date of the ordinary drawing to eighteen months. The Fund also undertook to review the formula upon which the export shortfall is calculated (though in fact the review, in March 1977, led to no changes) and to review the CFF as a whole in the light of experience, or whenever drawings in any twelve-month period exceed SDR 1500 million or outstanding drawings exceed SDR 3000 million.

The basic conditions governing access to the CFF remain unchanged under the 1975 liberalisation. Access still remains based on the requirements that the export shortfall should be short-term in character, that the member should not be responsible for the shortfall, and that the member should co-operate with the Fund in finding appropriate solutions.[11] No change was made, under the 1975 liberalisation, to the status of the CFF as an additional facility, over and above ordinary tranche drawings, or to the provisions which apply to repurchasing.

The buffer stock financing facility

Whereas the CFF attempts to deal *ex post* with the implications of fluctuations in export receipts, international commodity agreements attempt, *ex ante*, to maintain prices and export receipts within agreed ranges. In response to a resolution adopted at the 1967 Annual Meeting of the Fund, the staff of the Fund, in consultation with the staff of the World Bank, undertook a study of the problem of commodity-price stabilisation. As a result of this investigation, in June 1969 the Fund introduced its Buffer Stock Financing Facility (BSFF). Through this facility the IMF assists members in financing their contributions to international buffer-stock schemes. Under the BSFF, drawings from the Fund, which are made with the purpose of financing buffer stocks in connection with international commodity agreements, may be made by members for amounts of up to 50 per cent of the relevant quota, provided that the combined drawings under the BSFF and the CFF do not exceed 75 per cent of the quota.[12]

The BSFF first came into operation in 1970. The Fourth International Tin Agreement provided for a buffer stock to be financed by the participating producers. The producers' contributions could have totalled about $65 million, although initially the compulsory contributions came to about $24 million. Under a decision of November 1970, the Fund provided assistance in connection with the scheme, and as a result each participating producer country had to meet not less than one-third of its contribution from non-IMF sources. At a maximum, then, Fund assistance with respect to this particular commodity agreement could have reached about $16 million of the initial contributions. The BSFF has subsequently been made available to members making loans to the International Cocoa Council.

The BSFF is, however, subject to four conditions. These are:

(i)   finance can be provided only to individual members participating in buffer-stock schemes and not to the international organisations which control the buffer stock;

(ii) before a member is permitted to draw from the Fund under the BSFF it must need to do so for balance-of-payments reasons;

(iii) drawings must be repaid within three to five years, or earlier if the buffer stock should reimburse the contributions of its members; and

(iv) the member country must agree to co-operate with the Fund in finding solutions, if required, to its balance-of-payments difficulties.

Further limitations on the use of the facility are that the buffer-stock scheme must conform to certain standards laid down by the United Nations, and that drawings from the Fund must be confined to the reimbursement of contributions made by participants in buffer-stock schemes for the purpose of financing either the purchase of the buffer stock or operating expenditure.

Unlike the CFF, which is completely separate from the gold and credit tranches, the BSFF does impinge on these normal drawings. If a member has drawn 25 per cent of its quota in order to finance contributions to a buffer-stock scheme, that member loses its right to an automatic drawing on the gold tranche. An ordinary drawing additional to a BSFF drawing of 25 per cent is treated as a drawing on the first credit tranche.[13] Like CFF drawings, on the other hand, BSFF drawings effectively do not count towards the 200-per-cent-of-quota quantitative limit on drawings from the Fund.

The extended fund facility

One of the proposals put forward by the Committee on Reform of the International Monetary System and Related Issues (the Committee of Twenty) was that the IMF should introduce a facility through which LDCs could obtain resources which would have a longer repayment period than normal drawings on the Fund. In large measure the Extended Fund Facility (EFF), which was established by an Executive Board decision in September 1974, and approved by the IMF in July 1975, represents a response to this proposal.

The EFF, as the Committee intended, is designed to be of particular benefit to LDCs. Its purpose is to provide medium-term assistance to those members of the IMF who find themselves in the sorts of balance-of-payments difficulties where the required economic policies are of a longer-term nature than those which could be supported by ordinary tranche drawings on the Fund. The 'special circumstances' under which the Fund has stated that it would regard an EFF drawing as appropriate include, first, 'an economy suffering serious payments imbalance relating to structural maladjustments in production and trade and where prices and cost distortions have been widespread', and, second, 'an economy characterized by slow growth and an inherently weak balance of payments position which prevents pursuit of an active development policy'.

Fund resources made available under the EFF are meant to support fairly comprehensive attempts to correct such structural imbalances, and in particular to support attempts which, 'mobilize resources and improve the utilization of them and . . . reduce reliance on external restrictions'. The EFF thereby counts as a significant extra dimension to Fund involvement with the formulation of economic policy in member countries, since prior to the introduction of the EFF the Fund had been directly and exclusively interested in financial stabilisation policies and was not much interested in policies designed to cure basic structural shortcomings.

The EFF displays certain key features. First, requests for drawing on this facility will be met only if it is felt by the Fund that longer-term policies which cannot be supported by ordinary tranche drawings are appropriate. Second, a member drawing on the EFF is expected to present an economic programme setting out objectives and policies for the duration of the extended arrangement, and a more detailed statement of proposed policy actions for the first twelve months of the arrangement and each twelve-month period thereafter. Drawings on the EFF are arranged on an instalment basis, so that the granting of later instalments depends on satisfactory performance in terms of implementing previously agreed policies. Third, the EFF allows drawings on the Fund to be spread over a three-year period, as compared with a maximum of one year under the more conventional stand-by arrangements. Fourth, drawings under the EFF may reach a maximum of 140 per cent of a member's quota over the three-year period, subject to the constraint that the Fund's holdings of the member's currency should not rise above 265 per cent of the member's quota (excluding holdings contracted under the CFF, BSFF or Oil Facility[14]). This makes the EFF the largest single source of finance available through the IMF. Ordinary drawings are limited to 25 per cent of quota in any one year and a ceiling of 200 per cent of quota.[15] A fifth and final feature of the EFF is that, whereas with the other Fund Facilities members are expected to make repurchases within a period of between three and five years after the drawing, under the EFF repurchases must be made, normally in sixteen equal instalments, over a period of between four and eight years.[16]

The oil facility and subsidy account

The Oil Facility (OF) was established by the IMF in June 1974 with a proposed lifetime of approximately two years and with the objective of helping countries to cope with the balance-of-payments implications of the rise in the price of oil. The OF, like the EFF, represented a new sphere of involvement for the Fund. From 1963 the IMF has possessed, in the specific form of the CFF, a means whereby it can help insulate countries from the balance-of-payments implications of a fall in their export prices. With the OF the IMF now attempted in some way to insulate economies from the balance-of-payments implications of a rise in the price of imports, or, more specifically, one particular import.

Largely because it was financed by means of the IMF borrowing from members, the OF proved to be rather more *ad hoc* than other facilities in the Fund, and existed on an approximately yearly basis. The resources made available to IMF members under the OF were supplementary to any assistance which they might have obtained through ordinary drawings on the Fund or drawings under the other special facilities available in the Fund.

To begin with, and in the case of the 1974 OF, purchases were in the main based on the increase in the cost of the members' net imports of petroleum and petroleum products over and above the cost of similar imports in 1972. Purchases under OF were not permitted to exceed 75 per cent of quota.

The 1975 OF differed in certain ways from its predecessor. These differences related first of all to the formula which was used to calculate a member's permitted access to the OF; second, to the conditions imposed by the Fund, which governed access to the facility; and, third, to the interest rate on drawings (and indeed borrowings by the Fund for the purpose of financing the OF). Access to the OF, 1975 version, was not permitted to exceed 125 per cent of a member's quota or 85 per cent of the calculated increase in the oil-import cost of a member, whichever of these two figures turned out to be the lower.[17] As compared with the 1974 OF, this new formula for determining access gave greater weight to the size of a member's quota and less weight to the cost of oil imports.[18] Furthermore the formula used in 1974 provided for a deduction in the size of access to the OF of an amount equivalent to 10 per cent of the member's international reserves at the end of 1973. The 1975 formula no longer incorporated such a formal deduction but instead the Fund, in its assessment of the member's balance-of-payments need for liquidity, evaluated the degree to which the member might be expected to use owned reserves to finance balance-of-payments deficits. Unlike the 1974 OF, access to the 1975 OF was subject to minimum limits. It was agreed that the total access of any member should not drop below one-third of the increase in its calculated oil-import cost or below the maximum access that the member would have been permitted under the 1974 OF.

The conditions applying to the use of the OF were in 1975 made somewhat stricter than they had been in 1974. Whereas under the 1974 facility members were expected to consult with the Fund concerning their prospects and policies with regard to oil and the balance of payments, under the 1975 facility the Fund more formally assessed the adequacy of proposed balance-of-payments policies. Additionally, under the 1975 OF, policies relating to the conservation of oil and the development of alternative sources of energy had to be reported to the Fund. Under both versions of the OF, access was not to be gained unless the requesting member avoided the introduction or intensification of restrictions on international transactions.

The condition applying to repurchase, again under both versions of the facility, was that all drawings had to be repurchased within three to seven years after the date of drawing. Whereas the interest rate on outstanding drawings had under the 1974 OF been 7 per cent, under the 1975 OF it centred around $7\frac{3}{4}$ per cent.[19]

In an attempt to reduce the interest-rate burden associated with OF drawings, in August 1975 the Fund established a Subsidy Account, the purpose of which is to make financial assistance available to those LDCs, with the lowest per capita national incomes, that had been most seriously affected by adverse world economic developments. The Subsidy Account is financed by contributions mainly from oil-exporting and industrial countries. Disbursements under the Account were scheduled to begin in May 1976.

Identification of the most seriously affected countries was made the responsibility of the United Nations Emergency Operation (UNEO), which was itself established in May 1974 following the Sixth Special Session of the General Assembly of the United Nations, held in April 1974, at which the problems facing oil-importing LDCs as a result of the rise in oil prices constituted the central issue. For a number of reasons the implications of the rise in the price of oil are rather more strategic for LDCs than for developed countries, although clearly, to some extent, the nature of the problems is common to both groups of countries.

The oil-price rise has caused problems for oil-importing LDCs in terms of both their balance of payments and their development. With regard to the balance of payments the rise in the price of oil has served to increase the price of many, if not most, imports. Certainly the prices of petroleum, petroleum products such as fertilisers, and manufactured goods and capital goods have risen. Furthermore, in LDCs where the scope for import substitution, particularly with regard to energy, is limited in the short to medium term, the demand for such goods tends to be price-inelastic. Such price-inelasticity implies a really rather cruel dilemma for policy-makers, inasmuch as basically they have had to choose between improving the balance-of-payments position, following the deterioration in their terms of trade, and maintaining economic development and the domestic standard of living. Other things remaining constant, a rise in the price of imports implies either a deterioration in the balance of payments (in cases where the demand for imports is price-inelastic), or a deterioration in living standards (in cases where the demand for imports is price-elastic). This reduction in the standard of living may be very marked when imported goods are crucial for development, or where the authorities attempt to reduce the price-inelastic demand for imported goods through domestic deflation. Take food production as one example of the effect of the oil-price rise on oil-importing LDCs. Food production is significant to many LDCs, both from the point of view of domestic consumption, being a major determinant of living standards, and from the point of view of exportation. To the extent that the importation of fertilisers is reduced as a result of the increase in their price, considerable difficulties are created in sustaining existing levels of food production. This in turn implies lower food exports, and/or a reduction in the level of domestic food consumption; and thus, *ceteris paribus*, falling living standards. Unfortunately, for some of the poorest LDCs the rise in the price of oil happened to coincide with a period of drought (particularly in parts of Africa), which caused a further shortfall in domestic food production.

Many LDCs have been unable to compensate for the impact which increasing import prices have had on their balance of payments by means of increasing the value of their exports. This is largely because the world recession, which in theory may also be partly explained in terms of the oil-price rise,[20] has reduced the developed countries' demand for imports – if not absolutely, then at least below trend level.

Although, fairly clearly, some raw-material exporting and, in particular, mineral-exporting LDCs benefited from the upswing in commodity prices in the early 1970s, other LDCs lost in every way. Import prices rose, whilst export prices and/or the value of exports fell. Significantly, it tended to be the poorest countries, which import very substantial quantities of fuel, food and fertilisers, and which tend to have the lowest elasticities of import substitution, that suffered the most, in terms of either the balance of payments or development or both. Assuming diminishing marginal utility of national income, any given reduction in total domestic expenditure in these countries implies a larger reduction in social welfare than would an equivalent reduction in expenditure in wealthier, more developed countries.

The UNEO defined as the most seriously affected countries those which have a per capita national income of less than $400 per year, and which face severe balance-of-payments problems on the basis of projected import and export performance.[21] Those countries which on average have basic balance-of-payments deficits of at least 5 per cent of their import value also come within this category, and it is for them that the Subsidy Account was designed.

The Trust Fund

In May 1976 the IMF announced the establishment of a Trust Fund, the basic purpose of which is to provide certain eligible LDCs with conditional but concessionary balance-of-payments financing assistance. The Trust Fund's resources are to be derived largely from gold sales by the IMF, but also from loans and voluntary contributions. The scheme is thereby related to the IMF's objective of reducing the role of gold in the international monetary system.

The details of the Trust Fund are as follows: First, assistance will be available to eligible members of the IMF either from the beginning of July 1976 to the end of June 1978, or from the beginning of July 1978 to the end of June 1980, or over both of these periods. The assistance to be provided will take the form of 'additional balance of payments assistance on concessional terms to support the efforts of eligible members that qualify for assistance to carry out programmes of balance of payments adjustment'.[22] Second, the Trust Fund will partly be financed through loans, contributions and income from investment; but in the main it will be financed from the profits which the IMF will make by selling at market prices one-sixth (25 million ounces) of its holding of gold over a period of four years.[23] Third, members of the IMF eligible for assistance from the Trust Fund are those LDCs with the lowest per capita national incomes, and in the most difficult economic positions. Fourth, eligible members, basically the least-developed countries, will, however, have access to financial assistance from the Trust Fund only if they meet certain conditions. To begin with, the Trustee of the Trust Fund, or in other words the IMF, has to be satisfied that the requesting member does possess a 'need' for balance-of-payments assistance, assessed on the basis of its balance of payments and reserve position, and also that the member is making 'reasonable effort' to strengthen its balance of payments. Reasonable effort is interpreted to mean that the member has already, under a stand-by agreement, EFF drawing or credit-tranche drawing, supplied the IMF with an acceptable economic programme for a twelve-month period approximately similar to the period covered by the Trust Fund loan; or, if such a programme has not already been presented, that one will be. Acceptability of a proposed economic programme will be determined by criteria similar to those used for assessing requests under the first credit tranche, and the conditions are therefore not very severe. Although actual performance will not normally affect a Trust Fund disbursement once agreed, it may influence the future availability of loans. Fifth, repayments of Trust Fund loans are to be made not later than between six and ten years after the date of the disbursement. Within this period payments may, however, be rescheduled in a way which will prevent 'serious hardship' for the member. Sixth, the maximum access of eligible members to Trust Fund loans will be fixed as a percentage of their IMF quota as of the end of 1975. Seventh, the Trust Fund may invest currency balances in international financial organisations or directly in member countries;

and, indeed, is empowered to undertake other activities connected with the profits derived from selling gold and for the benefit of LDCs subject to the proviso that these other activities do not take the IMF outside its conventional sphere of involvement.

Concluding Remarks

It may be seen from this review of the sources of IMF finance available to LDCs that a number of channels for assistance do exist. Questions, however, may immediately be posed concerning the extent to which these sources of finance have been used, and the extent to which the facilities and arrangements currently in existence meet the needs of the developing world. These are questions which we move on to discuss in the next chapter.

8 An Evaluation of IMF-based Sources of International Liquidity for LDCs

The Facilities in the General Account

Through its various facilities, LDCs have made considerable use of the IMF as a source of international finance. Quantitatively the IMF has become a particularly significant source of finance in the middle 1970s. The general pattern of drawings on the Fund may be gleaned from Table 8.1. This table shows the fluctuations in drawings on the Fund which have occurred over the period 1952–76. It is also a fact that, more often than not, drawings on the Fund by industrial countries have exceeded drawings by LDCs.[1] It is interesting to note, as an extreme example of this, that in 1961, when LDCs as a group drew the historically large amount of SDR 687·5 million from the Fund, the United Kingdom alone drew SDR 1500 million. The relatively large use of Fund resources by industrial countries tends, however, to reflect large drawings by a few countries rather than more general use by industrial countries. In eight of the ten years that drawings by LDCs exceeded those by industrial countries, drawings by industrial countries were zero.

As Table 8.1 reveals, there has been considerable intra-group variation in the use made of the Fund by LDCs. Whilst some LDCs, such as Argentina, Chile, India, Pakistan and the Sudan, have made frequent, and often large, drawings on the Fund, others, such as Thailand, Upper Volta and Paraguay, have had little if any recourse to the Fund. It clearly emerges from Table 8.1, however, that the vast majority of LDCs did draw on Fund resources in 1974, 1975 and 1976.

Table 8.1 reveals other interesting features. In general it is the LDCs of Latin America and the Caribbean which have made greatest use of the IMF, although in the mid-1960s and in 1974, 1975 and 1976 it was Asian

LDCs which drew most from the Fund. Again, whilst oil-exporting LDCs, as a group, made fairly regular use of Fund resources prior to 1973, (indeed in 1970 almost one-third of drawings on the IMF by LDCs were by oil-exporting LDCs), since 1973 the picture has changed radically. In 1974 and 1976 there were no drawings on the Fund by these countries, whilst in 1975 Indonesia drew SDR 80 million and Oman SDR 0·3 million from the Fund, representing less than 4 per cent of total LDC drawings.

A further indication of the use of Fund resources is provided by Table 8.2, which shows the total cumulative value of drawings on the IMF, as of December 1976, broken down by country group and individual countries. Table 8.2 demonstrates that total drawings by non oil-exporting LDCs have represented only about 58 per cent of total drawings by industrial countries, although it is true that the proportion of drawings by LDCs is growing. Latin American and Asian LDCs emerge as the principal LDC users of Fund finance, although the Asian cumulative total is heavily weighted by relatively large drawings in 1974, 1975 and 1976. Non oil-exporting Middle Eastern LDCs, and perhaps in particular African LDCs, appear to be relatively low users of IMF finance.

Table 8.2 shows that, of the various sources of finance within the General Account of the IMF, taking the position up until the end of 1976, ordinary tranche drawings have represented the single most important source of finance for LDCs, providing non oil-exporting LDCs with SDR 7853·3 million.[2] Quantitatively about one-third as important as ordinary tranche drawings have been the Compensatory Financing Facility (CFF) and the Oil Facility (OF); whilst the Buffer Stock Financing Facility (BSFF) and the Extended Fund Facility (EFF) appear as having been relatively insignificant. This cumulative picture, however, conceals a good deal. First, the aggregate LDC picture is not representative of all LDCs. Cyprus, Jordan, Bangladesh, Cambodia, Malaysia, Thailand, Papua New Guinea, Western Samoa, Cameroon, the Central African Empire, Chad, Ivory Coast, Kenya, the Malagasy Republic, Mauritania, Senegal, Tanzania, Togo, Uganda, Zaire and Zambia have all relied more heavily on CFF and/or OF drawings than on ordinary drawings. Other LDCs, such as the Philippines and, to a lesser extent, Kenya, have made significant use of the EFF, whilst the major tin-exporting LDCs have derived significant assistance from the BSFF. Second, the cumulative picture presented in Table 8.2 fails to depict the pattern of drawings over time. This will be discussed in detail in a moment when we examine the use of specific facilities in the Fund.

TABLE 8.1
Fund Transactions, Drawings
(SDR millions)

	1952	1953	1954	1955	1956	1957	1958	1959	1960	1961	196:
Less-developed areas	40·6	80·5	62·5	27·5	118·6	388·3	97·5	129·8	260·5	687·6	268
Oil-exporting countries	2·2	–	15·0	17·5	74·7	–	–	5·0	45·0	68·8	21·
Indonesia	–	–	15·0	–	55·0	–	–	–	–	61·3	21·
Iran	2·2	–	–	17·5	19·7	–	–	5·0	45·0	7·5	–
Iraq	–	–	–	–	–	–	–	–	–	–	–
Nigeria	–	–	–	–	–	–	–	–	–	–	–
Other Western Hemisphere	38·4	80·5	47·5	–	8·9	169·6	92·5	114·8	147·0	347·5	95·
Argentina	–	–	–	–	–	75·0	–	72·5	70·0	60·0	50·
Bolivia	–	2·5	–	–	3·0	1·0	2·0	3·4	1·0	2·0	3·
Brazil	37·5	65·5	–	–	–	37·5	54·8	–	47·7	60·0	–
Chile	–	12·5	–	–	–	31·1	10·7	0·7	–	76·0	–
Colombia	–	–	25·0	–	–	5·0	10·0	–	–	65·0	7·
Costa Rica	–	–	–	–	–	–	–	–	–	7·5	2·
Dominican Rep.	–	–	–	–	–	–	–	–	9·0	–	–
Ecuador	–	–	–	–	–	5·0	–	–	–	14·0	4·
El Salvador	–	–	–	–	2·5	–	–	5·5	13·3	8·0	–
Guatemala	–	–	–	–	–	–	–	–	–	–	5·
Haiti	–	–	–	–	–	1·0	2·5	1·9	–	1·5	3·
Honduras	–	–	–	–	–	6·3	–	3·8	5·0	2·5	5·
Mexico	–	–	22·5	–	–	–	–	22·5	–	45·0	–
Nicaragua	–	–	–	–	1·9	3·8	1·9	–	–	6·0	–
Panama	–	–	–	–	–	–	–	–	–	–	–
Paraguay	0·9	–	–	–	1·5	4·0	0·8	–	1·0	–	–
Peru	–	–	–	–	–	–	10·0	4·5	–	–	–
Uruguay	–	–	–	–	–	–	–	–	–	–	15·0
Barbados	–	–	–	–	–	–	–	–	–	–	–
Grenada	–	–	–	–	–	–	–	–	–	–	–
Guyana	–	–	–	–	–	–	–	–	–	–	–
Jamaica	–	–	–	–	–	–	–	–	–	–	–
Trinidad and Tobago	–	–	–	–	–	–	–	–	–	–	–
Other Middle East	–	–	–	–	15·0	18·8	–	–	49·8	10·0	73·
Bahrain	–	–	–	–	–	–	–	–	–	–	–
Cyprus	–	–	–	–	–	–	–	–	–	–	–
Egypt	–	–	–	–	15·0	15·0	–	–	34·8	10·0	67·4
Israel	–	–	–	–	–	3·8	–	–	–	–	–
Jordan	–	–	–	–	–	–	–	–	–	–	–
Syria	–	–	–	–	–	–	–	–	15·0	–	5·6
Yemen Arab Rep.	–	–	–	–	–	–	–	–	–	–	–
Yemen, People's Dem. Rep.	–	–	–	–	–	–	–	–	–	–	–
Other Asia	–	–	–	10·0	20·0	200·0	–	8·8	18·8	261·3	64·6
Afghanistan	–	–	–	–	–	–	–	–	–	–	–
Bangladesh	–	–	–	–	–	–	–	–	–	–	–

able 8.1 cont.

1963	1964	1965	1966	1967	1968	1969	1970	1971	1972	1973	1974	1975	1976
81·7	180·9	486·5	556·3	410·0	688·6	385·2	326·3	427·0	796·1	315·1	1700·7	2038·9	2749·0
20·0	17·5	–	–	40·0	100·8	65·8	90·8	2·9	4·2	–	–	80·0	–
20·0	–	–	–	–	45·0	65·8	38·0	2·9	2·7	–	–	80·0	–
–	17·5	–	–	–	46·5	–	16·8	–	–	–	–	–	–
–	–	–	–	40·0	–	–	27·3	–	–	–	–	–	–
–	–	–	–	–	9·3	–	8·8	–	1·5	–	–	–	–
31·5	62·5	147·2	174·0	122·7	273·5	177·2	124·1	173·3	447·9	89·0	308·9	610·2	1192·6
50·0	–	–	47·5	–	–	–	–	5·2	284·0	–	–	311·3	269·5
4·0	–	–	–	–	12·0	11·0	–	4·5	4·3	18·2	–	4·7	–
60·0	–	75·0	–	–	75·0	–	–	–	–	–	–	–	–
40·0	20·0	36·0	30·0	10·0	43·3	29·0	–	77·5	41·0	–	120·5	176·8	124·4
48·5	7·5	–	37·8	71·4	34·8	33·3	29·3	30·0	–	–	–	–	–
10·0	–	10·0	6·8	2·8	–	–	1·8	6·0	–	–	21·5	12·0	6·8
–	15·0	5·0	6·6	–	–	14·0	–	7·5	–	–	10·8	10·8	21·5
–	–	11·0	6·3	–	–	18·0	10·0	–	8·9	8·9	–	–	17·6
–	–	–	20·0	5·0	3·0	12·3	–	9·0	8·8	–	22·4	–	–
–	–	5·0	7·0	10·0	3·0	6·0	–	–	–	–	–	–	–
5·0	3·0	2·5	4·6	2·3	–	1·5	–	–	–	3·7	7·5	4·5	4·9
2·5	5·0	–	2·5	–	–	–	6·3	–	–	–	23·0	–	–
–	–	–	–	–	–	–	–	–	–	–	–	–	416·9
11·5	12·0	–	–	–	19·0	14·0	10·0	3·0	4·0	12·0	3·3	12·2	–
–	–	2·7	–	–	3·0	6·4	–	1·0	–	–	16·4	10·2	25·1
–	–	–	–	–	–	–	–	–	–	–	–	–	–
–	–	–	–	21·3	46·3	30·0	18·0	16·0	61·5	–	–	–	189·5
–	–	–	5·0	–	29·5	1·8	40·4	9·5	22·3	16·4	65·3	53·2	38·0
–	–	–	–	–	–	–	–	–	–	–	–	1·3	0·4
–	–	–	–	–	–	–	–	4·0	–	4·6	5·0	–	22·3
–	–	–	–	–	–	–	3·8	–	13·3	18·7	13·3	13·3	55·7
–	–	–	–	–	4·8	–	4·8	–	–	6·6	–	–	–
21·0	58·0	15·0	11·7	9·5	63·0	54·5	21·0	56·5	25·0	49·9	131·0	191·8	255·8
–	–	–	–	–	–	–	–	–	–	–	–	–	5·0
–	2·0	–	0·9	–	–	–	–	–	–	–	12·9	1·7	35·0
21·0	25·0	15·0	7·5	–	63·0	–	17·5	32·0	–	47·0	40·0	–	125·7
–	12·5	–	–	–	–	45·0	–	20·0	–	–	65·0	175·8	77·0
–	–	–	–	–	–	–	–	4·5	–	2·9	–	–	–
–	18·5	–	3·3	9·5	–	9·5	3·0	–	25·0	–	–	–	–
–	–	–	–	–	–	–	0·5	–	–	–	–	–	–
–	–	–	–	–	–	–	–	–	–	–	13·1	14·3	13·2
5·6	5·6	278·2	273·8	162·3	152·6	61·0	53·5	140·8	215·2	145·4	1025·9	782·8	776·4
5·6	5·6	1·7	9·1	4·0	4·8	13·0	4·0	–	–	7·5	2·5	8·5	–
–	–	–	–	–	–	–	–	–	62·5	0·8	71·2	58·8	97·2

Table 8.1 cont.

	1952	1953	1954	1955	1956	1957	1958	1959	1960	1961	19
Burma	–	–	–	–	15·0	–	–	–	–	–	–
Cambodia	–	–	–	–	–	–	–	–	–	–	
China, Rep. of	–	–	–	–	–	–	–	–	–	–	
India	–	–	–	–	–	200·0	–	–	–	250·0	2!
Korea	–	–	–	–	–	–	–	–	–	–	
Laos	–	–	–	–	–	–	–	–	–	–	–
Malaysia	–	–	–	–	–	–	–	–	–	–	–
Nepal	–	–	–	–	–	–	–	–	–	–	–
Pakistan	–	–	–	–	–	–	–	–	12·5	–	–
Philippines	–	–	–	10·0	5·0	–	–	8·8	6·3	–	28
Sri Lanka	–	–	–	–	–	–	–	–	–	11·3	1▶
Thailand	–	–	–	–	–	–	–	–	–	–	–
Vietnam	–	–	–	–	–	–	–	–	–	–	–
Fiji	–	–	–	–	–	–	–	–	–	–	–
Papua New Guinea	–	–	–	–	–	–	–	–	–	–	–
Western Samoa	–	–	–	–	–	–	–	–	–	–	–
Other Africa	–	–	–	–	–	–	5·0	1·3	–	–	14
Burundi	–	–	–	–	–	–	–	–	–	–	–
Cameroon	–	–	–	–	–	–	–	–	–	–	–
Central African Empire	–	–	–	–	–	–	–	–	–	–	
Chad	–	–	–	–	–	–	–	–	–	–	–
Congo People's Rep.	–	–	–	–	–	–	–	–	–	–	–
Equatorial Guinea	–	–	–	–	–	–	–	–	–	–	–
Gambia	–	–	–	–	–	–	–	–	–	–	
Ghana	–	–	–	–	–	–	–	–	–	–	14
Guinea Rep.	–	–	–	–	–	–	–	–	–	–	–
Ivory Coast	–	–	–	–	–	–	–	–	–	–	–
Kenya	–	–	–	–	–	–	–	–	–	–	–
Lesotho	–	–	–	–	–	–	–	–	–	–	–
Liberia	–	–	–	–	–	–	–	–	–	–	–
Malagasy Rep.	–	–	–	–	–	–	–	–	–	–	–
Malawi	–	–	–	–	–	–	–	–	–	–	–
Mali Rep.	–	–	–	–	–	–	–	–	–	–	–
Mauritania	–	–	–	–	–	–	–	–	–	–	–
Mauritius	–	–	–	–	–	–	–	–	–	–	–
Morocco	–	–	–	–	–	–	–	–	–	–	–
Rwanda	–	–	–	–	–	–	–	–	–	–	–
Senegal	–	–	–	–	–	–	–	–	–	–	–
Sierra Leone	–	–	–	–	–	–	–	–	–	–	–
Somalia	–	–	–	–	–	–	–	–	–	–	–
Sudan	–	–	–	–	–	–	5·0	1·3	–	–	
Swaziland	–	–	–	–	–	–	–	–	–	–	–
Tanzania	–	–	–	–	–	–	–	–	–	–	–
Togo	–	–	–	–	–	–	–	–	–	–	–
Tunisia	–	–	–	–	–	–	–	–	–	–	–
Uganda	–	–	–	–	–	–	–	–	–	–	–
Upper Volta	–	–	–	–	–	–	–	–	–	–	–
Zaire	–	–	–	–	–	–	–	–	–	–	–
Zambia	–	–	–	–	–	–	–	–	–	–	–

Source. **IMF,** *International Financial Statistics.*

Table 8.1 cont.

1963	1964	1965	1966	1967	1968	1969	1970	1971	1972	1973	1974	1975	1976
—	—	—	—	15·0	4·5	—	12·0	6·5	—	13·5	29·5	9·5	—
—	—	—	—	—	—	—	—	6·3	6·3	6·3	—	—	—
—	—	—	—	—	—	—	—	59·9	—	—	—	59·9	—
—	—	200·0	225·0	90·0	—	—	—	—	—	—	573·2	201·3	—
—	—	—	—	—	12·5	—	—	7·5	—	—	130·0	107·3	104·4
—	—	—	—	—	—	—	0·5	—	—	—	—	6·5	3·3
—	—	—	—	—	—	—	—	11·7	—	—	—	—	93·0
—	—	—	—	—	—	—	—	—	—	—	—	—	7·6
—	—	53·5	9·5	—	40·0	35·0	—	—	84·0	60·0	129·9	161·4	107·2
—	—	—	—	27·5	55·0	—	27·5	35·0	35·0	38·8	40·0	125·9	222·7
—	—	23·0	30·3	25·8	35·8	13·0	9·5	14·0	25·3	18·6	46·9	42·1	28·2
—	—	—	—	—	—	—	—	—	2·2	—	—	—	67·0
—	—	—	—	—	—	—	—	—	—	—	—	—	15·5
—	—	—	—	—	—	—	—	—	—	—	2·6	—	—
—	—	—	—	—	—	—	—	—	—	—	—	—	29·8
—	—	—	—	—	—	—	—	—	—	—	—	1·6	0·7
3·6	37·3	46·1	96·8	75·6	98·7	36·7	36·9	53·6	103·8	31·0	235·0	374·2	524·2
—	—	2·0	3·9	5·0	5·0	3·5	2·5	1·5	—	—	2·0	1·3	—
—	—	—	—	—	—	—	—	—	—	—	11·5	7·5	21·8
—	—	—	—	—	—	—	—	1·3	—	—	3·2	2·3	6·1
—	—	—	—	—	—	—	3·8	—	—	—	5·0	—	6·5
—	—	—	—	—	—	—	—	—	—	—	—	—	—
—	—	—	—	—	—	—	—	1·0	—	—	—	—	—
—	—	—	—	—	—	—	—	—	—	—	—	—	—
—	—	—	52·2	25·0	10·0	5·0	2·0	—	—	—	—	51·9	—
—	—	—	1·0	—	—	3·8	4·2	—	—	—	12·2	—	—
—	—	—	—	—	—	—	—	—	—	—	21·9	—	36·4
—	—	—	—	—	—	—	—	—	—	—	44·4	48·5	27·1
—	—	—	—	—	—	0·6	—	—	—	—	—	—	—
3·6	3·8	3·0	5·2	5·2	3·4	1·4	2·0	1·0	—	2·8	—	—	4·6
—	—	—	—	—	—	—	—	—	—	—	8·5	10·9	—
—	—	—	—	—	—	1·0	—	—	—	—	—	6·1	1·4
—	5·0	5·0	1·0	3·0	4·0	2·5	1·5	2·5	2·0	—	4·0	1·0	4·0
—	—	—	—	—	—	—	—	1·0	—	—	1·0	2·1	11·8
—	—	—	—	—	4·0	—	—	—	—	—	5·5	—	—
—	13·1	—	—	—	50·0	10·0	10·0	8·3	—	—	—	—	143·7
—	—	—	5·0	2·0	3·0	2·0	—	—	2·1	—	—	—	—
—	—	—	—	—	—	—	—	—	—	—	4·8	25·4	—
—	—	—	1·5	5·4	—	—	—	—	—	—	10·6	0·6	17·5
—	4·7	5·6	0·9	4·0	3·7	—	—	—	—	—	—	—	—
—	5·5	18·8	17·5	19·0	10·0	2·5	—	—	32·5	9·0	45·7	48·3	26·7
—	—	—	—	—	—	1·2	—	—	—	0·2	0·5	—	—
—	—	—	—	—	—	—	—	—	—	—	49·3	23·8	21·0
—	—	—	—	—	—	—	—	—	—	—	—	—	7·5
—	5·3	11·8	8·5	7·0	9·6	2·0	7·5	2·5	—	—	—	—	—
—	—	—	—	—	—	—	—	16·5	—	—	5·0	14·2	20·0
—	—	—	—	—	—	—	0·8	—	—	—	—	—	—
—	—	—	—	—	—	—	—	—	28·3	—	—	73·3	130·0
—	—	—	—	—	—	—	—	19·0	38·0	19·0	—	56·9	38·3

TABLE 8.2
Fund Accounts: Position to Date at 31 December 1976
(SDR millions)

	Total drawings to date	Tranche drawings to date	CFF drawings to date	OF drawings to date	BSFF drawings to date	EFF drawings to date
Oil-exporting countries	677·8	653·2	17·5	–	7·1	–
Algeria	–	–	–	–	–	–
Indonesia	406·8	401·3	–	–	5·6	–
Iran	184·2	184·2	–	–	–	–
Iraq	67·3	49·8	17·5	–	–	–
Kuwait	–	–	–	–	–	–
Libya	–	–	–	–	–	–
Nigeria	19·5	18·0	–	–	1·5	–
Oman	–	–	–	–	–	–
Qatar	–	–	–	–	–	–
Saudi Arabia	–	–	–	–	–	–
United Arab Emirates	–	–	–	–	–	–
Venezuela						
Other Less-developed Areas	13045·1	7853·3	2532·6	2538·9	22·9	97·7
Other Western Hemisphere	5375·4	3769·2	974·6	618·2	13·5	–
Argentina	1295·1	935·0	284·0	76·1	–	–
Bolivia	77·0	63·5	–	–	13·5	–
Brazil	578·5	518·5	60·0	–	–	–
Chile	888·2	486·5	158·0	243·7	–	–
Colombia	404·9	384·1	20·8	–	–	–
Costa Rica	88·8	51·2	–	37·7	–	–
Dominican Rep.	100·1	72·0	28·1	–	–	–
Ecuador	103·6	97·4	6·3	–	–	–
El Salvador	109·7	85·5	6·3	17·9	–	–
Guatemala	36·0	29·8	6·3	–	–	–
Haiti	49·7	38·4	2·3	9·0	–	–
Honduras	61·8	45·0	–	16·8	–	–
Mexico	529·4	344·4	185·0	–	–	–
Nicaragua	115·0	99·5	–	15·5	–	–
Panama	64·7	22·1	18·0	24·6	–	–
Paraguay	8·1	8·1	–	–	–	–
Peru	397·0	252·1	92·3	52·7	–	–
Uruguay	296·3	149·0	52·7	94·7	–	–
Bahamas	–	–	–	–	–	–
Barbados	–	–	–	–	–	–
Grenada	1·7	1·2	–	0·5	–	–
Guyana	35·8	20·8	15·0	–	–	–
Jamaica	117·9	49·0	39·8	29·2	–	–
Trinidad and Tobago	16·1	16·1	–	–	–	–

Table 8.2 cont.

	Total drawings to date	Tranche drawings to date	CFF drawings to date	OF drawings to date	BSFF drawings to date	EFF drawings to date
Other Middle East	1133·1	614·6	289·8	228·8	–	–
Bahrain	5·0	5·0	–	–	–	–
Cyprus	52·5	9·4	13·0	30·1	–	–
Egypt	538·9	327·2	180·0	31·7	–	–
Israel	399·0	190·8	65·0	143·3	–	–
Jordan	7·4	–	7·4	–	–	–
Lebanon	–	–	–	–	–	–
Syria	89·4	67·4	22·0	–	–	–
Yemen,Arab Rep.	0·5	0·5	–	–	–	–
Yemen People's Dem. Rep.	40·6	14·3	2·5	23·8	–	–
Other Asia	4762·2	2612·9	822·7	1227·2	9·4	90·0
Afghanistan	66·3	61·5	4·8	–	–	–
Bangladesh	290·4	96·9	101·6	92·0	–	–
Burma	105·5	76·5	29·0	–	–	–
Cambodia	18·8	6·3	12·5	–	–	–
China, Rep. of	119·7	119·7	–	–	–	–
India	1864·5	1311·2	152·0	401·3	–	–
Korea	361·7	69·0	40·0	252·7	–	–
Laos	10·2	3·7	6·5	–	–	–
Malaysia	104·7	4·4	93·0	–	7·3	–
Nepal	7·6	7·6	–	–	–	–
Pakistan	693·0	366·5	90·5	236·0	–	–
Philippines	665·6	307·4	116·3	152·0	–	90·0
Singapore	–	–	–	–	–	–
Sri Lanka	334·8	158·6	98·6	77·6	–	–
Thailand	69·2	–	67·0	–	2·1	–
Vietnam	15·5	15·5	–	–	–	–
Fiji	2·6	2·3	–	0·3	–	–
Papua New Guinea	29·8	5·0	10·0	14·8	–	–
Western Samoa	2·3	0·9	1·0	0·4	–	–
Other Africa	1774·4	856·6	445·5	464·4	–	7·7
Benin	–	–	–	–	–	–
Botswana	–	–	–	–	–	–
Burundi	26·8	23·1	2·5	1·2	–	–
Cameroon	40·8	6·9	17·5	16·4	–	–
Central African Empire	13·0	1·9	5·1	6·0	–	–
Chad	15·3	6·6	6·5	2·2	–	–
Comoros	–	–	–	–	–	–
Congo People's Rep.	–	–	–	–	–	–
Equatorial Guinea	1·0	1·0	–	–	–	–
Ethiopia	0·6	0·6	–	–	–	–
Gabon	–	–	–	–	–	–
Gambia	–	–	–	–	–	–
Ghana	160·3	104·4	17·3	38·6	–	–

Table 8.2 cont.   (SDR millions)

	Total drawings to date	Tranche drawings to date	CFF drawings to date	OF drawings to date	BSFF drawings to date	EFF drawings to date
Other Africa (*cont.*)						
Guinea Rep.	21·2	11·7	6·0	3·5	–	–
Ivory Coast	58·3	10·8	26·0	21·5	–	–
Kenya	120·0	24·3	24·0	63·9	–	7·7
Lesotho	0·6	0·6	–	–	–	–
Liberia	35·9	35·9	–	–	–	–
Malagasy Rep.	19·3	5·0	–	14·3	–	–
Malawi	8·4	4·7	–	3·7	–	–
Mali Rep.	35·4	26·4	–	9·0	–	–
Mauritania	16·0	4·1	6·5	5·3	–	–
Mauritius	9·5	9·5	–	–	–	–
Morocco	235·1	160·6	56·5	18·0	–	–
Niger	–	–	–	–	–	–
Rwanda	14·1	14·1	–	–	–	–
Senegal	30·2	4·8	–	25·4	–	–
Sierra Leone	35·5	13·1	12·5	9·9	–	–
Somalia	18·9	18·9	–	–	–	–
Sudan	241·7	138·7	56·0	47·0	–	–
Swaziland	1·8	1·8	–	–	–	–
Tanzania	94·1	21·0	21·0	52·1	–	–
Togo	7·5	–	7·5	–	–	–
Tunisia	54·2	54·2	–	–	–	–
Uganda	55·7	16·5	20·0	19·2	–	–
Upper Volta	0·8	0·8	–	–	–	–
Zaire	231·5	69·3	84·7	77·5	–	–
Zambia	171·2	65·5	76·0	29·7	–	–

Source. IMF, *International Financial Statistics.*

Broadly speaking, up until 1972 ordinary tranche drawings represented far and away the most significant source of finance for LDCs. For instance, it was only in 1963, 1967, 1972, 1973 and 1976 that drawings under the CFF accounted for more than 10 per cent of total LDC drawings. For seven of the remaining years in the period 1963–1976, drawings under the CFF accounted for less than 7·5 per cent of total LDC drawings.

In 1976 there was a major change in the relative importance of the various sources of IMF-based finance to LDCs. In that year LDCs used Fund credit to the value of SDR 5283·6 million, of which only SDR 1012 million was accounted for by credit tranche drawings, while net CFF drawings were SDR 1770·6 million and net OF drawings totalled SDR 2338·5 million. In 1976, then, both the CFF and OF represented more significant sources of finance to LDCs than the ordinary credit tranches in the Fund; and this was the pattern for all LDCs except Grenada, Afghanistan, Burma and Nepal.

Investigating 1976 more closely, in that year thirty-five LDCs (of which thirty-three had Reserve Positions in the Fund) did not draw on the Fund; twenty-four LDCs made a credit-tranche drawing, but only in the cases of Israel, Bangladesh, Pakistan and the Sudan did the drawing venture beyond the first credit tranche. In the case of eleven of the twenty-four credit-tranche drawings, a stand-by arrangement had been agreed. Forty LDCs drew resources under the CFF and forty-four under the OF. Of twenty-six LDCs for which the Fund was holding domestic currency to the extent of 100 per cent of quota (thus giving these countries no Reserve Position), twenty-four were using some form of Fund credit. With the exceptions of Afghanistan and Nepal, all LDCs that were using their credit branches were also drawing on the Fund under either the CFF or OF or both. The detailed evidence relating to the status of all LDCs in 1976 is presented in Table 8.3[3]

The compensatory financing facility

Information concerning the use of the CFF is presented in Table 8.4. It may be seen from this table that, before the liberalisation of the CFF in 1966, only Brazil, Egypt and the Sudan had made use of the facility. Following the liberalisation, seven LDCs drew on the CFF in 1967. During the remainder of the 1960s, however, the facility was little used and in 1970 a meagre total of SDR 2·5 million was drawn, representing just one drawing by Burundi. Record drawings under the CFF of almost SDR 300 million were experienced in 1972, with ten LDCs using the facility, but this was an exception to the general pattern. Until 1976, then, the CFF had been used by relatively few LDCs, and only a few countries (for instance, Argentina) had made any drawings that could be considered at all large. In fact, over the period 1963–75 fifty-one drawings under the CFF had been made by thirty LDCs; a total of SDR 1096·6 million had been drawn, making the average drawing SDR 21·5 million.

In 1976, following the further liberalisation of the CFF, there occurred a dramatic change: thirty-seven LDCs drew a total of SDR 1453·8 million under the facility, giving an average drawing of SDR 39·3 million. In 1976 the size of the average drawing almost doubled, whilst the number of LDCs making use of the Fund almost quadrupled as compared with the previous record year of 1972.

TABLE 8.3

Fund Accounts: Position to Date at 31 December 1976
(SDR millions)

	Fund holdings of currency adjusted	Percentage of quota	Reserve Position in Fund	Use of Fund credit	Net credit tranche drawings	Net CFF drawings	Net OF drawings	Net EFF drawings	Stand-by arrangements		EFF arrangements	
									Agreed	Available	Agreed	Available
Oil-exporting countries	788·2	55·5	5428·0	—	—	—	—	—	—	—	—	—
Algeria	96·5	74·2	33·5	—	—	—	—	—	—	—	—	—
Indonesia	260·0	100·0	—	—	—	—	—	—	—	—	—	—
Iran	124·0	64·6	998·0	—	—	—	—	—	—	—	—	—
Iraq	81·7	75·0	27·3	—	—	—	—	—	—	—	—	—
Kuwait	7·3	11·3	742·7	—	—	—	—	—	—	—	—	—
Libya	18·0	74·8	6·0	—	—	—	—	—	—	—	—	—
Nigeria	101·2	75·0	333·8	—	—	—	—	—	—	—	—	—
Oman	2·1	30·3	25·0	—	—	—	—	—	—	—	—	—
Qatar	3·8	19·1	16·2	—	—	—	—	—	—	—	—	—
Saudi Arabia	78·2	58·4	2205·8	—	—	—	—	—	—	—	—	—
United Arab Emirates	0·9	6·1	114·1	—	—	—	—	—	—	—	—	—
Venezuela	14·4	4·4	925·6	—	—	—	—	—	—	—	—	—
Other Less-Developed Areas	7380·6	110·3	447·4	5283·6	1012·4	1770·6	2338·5	97·7	458·9	226·2	140·0	42·4
Other Western Hemisphere	2421·5	106·7	267·6	1695·1	408·9	685·0	618·2	—	310·7	144·0	—	—
Argentina	599·5	136·3	—	455·6	159·5	220·0	76·1	—	260·0	100·5	—	—
Bolivia	30·6	82·6	6·4	—	—	—	—	—	—	—	—	—
Brazil	277·8	63·1	162·2	—	—	—	—	—	—	—	—	—
Chile	217·5	137·7	—	402·2	59·5	99·0	243·7	—	—	—	—	—
Colombia	111·8	71·2	45·3	—	—	—	—	—	—	—	—	—
Costa Rica	32·0	100·0	—	32·3	—	—	37·7	—	11·6	11·6	—	—
Dominican Rep.	43·0	100·0	—	21·5	—	21·5	—	—	—	—	—	—
Ecuador	33·0	100·0	—	—	—	—	—	—	—	—	—	—
El Salvador	35·0	100·0	—	12·8	—	—	17·9	—	—	—	—	—
Guatemala	24·0	66·7	12·0	—	—	—	—	—	—	—	—	—
Haiti	22·4	118·1	—	12·4	3·2	—	9·0	—	6·9	6·9	—	—
Honduras	25·0	100·0	—	16·8	—	—	16·8	—	—	—	—	—
Mexico	504·1	136·3	—	319·1	134·1	185·0	—	—	—	—	—	—

	(1)	(2)	(3)	(4)	(5)	(6)	(7)	(8)	(9)	(10)	(11)	(12)	(13)
Nicaragua	27·0	100·0	—	8·7	—	—	15·5	—	—	—	—	—	—
Panama	36·0	100·0	—	42·6	—	18·0	24·6	—	—	—	—	—	—
Paraguay	13·2	69·6	5·8	—	44·6	61·5	52·7	—	25·0	—	—	—	—
Peru	167·6	136·3	—	158·8	—	30·3	94·7	—	—	25·0	—	—	—
Uruguay	69·0	100·0	—	124·9	—	—	—	—	—	—	—	—	—
Bahamas	15·0	75·0	5·0	—	—	—	—	—	—	—	—	—	—
Barbados	9·7	74·9	3·3	—	—	—	—	—	—	—	—	—	—
Grenada	2·7	136·0	—	1·2	0·7	10·0	0·5	—	—	—	—	—	—
Guyana	27·3	136·3	—	17·3	7·3	39·8	—	—	7·3	—	—	—	—
Jamaica	53·0	100·0	—	68·9	—	—	29·2	—	—	—	—	—	—
Trinidad and Tobago	45·3	71·8	27·8	—	—	—	—	—	—	—	—	—	—
Other Middle East	540·0	113·7	27·8	543·1	87·5	221·5	228·8	—	—	—	—	—	—
Bahrain	5·3	52·6	—	—	—	—	—	—	—	—	—	—	—
Cyprus	26·0	100·0	4·7	43·1	—	13·0	30·1	—	—	—	—	—	—
Egypt	193·2	102·8	—	177·9	—	141·0	31·7	—	29·3	17·3	—	—	—
Israel	207·0	159·2	—	285·3	77·0	65·0	143·3	—	—	—	—	—	—
Jordan	17·2	75·0	5·8	—	—	—	—	—	—	—	—	—	—
Lebanon	6·7	74·8	2·3	—	—	—	—	—	—	—	—	—	—
Syria	37·5	75·0	12·5	—	—	—	—	—	—	—	—	—	—
Yemen, Arab. Rep.	7·5	75·0	2·5	—	10·5	2·5	23·8	90·0	29·3	17·3	—	—	—
Yemen, People's Dem. Rep.	39·5	136·2	—	36·8	—	—	—	—	—	—	—	—	—
Other Asia	3156·5	113·4	99·9	2112·5	367·5	523·6	1026·9	—	—	—	—	—	—
Afghanistan	38·8	104·7	—	1·8	1·8	70·3	92·0	90·0	4·5	—	90·0	—	—
Bangladesh	198·5	158·8	—	235·8	72·7	15·0	—	—	—	—	—	—	—
Burma	79·5	132·5	—	34·5	19·5	12·5	—	—	—	—	—	—	—
Cambodia	25·0	100·0	—	12·5	—	—	—	—	—	—	—	—	—
China, Rep. of	550·0	100·0	—	—	—	—	—	—	—	—	—	—	—
India	1145·0	121·8	—	406·3	118·7	—	201·3	—	—	—	—	—	—
Korea	89·0	111·2	—	301·7	9·0	40·0	252·7	—	—	—	—	—	—
Laos	13·0	100·0	—	6·5	—	6·5	—	—	—	—	—	—	—
Malaysia	132·2	71·1	53·8	93·0	—	93·0	—	—	—	—	—	—	—
Nepal	16·9	136·2	—	4·5	4·5	90·5	—	—	4·5	—	—	—	—
Pakistan	348·0	148·1	—	439·6	111·8	77·5	236·0	—	—	—	—	—	—
Philippines	183·9	118·6	—	348·4	28·9	—	152·0	90·0	—	—	90·0	—	—
Singapore	27·7	74·7	9·4	—	—	—	—	—	—	—	—	—	—
Sri Lanka	114·3	116·7	—	134·3	—	40·3	77·6	—	—	—	—	—	—

Table 8.3 cont.

	Fund holdings of currency adjusted	Percentage of quota	Reserve Position in Fund	Use of Fund credit	Net credit tranche drawings	Net CFF drawings	Net OF drawings	Net EFF drawings	Stand-by arrangements Agreed	Stand-by arrangements Available	EFF arrangements Agreed	EFF arrangements Available
Thailand	100·5	75·0	33·5	67·0	—	67·0	—	—	—	—	—	—
Vietnam	62·0	100·0	—	—	—	—	—	—	—	—	—	—
Fiji	9·8	75·0	3·3	—	—	—	—	—	·-	—	—	—
Papua New Guinea	20·0	100·0	—	24·8	—	10·0	14·8	—	—	—	—	—
Western Samoa	2·5	125·0	—	1·9	0·5	1·0	0·4	—	—	—	—	—
Other Africa	1262·6	108·6	52·1	932·9	148·5	340·5	464·6	7·7	114·5	65·0	50·1	42·4
Benin	10·9	83·6	2·1	—	—	—	—	—	—	—	—	—
Botswana	4·4	87·8	0·6	—	—	—	—	—	—	6·5	—	—
Burundi	19·0	100·1	—	1·2	—	—	1·2	—	6·5	—	—	—
Cameroon	35·0	99·9	—	33·9	—	17·5	16·4	—	—	—	—	—
Central African Empire	13·0	100·0	—	9·6	—	5·1	6·0	—	—	—	—	—
Chad	13·8	105·9	—	9·5	0·8	6·5	2·2	—	—	—	—	—
Comoros	1·9	100·0	—	—	—	—	—	—	—	—	—	—
Congo, People's Rep.	11·0	84·4	2·0	—	—	—	—	—	—	—	—	—
Equatorial Guinea	6·2	78·0	1·8	—	—	—	—	—	—	—	—	—
Ethiopia	20·2	74·7	6·8	—	—	—	—	—	—	—	—	—
Gabon	12·5	83·1	2·5	—	—	—	—	—	—	—	—	—
Gambia	5·3	75·1	1·7	—	—	—	—	—	—	—	—	—
Ghana	87·0	100·0	—	38·6	—	—	38·6	—	—	—	—	—
Guinea Rep.	24·0	100·0	—	7·1	—	6·0	3·5	—	—	—	—	—
Ivory Coast	52·0	100·0	—	23·4	—	12·6	21·5	—	—	—	—	—
Kenya	48·0	100·0	—	85·0	—	24·0	63·9	7·7	—	—	50·1	42·4
Lesotho	3·8	75·0	1·3	—	—	—	—	—	—	—	—	—
Liberia	29·0	100·0	—	—	—	—	—	—	5·0	5·0	—	—
Malagasy Rep	26·0	100·0	—	14·3	—	—	14·3	—	—	—	—	—
Malawi	15·0	99·9	—	3·7	—	—	3·7	—	—	—	—	—
Mali Rep.	25·7	117·0	—	12·7	—	—	9·0	—	—	—	—	—
Mauritania	13·0	100·0	—	11·8	—	6·5	5·3	—	—	—	—	—
Mauritius	16·5	75·0	5·5	—	—	—	—	—	—	—	—	—

Morocco	154·0	136·3	—	115·5	40·9	56·5	18·0	—	—	—	—
Niger	10·9	83·7	2·1	—	—	—	—	—	—	—	—
Rwanda	16·9	89·1	2·1	—	—	—	—	—	—	—	—
Senegal	34·0	100·0	—	25·4	—	—	—	—	—	—	—
Sierra Leone	25·1	100·2	—	22·4	—	12·5	25·4	—	—	—	—
Somalia	14·8	77·7	4·2	—	—	—	9·9	—	—	—	—
Sudan	99·4	138·0	—	119·1	27·5	44·7	47·0	—	—	—	—
Swaziland	6·0	75·0	2·0	—	—	—	—	—	—	—	—
Tanzania	52·5	125·1	—	83·6	10·5	21·0	52·1	—	—	—	—
Togo	12·9	86·3	2·1	7·5	—	7·5	—	—	—	—	—
Tunisia	36·0	75·0	12·0	—	—	—	—	—	—	—	—
Uganda	40·0	100·0	—	32·7	—	20·0	19·2	—	—	—	—
Upper Volta	9·7	74·9	3·3	—	—	—	—	—	—	—	—
Zaire	154·0	136·3	—	180·6	41·0	62·1	77·5	41·0	—	—	—
Zambia	103·5	136·2	—	95·2	27·5	38·0	29·7	62·0	53·5	—	—

Source. IMF, *International Financial Statistics.*

TABLE 8.4
Compensatory Drawings
(SDR millions)

	1963	1964	1965	1966	1967	1968	1969	1970	1971	1972	1973	1974	1975	1976
Less-developed areas	76·0	—	11·3	23·9	165·2	64·8	12·5	2·5	69·5	299·4	113·5	107·2	150·8	1453·8
Oil exporting countries	—	—	—	—	17·5	—	6·3	—	—	—	—	—	—	—
Ecuador	—	—	—	—	—	—	6·3	—	—	—	—	—	—	—
Iraq	—	—	—	—	17·5	—	—	—	—	—	—	—	—	—
Other less developed areas	76·0	—	11·3	23·9	147·7	64·8	6·3	2·5	69·5	299·4	113·5	107·2	150·8	1453·8
Other Western Hemisphere	60·0	—	—	6·6	21·2	17·7	6·3	—	39·5	151·5	—	18·3	110·0	537·4
Argentina	—	—	—	—	—	—	—	—	—	64·0	—	—	110·0	110·0
Brazil	60·0	—	—	—	—	—	—	—	—	—	—	—	—	—
Chile	—	—	—	—	—	—	—	—	39·5	39·5	—	—	—	79·0
Colombia	—	—	—	—	18·9	1·9	—	—	—	—	—	—	—	—
Costa Rica	—	—	—	—	—	—	—	—	—	—	—	—	—	—
Dominican Rep.	—	—	—	6·6	—	—	—	—	—	—	—	—	—	21·5
El Salvador	—	—	—	—	—	—	6·3	—	—	—	—	—	—	—
Guatemala	—	—	—	—	—	6·3	—	—	—	—	—	—	—	—
Haiti	—	—	—	—	2·3	—	—	—	—	—	—	—	—	—
Honduras	—	—	—	—	—	—	—	—	—	—	—	—	—	—
Mexico	—	—	—	—	—	—	—	—	—	—	—	—	—	185·0
Nicaragua	—	—	—	—	—	—	—	—	—	—	—	—	—	—
Panama	—	—	—	—	—	—	—	—	—	—	—	—	—	18·0
Peru	—	—	—	—	—	—	—	—	—	30·8	—	—	—	61·5
Uruguay	—	—	—	—	—	9·5	—	—	—	17·3	—	—	—	25·9

Grenada	—	—	—	—	—	—	—	—	—	—	—	—	—
Guyana	—	—	—	—	—	—	—	—	—	—	5·0	—	10·0
Jamaica	—	—	—	—	—	—	—	—	—	—	13·3	—	26·5
Other Middle East	16·0	—	—	—	—	9·5	23·0	—	4·5	12·5	49·9	—	—	174·5
Cyprus	16·0	—	—	—	—	—	—	—	—	—	—	—	13·0
Egypt	—	—	—	—	—	—	23·0	—	—	—	47·0	—	94·0
Israel	—	—	—	—	—	—	—	—	—	—	—	—	65·0
Jordan	—	—	—	—	—	—	—	—	4·5	—	2·9	—	—
Syria	—	—	—	—	—	9·5	—	—	—	12·5	—	—	—
Yemen, People's Dem. Rep.	—	—	—	—	—	—	—	—	—	—	—	—	2·5
Other Asia	—	—	—	—	—	117·0	24·1	—	6·5	88·2	63·6	82·9	3·8	436·6
Afghanistan	—	—	—	—	—	—	4·8	—	—	—	—	—	—
Bangladesh	—	—	—	—	—	—	—	—	—	62·5	—	—	39·1
Burma	—	—	—	—	—	7·5	—	—	6·5	—	—	15·0	—
Cambodia	—	—	—	—	—	—	—	—	—	6·3	6·3	—	—
India	—	—	—	—	—	90·0	—	—	—	—	—	62·0	—
Korea	—	—	—	—	—	—	—	—	—	—	—	—	40·0
Laos	—	—	—	—	—	—	—	—	—	—	—	—	3·3	3·3
Malaysia	—	—	—	—	—	—	—	—	—	—	—	—	93·0
Pakistan	—	—	—	—	—	—	—	—	—	—	—	—	90·5
Philippines	—	—	—	—	—	—	—	—	—	—	38·8	—	77·5
Sri Lanka	—	—	—	—	—	19·5	19·3	—	—	19·5	18·6	5·9	—	15·8
Thailand	—	—	—	—	—	—	—	—	—	—	—	—	67·0
Fiji	—	—	—	—	—	—	—	—	—	—	—	—	—
Papua New Guinea	—	—	—	—	—	—	—	—	—	—	—	—	10·0
Western Samoa	—	—	—	—	—	—	—	—	—	—	—	—	0·5	0·5
Other Africa	—	—	—	17·3	—	—	—	2·5	19·0	47·2	—	6·0	37·0	305·3
Burundi	—	—	—	11·3	—	—	—	2·5	—	—	—	—	—

Table 8.4 cont.

	1963	1964	1965	1966	1967	1968	1969	1970	1971	1972	1973	1974	1975	1976
Other Africa (cont.)														
Cameroon	—	—	—	—	—	—	—	—	—	—	—	—	—	17·5
Central African Empire	—	—	—	—	—	—	—	—	—	—	—	—	—	—
Chad	—	—	—	—	—	—	—	—	—	—	—	—	—	5·1
Ghana	—	—	—	17·3	—	—	—	—	—	—	—	—	—	6·5
Guinea Rep.	—	—	—	—	—	—	—	—	—	—	—	6·0	—	—
Ivory Coast	—	—	—	—	—	—	—	—	—	—	—	—	—	26·0
Kenya	—	—	—	—	—	—	—	—	—	—	—	—	—	24·0
Malagasy Rep.	—	—	—	—	—	—	—	—	—	—	—	—	—	—
Malawi	—	—	—	—	—	—	—	—	—	—	—	—	—	—
Mali Rep.	—	—	—	—	—	—	—	—	—	—	—	—	—	—
Mauritius	—	—	—	—	—	—	—	—	—	—	—	—	—	6·5
Morocco	—	—	—	—	—	—	—	—	—	—	—	—	—	56·5
Senegal	—	—	—	—	—	—	—	—	—	—	—	—	—	—
Sierra Leone	—	—	—	—	—	—	—	—	—	—	—	—	—	12·5
Sudan	—	—	—	—	—	—	—	—	—	—	—	—	18·0	26·7
Tanzania	—	—	—	—	—	—	—	—	—	—	—	—	—	21·0
Togo	—	—	—	—	—	—	—	—	—	—	—	—	—	7·5
Uganda	—	—	—	—	—	—	—	—	—	—	—	—	—	20·0
Zaire	—	—	11·3	—	—	—	—	—	—	28·2	—	—	—	56·5
Zambia	—	—	—	—	—	—	—	—	19·0	19·0	—	—	19·0	19·0

Source. IMF, International Financial Statistics.

Amongst non oil-exporting LDCs, Latin American and Caribbean LDCs, with drawings of SDR 974·6 million, have made the greatest use of the CFF, Middle Eastern LDCs have drawn SDR 289·8 million, Asian LDCs have drawn SDR 822.7 million, and African LDCs have drawn SDR 445·5 million.

The buffer stock financing facility

The BSFF has in general been little used by LDCs. As of the end of 1976, only SDR 30·0 million had been drawn under the facility, and only Indonesia (SDR 5.6 million) Nigeria (SDR 1.5 million), Bolivia (SDR 3.5 million), Malaysia (SDR 7.3 million) and Thailand (SDR 2.1 million) had made BSFF drawings.

The oil facility

As Table 8.5 confirms, in the course of its short existence the OF was greatly used by LDCs. By the end of 1976 forty-five LDCs had drawn a total of SDR 2538.9 million under the facility. This means that 50 per cent of all non oil-exporting LDCs in the IMF had made OF drawings by December 1976. Interestingly from a distributional point of view, it has been the non oil-exporting Asian LDCs that have made the greatest use of the OF, with drawings totalling SDR 1227·2 million by the end of 1976. Western Hemisphere LDCs had by this time drawn SDR 618·2 million, whilst Middle Eastern and African LDCs had drawn SDR 228·8 million and SDR 464·6 million respectively. The large drawings by Asian LDCs, however, reflect not that a relatively high proportion of Asian LDCs used the facility but that the LDCs that used it (in particular, India, Korea and Pakistan, and, to a slightly lesser extent, Bangladesh and Sri Lanka) made large drawings.

Even though LDCs have made considerable use of the OF, it remains interesting that the value of drawings by just two industrial countries, Italy and the United Kingdom, almost equals the value of drawings by forty-five LDCs.

The extended fund facility

The EFF is still in its infancy. By the end of 1976, LDCs had drawn SDR 97·7 million under the facility, this total representing two drawings: one of SDR 90.0 million by the Philippines and the other of SDR 7·7 million by Kenya. The Philippines have in fact agreed a three-year EFF

TABLE 8.5
Oil Facility Drawings
(SDR millions)

	1974	1975	1976
Other less-developed areas	764·5	1274·4	500·1
Other Western Hemisphere	156·1	306·1	156·1
Argentina	–	76·1	–
Brazil	–	–	–
Chile	41·5	156·8	45·4
Colombia	–	–	–
Costa Rica	18·8	12·0	6·8
Dominican Rep.	–	–	–
Ecuador	–	–	–
El Salvador	17·9	–	–
Guatemala	–	–	–
Haiti	3·8	2·6	2·6
Honduras	16·8	–	–
Mexico	–	–	–
Nicaragua	3·3	12·2	–
Panama	7·4	10·2	7·1
Peru	–	–	52·7
Uruguay	46·6	35·9	12·1
Grenada	–	0·3	0·2
Guyana	–	–	–
Jamaica	–	–	29·2
Other Middle East	15·7	152·1	61·1
Cyprus	6·4	1·7	22·0
Egypt	–	–	31·7
Israel	–	143·3	–
Jordan	–	–	–
Syria	–	–	–
Yemen, People's Dem. Rep.	9·3	7·1	7·4
Other Asia	462·7	577·3	187·2
Bangladesh	40·4	36·9	14·7
Cambodia	–	–	–
Burma	–	–	–
India	200·0	201·3	–
Korea	90·0	107·3	55·4
Laos	–	–	–
Malaysia	–	–	–
Pakistan	97·9	103·4	34·7
Philippines	–	96·9	55·2

Table 8.5 cont.

	1974	1975	1976
Other Asia (cont.)			
Sri Lanka	34·0	31·3	12·4
Thailand	–	–	–
Fiji	0·3	–	–
Papua New Guinea	–	–	14·8
Western Samoa	–	0·3	0·2
Other Africa	130·0	238·9	95·7
Burundi	–	1·2	–
Cameroon	4·6	7·5	4·3
Central African Empire	2·7	2·3	1·0
Chad	2·2	–	–
Ghana	–	38·6	–
Guinea Rep.	3·5	–	–
Ivory Coast	11·2	–	10·4
Kenya	32·0	28·8	3·1
Malagasy Rep.	3·5	10·9	–
Malawi	–	2·4	1·4
Mali Rep.	4·0	1·0	4·0
Mauritania	–	–	5·3
Morocco	–	–	18·0
Senegal	–	25·4	–
Sierra Leone	4·3	0·6	5·0
Sudan	28·7	18·3	–
Tanzania	28·4	23·8	–
Togo	–	–	–
Uganda	5·0	14·2	–
Zaire	–	45·0	32·5
Zambia	–	18·9	10·8

Source. IMF, *International Financial Statistics.*

arrangement for a total of SDR 217.0 million whilst Kenya has a similar three-year arrangement for a total of SDR 67.2 million.

Evaluation of General Account Sources of International Finance

An evaluation of the IMF General Account as a source of international liquidity for LDCs involves both quantitative and qualitative aspects. In the previous section we saw that, quantitatively speaking, until 1976 LDCs made relatively little use of the IMF. The qualitative aspect of the evaluation concerns the nature of the conditions under which drawings have been made. The two aspects of the evaluation are, of course, interrelated: the imposition of harsh conditions by the IMF may deter countries from drawing on the Fund and may therefore serve to keep down the size of actual drawings.

A low level of actual usage could reflect not only that LDC members of the IMF have failed to qualify for assistance on the basis of the requirements of the various facilities, in the main because of satisfactory balance-of-payments performance, but also that, even though they qualify on the basis of the access criteria agreed, they prefer to use measures other than IMF financial assistance. Examples of the latter situation include Brazil and Colombia. Even though these countries possess sizable Reserve Positions in the Fund, such that drawings would initially come within the scope of the gold and super gold tranches, a preference has been demonstrated for adjustment by means of flexible exchange rates. Again, the two factors which might account for a low level of drawings may be interrelated, since alternative action may be taken in advance of anticipated balance-of-payments deficits. This might happen where, although corrective measures would no doubt involve welfare costs, these costs are estimated to be less than the overall cost of IMF credit. This is particularly likely to be the case if a country views IMF policies as inappropriate to the realisation of its own objectives.

IMF credit is conditional in two respects. First, access is constrained quantitatively by such things as the size of the member's quota. A question here is whether the determinants of access provide an accurate indicator of financial need. The second aspect of conditionality relates to the fact that the largest part of Fund credit is granted only on the acceptance, by drawing members, of certain policy requirements. A question here is whether the requirements are appropriate to LDCs. Let us move on to examine each of these questions by studying the access which LDCs have to IMF finance under the quota system.

The quota system

Quotas are significant because they determine, first, a member's voting rights in the Fund; second, the extent of a member's ordinary drawing rights with the Fund; third, the extent of a member's access to other special facilities in the Fund, such as the CFF, BSFF and EFF; fourth, the size of a member's SDR allocation; and fifth, the size of a member's subscription to the Fund.

The quotas initially used by the IMF were rather loosely based on a formula worked out for the United States Treasury by Raymond Mikesell. Quotas were fixed at approximately 90 per cent of

> 2 per cent of national income in 1940
>
> *plus* 5 per cent of gold and dollar balances on 1 July 1943
>
> *plus* 10 per cent of the maximum variation in exports between 1934 and 1938
>
> *plus* 10 per cent of average imports between 1934 and 1938

the resulting total being increased in the same ratio as that which the country's average annual exports in the periods between 1934 and 1938 bore to its national income. The reason for calculating quotas at 90 per cent of a certain figure was to leave some leeway for an addition to any quota which did not adequately reflect the economic weight of any particular country.

In fact it has been shown[4] that to a considerable extent the quota formula was spurious, since it had previously been agreed between the US and UK Treasuries that the total amount of quotas should be about $8000m, that the US quota should be about $2500m and that the UK quota should be about half that of the US one. Furthermore, it had been agreed that the USSR and China should have the third and fourth largest quotas respectively. It has been suggested by Marquez (1970) that a trial-and-error process was used to derive a quota formula which would generate the desired results. At it turned out, quotas were not rigidly based on the formula, but instead the formula was taken as a point of departure for negotiations.[5]

The Articles of Agreement provided for a five-yearly general review of quotas, and also allowed individual quotas to be reviewed at any time merely at the request of the member concerned. Apart from one or two modifications, however, there was little change in quotas over the period 1946–55. In 1955 however, the Second General Review of Quotas revealed that a number of members with small quotas wished to increase them. To meet this desire the Fund pursued a 'Small Quotas Policy' by which it provided that quotas below $5 million could be increased to $7.5 million, quotas of $5–8 million could be increased to $10 million, quotas of $10 million could be increased to $15 million, and quotas of $15 million could be increased to $20 million.

In 1957, however, the fact that most drawings on the Fund had necessitated waivers encouraged the Fund to consider whether quotas were generally too small.[6] Such a view was supported by a staff report,

International Reserves and Liquidity. As a result of this and other deliberations, in 1959 there was a general 50 per cent increase in quotas, although in fact some members increased their quotas by more, some by less, and some not at all. One implication of the general increase in quotas was that no member was required to have a quota of less than $11·25 million. For many small countries a quota of $11·25 million exceeded the quota which would have been derived for the Bretton Woods formula.

Subsequent to the general increase in quotas in 1959, and following requests by the UAR, Syria and El Salvador for increases to their quotas, attention shifted to the specific problem of export instability. Staff research tended to support the argument that members with small quotas had failed to maintain the appropriateness of their quota position in comparison with the industrial countries (see Horsefield, 1969a).A major reason for this was the variability of the exports of small-quota countries (mostly LDCs). Largely in connection with the Fund's policies on compensatory finance, the Bretton Woods formula was revised during 1962 and 1963, the intention of the revision being to increase the relative share of small quotas in the total of Fund quotas. It was also decided that members experiencing export fluctuations to a degree not adequately alleviated by the provision of the CFF should be permitted to increase their quotas.

In 1965 the Fourth General Review of Quotas showed that the total size of quotas was again inadequate in relation to the potential demands on Fund resources and quotas were increased by 25 per cent. As a result the normal minimum quota became $15 million.

In 1969, in the Fifth General Review of Quotas, it was again proposed to increase quotas. A 35.5 per cent increase in quotas was approved in 1970. Although the overall increase in quotas was 35.5 per cent, the opportunity was taken to adjust individual quotas on the basis of 'extensive and rather complex calculations resulting from quota formulas, bearing in mind that formulas and the resulting calculations are only a guide to the determination of quotas'.[7]

The Sixth General Review of Quotas was approved by the Governors of the IMF in 1976. The quota adjustment involved changes in the quota total, the distribution of quota shares and the mode of subscription payment. The quota total was increased under the Sixth General Review by approximately 32·5 per cent from SDR 29,200 million to SDR 39,000 million. The quota share of oil-exporting countries was doubled from 5 per cent to 10 per cent, whilst the collective share of other LDCs was maintained at 20·85 per cent. It was agreed that the 25 per cent of a member's subscription which previously had had to be paid in gold, should in future be paid either in SDRs, or in currencies of certain other members of the Fund (subject to their agreement) or in the member's own currency. Thus it is now possible for a member to pay its entire subscription in its own currency, with no obligation to repurchase.[8] This change in the mode of payment is quite significant for LDC members whose currency is held by the Fund in excess ·of 100 per cent of the relevant quota, since, previously, the only way in which they had been able to derive the extra conditional liquidity associated with a quota increase was to sacrifice a measure of unconditional liquidity, by paying out gold.[9]

A major criticism of the quota system from the viewpoint of LDCs relates to the nature of the formula upon which quotas are based. Since quotas take little explicit recognition of the industrial and trading structure which many LDCs have — for instance, their reliance on a few key exports, and the resulting variability in trade — they tend to understate the need of LDCs for international financial assistance. A more widely based formula for the fixing of quotas, one that did take such factors into consideration and give them weight, would no doubt result in an increase in the quotas of LDCs. Whilst an increase in quotas could provide significant benefits to LDCs, little cost, in the form, say, of inflation, would be imposed on the developed countries, since the absolute values involved would be small.

The need for IMF-based financial assistance depends on the variability of the balance of payments, the availability of alternative sources of liquidity, the terms on which such assistance is granted, and the costs of adjustment. On all these counts the need of LDCs for financial assistance from the IMF could legitimately be assessed as exceeding that of developed countries. LDCs in general possess relatively low levels of owned reserves, have little access to commercial funds and have a relatively high marginal productivity of funds. The failure of the international monetary system to provide LDCs with adequate liquidity may have forced them to take inappropriate corrective action and to over-use short- and medium-term suppliers' credits.[10] Certainly, during the first half of the 1970s the ratio of quotas to imports fell by almost 50 per cent in LDCs, inflation serving to reduce the real value of quotas. Even the Sixth General Review of Quotas failed to restore the quota — import ratio to earlier levels. Of course, it should be remembered that the value of exports also rose during this period, thus helping to neutralise the impact of rising import values on the balance of payments. The adequacy of Fund finance should be related to the incidence of deficits rather than simply the size of the components of the balance of payments. However, the fall in the quota–import ratio remains indicative of a failure adequately to adjust to an inflationary environment. Indeed, since LDC exports rose less rapidly than LDC imports, the incidence of deficits rose, and, therefore to maintain the degree of protection against deficits, quotas should have risen in tandem. This did not happen.

Another aspect of IMF credit relates to the repayment provisions. LDCs would no doubt favour a system whereby repayments are linked to the state of the balance of payments, the terms of trade and the amount of aid received. Certainly a fixed repayment period of between three and five years may misinterpret the nature of the balance-of-payments problems facing LDCs. In many cases these problems will have been caused by exogenous fluctuations in demand and supply over which LDCs have limited control and about which they can do little in the short- to medium-term. Given the low levels of income in LDCs, it could be maintained that the quota system has not been adequate in insulating these countries from the implications of such external disturbances. The relatively low level of income in LDCs could, in addition, constitute an egalitarian reason why LDCs might be asked to pay a lower rate of interest of their purchases from the IMF than developed countries pay.[11]

The conditions imposed by the IMF on the recipients of its financial assistance reflect the Fund as a short-term balance-of-payments stabilisation agency rather than a long-term development one. In certain circumstances short-term balance-of-payments stabilisation may not conflict with long-term development (indeed the 'Fund view' demonstrates a belief in their compatability), but in other circumstances the two objectives may conflict. In such cases the conditions attached to Fund assistance are likely to be viewed as inappropriate by LDCs whose main concern is the growth and development of their economies.[12]

The conditions stipulated by the IMF, as reflected in the published 'letters of intent', and 'performance criteria', usually involve some measure of domestic aggregate-demand deflation and trade and payments liberalisation. It might, of course, be expected that these broad categories of policy would go hand in hand, since the pursuit of a liberal system of trade and payments necessitates an alternative mechanism for reducing the demand for foreign exchange; aggregate-demand deflation is one such alternative. The IMF's observed preference for demand-deflationary policies in turn reflects the defined objectives of the Fund in terms of establishing balance-of-payments equilibria and a free system of multilateral payments.

Demand deflation, which is designed to reduce imports to a level consistent with balance-of-payments equilibrium, may yield welfare benefits by lowering the rate of inflation; though even in this context it is by no means self-evident that a moderate rate of inflation is undesirable in a developing economy, either because it helps to generate domestic saving and thereby provide finance for investment, or because in conditions of downward price rigidity price increases are required in order to provide resource allocational indicators.[13] Similarly, trade liberalisation may involve LDCs in welfare costs,[14] not least in terms of the deterioration in the balance of payments which may ensue where the liberalisation is unilateral. In fact, it might be argued that the balance-of-payments policy most relevant to LDCs is trade liberalisation in developed countries. This would help LDCs to correct their balance-of-payments deficits through export expansion rather than import contraction. Clearly, in certain situations – for instance, where domestic-demand inflation is not a major problem, the level of unemployment is high, and the rate of growth is low – export expansion would have benefits not only for the balance of payments but also for the domestic economy.[15]

In the situation in which many LDCs find themselves, the use of trade controls and/or some form of multiple-exchange practice might be quite sensible. Import controls and multiple-exchange practices may help to improve the balance of payments at a lower cost in terms of inflation than would the alternative of exchange-rate depreciation, or at a lower cost in terms of unemployment and forgone domestic production than would the alternative of demand deflation. Although import restriction might harm future growth prospects, it would not rely on a reduction in current income to bring about payments equilibrium, as does an internal demand-contractionary policy. Futhermore, trade liberalisation may impede the growth of the indigenous manufacturing sector, which, before a certain stage of development, may have difficulty in competing with foreign producers who, because of their larger scale, possess lower unit costs.

Trade liberalisation and internal-demand deflation have, according to Payer (1974), generated still other undesirable consequences for LDCs. These have been: a takeover of domestic production by foreign-owned multinationals (caused by falling domestic sales and increasing costs); a simultaneously cost-inflationary and demand-deflationary situation stemming from an attempt to balance the budget by raising the price of public utility goods and services; an increase in the debt-service payments arising from the foreign borrowing undertaken in an attempt to fill the foreign-exchange gap created by trade and payments liberalisation; and the increased importation of non-essential goods.

A perhaps rather more fundamental criticism is, as noted earlier, that the conditions stipulated by the Fund misinterpret the basic cause of balance-of-payments deficits in many LDCs. The Fund's policy approach is implicitly designed to deal with disequilibria which have been generated internally, where, given time, it is within the scope of each country to remove or reduce the causal elements of the disequilibrium. No doubt in some LDCs balance-of-payments difficulties have been caused or enhanced by domestic excesses and in such cases the Fund view may be quite appropriate. Indeed the Fund may fulfil a useful role in directing such countries towards the appropriate domestic policies and in providing the financial assistance needed to facilitate the required internal adjustment. In many instances, however, balance-of-payments difficulties in LDCs are caused not by internal mismanagement but by exogenous variations in the demand for and supply of key commodities. The balance-of-payments problems then reflect the industrial and trading structure of the countries and not over-expansionary domestic-demand management. In these circumstances conventional Fund policy may impose considerable short- and long-term costs on LDCs. For instance, an LDC experiencing balance-of-payments difficulties caused by a demand-induced fall in export earnings is likely to be already experiencing a fall in income and a rise in unemployment. The prescription of further demand deflation will impose extra costs in these directions. In addition, monetary and fiscal contraction is likely to impair industrial development and diversification and thereby prevent the LDC from reducing the incidence of, and its vulnerability to, future fluctuations in foreign-trade earnings and payments. Also, to the extent that there exists an 'external commodity cycle',[16] short-term adjustments in domestic demand may not even be necessary if a slightly longer-term view is taken. In the long run, deficits generated by the commodity cycle will be self-correcting, and what is required is a longer-term facility for financing the non-synchronisation between import payments and export earnings under which immediate adjustment is not requested.[17]

It emerges, then, that the policies conventionally supported by the IMF are not necessarily the ones most appropriate to LDCs. This, of course, would not matter if, after promising to adopt such policies, in order to secure Fund assistance, LDCs looked rather more to their own needs as they see them. Evidence collected by Reichmann and Stillson (1977) suggests, however, that this is not the situation. It does appear from this evidence that, in the clear majority of cases, LDCs which draw on the IMF do effectively put into practice the policies advocated by the Fund.

The compensatory financing facility

The CFF scheme has attracted three types of criticism: first, as to the manner in which an export shortfall is measured; second, as to the appropriateness of a short-term expedient such as the CFF for dealing with problems that are essentially long term; and third, as to the adequacy of the CFF even as a short-term facility.

The basic problem in measuring the size of an export shortfall lies in estimating what export earnings would have been in any particular year in normal circumstances. The IMF has approached this problem by assuming that the value of exports in any year will be an average of export values in the years of the period from two years before the year in question to two years after it. The CFF is therefore based on a five-year moving average centred on the shortfall year. Since information about future export earnings is not available, an estimate of normal export earnings in any particular year has often been made on the basis of historical data.[18] In addition, however, the Fund has attempted to forecast future export receipts. Before 1976 this had been done by considering the likely output of a country's principal exports, forecasting the state of markets for them and deducing from these forecasts what the country's export earnings were likely to be in each of the two years following the shortfall year. Following the 1975 liberalisation, export earnings for the two post-shortfall years have been 'deemed to be equal to the earnings in the two pre-shortfall years multiplied by the ratio of the sum of the earnings in the most recent three years to that in the three preceding years'.[19]

Since the size of a member's access to the CFF partly depends on the size of the estimated export shortfall, the way in which the trend export performance is measured is important, as is the absence of bias from the calculation. Where the trend is estimated accurately, export shortfalls and excesses will, over the long run, cancel one another out, but if the trend estimate is biased this will not be the case. If the normal export value is underestimated, access to compensatory finance will be reduced and there will be net export excesses. If the trend is overestimated, the value of shortfalls will rise and the value of excesses will fall: the existence of net shortfalls over the long term will create problems for repayment. The CFF estimation technique will give an unbiased result if earnings increase by a constant absolute amount. Where, however, earnings grow at a constant rate, the arithmetic average used by the IMF will result in a biased estimate of trend. In these circumstances, a moving geometric average of export earnings centred on the shortfall year would be more appropriate.

To illustrate the point that an inappropriate method of estimating the trend can lead to systematic over- or underestimation of normal export earnings in any year, imagine a situation where export earnings are growing at an annual rate of 100 per cent, such that over a five-year period they are 25, 50, 100, 200 and 400. Application of the CFF method to this series will result in an estimated trend value for year three of 155, whilst the appropriate trend value is actually 100. If, as appears to be the case, total export earnings have tended to grow at a constant rate rather than by constant absolute amounts, it follows that the CFF method of estimating trend is inappropriate and leads to the accumulation of debt.[20] Of course, if earnings stagnate, with a trend growth of zero, the problem of biased estimators disappears.

The CFF method of estimating the export shortfall may also be regarded as unsatisfactory in that it includes data for the shortfall year. This will result in underestimation, since the shortfall will be measured against a trend which itself gives a 20 per cent weighting to the shortfall.

One restriction on the use of the CFF which was embedded in the 1966 CFF arrangements but abandoned by the 1975 liberalization was that estimated export growth was effectively limited to a maximum of just over 3 per cent per year. Since, in most cases, the actual growth of nominal export earnings far exceeded an annual rate of 3 per cent, particularly, of course, during a period of inflation, this constraint on the measurement of export shortfalls was very significant, and served to reduce the real value of LDCs' access to the CFF.[21] The 1975 liberalisation, which removed the forecasting limit, was therefore important in terms of permitting estimated export shortfalls to be very much larger. Furthermore, the 1975 decision allowed earlier drawings to be made, since under this decision member countries were permitted to estimate data for half of the shortfall year. At the same time, quota limits on CFF drawings were retained (even though the limits were raised), thus ensuring that an overall constraint on drawings remained.

It has been estimated that, had the rules governing the CFF remained unchanged in 1976, the amount drawn under the facility would have been reduced from SDR 2350 million to SDR 500 million. Both the elimination of the forecasting limit and the increase in quota limits had a major quantitative impact on the use of the CFF. On its own, the elimination of the forecasting limit would have permitted drawings in 1976 to rise by SDR 1500 million, whilst, again on its own, the increase in quota limits would have allowed drawings to rise by SDR 1200 million.[22] The early-drawing procedure also contributed to the expansion of drawings in 1976.[23] Without this procedure six LDCs that did draw on the Fund under the CFF in 1976 would not have been able to do so, because of insufficient data.

The inadequacy of the CFF as a short-term measure has usually been argued on the basis of four reasons. First, the scheme is quantitatively inadequate in relation to the size of the problem.[24] Second, since the CFF applies only to shortfalls in export receipts caused by either a fall in price or in quantity sold, it does not compensate for those payments difficulties which are caused by externally generated increases in import prices, or by bad harvests which force a member country to make additional outlays on food imports. Thus, in relating only to export shortfalls and not, more generally, to a deterioration in the terms of trade, the IMF has tended to neglect increases in import expenditure, which from a balance-of-payments and/or development angle may be equally damaging. Indeed, it is quite possible that a country's balance-of-payments position will be deteriorating at the same time as export earnings are rising, or are showing an excess over trend, simply because an increase in import prices may cause the real value of exports, expressed in terms of imports, to fall. If the purpose behind the CFF is to protect countries against fluctuations caused to their foreign-exchange holdings by external pressures that are largely beyond their control, then it would appear logical to protect against rising import prices as well as against falling export prices. Third, the CFF implicitly assumes that a drawing member can reverse and offset a shortfall in export receipts within three years. There appears to be no strong theoretical or empirical justification for such an assumption. Fourth, the trade basis of the CFF results in a skewed distribution of benefits. The low-income LDCs receive a relatively small proportion of CFF assistance even as a percentage of GNP.[25] There may be a case for reorganising the CFF in a way that brings about a more egalitarian distribution of financial assistance. This could be achieved by making the terms of access to the CFF dependent on country status.

Perhaps the principal criticism of the CFF scheme, though, is that it fails to deal with the more fundamental, long-term problems which face LDCs, problems such as worsening terms of trade, the existing structure of production and trade, and in particular the heavy concentration on the export of one or two commodities.[26] To halt a decline in the terms of trade or to neutralise its adverse implications requires a change in the structure of trade and production, but in order to bring about such changes long-term finance and capital is needed. The provision of such finance, however, cannot be reconciled with the philosophy of the Fund as a short-term balance-of-payments stabilisation agency. From this viewpoint it is unfortunate that the scheme for Supplementary Financial Measures discussed at the first meeting of the UNCTAD[27] was not pursued. The idea behind the SFM scheme was to provide longer-term compensation to countries in which unexpected shortfalls in export receipts adversely affected the implementation of an IBRD-vetted development plan. The availability, of SFM, so it was thought by proposers of the scheme, might serve to improve the planning of development and the reliability of such plans. Although the SFM would not in themselves have provided long-term aid, they would have lent some long-term stability to the development process and have helped avoid the disruption of development caused by export shortfalls. One proposed feature of the SFM was that the availability of assistance would be negotiated before a particular development plan was embarked upon, so that the LDCs involved would thereby be assured of the immediate and certain supply of resources as and when required. By protecting development plans, the SFM, unlike the CFF, would have gone some way towards ensuring that a user of the measures would stand less chance of experiencing future instability in export earnings. The scheme for SFM might well have fostered the closer link between the IMF, as a provider of short-term stabilisation assistance, and the IBRD, as a provider of longer-term finance, that many commentators have considered to be highly desirable.[28] Inasmuch as the use of the CFF does reflect export concentration,[29] the long-term answer to the related balance-of-payments difficulties is to reduce the price instability of primary products, or to assist LDCs in the diversification of their export base, which would weaken the causal link between commodity instability and export-earnings and balance-of-trade instability.

The buffer stock financing facility

The principal criticism that can be directed at the BSFF is implied by the fact that the facility has been so little used. The low level of usage in turn reflects the difficulties which surround the organisation of international buffer-stock schemes.[30]

The oil facility

Although the OF was a short-term expedient designed by the IMF to help member countries deal with some of the balance-of-payments problems caused by the rise in the price of oil, the facility incorporated a number of interesting features. One was the way in which the OF complemented the CFF. Whilst the latter concentrates exclusively on the balance-of-payments problems caused by an export shortfall, the OF concentrated on the implications of a rise in the price of imports. A second feature was that the OF begot the Subsidy Account, which was designed and intended to make OF drawings in effect concessionary for the poorest LDCs in the world. Since both insulation from the implications of increases in import prices and subsidisation of interest rates could be regarded as significant steps forward in the relationship between the LDCs and the international monetary system, a major criticism of the OF is that its existence was temporary and that it was concerned only with oil.

Further rather more general comments of a quantitative nature could, of course, be made. The provisions of the OF were such that member countries were not fully compensated for the short-term balance-of-payments effects of the oil-price rise. The implications of this were that members had to find alternative sources of finance, or adjust their economies in a way that from a long-term point of view might not be desirable. For many LDCs, the availability of alternative, commercial sources of finance was and is fairly strictly limited, and in any case the cost of commercial finance is high relative to that of IMF finance; furthermore, the costs of adjustment are likely to be higher in LDCs than in developed countries. Even the repayment provisions of the OF required quite rapid adjustment to be made. At best, from the point of view of non oil-exporting LDCs, the OF operated as an imperfect recycling device.

The extended fund facility

It is perhaps rather premature to evaluate the EFF. At the time of writing, only two drawings have been made under this facility since its introduction in 1974. In prospect, however, the EFF offers a significant advance in the provision of international finance to LDCs. The facility explicitly recognises that LDCs may require longer-term finance than is provided by conventional credit-tranche drawings. Related to this, it further recognises that many observed balance-of-payments difficulties may constitute the manifestation of structural misallocation. Finally, the EFF specifically views the balance of payments in the context of development policy.[31]

EFF finance, in common with almost all IMF-based finance, is conditional, and is granted in support of acceptable domestic economic policies.[32] From the point of view of LDCs, the usefulness of the EFF will largely depend on what policies the Fund sees as appropriate in particular situations and what policies it is prepared to support. In this respect the EFF is similar to the credit tranches and stand-by agreements. The EFF is dissimilar to these other facilities in terms of the amount that may be drawn (the EFF allows for larger drawings), the period over which the arrangement exists, (three years as opposed to one year), and the period of time over which repurchases are conducted (four to eight years as opposed to three to five).

In many respects the EFF as just outlined should at least to a degree meet some of the criticisms that have been directed at other IMF facilities. Even so, the EFF still rests on the implicit assumption that required structural modification can be achieved within three years; it still concentrates attention and puts emphasis on the balance of payments, rather than development, although accepting that medium-term policies may be required to correct balance-of-payments deficits; and it still fails formally to provide LDCs with a co-ordinated package of development aid and international financial support. In this sense the EFF may be assessed as falling some way short of schemes for a development insurance fund or, indeed, supplementary financing measures. Furthermore, the EFF might be criticised on grounds similar to those put forward by critics of the conditionality of Fund assistance, if it could be shown that the policies advocated by the IMF have achieved balance-of-payments equilibrium at the cost of development. The Fund, of course, views development and balance-of-payments equilibrium as complementary.

An indication of the relevance of this potential criticism may be gleaned from examining the two cases of EFF drawings. In particular, let us examine the case of Kenya. Since independence in 1964 and up until 1970, Kenya displayed a real annual growth rate of about 6·5 per cent, and overall balance-of-payments surpluses. In the 1970s the growth rate fell substantially and for most of the time the balance of payments moved into deficit. The Fund's diagnosis of the deterioration in Kenya's economic situation noted a number of trends. These included an emerging resource constraint, with investment exceeding saving; a preference for industrial development, to the relative neglect of agriculture; and a movement towards capital-intensive techniques. These trends were seen as having been caused by tariff policy, which accorded significant protection to manufacturing industry; official action which served to keep down the prices of staple foodstuffs; and an increase in wages relative to the price of capital goods. One outcome of these trends, according to the Fund, was a rise in imports, partly reflecting capital-intensive industrialisation and partly reflecting the increased demand for consumers goods.

The economic programme that the Fund supported included as targets an average rate of real GDP growth of at least 5 per cent per annum; a rate of inflation significantly below the world rate; and the elimination, within five years, of the need for balance-of-payments assistance. The policies designed to realise these targets involved the control of private consumption through various taxes, including sales tax, capital gains tax, and an urban property tax; the control of public consumption; the enforcement of wage guidelines; a redirection of government expenditure towards the less capital-intensive agricultural sector; an adjustment in tariff policy designed to reduce the inducements being offered to capital-intensive and import-intensive production; and a credit policy to moderate domestic demand.

Although the approved economic policy does indeed involve aggregate deflationary aspects such as credit control and fiscal contraction, the programme also involves significant and seemingly relevant structural elements which are intended to encourage stable development. Furthermore, it is interesting to note that the Fund and the IBRD made co-ordinated policy recommendations to the Kenyan government, which received, in addition to the EFF drawing on the Fund, an IBRD loan of $30 million. In combination, the IBRD loan and the EFF drawing are designed to permit Kenya to pursue appropriate long-term structural policies without the encroachment of short-term development or balance-of-payments constraints. In effect, this close co-operation between the IMF and the IBRD comes some way towards the more formal aid and financing approach suggested earlier in this chapter. Under such an approach, LDCs would know that approved development plans would not have to be sacrificed or modified for short-term balance-of-payments reasons, and that development aid provided by the IBRD would be supported by balance-of-payments finance provided by the IMF.

TABLE 8.6
Participants' SDR Positions at 31 December 1976
(SDR millions)

	Allocations	Net acquisition or net use	Holdings	Holdings as percentage of allocations
All countries	9314·8	−659·4	8655·5	92·9
Industrial countries	6177·7	789·7	6967·4	112·8
Other Europe	405·1	−141·4	263·7	65·1
Australia, NZ, S. Africa	384·0	−297·7	86·3	22·5
Oil-exporting countries	374·2	−46·9	327·3	87·5
Algeria	40·3	2·8	43·1	106·9
Bahrain	−	−	−	−
Indonesia	90·2	−86·1	4·1	4·5
Iran	61·9	2·4	64·3	103·9
Iraq	23·2	4·8	28·0	120·5
Kuwait	−	−	−	−
Libya	−	−	−	−
Nigeria	45·6	15·6	61·2	134·2
Oman	0·7	−	0·7	100·0
Qatar	−	−	−	−
Saudi Arabia	−	−	−	−
United Arab Emirates	−	−	−	−
Venezuela	112·3	13·7	126·0	112·2
Other less-developed Areas	1974·0	−963·1	1010·8	51·2
Other Western Hemisphere	766·8	−367·4	399·4	52·1
Argentina	152·5	−74·3	78·2	51·3
Bolivia	12·8	−5·9	6·9	54·0
Brazil	152·5	18·4	171·0	112·1
Chile	54·7	−6·4	48·3	88·3
Colombia	54·4	−30·1	24·3	44·7
Costa Rica	11·0	−9·8	1·2	11·3
Dominican Rep.	14·5	−8·5	6·0	41·4
Ecuador	11·2	−5·0	6·3	55·7
El Salvador	11·7	−7·6	4·0	34·6
Guatemala	11·9	−0·4	11·4	96·4
Haiti	6·6	−5·3	·1·2	18·9
Honduras	8·5	−5·9	2·7	31·2
Mexico	124·2	−123·3	0·9	0·7
Nicaragua	8·9	−5·5	3·5	38·8

Table 8.6 cont.

	Allocations	Net acquisition or net use	Holdings	Holdings as percentage of allocations
Other Western Hemisphere (cont.)				
Panama	12·4	− 7·2	5·2	42·0
Paraguay	6·6	−	6·6	100·0
Peru	40·5	− 37·2	3·3	8·2
Uruguay	23·9	− 20·2	3·7	15·5
Bahamas	−	−	−	−
Barbados	2·8	−	2·8	100·0
Grenada	−	0·1	0·1	−
Guyana	6·8	− 3·2	3·5	52·2
Jamaica	17·7	− 16·9	0·8	4·4
Trinidad and Tobago	20·8	− 13·2	7·6	36·4
Other Middle East	153·6	− 97·4	56·2	36·6
Cyprus	8·9	− 1·0	7·9	89·0
Egypt	65·2	− 44·9	20·3	31·1
Israel	42·8	− 34·2	8·7	20·2
Jordan	7·6	− 0·2	7·4	97·2
Lebanon	−	−	−	−
Syria	17·0	− 10·3	6·8	39·8
Yemen, Arab Rep.	2·1	−	2·1	100·0
Yemen, People's Dem. Rep.	9·9	− 6·8	3·0	30·8
Other Asia	674·9	− 290·4	384·4	57·0
Afghanistan	12·8	− 7·6	5·1	40·2
Bangladesh	−	16·1	16·1	−
Burma	20·8	− 13·2	7·6	36·5
Cambodia	8·5	− 8·2	0·3	3·9
China, Rep. of	−	−	−	−
India	326·2	− 137·1	189·1	58·0
Korea	22·2	− 15·4	6·8	30·6
Laos	4·5	− 3·0	1·5	32·8
Malaysia	60·6	4·5	65·1	107·4
Nepal	2·2	− 0·1	2·1	95·5
Pakistan	81·6	− 49·7	32·0	39·2
Philippines	51·5	− 37·9	13·6	26·4
Singapore	−	−	−	−
Sri Lanka	34·0	− 21·6	12·4	36·6
Thailand	28·5	0·4	28·9	101·4
Vietnam	19·8	− 19·0	0·7	3·7
Fiji	1·4	− 0·1	1·3	96·4
Papua New Guinea	−	1·7	1·7	−
Western Samoa	0·2	− 0·2	−	−

Table 8.6 cont.

	Allocations	Net acquisition or net use	Holdings	Holdings as percentage of allocations
Other Africa	378·7	− 207·9	170·8	45·1
Benin	4·5	−	4·5	100·0
Botswana	1·6	−	1·5	100·0
Burundi	6·6	− 3·5	3·0	46·1
Cameroon	10·5	− 1·7	8·8	83·6
Central African Empire	4·4	− 2·7	1·6	37·2
Chad	4·5	− 2·5	1·9	42·9
Comoros	−	−	−	−
Congo, People's Rep.	4·5	− 2·4	2·1	46·3
Equatorial Guinea	2·7	− 0·9	1·8	65·3
Ethiopia	−	−	−	−
Gabon	4·8	− 0·2	4·6	96·5
Gambia	2·3	− 0·3	2·0	85·8
Ghana	30·1	− 23·5	6·7	22·1
Guinea Rep.	8·3	− 5·4	2·9	34·5
Ivory Coast	14·3	− 2·5	11·8	82·4
Kenya	15·6	− 12·8	2·8	17·8
Lesotho	1·6	− 1·1	0·5	31·8
Liberia	9·5	− 6·0	3·5	36·9
Malagasy Rep.	8·7	− 6·9	1·9	21·3
Malawi	5·1	− 0·8	4·3	84·8
Mali Rep.	7·5	− 4·8	2·8	36·5
Mauritania	4·5	− 3·3	1·2	26·7
Mauritius	7·4	− 4·7	2·7	36·5
Morocco	39·2	− 28·8	10·4	26·5
Niger	4·5	− 0·1	4·4	98·7
Rwanda	6·6	− 4·2	2·4	36·4
Senegal	11·4	− 10·3	1·2	10·1
Sierra Leone	7·8	− 4·9	2·9	37·4
Somalia	6·6	− 2·3	4·3	65·0
Sudan	24·9	− 24·9	−	−
Swaziland	2·7	− 1·8	0·9	34·7
Tanzania	14·3	− 9·3	5·1	35·3
Togo	5·1	− 0·1	5·0	98·2
Tunisia	14·7	− 4·7	10·0	67·8
Uganda	13·9	− 13·0	0·9	6·4
Upper Volta	4·5	−	4·4	99·6
Zaire	39·2	− 12·1	27·1	69·2
Zambia	24·6	− 5·4	19·2	77·9

Source. IMF, *International Financial Statistics*

The SDR Account

In addition to the sources of international finance through the General Account, LDCs have obtained extra liquidity in the form of SDRs. The SDR facility, which was introduced in 1970 in order to provide the international monetary system with a source of liquidity which was independent of both the unregulated outcome of the US balance of payments and current gold production and the attitudes of speculators, has provided the participants in the scheme with significant, though comparatively small, amounts of liquidity. As of December 1976, a total of SDR 9315 million had been allocated, of which SDR 1974 million had been allocated to non oil-exporting LDCs. On average, each industrial country has received SDR 441 million whilst each non oil-exporting LDC has received only SDR 25 million. On the other hand, LDCs have generally made greater proportionate use of the facility than have industrial countries. During the first basic period of allocation, 1970–3, LDCs, including oil-exporting LDCs, were net users of SDRs to the value of SDR 835 million, with fifty-nine of the eighty-four participating LDCs having used them. With the exceptions of the United Kingdom, the United States, France and Italy, industrial countries made net acquisitions of SDRs. By December 1976, and of a total allocation of SDR 2348 million, LDCs had made a net use of SDR 1010 million. By the same time industrial countries, as a group, had made a net acquisition of SDR 790 million.[33]

The pattern of SDR use and acquisition amongst LDCs is presented in Table 8.6. It emerges from this table that, whilst, in general, non oil-exporting LDCs have used 48·8 per cent of their allocated SDRs, there has been great variation. This diversity is illustrated more sharply in Table 8.7, which shows that, while only three non oil-exporting LDCs have acquired SDRs, seventy-two have made net use of them; in nineteen of these cases, net use has been so great as to make reconstitution necessary.

The benefits of the SDR scheme for LDCs

LDCs are likely to benefit from the SDR facility in a number of ways: first, by holding allocated SDRs and thereby adding to reserves (the benefit representing the opportunity cost of reserve acquisition by alternative means); second, by using SDRs to pay off debts with the IMF, thereby avoiding the opportunity cost associated with raising the

TABLE 8.7
Net Use of SDRs by Non Oil-Exporting LDCs, As of December 1976

Net acquisitions (holdings over 100 per cent of allocation)	No net use or acquisition (holdings equal to 100 per cent of allocation)	Net use, but above reconstitution level (holdings 30–100 per cent of allocation)	Net use and below reconstitution level (holdings less than 30 per cent of allocation)
Brazil	Paraguay	Argentina	Costa Rica
Malaysia	Barbados	Bolivia	Haiti
Thailand	Yemen, Arab Rep.	Chile	Mexico
	Benin	Colombia	Peru
	Botswana	Dominican Rep.	Uruguay
		Ecuador	Jamaica
		El Salvador	Israel
		Guatemala	Cambodia
		Honduras	Philippines
		Nicaragua	Vietnam
		Panama	Western Samoa
		Guyana	Ghana
		Trinidad and Tobago	Kenya
		Cyprus	Malagasy Rep.
		Egypt	Mauritania
		Jordan	Morocco
		Syria	Senegal
		Yemen, People's Dem. Rep.	Sudan
		Afghanistan	Uganda
		Burma	
		India	
		Korea	
		Laos	
		Nepal	
		Pakistan	
		Sri Lanka	
		Fiji	
		Burundi	
		Cameroon	
		Central African Empire	
		Chad	
		Congo	
		Equatorial Guinea	
		Gabon	
		Gambia	

Table 8.7 cont.

Net acquisitions (holdings over 100 per cent of allocation)	No net use or acquisition (holdings equal to 100 per cent of allocation)	Net use, but above reconstitution level (holdings 30–100 per cent of allocation)	Net use and below reconstitution level (holdings less than 30 per cent of allocation)
		Guinea Rep.	
		Ivory Coast	
		Lesotho	
		Liberia	
		Malawi	
		Mali Rep.	
		Mauritius	
		Niger	
		Rwanda	
		Sierra Leone	
		Somalia	
		Swaziland	
		Tanzania	
		Togo	
		Tunisia	
		Upper Volta	
		Zaire	
		Zambia	

necessary foreign exchange; and, third, by using SDRs to acquire convertible currencies, which may then be used to buy real goods and services.[34] LDCs may also gain in development terms from the actions and policies induced in developed countries as a response to SDR allocations; actions which could result in an increased capacity for LDCs both to earn foreign exchange by means of exporting to developed countries, and to acquire foreign exchange through increased investment in, and aid to, LDCs by developed countries. Although such indirect benefits may be substantial,[35] they are, unfortunately, difficult to measure. The other benefits are perhaps more susceptible to quantification.

Particularly interesting in this context is the size of the real-resource gain to LDCs which has resulted from the SDR scheme. The potential real-resource gain over a five-year period, bearing in mind the 30 per cent reconstitution provision, is equal to 70 per cent of the initial SDR allocation. Allowing for the fact that net users of SDRs pay interest on their net use, it follows that

$$P = \frac{70}{100}Q(A) - I^* \tag{1}$$

where P is the total potential permanent real-resource transfer equivalent of SDR allocation, Q is the relevant quota value, A is the SDR allocation expressed as a percentage of the quota, and I^* represents the interest payments associated with full potential SDR net use. More generally,

$$I = r(N) \tag{2}$$

where r is the rate of interest charged to net users of SDRs and N represents the value of SDRs actually used by a participant or group of participants in the SDR scheme. In equation (1), P varies positively with both Q and A and inversely with I^*, whilst I^* varies positively with r.

The *realised* real-resource transfer resulting from the SDR scheme is a less straightforward concept, since changes in SDR holdings which might be used to show real-resource gains do not necessarily provide precise information on the direction and nature of resource flows.

Real-resource transfers will occur as a result of SDR allocation for as long as the SDRs are used to acquire foreign exchange which is then spent on goods and services. SDR recipients are not, of course, compelled to spend SDRs. They may hold them, or they may transfer them to the General Account of the IMF in order to meet repurchases or pay charges, or they may use them to meet interest charges. Thus

$$R = Q(A) - T^G - H \tag{3}$$

or

$$R^* = Q(A) - H \tag{3a}$$

where R is the total realised real-resource transfer equivalent of SDR allocation, T^G represents transfers to the General Account, defined here to include interest charges, and H represents that part of the SDR allocation added to reserves. Transfers to the General Account represent debt cancellation, and measure additional aid only to the extent that a participant's need to raise foreign exchange is thereby removed, thus allowing the cancellation of future negative real-resource flows. R and R^* give the alternative ways of estimating the realised real-resource transfer, one including and the other excluding T^G.

In the short term it is possible that $R > P$, but in these circumstances reconstitution will be required. When $R < P$, the SDR recipient or group of recipients is not using all its potential access to real resources.

Ignoring, for a moment, certain problems of aggregation, to which we shall return, and taking figures from *International Financial Statistics*, the situation for non oil-exporting LDCs as a group on 31 December 1976 (all figures expressed in SDR millions) was that

$$Q(A) = 1974\cdot0$$

$$\frac{70[Q(A)]}{100} = 1381\cdot8$$

$$T^G = 659\cdot3$$

$$H = 1010\cdot8$$

$$\therefore R = 1974\cdot0 - 659\cdot3 - 1010\cdot8 = 303\cdot9$$

$$\text{or } R^* = 1974\cdot0 - 1010\cdot8 = 963\cdot2$$

These figures, which are based on IMF SDR net-acquisition and net-use data, may, however, fail to give an accurate picture of real-resource flows. The *ex post* data relating to SDR net use and acquisition which appear in *International Financial Statistics* are comparative-static in nature. The data provide information about the current position of SDR participants, but do not provide information about the channels through which these positions were reached. In an attempt to understand why this omission is significant it may be helpful to explain the process by which SDR-related real-resource transfers are activated. A participant wishing to engineer a real-resource transfer will, through the IMF, exchange SDRs for convertible currencies, which may then be spent.[36] The spending participant will not necessarily, however, spend this convertible currency in the country or countries that acquire its activated SDRs. Thus it is quite possible that country A may draw currencies from country B and spend them in country C. Country A will lose reserves but will gain real resources. In country B, the composition of reserves may change if foreign exchange as opposed to domestic currency is swapped for SDRs, while country C will acquire foreign-exchange reserves but will lose real resources. Only where country B and country C are one and the same will the observed acquisition of SDRs also imply an equivalent real-resource loss. In fact it is quite likely that the participants which sacrifice real resources will also be the ones which acquire SDRs. This is likely not because the acquisition of SDRs in itself causes a loss of real resources, but because those surplus countries which acquire reserves through net exportation (at a real-resource cost) will in all probability be those designated by the Fund to accept SDRs in excess of their cumulative allocation.

One outcome of this state of affairs is that any particular reported position of SDR participants may be consistent with a number of real-resource flow patterns. This will be true both within and between IMF country groups. As a general illustration of the point let us take the position for SDR participants on 31 July 1973. This is shown in Table 8.8.

TABLE 8.8

Participants' SDR Positions, 31 July 1973, 28 February 1975 and 31 December 1976 (SDR millions)

	Total allocations	Net acquisition or use (−) (31.7.73)	Net acquisition or use (−) (20.2.75)	Net acquisition or use (−) (31.12.76)
Industrial countries	6177·7	433·2	624·7	789·7
Other developed areas	789·1	−115·5	−288·8	−439·1
Less-developed areas	2348·0	−835·2	−792·1	−1010·0
Fund holdings		527·5	436·3	659·3

Source. IMF, *International Financial Statistics.*

This *ex post* position could be consistent with a range of resource-flow patterns. At one extreme it would be consistent with less-developed plus other developed areas realising a real-resource transfer of SDR 950·7 million from industrial countries, and the latter transferring SDR 527.5 million to the General Account.[37] It would also be consistent with less-developed and other developed areas realising a real-resource transfer of only SDR 307·7 million from industrial countries, and transferring SDR 527.5 million to the General Account. The position reported in the table, is, of course, also consistent with any set of events lying between these two extremes. Until the size of the LDC's SDR transfer to the General Account is known, it is not possible to make an accurate estimate of the size of their realised real-resource gain. Indeed, it is possible in theory, though rather unlikely in practice, that, whilst it is the developed countries that have acquired SDRs, the real-resource movements have been *within* the LDC group. The fact remains, however, that the net use of SDRs by LDCs need not imply an equivalent transfer of real resources from industrial countries to the LDCs.

The conclusion emerges that *International Financial Statistics* data only provide direct information about which participants acquired SDRs and which participants used them over a particular period of time. *At best*, the data only *imply* the direction, pattern and size of real-resource flows. To the extent that 'shuffling around' of SDR holdings will carry on for some time after their actual creation, the picture provided of real-resource flows, as indicated in net-use and net-acquisition data, may in any case tend to change. Equilibrium, even if achieved, is hardly likely to be stable. To illustrate this point, Table 8.8 provides additional information on participants' SDR positions in February 1975 and December 1976.

It would appear that between July 1973 and February 1975 LDCs, as a group, acquired SDRs. In making precise claims regarding the implications of the SDR scheme for the transfer of real resources from developed countries to LDCs, caution and careful analysis is clearly advisable. When, however, it is remembered that a substantial portion of the industrial countries' use of SDRs reflects the amortisation by the United States of previously accumulated, externally held dollar liabilities and the cancellation of previously accumulated debt by the United Kingdom, then, also bearing in mind LDCs' trade patterns, and particularly import patterns, it does seem reasonable to assume that the operation of the SDR scheme has brought about a considerable transfer of real resources from industrial countries to LDCs. LDCs have not had to pay for these real resources either in terms of running down their reserves or in terms of selling exports. The only cost to LDCs of using SDRs is the modest interest rate on their use, and the opportunity cost which represents the lost opportunity of increasing balance-of-payments security by increasing reserves. What can be unambiguously stated is that LDCs do seem to have benefited from the SDR scheme, by increased reserves, cancellation of debt with the IMF, and net inflows of real resources.

It is also fairly clear from Table 8.6 that not all LDCs have distributed the benefits equally between the various sources of benefit. This is demonstrated by the wide range of propensities to spend or use SDRs. Some LDCs, such as the Sudan and Western Samoa, have spent all their SDRs, thus taking no benefit in the form of positive reserve accumulation (though, clearly, SDRs may have prevented reserves from falling), whilst others, such as Brazil, Malaysia, Thailand, Paraguay, Barbados, the Yemen Arab Republic, Benin and Botswana, have in net terms, accumulated at least their entire allocation of SDRs, taking the whole of the benefit in terms of an addition to reserves.

The determination of SDR use

What accounts for the observed differences in LDCs' behaviour with respect to SDRs, or, in other words, what are the major determinants of SDR use? This is a question that has been examined by Leipziger (1975). He sets up a model which relates a country's SDR use to the state of the balance of payments, changes in reserve-asset levels, the composition of reserve-asset portfolios and the exogeneously determined supply of SDRs. On the basis of a cross-country regression analysis, Leipziger finds significant evidence that SDR use is positively related to the size of SDR allocations, the size of balance-of-payments deficits, and the ratio of foreign exchange to gold in reserve portfolios; and that it is negatively related to changes in the level of other reserve assets. These findings are consistent with *a priori* reasoning and suggest that SDRs are viewed as substitutes for foreign exchange and complements to gold.[38]

The observation that Western Hemisphere LDCs were showing a marked increasing marginal propensity to use SDRs, whilst in other LDCs this propensity was rising less rapidly (African LDCs) or falling (Middle Eastern and Asian LDCs), led Leipziger to test whether the determinants of SDR use were significantly different as between groups of LDCs.[39] He found that they were, and concluded therefore that LDCs should not be considered as homogeneous with respect to their response, in terms of SDR use, to a given set of economic parameters. In Latin American LDCs the general model performed well, but amongst the other LDCs it was discovered that SDR use was significantly influenced only by the balance of payments and SDR allocations, and even then it was less responsive to changes in these variables than it was in Latin American LDCs. It also emerges from Leipziger's study that LDCs appear to be more reluctant to use SDRs than foreign exchange to finance balance-of-payments deficits, but less reluctant to use SDRs than gold.

The distribution formula for SDRs

SDRs are currently allocated to participants in the SDR scheme on the basis of their quotas in the IMF. Allocations are expressed as a percentage of quotas on the day before the allocation is made. Thus the rate of allocation for the first year of the basic period of the SDR scheme was 16·8 per cent of quotas on 31 December 1969. The exercise of determining IMF quotas is, as we have already noted, not very precise, but individual quotas are approximately related to factors such as national income, the level of international reserves held and the magnitude and stability of the balance of payments.

Arguably, the use of quotas to decide the allocation of SDRs was determined first by considerations of expediency and a desire to get the scheme accepted and operating as soon as possible, and second by a general lack of concern over the distribution of SDRs. At the time that the SDR scheme was established, emphasis was being placed on the issue of the *global* adequacy of international liquidity rather than its distribution. In retrospect it may be suggested that the quota formula provides a singularly inappropriate basis upon which to determine the allocation of SDRs. Let us examine why this should be so.

First, to a certain extent, quotas still reflect the relative political bargaining power of IMF members rather than their economic demand for reserves as such. Even the economic criteria used tend to be based on old data. Second, quotas are designed to determine the extent of members' drawings from the General Account of the IMF. Essentially the General Account provides backed, conditional and short- to medium-term credit. As a result, quotas have tended to be biased towards countries possessing large reserves and convertible currencies. Although reserve creation occurs as a by-product of the use of the General Account, it is the prime stated objective of the Special Account. This account provides unbacked, unconditional and largely non-repayable funds. [40] Considerations relevant to determining the optimal allocation of credit facilities in the form of drawings on the General Account, such as the ability to repay, need not be relevant to the determination of the optimal allocation of owned reserves. Indeed, as we shall see, it is quite possible that opposite considerations will be appropriate in each of the two instances. Third, since SDRs constitute an international reserve asset the significance of which is crucially dependent on the willingness of the international community to accept them, and since the creation of SDRs was the result of international monetary co-operation, it might be argued that SDRs should be used for internationally agreed purposes and not to support such nationalistic and anti-social economic policies as certain countries might wish to pursue. [41] By allocating SDRs almost automatically and unconditionally to countries on the basis of quotas, the international community fairly effectively forgoes the opportunity to exert control over the uses to which SDRs are put. Fourth, but leading on from this third point, it could be suggested that, by tying SDR allocations to quotas, the IMF limits its ability to change the relative significance of conditional as against unconditional finance, either in general or in particular cases. If it is thought that conditional and unconditional finance perform different and seperate functions, it may be thought unwise to tie the two together. In the case of particular countries it may be wanted to increase owned reserves but not conditional finance, or the other way around. The current system for distributing SDRs does not conveniently permit this. This system of allocation does not allow for distributional selectivity other than that incorporated in the quota system.

The question now arises of what factors should determine the distribution of new reserves, and the extent to which this distribution is realised by the use of quotas. In an attempt to answer these questions, it may be noted that reserves are held as a precautionary stock of international purchasing power. Inasmuch as a country's reserves represent stored-up command over real and financial resources, they may be seen as a form of national wealth. From this point of view, it might be maintained that new reserves should be distributed on the basis of relative wealth measured, say, by income per capita. The establishment of a negative association between current wealth and new reserve allocation would, by allocating new owned reserves to poorer countries, engineer a movement towards a more equal international distribution of wealth. The quota formula, however, which was designed to determine conditional drawings on the Fund rather than to allocate largely unconditional purchasing power, distributes most of the command over resources represented by SDRs to rich countries, which have the highest quotas. Thus, the current system of SDR distribution initially tends to widen international wealth inequalities rather than to narrow them.

Extending the conceptualisation of reserves as wealth, reserves may be seen as a means of financing future balance-of-payments deficits. On the basis of this notion of reserves, it might be maintained that new reserves should be allocated to those countries which, in the first instance, are most likely to experience balance-of-payments instability or, more precisely, deficits, and which, in the second instance, experience the highest adjustment costs. Arguably, LDCs fit into both these categories.[42] For instance, factors such as the low level of development, the high concentration of production, the low level of factor mobility, the price inelasticity of demand for exports and imports and the inelasticity of supply of exports and import substitutes all tend to increase the costs of adjustment in LDCs. Furthermore, limited access to international capital markets, and the relatively high opportunity cost of reserve acquisition combine to provide a strong case for biasing the distribution of new reserves-to-hold in favour of LDCs. Although the quota formula takes some account of balance-of-payments instability, it takes little or no account of the cost of adjustment.

A broad conclusion might be that IMF quotas do not significantly reflect factors, such as wealth and the cost of adjustment, which theoretically should influence the distribution of SDRs. [43] As a result of basing allocations on national income and trade, the quota formula tends to bias the initial distribution of SDRs in favour of developed countries.

The Trust Fund

The first interim Trust Fund loan disbursements were made in January 1977 to twelve eligible LDCs—the Trust Fund's resources having come from five gold auctions. Six further auctions served to increase the Trust Fund's resources from SDR 198 million to SDR 402 million by mid 1977 and enabled another twelve of the sixty-one eligible LDCs to be assisted through the second interim loan disbursement. Table 8.9 shows the standing of the Trust Fund's disbursements as of July 1977; further loan disbursements, at six monthly intervals, are planned. The SDR 402 million available for loans following the first eleven gold auctions represents just over 10 per cent of the total quotas of the sixty-one LDCs eligible for Trust Fund assistance.

As Table 8.9 reveals, the Trust Fund represents both a relatively and an absolutely important source of financial assistance for a number of LDCs.[44] Advantages of the Trust Fund from the viewpoint of those LDCs eligible for assistance are that, first, Trust Fund loans are additional to normal drawings; second, loans are made at a concessionary interest rate; third, loans are subject to a relatively long repayment period; and, fourth, assistance is concentrated on the least-developed countries. Potential limitations relate to the size of total loan disbursements, which seem likely to be effectively constrained by the size of the profits derived from selling IMF gold, and the conditionality of the finance provided by the Trust Fund, though the conditions are in fact quite moderate. A significant feature of the Trust Fund is that its establishment has demonstrated a willingness by the IMF to use international monetary reform, in this case the reduction in the role of gold in international monetary affairs, for the specific benefit of the poorest countries in the world. Acceptance of such a principle has implications for the SDR–aid link proposal which is discussed in Chapter 11.

TABLE 8.9

Trust Fund's First Period Loan Disbursements, 1 July 1976 to 30 June 1978
(SDR millions)

Country	Total disbursements	First interim disbursements	Second interim disbursements
Bangladesh	13·375	–	13.375
Burma	6·420	–	6·420
Burundi	2·033	1·007	1·026
Congo	1·391	0·689	0·702
Egypt	20·116	–	20·116
Gambia	0·749	–	0·749
Grenada	0·214	–	0·214
Guinea	2·568	–	2·568
Haiti	2·033	1·007	1·026
Kenya	5·136	2·544	2·592
Lesotho	0·535	–	0·535
Liberia	3·103	1·537	1·566
Malawi	1·605	–	1·605
Mauritania	1·391	–	1·391
Morocco	12·091	5·989	6·102
Nepal	1·498	0·742	0·756
Pakistan	25·145	–	25·145
Philippines	16·585	8·215	8·370
Sierra Leone	2·675	–	2·675
Tanzania	4·494	2·226	2·268
Thailand	14·338	–	14·338
Western Samoa	0·214	0·106	0·108
Yemen, People's Dem. Rep.	3·103	1·537	1·566
Zaire	12·091	5·989	6·102
Total	152·903	31·588	121·315

Source. IMF Survey, 1 August 1977

Concluding Remarks

LDCs as a group have made considerable and growing use of IMF
facilities under both the General and the Special Account, and there can
be little doubt that they have benefited from the availability of such
assistance. However, the facilities that currently exist in the IMF may,
from the viewpoint of LDCs, be criticised on a number of counts, and it
is possible to suggest modifications to these existing facilities, and to put
forward ideas for new facilities, which would operate to the advantage

of LDCs whilst imposing little if any cost on developed countries. Over recent years, however, attention has been focused on two particular areas of reform. The first concerns the way in which the international monetary system might be used to help deal with the commodities problem, which causes or contributes to many of the balance-of-payments difficulties experienced by LDCs. The second concerns the notion of linking the allocation of SDRs with the provision of aid. We move on to examine these issues in Chapters 10 and 11. Before that, in the next chapter, we examine the use that LDCs have made of private sources of international financial assistance.

9 Private Sources of International Finance for LDCs

In addition to the IMF, there are various other sources of finance available to LDCs. Finance may be borrowed either officially, from foreign governments and international organisations, or privately, through international capital markets. Private borrowing may be in the form of bond issues or shorter-term credits. A certain proportion of short-term credit will be associated with trade and will be in the form of suppliers' credit, but a further source of private finance arises out of commercial borrowing from foreign banks, primarily operating through the Eurocurrency market.

Although LDCs still receive a very substantial amount of financial assistance through official channels, the significance of official financing relative to other sources of finance declined in the first half of the 1970s. Table 9.1 reveals the increasing role of private banks in financing the current-account deficits of non oil-exporting LDCs. Over the period 1968–75, while official borrowing rose at an annual average of 25·3 per cent, private long-term borrowing from banks located abroad rose by an annual average of 61·3 per cent, with most of the increase occurring after 1971, and in particular after 1973. Again, while in 1970 official financing constituted about 70 per cent of all borrowing conducted by LDCs, by 1975 the figure had fallen to only just over 60 per cent. During the same period the share of private borrowing rose from just under 30 per cent to almost 40 per cent.[1] Indeed of the loan commitments or debt contracted by all LDCs during 1975, 53·5 per cent was with private creditors, 19·5 per cent with international organisations, and 27 per cent with governments. During 1970, 42·8 per cent of total loan commitments had been with private creditors, 21·1 per cent with international organisations, and 36·1 per cent with governments. By the mid 1970s LDCs constituted the single most significant group of borrowers in the Eurocurrency market, accounting for well over 50 per cent of all

TABLE 9.1

Financing of Current Account Deficits in Non Oil-Exporting LDCs, 1968–75
(US$ thousand millions)

	1968	1969	1970	1971	1972	1973	1974	1975
Current account deficit	6·8	5·9	8·7	11·4	9·2	9·9	28·4	37·0
Financing through transactions that do not affect net debt positions	3·1	3·3	3·8	4·5	5·1	7·8	9·1	10·0
Net unrequited transfers received by governments of non-oil developing countries	1·8	1·8	1·9	2·2	2·3	4·4	4·9	6·1
Direct investment flows, net	1·3	1·5	1·2	1·7	2·2	3·4	4·2	3·9
SDR allocations and gold monetisation, net	–	–	0·7	0·6	0·6	–	–	–
Net borrowing and use of reserves	3·7	2·6	4·9	6·9	4·1	2·1	19·3	27·0
Reduction of reserve assets (accumulation, −)	−1·3	−1·2	−2·2	−1·3	−6·4	−8·1	−2·5	0·8
Net external borrowing	5·0	3·8	7·1	8·2	10·5	10·2	21·8	26·2
Long-term loans received by governments from official sources, net	2·6	2·8	3·1	3·3	3·6	5·1	7·6	12·6
Other long-term borrowing from non-residents, net	1·0	1·1	1·9	2·6	4·4	4·5	8·7	9·3
From private banks abroad	0·3	0·4	0·4	1·2	2·1	3·7	7·0	8·5
Through suppliers' credits	0·7	0·8	0·7	0·2	0·3	0·3	0·8	1·3
Other sources	–	−0·1	0·8	1·2	2·0	0·5	0·9	−0·5
Use of reserve-related credit facilities, net[a]	0·2	–	−0·4	–	0·4	0·2	1·3	3·4
Other short-term borrowing, net	0·6	0·7	1·7	1·6	0·5	0·2	4·3	2·9
Residual errors and ommissions	0·6	−0·8	0·8	0·7	1·6	0·2	−0·1	−2·0

[a]Comprises use of Fund credit and short-term borrowing by monetary authorities from other monetary authorities.

Source. IMF, *Annual Report*, various years.

publicised credits; in fact, in the fourth quarter of 1976 LDCs took almost 75 per cent of Eurocurrency credit commitments. In absolute terms LDCs borrowed almost $17,500 million from the Eurocurrency market in 1976.

However, these aggregated figures are in some respects misleading, since LDCs have not all enjoyed the same access to Eurocurrency credits.

It might be anticipated that private banks, motivated by considerations of profitability and security, would prefer to lend to those LDCs which seem to offer the best developmental prospects: LDCs which are rich in resources, and therefore have the potential for development; which have diversified export sectors, and therefore tend to have a reasonable degree of export stability; and which have a good record in terms of growth. The empirical validity of such *a priori* reasoning may be supported by casual reference to the distribution pattern of Eurocurrency credits. The low-income LDCs, which have few resources, are heavily reliant on the export of one or two primary products, and possess poor growth records, have been by-passed by the rise in the availability of private credit.

Lending criteria may, however, be more rigorously examined (see Kapur (1977). Rationing of Eurocurrency credits to LDCs does not tend to be conducted purely, or even substantially, on the basis of price; there is no use of differential interest rates to reflect the varying assessments of the probabilities of default amongst LDCs. One reason for this is that, to a certain extent, an increase in the interest rate charged to less credit-worthy borrowers would itself raise the risk of default and therefore increase further the interest rate that lenders would require. Instead, credit is rationed on the basis of availability, with quantitative limits or exposure levels being used to equalise the default risk at the margin of lending. The limits tend to be based on the lenders' evaluation of credit-worthiness. These evaluations will themselves be determined by a number of factors. Kapur identifies five major determinants of a potential borrower's credit-worthiness: the level of international liquidity (measured by the ratio of gross international reserves to imports of goods and services); economic growth, (measured by the rate of growth of real GNP over recent time); the external debt situation (measured by the expected change in the debt-service ratio over the short-to medium term); export performance; and the existing level of private-banking exposure. The hypothesis which Kapur tests is that the flow of Eurocurrency credit is positively related to the rate of economic growth, export performance and the level of reserves, and negatively related to the estimated debt burden[2] and the existing degree of exposure. Not included in the model are political influences, and special lender—borrower relationships which would be difficult to quantify. Also ignored is the fact that lending behaviour may be influenced by the distribution of borrowing. Banks operating in the Eurocurrency markets may not only lend to LDCs but may also borrow from them.

The results obtained by Kapur on the basis of a cross-country regression analysis of data drawn from twenty-five LDCs that borrowed from the Eurocurrency market during the period 1972–74 largely confirm theoretical expectations. The flow of funds from the London Eurocurrency market is found to be significantly dependent in the expected ways on the current level of exports, and the expected growth in them, the projected change in the debt burden, the *rate* of economic growth, and current exposure levels. There seems to be little relationship, however, between the liquidity position of an LDC and the supply of Eurocredits.

The actual distribution of Eurocurrency borrowing amongst LDCs has been even more narrowly concentrated than the foregoing analysis might lead one to expect. In 1975, for example, Mexico and Brazil on their own accounted for well over half of total Eurocurrency credits to non oil-exporting LDCs; these countries were becoming heavily dependent on commercial borrowing, with approaching 50 per cent of their external debt in the form of private credit. The involvement of particular LDCs in the Eurocurrency market is shown in Table 9.2. The only exception to the general pattern of Eurocurrency borrowing outlined above is provided by Zaire, which, though a low-income LDC, reliant on the fluctuating export earnings of one commodity, has made significant use of the Eurocurrency market.

The distribution of borrowing from international capital markets as a whole is shown in Table 9.3. This table reveals that the skewed pattern of borrowing applies to both bonds and credits alike.[3] It also emerges from Table 9.3 that by far the largest share of LDCs' borrowing in international capital markets (over 90 per cent) has been in the form of Eurocurrency credits, although middle-income LDCs have been making increasing recourse to Eurobond financing.

LDCs' loan commitments for the period 1970–5 are shown in Table 9.4. The main points to emerge from this table are the sharp rise in loan commitments for LDCs as a group, and the varying significance of different sources of loans for different sub-groups of LDCs. In 1975, high-income, upper middle-income, and oil-exporting LDCs relied most heavily on private financial markets, where middle-income LDCs relied most heavily on loans from governments, and lower-income LDCs on loans from international organisations.

TABLE 9.2
Use of Commercial Credit by Non Oil-Exporting LDCs, end 1975
(US$ thousand millions)

| | Liabilities to commercial banks | |
	All banks[a]	US banks[b]
Brazil	14·8	9·2
Mexico	13·5	9·9
Argentina	3·2	2·1
Chile	0·8	0·6
Peru	2·3	1·5
Colombia	1·6	1·3
Korea, Rep. of	3·3	2·6
China, Rep. of	2·1	1·8
Turkey	1·0	n. a.
Philippines	2·0	1·8
Thailand	1·2	0·8
Zaire	0·8	n. a.
Subtotal	*46·6*	*31·6*
Other countries	12·7	6·9
Total	*59·3*	*38·5*

[a]Banks in the Group of Ten countries, plus Switzerland and foreign branches of US banks in Bahamas, Cayman Islands, Panama, Hong Kong and Singapore.
[b]US offices and foreign branches of US banks plus US offices of foreign banks.

Source. World Financial Markets (Morgan Guaranty Trust) Sep 1976.

TABLE 9.3
LDCs' Borrowing in International Capital Markets
(millions US dollars or equivalent)

Category of borrowing country[a]	Foreign bonds[b]		Eurobonds[c]		Euro-currency credits	Total bonds and credits
	Public	Private	Public	Private		
Developing						
1973	76·2	222·9	273·5	284·7	8,272·7	9,130·0
1974	16·2	242·9	109·4	4·0	9,616·1	9,988·6
1975	75·0	230·0	346·2	111·4	12,453·5	13,216·1
1976	468·9	170·6	1,068·5	121·4	17,465·4	19,294·8
Oil-exporting						
1973	—	—	—	—	324·9	324·9
1974	—	—	—	—	151·0	151·0

Table 9.3 cont.

Category of borrowing country[a]	Foreign bonds[b]		Eurobonds[c]		Euro-currency credits	Total bonds and credits
	Public	Private	Public	Private		
Oil-exporting (*cont.*)						
1975	–	–	–	–	6·3	6·3
1976	–	–	–	–	400·0	400·0
Higher-income						
1973	–	43·2	172·8	91·5	2,573·6	2,881·1
1974	–	78·7	67·2	4·0	3,250·7	3,400·6
1975	–	16·0	190·4	83·1	3,225·8	3,515·3
1976	33·9	52·4	413·9	20·3	6,408·8	6,929·3
Middle-income						
1973	73·7	179·7	100·7	150·2	4,939·3	5,443·6
1974	16·2	164·2	42·2	–	5,804·8	6,027·4
1975	75·0	196·5	155·8	28·3	7,540·7	7,996·3
1976	435·0	118·2	654·6	101·1	10,159·0	11,467·9
Lower-income						
1973	2·5	–	–	43·0	434·9	480·4
1974	–	–	–	–	409·6	409·6
1975	–	17·5	–	–	1,680·7	1,698·2
1976	–	–	–	–	497·6	497·6
Total borrowing in markets by all borrowers						
1973	3,001·2	2,345·3	3,275·5	1,426·4	20,726·0	30,774·4
1974	2,516·5	5,246·3	1,558·3	2,953·4	28,335·1	40,609·6
1975	7,397·5	4,876·5	6,731·9	3,787·6	20,553·6	43,347·1
1976	8,981·9	10,096·7	11,701·7	3,393·2	28,744·4	62,917·9

[a] The IMF subdivides its eighty-four developing-country members according to whether or not they export oil; those that do not are then classified by income group on the basis of their 1975 GNP per capita, in current US dollars. These groups are:

Higher-income ($1075 or above): Argentina, Cyprus, Greece, Jamaica, Malta, Portugal, Singapore, Spain, Uruguay and Yugoslavia.

Upper middle-income ($521–$1074): Brazil, Chile, the Republic of China, Colombia, Costa Rica, the Dominican Republic, Fiji, Guatemala, Guyana, the Republic of Korea, Malaysia, Mauritius, Mexico, Nicaragua, Panama, Paraguay, Peru, the Syrian Arab Republic, Tunisia, Turkey and Zambia.

Middle-income ($266–$520): Bolivia, Botswana, Cameroon, the People's Republic of the Congo, Egypt, El Salvador, Ghana, Honduras, Ivory Coast, Jordan, Liberia, Mauritania, Morocco, the Philippines, Senegal, the Sudan, Swaziland, Thailand and Togo.

Lower-income ($265 or less): Afghanistan, Bangladesh, Benin, Burma, Burundi, the Central African Empire, Chad, Ethiopia, Gambia, India, Kenya, Lesotho, the Malagasy Republic, Malawi, Mali, Niger, Pakistan, Rwanda, Sierra Leone, Somalia, Sri Lanka, Tanzania, Uganda, Upper Volta and Zaire.

Table 9.3 cont.

Oil-exporting developing countries: Algeria, Ecuador, Gabon, Indonesia, Iran, Iraq, Nigeria, Trinidad and Tobago, and Venezuela.

[b]The traditional foreign bond is one issued and placed in a country other than that of the borrower and denominated in the currency of the country in which it is issued. Regulations abound in the foreign-bond market.

[c]A Eurobond is one that is issued simultaneously in more than one market by international syndicates of underwriters or selling groups. The bond is denominated in third-country currency. The Eurobond market (and in particular the Eurodollar bond market) is generally relatively free from regulations.

Source. World Bank, *Borrowing in International Capital Markets* (EC-181), various issues.

TABLE 9.4

Loan Commitments of Eighty-Four Developing Countries
(US$ thousand millions)

	1970	*1971*	*1972*	*1973*	*1974*	*1975*
Non-oil exporting countries						
Higher-income	1·3	2·4	2·5	2·0	5·4	4·3
International organisations	0·3	0·5	0·3	0·3	0·4	0·8
Loans from governments	0·3	0·5	0·5	0·5	1·5	0·7
Financial markets	0·5	1·1	1·4	1·0	2·9	2·2
Suppliers' credits	0·3	0·2	0·3	0·2	0·6	0·5
Upper-middle-income	5·4	5·5	7·5	10·3	15·1	15·1
International organisations	1·2	1·3	1·8	1·9	2·3	2·7
Loans from governments	1·3	1·5	2·3	2·1	3·0	3·0
Financial markets	1·5	1·9	2·7	5·5	8·5	8·2
Suppliers' credits	1·3	0·9	0·8	0·8	1·4	1·3
Middle-income	1·1	1·3	2·0	2·3	4·9	6·9
International organisations	0·3	0·3	0·5	0·7	1·3	1·5
Loans from governments	0·5	0·6	1·0	1·0	2·1	3·8
Financial markets	0·2	0·2	0·3	0·4	1·2	1·1
Suppliers' credits	0·1	0·2	0·2	0·3	0·4	0·5
Lower-income	2·9	2·1	2·8	4·8	7·1	4·8
International organisations	0·6	0·7	0·7	1·2	1·9	2·3
Loans from governments	1·7	1·2	1·7	2·6	4·2	2·2
Financial markets	0·1	0·1	0·2	0·6	0·7	0·2
Suppliers' credits	0·4	0·1	0·2	0·4	0·3	0·1
Oil-exporting countries	2·5	3·4	4·0	6·9	5·3	8·9
International organisations	0·4	0·4	0·4	0·8	0·8	0·6
Loans from governments	1·0	1·5	1·7	2·5	1·0	1·0
Financial markets	0·4	0·7	1·2	3·0	1·0	4·7
Suppliers' credits	0·8	0·9	0·7	0·6	2·4	2·6

Table 9.4 cont.

	1970	1971	1972	1973	1974	1975
84 developing countries	13·3	14·7	18·9	26·4	37·7	40·0
International organisations	2·8	3·1	3·7	4·9	6·7	7·8
Loans from governments	4·8	5·2	7·3	8·6	11·7	10·8
Financial markets	2·8	4·1	5·7	10·6	14·2	16·4
Suppliers' credits	2·9	2·3	2·1	2·3	5·0	5·0

Source. World Bank, *World Debt Tables* (EC-167/77)

Reasons for the Growth of Commercial Borrowing by LDCs

The explanation of the growth in the use of Eurocurrency credits by LDCs may be found in a combination of supply and demand factors. Let us first examine these factors prior to the oil-price rise, then subsequent to it. Prior to 1973, and on the demand side, a number of factors were at work. First, the borrowing of multinational corporations, which had expanded their activities in certain LDCs in the late 1960s and early 1970s, caused an inflow of funds to these LDCs. Second, the slow growth in official aid, and the redirection of aid towards low-income LDCs encouraged middle- and high-income LDCs to turn to commercial markets for financing. Third, the growth in world trade, and in particular the rapid expansion in LDC export receipts in the early 1970s, served to increase the capital requirements of LDCs (though, of course, it also served to increase their foreign-exchange earnings). Fourth, the gap between commercial interest rates and some official rates narrowed in the late 1960s and early 1970s and this made commercial borrowing relatively more attractive than it had previously been.

On the supply side, whilst the growth of the Eurocurrency market facilitated the movement of funds to LDCs, it was the expansion in the syndicated part of the market in the early 1970s which enabled individual banks to spread risks and lower 'tolerance levels', and which therefore encouraged them markedly to increase their lending to LDCs. In addition to this change within the Eurocurrency market, the improving export and growth performance of LDCs in the early 1970s clearly made them more attractive to lenders.

Keeping on the supply side, let us now look at the period following the oil-price rise. This rise served to generate excess revenue in oil-exporting countries. These countries, which exhibited a preference for keeping their revenues in a relatively liquid form, were reluctant to undertake direct foreign investment or extensive bilateral lending, and found the Eurocurrency market appealing precisely because of the degree of liquidity associated with it.

On the demand side, the oil-price rise simultaneously created balance-of-payments deficits in many oil-importing LDCs. The size of the deficits was such that traditional financing channels proved inadequate. Given that these deficit LDCs were reluctant to adjust their economies, they were forced to find new and alternative means of financing. This was the case even though many of the more conventional financing channels, and in particular those through the IMF, were expanded.

The rise in the price of oil therefore created an increase both in the supply of funds to, and in the demand for funds from, the Eurocurrency market. The market and the commercial banks operating in it have acted as intermediaries in providing a mechanism through which oil surpluses may be recycled from the oil-exporting LDCs to the high- and middle-income oil-importing LDCs.

The recession among industrial countries, itself largely caused by the oil-price rise, and the tightening of capital controls in certain European countries that was associated with it, tended to reduce the demand for Eurocurrency credits by this group of countries. Lower demand for credits combined with increased supply caused Eurocurrency market interest rates to fall and induced LDC borrowers to enter the market; indeed, some LDCs found that Eurocurrency interest rates fell below domestic rates.

Benefits Associated with Commercial Borrowing

From the viewpoint of LDCs, commercial borrowing has advantages over borrowing from the IMF inasmuch as it is free of conditions and therefore allows a greater degree of independence with regard to policy. Furthermore, since commercial borrowing can usually be negotiated fairly rapidly and drawn on without delay, it can conveniently be used to help cope with sudden pressures on the balance of payments. More generally, and as is the case with any form of financing, benefits accrue in the form of the adjustment costs that are thereby avoided. In the wake of the oil-price rise and without the option of commercial borrowing, certain middle-income LDCs would, for instance, have had to implement strict deflationary measures, which in turn would have curtailed, or impeded, growth and development. Commercial borrowing performed a useful function in enabling growth to be maintained even in the face of large payments deficits. Benefits may not, however, be limited to the borrowing countries only, since, if borrowing enables existing or expanded import levels to be financed, the countries supplying these imports will avoid the deflationary implications of a reduction in export demand.[4]

Although benefits may clearly be derived by those countries which make use of commercial borrowing, the nature of these benefits depends very much on the way in which the resources are employed. Where the credits are used to finance the importation of luxury consumer goods, the benefits are likely to be transitory, but, where borrowing is used to finance the import of capital goods, which facilitate domestic investment and structural adaptation, the benefits will be rather more lasting. Some of the LDCs that have made use of Eurocurrency borrowing in the 1970s have, or instance, been able to achieve self-sufficiency in energy.

Problems Associated with Commercial Borrowing

There are a number of problems associated with the use of commercial borrowing by LDCs. A first point to make relates to the distribution of commercial borrowing. Since Eurocurrency credits have, with few exceptions, been available to high- and middle-income LDCs but not to low-income LDCs, commercial borrowing has served to widen the gap between the two groups. Whereas high- and middle-income LDCs have, thanks to Eurocurrency credits, been able to sustain growth, the low-income LDCs have had no option but to draw conditional resources from the IMF, and to adjust their economies in a way that has reduced real domestic living standards.[5] In addition, the poorest LDCs may have lost in a rather more indirect fashion from the availability of commercial loans to high- and middle-income LDCs, since the strength of the case for a more general and permanent reform of the international monetary system has thereby been reduced. More general reform, such as the introduction of an SDR – aid link, would benefit the poorer as well as the richer LDCs.[6] Instead, the low-income LDCs have had to rely on what have been essentially *ad hoc* increases in the availability of concessionary assistance, insufficient to permit the maintenance, let alone the acceleration, of economic growth.

A second problem associated with commercial borrowing is that there may be a tendency for LDCs to become over-committed to it, not only in the sense that the economy may not be able to sustain the related debt financing, but also in the sense that necessary adjustment may be deferred.[7] Particularly in LDCs where export earnings are unstable, and where loans involve floating interest rates, the ease with which debts can be serviced is difficult to forecast accurately and the risks of default may be high.[8] Furthermore, there is no formal lender of last resort in the Eurocurrency market, and this introduces an extra degree of uncertainty into international monetary affairs, especially where borrowers are in vulnerable economic situations. Certainly some LDCs have become over-extended on their debt obligations as a result of excessive commercial borrowing. Zaire, which failed to service its Eurodebt in 1975, is a case in point. Default on servicing by one LDC may have ramifications for others which are in fact financially better managed, since lenders may, as a direct consequence of the default, become more reluctant to lend to LDCs as a group, or may at least be more inclined to impose some form of conditionality on loans.[9]

The debt-servicing problems of LDCs have been aggravated by the movement towards shorter maturities in the Eurocurrency market – a movement which has been particularly marked for loans to LDCs and which reflects an attempt by banks to avoid over-exposure in their lendings to these countries. Of total Eurocurrency credits to LDCs, the share of those with a maturity of one to six years rose from 8·1 per cent in 1973 to 74·8 per cent in 1975, whilst the share of loans with a maturity of more than ten years fell from 36·2 per cent to 1·7 per cent. A shortening of maturities creates problems for borrowers inasmuch as it leads to a bunching of maturities and a sharp rise in repayments. A rise in repayments increases both the likelihood of default, and in turn, that of the withdrawal of commercial banks from their LDC activities.[10]

The external-debt situation of LDCs is summarised in Table 9.5. It may be seen that LDCs, as a whole, and in nominal terms, have increased their external debt by almost 145 per cent over the period 1970–75.[11] Of the non oil-exporting LDCs, the upper middle-income group of countries accounts for by far the largest group share of external debt, and, in common with high-income LDCs owes most of its debt to private creditors.

Other problems associated with commercial borrowing are that there may be a foreign-exchange risk, especially under a system of flexible exchange rates;[12] inflows of Eurocurrencies may disrupt internal monetary management, through effects which they induce on the domestic money supply; and short to medium loans may be used by their recipients for long-term purposes such as project financing, with related illiquidity implications.

TABLE 9.5

The External Public Debt of Eighty-Four Developing Countries,[a] Debt Outstanding, Including Undisbursed
(US$ thousand millions)

	1970	1971	1972	1973	1974	1975
Non-oil exporting countries						
Higher-income	8·4	10·1	11·6	12·5	16·6	18·7
Official creditors	4·5	5·3	5·7	6·3	7·8	8·5
Private creditors	3·9	4·8	5·8	6·3	8·8	10·2
Upper middle-income	24·9	28·8	34·1	41·8	54·5	65·1
Official creditors	15·1	17·4	20·9	24·4	29·1	32·3
Private creditors	9·8	11·4	13·2	17·4	25·5	32·9
Middle-income	7·3	8·5	9·7	11·4	15·9	21·4
Official creditors	5·6	6·4	7·5	8·9	12·1	16·5
Private creditors	1·7	2·0	2·2	2·5	3·8	4·9
Lower-income	19·3	21·2	23·4	27·5	33·8	36·0
Official creditors	17·3	19·2	21·3	24·7	30·3	32·7
Private creditors	2·0	2·0	2·1	2·8	3·5	3·3
Oil-exporting developing coun-tries	11·2	15·0	18·1	23·8	27·1	33·1
Official creditors	7·8	10·2	12·1	15·0	16·4	16·8
Private creditors	3·4	4·8	6·0	8·8	10·7	16·4
84 developing countries	71·2	83·6	96·8	117·1	148·0	174·2
Official creditors	50·3	58·4	67·5	79·3	95·7	106·8
Private creditors	20·9	25·1	29·4	37·8	52·3	67·5

[a] *External public debts*, or 'official debts', are those contracted or guaranteed by the public sector of a debtor country and which are owed in foreign currency to creditors outside the country. They have an original or extended maturity of over one year. The public sector includes the national government and any of its political subdivisions, agencies, or autonomous public bodies. *Debt outstanding* includes the principal, net of past repayments, on both disbursed and undisbursed funds (amounts not yet drawn by receipients).

For low-income and middle-income countries, whose firms normally borrow funds externally with a guarantee by a public-sector institution in their country, the data presented reflect a fairly accurate picture of the country's external debt. For some high-income countries whose firms may borrow funds externally without the benefit of a guarantee by a public-sector institution, the external debt figures underestimate the actual external obligations.

Source. World Bank, *World Debt Tables* (EC-167–77)

More generally, there is a problem in that the availability of Euroloans to LDCs may not constitute a permanent feature of the international monetary system. The access which LDCs have enjoyed coincides with a period of excess supply in the Eurocurrency market. As soon as the supply of funds falls, or the demand from other, developed-country borrowers rises, LDCs, and in particular the marginal borrowers amongst them, may find that they are squeezed out of the market, even though their demand for funds is likely to remain strong, if for no other reason than to roll over or refinance existing debt as it reaches maturity. For LDCs with high roll-over ratios, a relatively small decline in the availability of funds from the Eurocurrency market could, other things remaining constant, imply a significant percentage reduction in net transfer, i.e. the proportion of disbursements not used for refinancing.

Concluding Remarks

Commercial borrowing has made a significant contribution to solving the balance-of-payments financing problems of a number of LDCs during the first half of the 1970s. If this source of financing is to be sustained, it seems likely that certain problems associated with private borrowing will have to be overcome. Furthermore, the international monetary system will have to deal with the financing difficulties of those LDCs which do not at present enjoy access to private capital markets.

The risks which commercial lenders face in dealing with LDCs could be reduced in a number of ways. Lenders could, for instance, impose IMF-type conditions on loans, or, more conveniently, adopt actual IMF conditions where borrowers are also drawing from the Fund. This has already been done in the case of Zaire. Alternatively, private lenders could make loans in conjunction with the IMF (parallel financing), as has happened with Argentina. Otherwise, private finance could be channelled through the IMF.

From the borrowers' point of view, while a strengthening of commercial credit would be beneficial, the imposition of conditions would reduce the quality of the loans received. Indeed, it has perhaps been the absence of conditions on commercial borrowing that has caused LDCs to find it an attractive proposition and preferable to conditional IMF-based finance. It would seem likely that in the future LDCs will have to choose between private financial assistance that is quantitatively more but qualitatively conditional, or quantitatively less but qualitatively unconditional. There are also distributional considerations here, for any mechanism that reduces the risks of lenders may encourage commercial lending to be spread more widely amongst

LDCs, possibly benefiting those LDCs that previously had to rely exclusively on the IMF.

More generally, confidence could be improved and the private market made more stable if the IMF formally stood ready to act as a lender of last resort. Under such a system, borrowers of private capital would initially have freedom of policy choice; but further finance would become subject to strict conditions if the borrowing country were forced to turn to the IMF in its capacity as lender of last resort. To some extent this role has already been performed by the IMF through its various facilities, but only in an informal way.

The debt problems of LDCs partially involve the inappropriate use of short-term finance. While short-term finance is appropriate for dealing with short-term balance-of-payments difficulties, many of the difficulties which LDCs encounter call for long-term development, and long-term finance is therefore required. But private lenders may not wish to take on long-term commitments in LDCs, because of the uncertainty involved; and, in any case, LDCs may not be able to afford long-term commercial interest rates. The degree of uncertainty could be reduced if the developed or oil-exporting countries were to guarantee the repayment of loans. At the same time, the grant element to LDCs could be increased by these countries' subsidising the commercial interest rates paid by LDCs. Interest-rate subsidisation, inasmuch as it would ameliorate the debt problems of LDCs, would also serve to reduce the risks associated with lending to them.[13]

For the low-income LDCs which have relied almost exclusively on inflows of official concessionary finance, there is considerable scope for improving access to international long-term capital markets.[14] Even in terms of concessionary lending, member countries of the Development Assistance Committee have consistently failed to reach target aid levels, and it is therefore very probable that the availability of concessionary finance through the IMF will be a crucial factor in determining the rate of economic growth of these countries at least until they have achieved a moderate stage of development.

10 The Commodities Problem and the International Monetary System

There are various dimensions to the commodities problem as seen by LDCs. The first of these relates to instability in export and import prices; the second relates to instability in export earnings and import expenditures and therefore the balance of payments; and the third relates to changes in the terms of trade, in particular the supposed secular decline in the price of primary products relative to the price of manufactures. In a number of ways the international monetary system may help in providing solutions to, or at least palliatives for, certain aspects of these problems. As currently constituted, the IMF can help through the CFF, which is specifically concerned with the financing of export shortfalls; the BSFF, which is designed to assist countries with the balance-of-payments implications of making contributions to international buffer-stock schemes; and the EFF, which provides longer-term assistance for dealing with those balance-of-payments problems of a largely structural variety. In addition, the OF, during its short lifetime, provided financial help for dealing with the balance-of-payments repercussions of the sudden rise in the price of oil imports; and, outside the IMF, the Stabex scheme operated by the European Economic Community provides some financial compensation to LDCs for export-commodity shortfalls.

There are basically two approaches to the commodities problem outlined above that are of interest from the viewpoint of the international monetary system. The first is the compensatory financing approach. This approach can be applied either to shortfalls in export earnings or to excesses in import expenditure. In practice it has been applied to shortfalls in either total export earnings, as is the case with the IMF's CFF, or export earnings from individual commodities, as is the case with the EEC's Stabex scheme. The second approach to the commodities problem is the buffer-stock approach. This approach may be applied to the problem of commodity-price stabilisation, which in certain cases will imply earnings stabilisation, or to the problem of inducing a long-term change in the relative price of primary commodities.

In some cases these two approaches to the commodity problem are largely interchangeable, and simply reflect a different emphasis. The compensatory technique attempts to deal with the earnings instability aspect of the commodity problem in an *ex post* fashion, as and when the problem has arisen, by neutralising the effects of export instability on the balance of payments. The buffer-stock technique, on the other hand, endeavours, in an *ex ante* way, to prevent export-price instability from arising. There are circumstances, however, under which buffer-stock export-price stabilisation will fail to engender stability in export earnings, and in such cases compensatory financing, which is specifically oriented towards earnings, will be required in addition to buffer stocks. Furthermore, where a major policy objective is to alter relative prices, the buffer-stock approach is appropriate and compensatory financing is not. Since, then, the compensatory-financing and buffer-stock approaches to the commodities problem are not perfect substitutes for one another it is not surprising that many advocates of a form of international monetary reform which is directed towards solving the problems of LDCs see the two approaches as complementary components of the reformed system.

An example of such advocacy is the UNCTAD Integrated Programme for Commodities, which has among its objectives the reduction of fluctuations in LDC's export earnings; adequate growth in LDCs' export receipts; and improved access to the markets of developed countries for the exports of LDCs. In order to help realise these objectives UNCTAD proposes, *inter alia*, the establishment of a common fund for the financing of international stocks, the setting up of a series of international commodity stocks or buffer stocks, and improved compensatory financing for the maintenance of stability in export earnings. With regard to buffer-stock arrangements, the UNCTAD has focused particular attention on ten core commodities: cocoa, coffee, copper, cotton, jute, rubber, sisal, sugar, tea and tin. It is suggested that buffer stocks could be organised for these commodities with the specific purpose of market regulation.[1] We now move on to examine the two approaches to the commodity problem.

Compensatory Financing

In theory, compensatory financing may fully offset export shortfalls and import excesses. If

$$CF = \alpha(X^N - X^A) + \beta(M^A - M^N)$$

where CF is the size of compensatory financing, X^N is the normal value of exports, X^A is the actual value of exports and α represents the degree of compensation, M^N is the normal value of imports, M^A is the actual value of imports and β represents the degree of compensation, all that is necessary for perfect compensation is that α and β both equal one. The only major intrinsic difficulty with respect to compensatory financing is to be found in estimating X^N and M^N. Most criticism of compensatory financing relates to specific aspects of particular compensatory schemes such as the CFF and the EEC Stabex scheme, rather than to the theory of compensation as such.[2]

Buffer Stocks

The question of buffer stocks is not a straightforward one. Although a neat theoretical case may be made for them, there is also something to be said against; so decisions regarding buffer stocks must rest on a careful evaluation of the associated costs and benefits. Perhaps we should briefly look at the case for and the case against international buffer stocks before moving on to examine the way in which the international monetary system could contribute to the operation, or more strictly the financing, of such schemes.

The case for buffer stocks

Much of the appeal of buffer stock schemes rests on their susceptability to simple economic analysis. Just as demand and supply analysis may be used to explain why price variations occur, the same analysis may be used to explain how such variations may be eliminated. Given that an equilibrium price emerges as a result of the interaction between demand and supply factors, the effect of autonomous changes in demand on price may be neutralised by offsetting changes in supply whilst the effect of autonomous changes is supply on price may be neutralised by offsetting changes in demand. An autonomous increase in supply would not then have any impact on price if demand increased equivalently. Similarly, an autonomous increase in demand would not have any impact on price if supply increased equivalently. It is the purpose of stabilisation or buffer-stock schemes to eliminate, by means of offsetting interventions in the market, cyclical price variations caused by fluctuations in demand and supply. In a situation of excess supply, the stabilisation agency would enter the market as a demander, and would accumulate a buffer stock of the commodity in question. In conditions of excess demand, the stabilisation agency would offload some of its buffer stock onto the market, thereby serving to increase supply. By acting in a fashion which compensates for excesses in the market, the buffer-stock scheme stabilises the market price. It is the quantity of the commodity held in the buffer stock which varies and not the price of the commodity.

A number of benefits may be claimed to result from price stabilisation. Some of these benefits will be derived by primary-product producers. First, the greater degree of certainty with regard to prices, and in some circumstances export earnings, that would follow on from buffer-stock arrangements would help producing countries in their domestic economic management. The availability of foreign exchange could become more predictable, and efficient development planning more feasible. Indeed, some commentators have maintained that, even where buffer stocks do not result in increased earnings stability, this is far outweighed in importance by the macroeconomic benefits (see UNCTAD, 1977). Second, the effect of buffer stocks in increasing the price stability of natural products would serve to improve the competitiveness of these products relative to synthetic substitutes, and thereby increase the long-term demand for them.

Other benefits would be derived by primary-product consumers. First, consuming countries would benefit in terms of a relatively assured supply of primary commodities, because of the supplementation of production by stock decumulation.[3] Second, a system of buffer stocks for key commodities would serve to reduce the incidence of major inflationary shocks emanating from sharp upward movements in commodity prices. Inasmuch as primary-product importing countries react to such surges of inflation by introducing demand-deflationary fiscal and monetary measures which cause output to fall and unemployment to rise, the removal of the commodity-price source of inflation generation would have real benefits in terms of raised or maintained output and employment. Commodity-price stability might then assist economic management not only in the producing countries but also in the consuming ones. This might be even more the case where primary-product price stabilisation induces greater stability in the producing countries' demand for imports of industrial goods from the primary-product consuming countries. Steadier growth and a lowered rate of inflation in industrial countries would, furthermore, exert a beneficial feedback effect on LDCs. Third, any reduction in price uncertainty induced by buffer-stock intervention could lower the costs of uncertainty, such as those imposed by inventory holding and forward transactions.[4]

More generally, a system of buffer-stock arrangements could result in a greater degree of world economic stability.[5] Evidence drawn from the early 1970s is consistent with the hypothesis that instability in commodity prices, which reflects variations in the demand for and supply of primary commodities, can play a major causal role in generating world economic instability. Since there is no reason to believe that demand and supply in commodity markets will be stagnant, especially where unstable expectations play a crucial role in influencing both demand and supply, an equilibrating mechanism is required. In principle, equilibrium may be achieved through the operation of the price mechanism. Thus, as demand emanating from the world's manufacturing sector exceeds output emanating from the primary sector, the price of primary products will tend to rise, and this will cause demand to fall and supply to expand. Similarly, as the supply of primary commodities outruns the demand for them, commodity prices will tend to fall, supply will fall and the demand for them will rise; manufacturers will experience a reduction in their costs and will expand both their output and their demand for inputs.

In practice, however, it seems as though this equilibrating device has operated in a perverse fashion. Since primary products are inputs to manufacturing, since changes in primary-product prices represent changes in costs to manufacturers, and since prices in the manufacturing sector are largely cost-determined, an increase in commodity prices tends to be reflected in higher manufactured good prices. As a result, a rise in the price of primary products relative to that of manufactured goods tends to be temporary, as is therefore the incentive to increase the supply of primary products and to contract the demand for them. In addition to the cost-inflationary implications, however, an increase in commodity prices tends to be world demand-deflationary, the deflation resulting both from the effects of the redistribution of world income to those with a higher propensity to save, and from the policy responses induced in primary-product importing countries following the increase in cost inflation. Aggregate demand deflation in the major primary-product importing countries is likely to reduce the demand for commodity imports, with the result that export earnings in producing countries may fall, even though their commodity terms of trade have improved. Over the longer run, then, excess demand for primary products results in an acceleration in the world rate of inflation, but no relative price change as between primary products and manufactured goods. Equilibrium is achieved not by relative price changes, but by income changes, which serve to reduce the demand for primary products. Should the reduction in aggregate demand overshoot its equilibrium level commodity prices will tend to fall. The fall in commodity prices may not, however, cause the demand for primary products to rise, even though real income in consuming countries will increase as a result. This expansionary influence on demand may be outweighed by the fact that export earnings in LDCs will tend to fall, and therefore the LDCs' demand for manufactured goods will also tend to fall; certainly there is no reason to believe that a fall in primary-product prices will automatically be associated with a rise in the level of activity in industrial countries.

It may be concluded from the above analysis that the market mechanism may act as an imperfect regulator for maintaining equilibrium between changes in the supply of and changes in the demand for primary products. Buffer stocks could provide a superior regulator. In a situation of excess demand for primary products, supply would be augmented from buffer stocks, prices would not rise, or at least would not rise by a large and sudden amount, and therefore the cost inflation and demand deflation associated with a rise in commodity prices would be avoided. In a situation of excess supply and with buffer-stock intervention, earnings in producing countries would not fall and therefore the demand for manufactured goods would be maintained.

It would seem, then, that primary-product producing countries, primary-product consuming countries, and the world in general stand to benefit from a system of buffer stocks. There are, however, counter-arguments.

The case against buffer stocks

The case against the use of buffer stocks as a price-stabilising device comprises a combination of theoretical, empirical and practical arguments. First, from a theoretical viewpoint, stabilising price may not always stabilise earnings. Buffer-stock intervention will tend to stabilise both price and earnings where price instability in the market is caused by variations in demand, but where price instability is caused by variations in supply this will not be the case; indeed, maintaining a stable price through market intervention may result in a larger fluctuation in earnings than would have existed in a free market. To illustrate this let us examine Figure 10.1, where it is assumed that the price elasticity of demand equals − 1 over the entire length of the demand curve. It may be seen that the impact of variations in supply on earnings are perfectly neutralised by offsetting variations in price. A low level of supply is

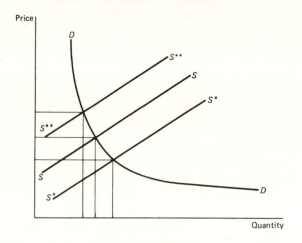

FIGURE 10.1

matched by a high price, and large supply is matched by a low price. In this instance, then, price instability serves to ensure earnings stability. Buffer-stock intervention in such a market could indeed stabilise price, but this would be at the cost of destabilising earnings. Following a leftward shift in the supply curve, earnings would fall: whilst, following a rightward shift on the supply curve, earnings would rise. In the case of buffer-stock intervention, variations in earnings positively reflect variations in supply, since price is fixed through the activities of the intervention agency (see Figure 10.2).

With either a price-elastic or price-inelastic demand curve, shifts in supply will of course cause instabilities in export earnings, even in a free market. Buffer-stock intervention in such cases will, however, tend either to exacerbate earnings instability or change the nature of the earnings instability. Earnings instability will be exacerbated where the

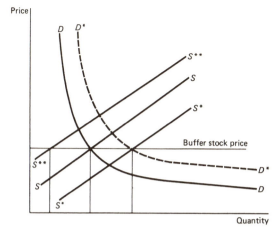

FIGURE 10.2

demand curve is price-elastic, although the higher is the price elasticity of demand the lower will be the degree of additional earnings instability caused by buffer-stock intervention in the market. Where the demand curve is inelastic with respect to price, buffer-stock intervention will change the nature of the relationship between variations in supply and variations in earnings. In a free market and with demand inelasticity a fall in supply will cause earnings to rise and an increase in supply will cause earnings to fall. With buffer-stock intervention, on the other hand, a fall in supply will also cause earnings to fall, whilst an increase in supply will cause earnings to increase. This change in the nature of the relationship between variations in supply and variations in earnings may be deemed undesirable, since the market will now fail to give producers appropriate equilibrating signals, either in terms of price or in terms of earnings. Following a supply glut, not only will price fail to fall, but earnings will rise, and producers may thereby be encouraged to increase supply in the future. Following a supply shortage, not only will price fail to rise, but earnings will fall, and this may serve to reduce future output. Furthermore, with buffer-stock intervention, the market signals facing consumers will fail to adjust to changes in the availability of supply, and this may also prevent a reduction in the discrepancy between demand and production.[6] Correction of the discrepancy may not be wanted in circumstances where the disequilibrium is of a cyclical or short-run nature, but a serious problem arises in contemporaneously distinguishing between those disequilibria that are only short run and those that are long run.[7]

It does seem possible that, in certain circumstances, the operation of buffer stocks will serve to bring about a reduction in the degree of price instability but will not necessarily reduce the degree of earnings instability. There is, however, little reason why this should constitute an insuperable hurdle to buffer-stock arrangements. In theory, price stability and earnings stability may be simultaneously achieved by buffer-stock intervention for those commodities where shifts in the demand curve form the principal cause of market instability. For commodities where price stability is inversely associated with earnings stability in a way and to an extent that is considered unacceptable, there is no theoretical reason why buffer-stock arrangements should not be complemented by a scheme for compensatory financing, which specifically sets out to stabilise earnings; indeed, a scheme of this sort could be organised in such a way that it redresses any unwanted income redistribution implicitly caused by the buffer-stock scheme. If price stability *per se* gives rise to certain benefits (quite separate from earnings stability), then, given that earnings stability may be achieved by other means, there seems no clear reason for abandoning the idea of buffer stocks as a means of stabilising price.

As noted above, however, there exists the problem of determining the price to be stabilised. In order to differentiate between cyclical and secular movements in price, it is necessary to be able to identify the price trend. This may be difficult to do on the basis of *ex ante* information. A great deal of uncertainty surrounds the future demand for and supply of many primary products and this creates a forecasting problem.[8] Where the buffer-stock agency miscalculates the trend, it is quite possible that its activities will raise the degree of price instability rather than reduce it. Where the intervention agency overestimates the long-run equilibrium price, it will experience a continuous accumulation of stocks and a continuous decumulation of financial resources. The same outcome would result if the agency were behaviourally reluctant to see the market price fall.[9] Similarly, where the intervention agency underestimates the long-run equilibrium price, this will result in a continuous decumulation of stocks. In either case the long-term existence of the agency may be open to question. In the first case, it would tend to run out of funds, thus forcing it to sell its stocks of the commodity and thereby causing price to fall. The price fall would be emphasised by the fact that the activities of the agency would have served to maintain production at a level above equilibrium. In the second case, the buffer-stock agency would eventually run out of its stocks of the commodity concerned and the market price would then have to rise. The rise in price would be emphasised because of the sub-equilibrium level of production implicitly encouraged by the activities of the agency, as well, perhaps, as by any attempts by the buffer-stock agency to replenish its stocks. The instability could be enhanced by the activities of private speculators who anticipate the collapse of the buffer stock.

In circumstances where private speculation in a particular commodity market is destabilising in terms of price, the intervention of an agency with superior powers of forecasting could serve to stabilise the market price through counter-speculation.[10] In deciding whether a buffer stock will stabilise price, a key issue is whether the stocking agency can forecast demand and supply, and therefore price, better than can private speculators. Some observers have expressed doubts over this;[11] and, indeed, it may be the case that for some commodities the extent of uncertainty effectively precludes forecasting with any degree of confidence. But for a significant range of primary commodities forecasting would appear to be a legitimate exercise, and a central agency availed of all relevant information should be able to forecast as accurately as anybody and more accurately than most, even though, in the case of an intervention agency, an extra variable becomes relevant to the calculation: the impact on demand and supply of the existence of the agency itself.

There are a number of other reasons why it might be deemed superior to have a system of international buffer stocks rather than one of privately-held speculative stocks.[12] The main reason is that the level of privately held stocks is likely to be socially sub-optimal, since not only may the private cost of stock-holding exceed the social cost, but, in addition, the social benefits of stocking may exceed the private benefits, which are expressed purely in terms of the speculators' profit. One beneficial externality which may be associated with international buffer-stock schemes is that their very existence may influence speculators' expectations in such a fashion that private speculators behave in a price-stabilising way. The extent to which this externality is derived will depend upon the speculators' confidence in the ability of the buffer-stock agency to defend its chosen price or price range.

Even if it is possible to overstate the theoretical case against buffer stocks, there still remains the practical problem that stocking involves storage, and that not all primary commodities may be stored without deterioration: some of them are perishable. For these commodities buffer-stocking arrangements are clearly inappropriate. Again, however, it is easy to overemphasise this limitation to buffer-stocking arrangements. Although there are indeed commodities, such as bananas, for which current technology does not permit storage, there are many products for which storage costs are 'negligible', 'low' or 'moderate'. Storage costs are negligible for copper, lead, manganese, tin and zinc; are low for cotton, jute, rubber, sisal, wool and sugar; and are moderate for cocoa, coffee and vegetable oils.[13] Hart (1976) maintains that a commodity is 'durable in storage' if it can be kept for at least one year with the sum of storage costs and grade loss not exceeding 5 per cent of the cost of fresh supplies. This description would fit most fibres, grains, metals, forest products and fuels.[14]

Another argument often used in the case against buffer stocks is the argument of experience. It may be observed that only one commodity agreement involving an element of buffer stocking has survived during the period since 1945: the International Tin Agreement (ITA).[15] However, as has recently been demonstrated by Smith and Schink (1976), this agreement has only marginally reduced the instability of tin prices and of producers' incomes. More significant than the buffer-stock aspect of the ITA have been the transactions of the United States stockpile, which is outside the tin agreement and which has served to defend ceiling prices, and the export-regulation aspects of the ITA, which have enabled floor prices to be defended through restriction of total supply. Evidence of previous failure is, of course, consistent with a number of hypotheses. On the one hand, it is consistent with the view that there is something intrinsically unworkable about buffer stocks. On the other hand, it is also consistent with the view that the circumstances necessary for the successful operation of buffer stocks have simply not been achieved. In the past it has been the conflict of interests between producers and consumers, and, indeed, between more and less efficient producers, as well as the inadequacy of finance, that has brought about the failure of most buffer-stock schemes. With a greater degree of commitment to commodity-price stabilisation, as it is realised or believed that all participants in stabilisation schemes will tend to experience net long-term benefits, and with more appropriate financial backing, it is not clear that history must continue to repeat itself with respect to buffer stocks.[16]

The terms of trade

One aspect of recent UNCTAD proposals for the introduction of a system of buffer stocks is that not only should stocking be used to stabilise price around the trend determined by the free operation of the market, but, in addition, the buying and selling behaviour of the stocking agency should be designed to encourage a secular increase in the price of primary products and thereby improve the terms of trade as between primary commodities and manufactured goods. In order to achieve an improvement in the terms of trade, it is envisaged that buffer stocks would be supported by a system of supply management, under which export quotas or taxes could be used to control the quantity supplied to the market. Without supply management, the maintenance of a price greater than the equilibrium one would cause over-production. By limiting output, producers will indeed tend to cause a rise in the market price and, where the demand curve is price-inelastic, in export earnings as well.[17]

A number of issues are involved in a proposal of this kind. Let us examine some of them. The first issue is really a non-issue and relates to the trend in LDCs' terms of trade.[18] It is not a relevant argument to say that the terms of trade of primary-product producing countries have been improving over recent years and that this makes any further improvement unnecessary. Apart from being factually dependent on the degree of disaggregation, if it is agreed that poverty should be relieved, one way to do this may be to bring about an improvement in the terms of trade of poor countries, irrespective of the current state of relative prices.[19]

The second issue relates to the effectiveness of buffer stocks and export controls in encouraging an improvement in the terms of trade of LDCs. Certainly, where synthetic substitutes are readily available, the demand curves facing producers of natural products are likely to be price-elastic, and for this reason the ability of producers to raise price may be limited. Again, the scope for increasing earnings will be influenced by the market share of the LDC producers: where this is small, unilateral action by LDCs as a group will tend not to be very effective.

The third issue concerns the view that an increase in the prices of primary products relative to those of manufactured goods may not benefit all LDCs; indeed, some primary-product importing LDCs may lose as a result. Whilst in theory this point is valid, there is little doubt that, if attention is concentrated on the UNCTAD's ten core commodities, an increase in the relative price of these commodities will redistribute income towards less-developed producing countries. In any case, a system of compensation could be established that would protect the import-reliant LDCs.[20]

The fourth issue is whether an increase in the relative price of primary products would cause an acceleration in the world rate of inflation and world instability, as evidence collected from the period immediately following 1973 might at first sight seem to suggest. More careful examination of this period, however, reveals that it was the large and sudden increase in commodity prices which generated instability, and, possibly, moved the rate of inflation above the threshold at which expectations became elastic. It is probable that consuming countries could adjust in a reasonably stable fashion to the gradual and predictable increase in primary-product prices that would be associated with commodity agreements.

The final issue relates to the way in which the supply of commodities might be controlled. Broadly speaking, there are two options, export quotas and export taxes. Export quotas have proved difficult to negotiate and have tended to break down either because of failure to secure full participation by all producing countries, thereby allowing non-participants to profit at the expense of participants by increasing their output at the higher price; or because of a failure by participants to control domestic output and, as a result, continually accumulate stocks; or because of failure to make the commodity agreement flexible enough to reflect changes in the pattern of production and trade in a way that does not penalise the relatively efficient producers.

Even where introduced and effective, export quotas may have undesirable consequences. Although they are likely to induce a re-distribution of income from consuming to producing countries, the redistribution may be from the relatively poor in rich countries to the relatively rich in poor countries; indeed, the income gains may not be derived by residents of LDCs at all, but rather by foreign business enterprise. The population in general in LDCs may, of course, gain indirectly in terms of any investment, development and diversification that is induced by export quotas, but such effects may be deemed unlikely. The gainers from export quotas may simply increase their consumption of foreign goods, or may invest abroad, or may invest in speculative luxury projects at home. Even where productive domestic investment is undertaken, this may well be in the commodity subject to the export quota rather than in alternative diversifying projects; indeed, inasmuch as export quotas raise or maintain the price of the commodity concerned, they tend to militate against diversification. So, although export quotas tend to raise export earnings in LDCs, they do not ensure that these extra resources will be used for developmental purposes. This is where export taxes become relevant. Taxes may be levied in addition to quotas or instead of them. Either way, export taxes may be used to offset excess supply;[21] to bring about an acceptable distribution of the extra earnings associated with higher commodity prices; and to channel the additional export earnings into diversification-oriented investment.

The Role of the International Monetary System

The connection between the commodity problem and the international monetary system lies in the provision of finance. The international monetary system could be designed in such a way that it provides the finance necessary for the operation of compensatory and buffer-stock schemes.[22] The precise nature of the connection may, however, vary, and it is in terms of such variations that it is possible to distinguish between the various proposals that have been suggested. For instance, in relation to the financing of buffer stocks, a proposal which has been put forward by the UNCTAD as part of the Integrated Commodity Programme envisages the IMF acting merely as a financial intermediary raising and distributing loans; other proposals go further than this and endeavour to relate commodity stabilisation to the regulation of the world's supply of international money. Schemes of the latter type see the IMF, or some similar agency, acting not merely as an intermediary, but as having the power to create the international finance that is required. Under such schemes, emphasis has either been put on the financing of buffer stocks, with variations in the supply of international reserves essentially constituting a side-effect (see, for example, Keynes, 1942), or on a form of commodity reserve currency which is rather more incidentally associated with the holding of stocks.

The Commodity-Reserve Currency

For more than a hundred years, economists have been discussing the principle of relating the international monetary system in some way to commodities. Much of the discussion, although perhaps not primarily concerned with the issue of commodity stabilisation, has had implications for it. Illustrative of the discussion is a plan that Professors Hart, Kaldor and Tinbergen (HKT) put forward in 1964 for an international commodity-reserve currency. They correctly identified the conflict which arose from within the gold-exchange system (GES) as a result of the simultaneous need, at that time, for extra liquidity and for confidence. In attempting to remedy this weakness of the GES, they suggested that the IMF should issue commodity-backed international reserves (bancor). The main purpose of the plan was to create an internationally acceptable reserve asset other than gold and key currencies. It was thought that by monetising primary commodities the backing required to make the new asset acceptable would be provided. Other, secondary features of the plan were, first, that by acquiring commodities from reserve-currency countries as well as from primary producers these currencies could be amortised over time; and, second, that by buying commodities in times of falling prices and selling them in times of rising prices the *overall* price of commodities would be stabilised.

The plan envisaged bancor being backed by a composite bundle of commodities, units of which would be bought and sold on the market. The composition of the bundle would be relatively constant. It was not a major intention of the scheme to eradicate instabilities in the prices of individual commodities, although it is likely, given the constitution of the HKT scheme, that such instabilities would be dampened, particularly where instabilities are commonly generated by variations in world aggregate demand. Purchases and sales under the HKT scheme, and under more recent versions of it,[23] would be in terms of the composite bundle of commodities rather than just individual commodities; thus, while the price of an individual commodity would tend to be stabilised under the scheme, provided that the commodity concerned were a component of the composite bundle, the stabilisation of individual commodity prices would not be as great as if transactions were concentrated on individual commodities. Indeed, under the HKT scheme, and the Hart 1976 version of it, the intension is that the relative prices of commodities would still vary.

The commodity-reserve plan has come in for considerable criticism. Essentially these criticisms relate to three features of the scheme. The first criticism relates to the fact that the scheme forgoes the opportunity of deriving the social saving which would be achieved by using a fiat international money. The second relates to the cost of maintaining and servicing the large commodity stockpile that would be required.[24] A large measure of the variation in cost estimations hinges on whether the buffer stocks associated with the commodity-reserve currency constitute the only stocks held, and whether the entire growth in the supply of world money is associated with commodity purchases. Clearly, where the commodity-reserve system exclusively holds stocks, and is the sole source of reserve growth, the size of the associated buffer stocks and the related storage costs will indeed be large. But, where other stocks are held outside the commodity-reserve system, and world liquidity growth is supplemented by other means, the costs of the commodity-reserve currency would be correspondingly reduced.

The third criticism relates to the problems which might arise from endeavouring to use one instrument – namely, the creation of bancor – to achieve both an adequate growth of international reserves and commodity-price stability. The validity of this criticism is perhaps questionable. Certainly, where two equivalent systems for expanding international reserves could be adopted, it is more efficient to choose the one which generates the greatest external net benefits. Where one scheme for expanding world reserves is inferior on monetary grounds but superior in terms of its external effects, the issue is less straightforward, and the desirability of the alternative schemes rests on a full evaluation of all the associated costs and benefits. In the case of the commodity-reserve currency, on purely monetary grounds this system of reserve creation is inferior to those systems based on fiat money, simply because of the social saving associated with fiat schemes.[25] However, the external benefits for LDCs may be greater, and are certainly more explicit in the case of a commodity-reserve currency.[26] From a world welfare point of view, which system is superior overall depends on the size of the relative costs and benefits and on their distribution. The issues raised here are involved and open to debate. Fortunately, the introduction and existence of the SDR facility overcomes many of the monetary costs associated with a commodity-reserve currency, but still permits the pursuit of certain developmental objectives. From a monetary point of view, a significant feature of the SDR is that it is unbacked; it is an 'outside' international asset which, to all intents and purposes, acts as money simply because, by international agreement, it is generally acceptable. As compared with commodity monies, and, indeed commodity-backed monies, the SDR gives rise to a social saving. The existence of the SDR provides reason to reappraise the possibility of linking the international monetary system with commodity-price stabilisation.

SDRs and the Financing of Commodity Stabilisation[27]

Unlike plans for commodity-reserve currencies, a link between the creation of SDRs and commodity stabilisation would not need to concern itself with the problem of the global adequacy of international liquidity. This problem may be left to the normal operations of the SDR facility, under which appropriate changes in the quantity of international liquidity are made by general consent through the creation (and perhaps cancellation) of SDRs.

The aim of a link between the SDR and commodity stabilisation would simply be to prevent large, short-term variations in the market prices of certain major primary products. In the process of stabilising primary-product prices, however, the SDR/commodity stabilisation (SDR–CS) link would tend to protect the international reserves of primary-product exporting countries (PPXCs) where the price of their exports would otherwise have fallen, and the reserves of primary-product importing countries (PPMCs) where the price of their imports would otherwise have risen. The SDR–CS link would remove one source of instability and uncertainty in the world economy.

The scheme in outline might work as follows. As the price of a particular primary product falls, a Commodity Stabilisation Agency (CSA) such as the IMF enters the market as a residual buyer. Most simply, the CSA could be provided with SDRs, which would then be used to finance the purchase. Alternatively, the CSA might convert SDRs credited to it by the Special Account of the IMF into foreign exchange. Assuming for the moment, however, that SDRs are directly used in the transaction, the outcome of this procedure would be (i) that the primary product price would be stabilised, (ii) that the PPXC would acquire SDRs, and (iii) that the CSA would acquire a stockpile of the primary product in question.

Assuming a supply curve which is inelastic at least in the short run, whether the PPXC would acquire *net* reserves as a result of the activities of the CSA would depend on whether the initial price fall was caused by a rightward shift in the supply curve, in which case it would, or a leftward shift in the demand curve, in which case it would not. In the latter case, the only change in the reserves of the PPXC as compared with a situation in which the price of the primary product had not fallen would be a change in the composition of reserves.

This analysis is illustrated in Figure 10.3 and 10.4. In Figure 10.3, as the supply curve shifts from S to S^1 the price falls from p^e to p^{e*}. If the objective of the CSA is to re-establish the old equilibrium price, it will enter the market as a buyer and act to shift the demand curve from D to D^1. At the new point of equilibrium it is clear that total export earnings (total revenue) will have risen as compared with either the initial equilibrium situation or that represented by the intersection of S^1 and D. If, however, it is the objective of the CSA to stabilise export earnings and not prices, then the CSA will be required to enter the market as a buyer (assuming that the demand curve is inelastic) but will operate so as to shift the demand curve not as far over to the right as D^1, but far enough

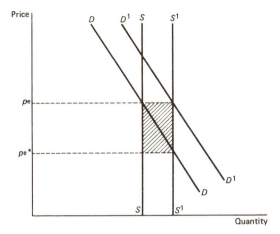

FIGURE 10.3

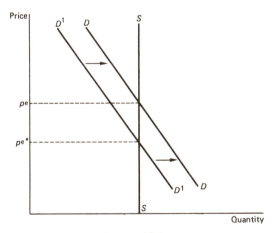

FIGURE 10.4

for the quantity demanded to rise sufficiently to offset the impact of the price fall on total revenue.

In Figure 10.4, whether the objective of the CSA is expressed in terms of price stability or in terms of the stability of export earnings is not significant. With either objective in view, the CSA will attempt to counteract perfectly the leftward shift in the demand curve from D to D^1 by increasing its own demand. Both the old equilibrium price and the old level of export earnings will simultaneously be re-established.

The benefit of the SDR—CS link to the PPXC is that its reserves would either rise or remain constant; they would not fall. Without the link, a fall in the primary-product price would, in all probability, lead to a fall in reserves. This would certainly be the outcome where the price fall resulted from a leftward shift in the demand curve; but it would also be the likely result of a price fall induced by a rightward shift in the supply curve, since the price elasticity of demand for most primary products is generally thought to be less than unity.

The cost of the SDR—CS link would be borne by the PPMCs in the sense that the operations of the CSA would prevent the primary-product price from falling. There may also be a real-resource cost to PPMCs if the PPXCs spend any *extra* reserves (SDRs) acquired. Where, however, PPXCs are at the same time LDCs, this feature of the scheme may be regarded by supporters of more conventional liquidity—aid link schemes[28] as a beneficial externality.

Now let us assume that demand and supply factors cause the price of our particular primary commodity to rise. The price rise may be owing to a rightward shift in the demand curve, a leftward shift in the supply curve, or both. In the absence of an SDR—CS link, what would happen? If the price rise had been caused by a rightward shift in the demand curve, then the foreign-exchange receipts of the PPXC would rise and the reserves of the PPMC would fall. On the other hand, if the price rise had been caused by a leftward shift in the supply curve, the impact on total revenue and reserves would depend on the price elasticity of demand. Where this is less than one, again the reserves of the PPXC would rise and those of the PPMC would fall.

If the CSA is in operation, however, then, as the price of the primary product rises, the CSA offloads its stocks of the commodity onto the market, thus serving to neutralise the rise in price. PPMCs buy these stocks, paying for them either in SDRs or in reserve currencies. Assuming for a moment that payment is made in SDRs, the outcome of CSA activity will be (i) that the CSA accumulates SDRs but de-cumulates its stocks of the primary product, and (ii) that PPMCs acquire the primary product but lose SDRs.

In the case of an upward movement in prices, the PPMCs benefit from the existence and involvement of the CSA, either by losing fewer reserves, or by gaining a greater real quantity of the primary product. The cost of CSA intervention is borne by the PPXC in terms of reserve-gain forgone.

At the end of the complete primary-product price cycle, the CSA will have recovered the full value of its initial SDR payment to PPXCs.

Indeed, the CSA will recover SDRs in excess of this initial payment, since the SDR selling prices of primary products supplied by the CSA to consumers will be greater than the SDR buying prices paid by the CSA to the primary-product producers.

A number of features of the SDR—CS link scheme should perhaps be emphasised.

First, the link relates to cyclical price variations. It is suggested not that the scheme should be used to prevent long-term relative price movements, but, rather, that it should be used to avoid short-term instability around secular trends in the terms of trade. To this end it is proposed that CSA price-intervention points should be flexible, with the intervention prices being related to market trends. Thus, for example, it is envisaged that a long-term rightward shift in a supply curve, or an equally permanent leftward shift in a demand curve, would be reflected in a fall in the market price for that commodity. The CSA would endeavour to estimate the long-run equilibrium price of a primary product by reference to demand and supply trends. Where short-run variations in either demand or supply resulted in deviations from this price, the CSA would intervene, buying when the market price fell a specified percentage below the long-run equilibrium price, and selling when the price rose a specified, though not necessarily equal, percentage above the long-run price. CSA prices could be adjusted downwards or upwards in the event of undesirable stock accumulations or decumulations.

Second, the SDR—CS link could conveniently be integrated with a scheme for the amortisation of reserve currencies. Integration could be achieved at either the price floor when the CSA is buying, or at the price ceiling when the CSA is selling. The 'price-floor version' of reserve-currency amortisation would involve the exchange, at the outset, of SDRs for reserve currencies, and then the use of these currencies to purchase primary products. The PPXCs which would receive these reserve currencies could then use them in the normal way to buy goods and services, except that the PPXCs would be constrained to spend the currencies in the appropriate reserve-currency countries. Integrating the SDR—CS link with a 'price-floor version' of reserve-currency amortisation would therefore involve an unfortunate and unnecessary element of tying.

This could be avoided by integrating the link with a 'price-ceiling version' of reserve-currency amortisation. Under this version, the CSA would accept reserve currencies in exchange and as payment for primary products. The CSA would then itself deposit these currencies with an amortisation account in the IMF in exchange for SDRs. Eventually the reserve-currency countries would be required to amortise the IMF's holding of their own domestic currencies.

A third important feature of the proposed SDR–CS link is that it would not preclude or interfere with SDR–aid link schemes, the rationale of which is more specifically the provision of development assistance. The SDR–CS scheme may be regarded as being additional and complementary to those other links, since it fulfils a different and non-competitive purpose.

Fourth and finally, the SDR–CS link represents a scheme from which most countries would benefit. All countries are, to some extent, PPMCs, whilst not all of them are PPXCs. At any particular stage in a primary-product price cycle, exclusive PPMCs will have an unambiguous stance, since they will either be gaining where the price is falling or losing where the price is rising. Given a universal movement in primary-product prices, countries which are at one and the same time both PPMCs and PPXCs may have an ambivalent attitude, since they may simultaneously be gaining from a rise in export prices and losing from a rise in import prices, or losing from a fall in export prices and gaining from a fall in import prices. Depending on the structure of trade and the direction and configuration of primary-product price movements, individual countries may either gain or lose. If countries are risk or uncertainty averters with regard to future reserve levels, they are likely to prefer stable and reasonably predictable prices, with neither the chance of gain nor the risk of loss. Although at points in the price cycle of a primary commodity certain countries may stand to gain from selling a highly priced good or buying a lowly priced one, gains enjoyed at some stages of the cycle will, assuming reserves yield a diminishing marginal rate of utility, fail to compensate for losses incurred at other stages. All countries are likely to find it easier to plan for growth and development in an environment in which primary-product prices are not subject to large and violent fluctuations.

Since all countries stand to gain from commodity stabilisation, it seems appropriate that the financing of stabilisation schemes should be provided centrally and multilaterally by an international agency such as the IMF. We have seen that SDRs could be used quite conveniently to finance market intervention, even though they are not yet accepted as a medium of exchange; so, to begin with at least, the stabilisation agency would have to convert them through the IMF into acceptable currency, which would then be used to purchase the buffer stock. As soon as there were a cyclical upturn in the price of the primary commodity, the agency would begin to sell its buffer stock and could then use the resulting accumulation of foreign exchange to buy back SDRs. A significant advantage of this system of financing buffer stocks is that it is consistent with the attempt to make SDRs the central reserve asset in any reformed international monetary system. The scheme could easily be modified to permit SDRs to be used directly in transactions, and could, as noted already, be integrated with reserve-currency amortisation.

Alternatively or additionally, the profits which the Trust Fund makes as a result of selling gold at a market price above the official price could be used to finance buffer-stock schemes, in part at least. Indeed, the Trust Fund, as currently constituted, is empowered to undertake activities other than the provision of direct balance-of-payments assistance, provided that these activities do not take the IMF outside its conventional sphere of involvement. The SDRs and acceptable foreign exchange that the Trust Fund receives in exchange for the gold which it sells would, under the scheme proposed, be transferred to a CSA, which would then behave in exactly the way already described. Indeed, the only major difference between the SDR and Trust Fund financing schemes relates to the initial provision of finance. In the case of the SDR scheme this comes from a direct allocation of SDRs, whilst in the case of the Trust Fund scheme it comes from the profits derived from selling gold.

The Size of the Financing Problem

There are a range of costs associated with operating a system of buffer stocks: these may be divided into private and social costs. Private costs include both the initial cost of stock acquisition and provision of storage facilities,[29] and the running costs of the buffer stock once it has been acquired. Gross private running costs include interest charges, where the buffer stock is financed by borrowing; the maintenance of an administrative and marketing structure; and losses associated with turnover transactions, where the buffer stock agency is selling commodities which have deteriorated in quality through storage, such that there is a continuing cost associated with maintaining any given quantity of them in store. Net private running costs are likely to be lower than gross private running costs, since the buffer stock will by nature make a profit in its commodity transactions. The wider the spread of the intervention prices, the greater will these trading profits tend to be; on the other hand, a high ceiling price will be associated with larger storage costs, whilst a low floor price and high ceiling price will generally reduce the effectiveness of the scheme in terms of its stabilising objectives. The gross social cost of buffer stocks may deviate from their gross private cost, since storage will involve an additional social cost in terms of the sacrifice of current consumption. Meanwhile, net social cost will also differ from net private cost. The reasons for this discrepancy are: first, the existence of centrally administered buffer stocks may obviate the need for other stocks; second, confidence in the long-term viability of the buffer stock may encourage private speculators to operate in a price-stabilising way; and, third, the world economy will tend to benefit from commodity stabilisation in terms of more stable development, more efficient use of resources, a lower rate of inflation and a higher level of employment.[30]

The size of resources needed to finance buffer stocks will essentially depend on the private net costs of setting up the scheme. These private net costs will in turn depend on the specific details of the buffer-stock arrangements. The first factor to be taken into account is the required degree of price stability, or, in other words, the acceptable amount of price variation. The lower that prices are allowed to fall before the stabilisation agency intervenes, the fewer will be the initial resources required. A second factor is the commodity coverage of the buffer-stock scheme. This concerns the number of commodities included in the scheme and the relationships between them. The fewer the commodities included, the smaller will tend to be the initial financing problem;[31] while, if the prices of all commodities covered by the scheme fall together, the size of the initial financing problem will be greater than if the prices of just a few of the commodities fall. The size of the financing problem will be minimised as the negative correlation between the price movements of commodities included in the scheme is maximised. If the prices of the various primary products incorporated in the scheme do move in different directions, it is quite possible that, once the scheme has been established, finance freed by selling stocks of one commodity may be used to finance the buying of stocks of another commodity.[32] However, the more closely and positively related are the prices of the commodities included in the scheme, the greater will be the initial financing requirements. Primary-product prices are more likely to move together the more significant are demand factors, as compared with supply factors, in generating price changes. This is because it is perhaps rather more probable that primary commodities will experience broadly similar shifts in demand than in supply.

A third factor bearing on the size of required finance is the relevant price elasticities of demand and supply, since these will effect the extent of commodity-price variation. The lower the elasticities, the greater will be the degree of price variability, and therefore the greater the initial amount of finance will need to be.

A fourth factor is the nature of private speculation. Where private speculators behave in a market-stabilising fashion, the size of agency buffer stocks will be reduced. The confidence of private speculators in the ability of the buffer-stock agency to stabilise the market may itself depend on the size of the financial resources available to the buffer-stock agency. Indeed, it could be that, the larger are the resources available to the buffer-stock agency, the lower will be the likelihood that these resources will be needed.

Clearly, then, it is not easy to define the amount of finance that would be needed to operate a buffer-stock scheme. Everything depends on the precise nature of the scheme itself. Estimated financing requirements range from $500 million to the $6000 million that the group of seventy-seven developing countries see as being ultimately required, to the $10,000 million to $12,000 million envisaged by other commentators.[33]

On the basis of a number of assumptions, the UNCTAD Secretariat (UNCTAD, 1976) has estimated that the financing required for the acquisition of buffer stocks of the ten core commodities of the Integrated Commodity Programme would be between $4500 million and $5000 million. The assumptions include: first, that the buffer stocks will commence operation in 1979; second, that the Common Fund will be the only source of financing; third, that price stabilisation will be the sole objective of the buffer stocks; fourth, that the price range would be 10 per cent either side of an estimated average price based on 1971–5 data or 1974–8 projections; fifth, that market activity in futures will not exist; and, sixth, that demand from industrial countries will expand normally. As would be anticipated, the UNCTAD's financing estimates do appear to be very sensitive to factors such as the chosen price target, and the commodities included.[34]

To some extent, arguments concerning the size of the initial financing problem may also be interpreted as dealing with the time period over which any system of buffer stocks is to be established. Provided that storage and administrative costs are not excessive, a stabilisation agency should be able to make a trading profit, which may then be used to expand the size and coverage of the buffer-stock scheme over a number of years. In any case, it may be advisable to begin a system of buffer-stock schemes on a relatively small scale, in order to gain experience, and this would naturally reduce the size of the initial financing problem.

Implications for World Economic Stability

It has been a common theme amongst advocates of the notion of linking the international monetary system in some way with commodities that such a link would encourage a greater degree of world economic stability.[35] Clearly, one of the principal functions of the international monetary system is to act as a stabilising factor in world economic development.. Although there might be legitimate discussion on the point, it would seem from casual observation that the stability which the Bretton Woods system induced during the 1950s and early 1960s has in recent years been lost.

In what ways, then, might a connection between the international monetary system and commodities generate stability? First, by stabilising short-run prices, a buffer-stock scheme will increase the ability of primary-product producing countries to plan development and may thereby generate a secular increase in supply. An increase in supply relative to demand will tend to reduce prices and hence lower the secular rate of world inflation.

Second, although the introduction of buffer stocks, which is, of course, most properly conducted at a time of excess commodity supply, is associated with an increase in the international supply of money, it should be remembered that an increase in money supply tends to be inflationary only when the money supply expands at a faster rate than real output.Under a buffer-stock scheme such as the one outlined in the previous section the supply of international money would tend to rise most during a period of generally low prices. Where low prices reflect below-trend demand, the increase in international reserves caused by buffer-stock intervention and the preservation of income levels in primary-product producing countries may help to sustain full employment in the world economy rather than cause inflation. The activities of the buffer stock could then prevent the transmission and exacerbation of recession. It is unlikely that increases in the quantity of international money generated as a result of an expansion in the supply of particular goods would be of a sufficiently universal significance to pose a serious inflationary threat; and, in any case, in a situation of general excess commodity supply the buffer-stock scheme may again be stabilising. In the absence of market intervention and in conditions of excess supply, commodity prices will tend to fall and adjustment in commodity markets will be effected by means of a cutback in supply. Demand may not rise, since developed countries will tend to experience a reduction in the demand for their exports, because of the lower incomes in primary-product producing countries. If, instead, a buffer-stock agency acts to increase incomes in primary-product producing countries by absorbing the extra production, effective demand for manufactured goods will rise. There will be an expansion in the exports of developed countries and this will generate a multiplier effect, which will cause the rate of absorption of primary commodities to increase until it balances the rate of production.[36]

During a period of cyclically high demand, when the problem of inflation is most potent, the buffer-stock scheme would be withdrawing more than the initial allocation of SDRs from circulation and would be increasing the real supply of primary products to world markets; the scheme would serve to negate the effect which high levels of demand would otherwise have on prices. The effect of rising commodity prices on income in producing countries, and the associated increase in demand for imports from developed countries, would also be offset by the operations of the buffer stock.

The monetary implications of the buffer-stock scheme emerge as being counter-cyclical, serving to expand monetary demand and the supply of international money during cyclical troughs, and to contract the supply of international money (as well as increase the level of real supply) during cyclical peaks. Furthermore, to the extent that the commodity-stabilisation scheme might be used to hasten the replacement of reserve currencies by one reserve asset, namely the SDR, the scheme would help to eradicate one of the major intermediate sources of world monetary instability.

Concluding Remarks

The commodities problem has significant implications for LDCs, being a major determinant of many of the balance-of-payments difficulties which they experience. Compensatory-financing and buffer-stocking arrangements may be used in an attempt to deal with certain aspects of the commodities problem, in particular the stabilisation of foreign-exchange receipts. The international monetary system has for a number of years provided some compensation for export shortfalls, and it has also provided some indirect support for buffer-stock schemes. Compensatory financing could, however, be further extended and liberalised to the advantage of LDCs. Although there are arguments both for and against buffer stocks, it would appear that in certain circumstances these could operate in a beneficial fashion. The international monetary system could make a major contribution by organising or providing the finance for such buffer-stocking arrangements. Such financing would tend to be tied to changes in the quantity of international liquidity. In the mid 1970s the solution of the commodities problem has emerged as a central economic and political theme in the developing world's pursuit of a new international economic order. Another central issue has been that of an SDR–aid link and it is to this that we turn in the next chapter.

11 The Link between SDRs and Aid

The Theory of Social Saving and Seigniorage

International money is made up a number of components, including gold and foreign exchange. The production costs involved with a commodity money, such as gold, may be largely avoided by replacing it with some form of fiat money. The replacement of gold by international fiat monies therefore gives rise to a considerable social saving in terms of the resources freed from producing money. Such replacement would appear to represent an unambiguous shift towards greater efficiency in international monetary arrangements. As the international monetary system has operated, however, not all countries have gained equally from the social saving implied by the movement which has taken place away from the gold standard and towards the foreign-exchange method of creating international money.

Under a gold-standard system, non gold-producing countries have to give up real resources in order to acquire gold. Gold-producing countries, on the other hand, stand to profit if the international value of gold exceeds its costs of production. This profit to the issuer of money is known as 'seigniorage'. Where the issuer of money makes no profit, no seigniorage exists. Seigniorage and social saving are distinct and separate concepts. Whilst the social saving represents the gain in real resources of moving from a commodity to a fiat money, seigniorage represents the difference between the cost of money creation and the value of the money created.

Under a gold-exchange system the extent of the seigniorage being gained by producers of internationally acceptable foreign exchange may at first glance appear to be even greater than under a gold-standard system, since production costs are lower. The size of the seigniorage is, however, reduced in so far as interest is paid to the holders of foreign exchange. Assuming that the real-resource cost of servicing monetary obligations is zero, seigniorage will exist while the return to money creation outweighs the interest paid to the holders of money. Other than the interest derived from holding foreign exchange, however, reserve acquisition by non-issuers of international money may be equally costly in terms of real resources whether a gold-standard or a gold-exchange system operates. Indeed, without the payment of interest on money holdings, non-issuing holders of international money would gain none of the social saving associated with the move to a gold-exchange system and all the social saving in terms of extra seigniorage would be gained by money issuers. To illustrate further, let us imagine a situation in which there is but one supplier of world money. Let us further assume that international money is originally made up of gold alone, but that later there is a switch to some form of fiat money, such as foreign exchange. In these circumstances the world supplier is in a position to gain the whole of the social saving in terms of additional seigniorage, since production costs have been reduced and monopoly profits have thereby been increased. In comparison, in a situation where there is no monopoly in the supply of world money, the profits to be derived from the production of international money will tend to entice other money issuers into the market, and will tend to bring about a fall in the amount of seigniorage gained by money suppliers and a spreading of the social saving to money holders through the payment of interest. With a competitive system of international money supply, then, the social saving associated with the substitution of fiat money for commodity money will be distributed to the holders of international money through interest payments. For as long as there is a degree of monopoly in international money supply, however, the issuers of money will be able to gain seigniorage and absorb a portion of the social saving for themselves, since the interest paid to money holders will not rise sufficiently to offset the returns to money creation.

It emerges that one significant question to which the discussion of social saving and seigniorage clearly gives rise is that of the distribution of social saving and seigniorage. It is to certain aspects of this question that this chapter is primarily addressed.

The international monetary system could be so organised as to ensure that seigniorage is distributed in a neutral fashion, i.e. that no permanently unrequited real-resource flows are generated as a result of the creation of international money. Neutrality may be brought about either by paying the holders of such money an appropriate rate of interest, or by distributing the new money in such a way that it is *held* by those initially receiving it rather than *spent*, such that seigniorage takes the form of the additional security afforded by increased reserve holdings.

As the gold-exchange system was worked in practice, however, the social saving and seigniorage which has been derived has not been distributed neutrally. The United States has been in a position to finance, in a relatively costless fashion, a transfer of real wealth to itself by creating dollars to be held as reserves outside the United States. Meanwhile, gold-producing countries have also been able to derive seigniorage. An international monetary system which distributes the social saving and seigniorage to its richer members may be criticised on grounds of equity. It might be suggested that equity would be better served by permitting LDCs to gain the benefits of the social saving and seigniorage. Considerations of equity and efficiency may, however, conflict, since the payment of a rate of interest on money holdings which lies below the opportunity cost of these holdings expressed in terms of the real return on resources will tend to restrict the holdings of international money to a 'sub-optimal' level, thus preventing the re-alisation of the full potential social saving from the use of fiat money.[1] A so-called 'optimal' system of international monetary creation would involve distributional neutrality, zero seigniorage at the margin of money creation, and the allocation of social saving to the holders of money. However, interpreting optimality more widely, to incorporate both efficiency and equity, serves to re-emphasise the significance of the distributional aspects of the creation of international money. Given the existing situation with regard to world income distribution, the equity gains from allocating seigniorage to LDCs may outweigh any losses expressed in terms of inefficiency. Any international monetary system has to deal consciously or subconsciously with the problem of the distribution of the seigniorage associated with the creation of in-ternational money.

The SDR scheme provides a ready mechanism through which the social saving and seigniorage associated with the creation of non-commodity international liquidity may be directed either wholly or in part towards LDCs.

SDRs and Informal Aid Link

The proposal for a link between the creation of international liquidity and the provision of aid hinges on the notion that to direct towards LDCs the benefit of the social saving involved in the use of fiat as against commodity money would represent a significant movement towards the establishment of a more egalitarian international community. SDRs represent a relatively costless means through which the international monetary system, via the IMF, can increase the supply of international liquidity at its own discretion.[2] By initially, in some way, allocating new issues of SDRs to LDCs, these countries will acquire command over real resources without having to make any direct real sacrifice; the increase in their reserves will be 'unearned'. As the SDR scheme was formulated, and as it currently operates, LDCs are allocated SDRs on the same terms as other participants in the scheme. The distribution formula results in the relatively few developed countries receiving about 75 per cent of newly created SDRs, while the many LDCs receive only 25 per cent. The average total allocation to each industrial country has been more than sixteen times as large as the average total allocation to each LDC, this difference in average total allocation being largely accounted for by the relative insignificance of LDCs in world trade, and the comparatively low levels of national income in these countries. Notwithstanding the relatively low level of their total allocation, however, SDRs have been of considerable importance to LDCs in their pursuit of development. Even though they have not been provided with a large share of drawing rights, they have in fact used what rights they possess in much larger proportions than have industrial countries and under the present constitution of the SDR scheme it is to net users of SDRs that seigniorage is distributed, inasmuch as net users derive a transfer of real resources. Over the first basic period of SDR allocation, LDCs were net users to the value of SDR 835 million, although this does not mean that they acquired real resources to this value, since some of the net use may have reflected interest payments and transfers to the General Account.[3] By the end of 1974 three out of every four LDCs participating in the SDR scheme had been net users of SDRs. Only a few LDCs made a net acquisition of SDRs. On the other hand, industrial countries as a whole have made a net acquisition of SDRs. When it is remembered that a substantial portion of the industrial countries' use of SDRs reflects the amortisation by the United States of previously accumulated externally held dollar liabilities, and the cancellation of previously accumulated debt by the United Kingdom, then these figures tend to suggest that the operation of the SDR scheme has brought about a considerable transfer of real resources to LDCs. Broadly speaking industrial countries have been accepting SDRs from LDCs in return for goods and services. The LDCs have received these real resources without having to pay for them by running down their often already meagre holdings of gold and foreign exchange, or by selling exports. The SDR scheme has thus served to increase the real resources available to LDCs in a manner which is practically costless to them. The only cost of using allocated SDRs is the relatively modest interest rate on their use and the opportunity cost of forgoing the balance-of-payments security which is afforded by an increase in reserve holding.

To establish a system by which LDCs might finance a transfer of real resources to themselves was not an original intention of the SDR scheme. Indeed, the Group of Ten countries specifically stated a preference for the SDR scheme to be neutral with respect to international resource transfers. In an attempt to provide the international monetary system with reserves to be held rather than spent, i.e. in an attempt to ensure neutrality, SDRs were allocated on the basis of IMF quotas, which are supposed to give an indication of individual countries' long-run demand for reserves to hold. In retrospect, however, it is difficult to see how any outcome other than a real-resource transfer to LDCs could have emerged. Certainly it is unlikely that many LDCs would be in a position to offer convertible currencies for other countries' SDRs and thus acquire SDRs. Looking to the future, and making two assumptions about the international monetary system – namely, that developed countries will be anxious to accumulate reserves at a rate faster than SDR allocation will permit, and that SDR allocation will constitute an important method by which total reserves are expanded – it seems likely that the transfer of real resources to LDCs will continue.

A number of factors govern the extent to which a transfer of real resources from developed to less-developed countries results from the distribution of SDRs.[4] In the first instance, wealth redistribution depends both on the proportion of any SDR allocation that is given to LDCs, and the demand-for-reserves functions in LDCs and developed countries. Where an SDR allocation results in LDCs' possessing excess reserves and developed countries' holding fewer reserves than desired, reserves will tend to move from LDCs to developed countries as the former spend their excess reserves on imports from the latter.

The resource-transfer effects of SDR distribution depend, further, on the nature and level of interest payments on SDRs. Where, in effect, LDC users of SDRs have to pay interest to developed-country receivers of SDRs, the extent of the real-resource transfer to LDCs will be reduced. The grant element in SDR allocation crucially depends on the rate of interest on SDR net use. Other things remaining constant, the grant element is inversely related to the rate of interest.[5] Where the rate of interest is zero, LDCs will benefit in terms of real resources to the full extent of the SDRs used.

The value of the SDR scheme to LDCs depends, however, not only on the volume of real resources transferred to them, but also on the marginal productivity of these resources, and the social discount rate. For as long as the marginal productivity of resources acquired through the net use of SDRs exceeds the rate of interest on SDRs, LDCs will tend to experience a real-resource benefit. An interesting question now arises. Is the benefit in real resources gained by LDCs as a result of SDR allocation counterbalanced by an equivalent loss in developed countries? The answer to this question depends on the relative marginal productivities of real resources and social discount rates in LDCs and developed countries. Assuming that social discount rates are similar, but that real resources *at the margin* are more productive in LDCs than in developed countries, it is quite possible that the value of the wealth gain in LDCs will exceed the value of the wealth loss in developed countries. It would be possible, under these circumstances, for LDCs to compensate developed countries for their real-resource loss (by paying interest on SDR use at a rate equal to the rate of return on real resources in developed countries) and still benefit. An increase in efficiency in the allocation of world resources would thereby be brought about by the careful distribution of SDRs.

It emerges from the above analysis that the proportion of seigniorage which LDCs derive from the creation of SDRs is positively related to the proportion of the total SDR allocation which they receive, and negatively related to the interest rate paid on SDRs. LDCs will gain all the seigniorage where SDRs are allocated exclusively to them and the interest rate is zero. However, the higher the proportion of SDRs which initially go to developed countries, or the closer that the interest rate is to the rate of return on real resources in the world as a whole, the more the seigniorage will go to developed countries. The actual amount of seigniorage which is available to be distributed will be positively related to the interest-rate elasticity of demand for SDRs to hold. The size of permanent real-resource transfers to LDCs rests partly on the proportion of SDRs allocated to LDCs. In turn, the distribution of SDRs as between LDCs and developed countries depends on the distribution formula used.[6]

Forerunners of the SDR–Aid Link

The notion of tying development assistance to liquidity creation has a long and well documented history.[7] Although as far back as 1943 the concept of a link was incorporated in the Keynes plan for an international clearing union, Stamp is usually credited with making the first explicit proposal for a link, in 1958. Basically, the original Stamp proposal was that the IMF should be given the power to issue Fund certificates, to be used primarily as a supplement to international liquidity but also as a form of development assistance. The idea was that any IMF member should be obliged to accept the certificates when tendered by the Fund or a central bank and provide its own domestic currency in exchange. Holders of certificates would, in turn, be able to exchange them into foreign currencies. In the first instance, the IMF would give certificates to a development agency such as the International Development Association (IDA), which would then allocate them to LDCs. LDCs receiving certificates would use them to finance imports by converting them into the foreign currencies required. Stamp subsequently modified his proposal in certain ways without altering its fundamental nature.

Rather more incidentally than in the case of the Stamp plan, in 1959 Triffin put forward a proposal for international monetary reform which incorporated a version of the link. Triffin's main concern was to suggest a form of international monetary system that would not rely on the use of national currencies as international reserves. To this end he proposed that the foreign-exchange component of reserves should be channelled into centralised deposits with the IMF. These deposits could then be used by the IMF, in line with normal banking procedures, to make advances or provide overdraft facilities in response to requests from member countries, or, at the initiative of the IMF, to undertake open market purchases and sales of securities and investments. Under the provisions of the Triffin plan, the IMF might lend assistance to LDCs by purchasing the financial obligations of development agencies such as the IBRD.

The link proposals of Stamp and Triffin spawned a number of often closely related schemes. In 1965, for instance, the UNCTAD issued a report recommending a link plan similar to that of Triffin's. Under the UNCTAD plan the IMF would issue Fund units to all member countries in exchange for deposits of domestic currency placed with the IMF. The Fund would then invest in IBRD bonds a portion of the currencies thereby acquired. The IBRD would in turn transfer some of its additional funds to the IDA, in order to finance 'soft' (i.e. long-term, low-interst) loans to LDCs.

A substantial modification to earlier proposals was incorporated into a link scheme advocated by Scitovsky in 1965. Like Stamp's plan,

Scitovsky's appeared in a number of versions. Essentially he suggested that units of new international currency should be created and allocated to countries experiencing difficulties in financing balance-of-payments deficits. The issue of new international currency by the IMF would be backed by these deficit countries' depositing domestic currency with the Fund. It was in the nature of Scitovsky's scheme, however, that the new international currency should intially be given not to deficit countries but to LDCs, with the intention that the currency should be used to finance development imports from the deficit countries. A strategic feature of the scheme was that an LDC receiving the new international currency could spend it *only* in the deficit country against whose domestic currency the new international currency had been issued. In effect, the deficit country would have to earn an increase in its reserves by supplying real resources to LDCs, whilst the LDCs would receive a 'tied grant'. A later version of the Scitovsky plan proposed that the newly created international currency units should be allocated to the IDA, which would spend this currency, only in the deficit countries which backed its issue, to finance approved development projects in LDCs.

Although certain versions of the aid link have found a degree of influential support (as for instance in the UNCTAD; the Pearson Commission on International Development; the House of Commons Select Committee on Overseas Aid; and the Sub-Committee on International Exchange and Payments, of the Joint Economic Committee of the US Congress), in general the link proposal did not find sufficient support for it to be included as an integral part of the SDR scheme at the time of its inception. Indeed, the Group of Ten, which for a considerable period of time supported a 'limited group' approach to the distribution of new reserve assets, remained adamant that such a link should not be made a *formal* part of the SDR scheme. Certain details of the SDR facility as described in the SDR-related amendment to the Articles of Agreement of the IMF (for instance, the ruling that development agencies should not be permitted to hold SDRs) may be interpreted as reflecting a desire to prevent the establishment of a link between liquidity creation and development assistance.

Inasmuch as the SDR facility does not involve currency backing for the new reserve asset and relies solely on the general acceptability of SDRs, certain link proposals, such as those of Triffin, Scitovsky, and the UNCTAD, have become less relevant. More recently, almost all proposals for linking liquidity creation to development aid have been presented in the context of the SDR scheme, and it is to a rather general examination of these proposals that we now turn.

Types of SDR–Aid Link

The 'inorganic' link

Schemes for linking the creation of international liquidity to the provision of development assistance are conventionally grouped into one of two categories. One set of proposals involves an 'inorganic' link through which developed countries would undertake to make voluntary contributions to development agencies at the time of each SDR allocation. Normally contributions would take the form of national currencies, would represent a uniform proportion of each contributor's SDR allocation, and would be made to a body such as the IDA, which would then use the currencies for financing development. Certain versions of the inorganic link incorporate a system of tied contributions. By this, contributed funds would in the first instance be spent only in the contributing country. Features of the inorganic link are: first, it would be relatively easy to implement, since it would involve no further amendment to the IMF's Articles of Agreement; second, parliamentary approval would have to be sought for each contribution; and, third, it would be possible for individual developed countries to opt out. The only difference between inorganic link schemes and autonomous decisions to increase normal aid is that under the inorganic link the decision to increase aid would be loosely related to the receipt of SDR allocations.

The 'organic' link

In contrast to the inorganic link, which relies on voluntary participation, schemes which come under the heading of an 'organic' link involve a more formalised connection between the creation of SDRs and aid and would entail some amendments to the IMF's Articles of Agreement. There are many variations on the theme of an 'organic link', but it is hoped that the following classification may prove illustrative. An organic link might take on any of the following forms.

(a) *A relative and absolute increase in the direct allocation of SDRs to LDCs.* This could be achieved either within the present scope of the SDR scheme, by increasing the quotas of LDCs, or outside the present scope of the scheme, by moving away altogether from the allocating of SDRs on the basis of IMF quotas. In Chapter 8, various ways in which the SDR distribution formula could be modified were discussed. The nature of the gain to LDCs resulting from such modifications would depend on the degree to which extra SDR allocations were held or spent. The benefit gained by holding SDRs, expressed in terms of an increase in reserves, might be represented by the opportunity cost of such an increase, whilst the benefit gained by spending SDRs might be represented by the real resources thereby acquired. However, the more LDCs that opt to spend their increased allocations of SDRs, the lower, because of the inflation induced as a result, is likely to be the amount of real resources acquired for a given number of SDRs. The question of whether SDRs are to be held or spent begs the further question of why countries need reserves.[8] In any distribution formula, variables relating to the incidence of balance-of-payments difficulties and the cost of adjustment provide information on the need for reserves to hold, whilst variables relating to the level of development and certain structural phenomena, such as the strategic significance of imports in the development process, perhaps refer as or more closely to the need for reserves to spend. It might be suggested that a demand for reserves to spend may more accurately be said to reflect a need for aid than to reflect a need for reserves. As a matter of fact, however, reserve creation does have incidental implications for development and organic link proposals specifically discuss the possibility of formalising the connections between reserve creation and development assistance. The effectiveness of a changed-distribution-formula version of the organic link in bringing about a transfer of real resources to LDCs rests on the LDC recipient's propensity to spend the extra SDRs. A feature of this form of organic link is that no aid agency would be involved as an intermediary.

(b) *A direct allocation of SDRs to development agencies.* Under this version of the organic link, a proportion or indeed the total amount of each SDR allocation would be channelled to development agencies, which would have accounts in the IMF's Special Account. The development agencies could then either exchange these SDRs for national currencies to be used to finance 'soft' loans, or transfer SDRs to the accounts of those countries supplying development goods, allowing these SDR recipients to pay domestic exporters in domestic currency. A significant feature of this version of the organic link is that, following initial parliamentary approval of the scheme, it would remove aid from national budgetary control.

(c) *An agreed contribution of SDRs to development agencies by developed countries only*.   In many ways this is similar to the version examined under (b). The significant difference is that to begin with all participants in the SDR scheme would be allocated SDRs in the normal way, but then *developed countries alone* would contribute a fixed proportion of their allocation to development agencies. The strategic feature of this scheme is that LDCs would not be expected to make an SDR contribution to the link.

As with the inorganic link, versions of the organic link may be presented in either a tied or an untied guise. In an untied guise, first-round spending of SDRs would be unrestricted, whilst in the tied scheme the location SDR spending would be restricted to those countries which express a willingness to pay the real-resource cost implied by an acquisition of earned SDRs.

Some Other Considerations Relevant to the Choice of SDR–Aid Link

Linking reserve-currency amortisation with aid

In international monetary discussions and arrangements, considerable support has been given to the proposal that the SDR should become the basic reserve asset in the international monetary system. Such a modification would have significant beneficial effects. For instance, it would eliminate the occurrence, as a result of crises of confidence, of destabilising speculative shifts between different reserve assets, and it would put the growth of international liquidity under purposive international control.

 As part of a move towards an SDR-based system, official holdings of reserve currencies could be deposited with the IMF in exchange for a special issue of SDRs. In every sense of the term, holdings of reserve currencies would thereby be 'funded'. In addition to paying interest on this funded debt, reserve-currency countries could then be requested to amortise the debt over time by transferring either allocated or earned SDRs to the IMF. The process of cancelling reserve-currency balances with the IMF would imply a steady reduction in the total quantity of reserve assets in the international monetary system to the value of the SDRs transferred to the IMF by the reserve-currency countries. This destruction of SDRs could be counterbalanced by appropriate discretionary SDR creation, or by grafting a form of aid link onto the system of reserve-currency amortisation. The link might work in the following manner.[9] The unrequited export surpluses required by the reserve-currency countries in order to acquire SDRs could be channelled to LDCs by means of the IMF's issuing to development agencies a special allocation of SDRs equal to the annual amortisation obligations accepted by the reserve-currency countries. Alternatively, the IMF could annually reactivate a proportion of the reserve currencies deposited with it, by making these available to development agencies to be spent on purchasing goods and services from the reserve-currency countries.

By creating SDRs equivalent to the amortisation obligations of the reserve-currency countries, the IMF could both prevent the decline in international liquidity that would otherwise take place, and ensure that an aid link would be operative even in years when there was no general allocation of SDRs.

In order to encourage monetary authorities to hold SDRs rather than alternative reserve assets, it is likely that SDRs will have to offer a competitive interest rate. The question of the interest rate to be paid to holders of SDRs and to be charged to users of SDRs raises a number important issues.

The interest rate on SDRs and the link

A case may be made out that SDRs should carry a competitive interest rate. To begin with, failure to pay a competitive rate will hinder the substitution of reserve currencies by SDRs. Again, the theory of the optimum quantity of money maintains that SDRs, since costless to produce, should be created for as long as they yield a positive marginal utility. Countries will, however, be willing to *hold* SDRs only if they yield a competitive interest rate. Even though arguments against the payment of market rates do exist, such as the claim that they would weaken the incentive for surplus countries to contribute to the adjustment process, a consensus of opinion does appear to exist in favour of competitive rates.[10]

The payment of a competitive rate of interest to the holders of SDRs has important implications for the SDR–aid link. To the extent that the payment of a competitive rate of interest to the holders of SDRs implies an equivalent increase in the interest paid by net users of SDRs, the increase in the interest rate will cause a reduction in the seigniorage gained by net users of SDRs. Even so, LDCs may still gain from the SDR facility, if the interest rate paid on SDR use lies below the rate that would otherwise have had to be paid for development finance, and below the rate of return on resources. If it is considered desirable not only to offer a competitive rate on SDR holdings, but also to increase the grant element in SDR allocation above the level it would be under a competitive rate system, or further to maximise the resource transfers to LDCs as net users of SDRs, it follows that a system for reconciling these conflicting objectives is necessary. Reconciliation could be achieved through some form of subsidisation under which LDCs would be treated on preferential terms. By subsidising the LDCs' interest payments on their net use of SDRs, the real-resource transfers implied by the link could be maintained or even increased without impairing the relative 'quality' of the SDR as a reserve asset to hold.

Without some modification to the current constitution of the SDR system, the objectives of the redistribution of wealth to LDCs, and the payment of a competitive interest rate may conflict even more sharply than is perhaps at first apparent. Under conditions where the rate of interest on SDRs exceeds the rate of growth of link allocations, the net transfer of resources to LDCs will, after a number of years, turn negative.[11] Assuming a constant annual rate of link allocations, the real transfer turn-round will come sooner the higher is the rate of interest on SDR use. Some fear has been expressed in the literature that the building up of large interest obligations by LDCs might pose the danger of default.[12] It is difficult, however, to think of circumstances under which it would be in an LDC's own interests to default, since the costs of such a policy in terms of international retaliation, and more particularly the almost certain sacrifice of future SDR allocations, are always likely to outweigh the benefits in terms of the interest payments avoided. In any case, the danger of default may conveniently be avoided in a number of ways. It may, for instance, be avoided by ensuring that interest payments represent a prior claim on new linked SDR allocations. Such a scheme would, of course, reduce the benefit of the link to LDCs. As has been seen, LDCs will gain most, in terms of real resource transfers, from the SDR link where the interest rate is zero.

Although it might therefore appear that, consistent with the adoption of the SDR as the key international monetary asset, LDCs would have a vested interest in keeping the rate on SDRs as low as possible, their attitude is in practice likely to be ambivalent. As users of SDRs, LDCs would no doubt prefer a low rate in order to maximise the real-resource gains from SDR allocation. On the other hand, as holders of SDRs LDCs would prefer them to carry an interest rate closer to that on reserve-currency assets. Ideally, LDCs would no doubt prefer an SDR scheme under which a competitive interest rate is paid to all holders but a lower rate is charged to LDC users. Such a scheme could be achieved if developed countries were prepared to subsidise the interest payments of LDCs on the net use of their SDRs.

Linking SDR allocation to commodity stabilisation

So far, most emphasis has been placed on SDR link proposals which link the allocation of SDRs fairly precisely with development finance. The link schemes discussed share the common feature that SDR allocation is related to the need for aid and for reserves to spend. Whilst it is difficult to make much operational sense of a distinction between reserves to hold and reserves to spend,[13] the distinction may provide a certain theoretical insight. In the case of many LDCs, the export reliance on a few primary products, and the tendency for the prices of these products to fluctuate present balance-of-payments difficulties. Arguably, such countries require reserves to hold in order to insure against forced adjustment in cases where primary-product price variations cause balance-of-payments deficits. The IMF could stand prepared to create such *precautionary* reserves, as and when required, in the form of SDRs. SDR allocation could then be linked in part at least to those balance-of-payments deficits in LDCs which have been caused by fluctuations in the prices of primary products. This type of SDR link could conveniently be related to a commodity-stabilisation scheme.[14] In the case of a price fall, an IMF commodity-stablision agency could enter the market as a buyer, paying for its purchases with newly created SDRs, and thus protecting the balance-of-payments positions of the LDCs concerned, both directly, in terms of the SDRs created, and indirectly, in terms of the supported price. As soon as prices rose, the CSA could offload its stocks onto the market, being paid in acceptable reserve assets. The scheme could adopt a number of forms, including that of being associated with a reserve-currency amortisation plan; but the essence of the scheme remains the same in all forms: namely, that SDRs are not provided to LDCs solely as aid to spend, irrespective of balance-of-payments positions, but rather as an activated precautionary international reserve designed to protect them against the implications of balance-of-payments deficits.

The Burden-Sharing Implications of the Link

Advocates of the link often use the argument that it represents a Pareto-efficient modification to the operation of the international monetary system. The arguments both for and against the link will be examined in some depth in the following two sections, but, if this claim is accurate, it may be illegitimate to imply that there is any 'burden' as such associated with the link. In this section, we investigate potential criteria for determining contributions to the link, and further look at the various implications of the link for balances of payments, real resources and international reserves.[15]

The initial distribution of contributions to the SDR link depends very much on the type of link adopted. Under most organic schemes, however, some criterion for determining the SDR contributions of countries would have to be decided. Three approaches may be identified. Under the first, each donating country would be required to relinquish the same proportion of its SDR allocation. Under the second, the proportion would be related to the country's contribution to IDA replenishment; and, under the third, the proportion would be related to GNP. Which approach is adopted depends on the fundamental question of whether contributions should be determined on a purely equitable basis in terms of the SDR scheme, or whether they should be determined more widely, in terms of ability to pay, or whether they should be determined by past willingness to provide aid.[16] To the extent that IMF quotas, IDA replenishments and GNPs are not perfectly positively correlated, the choice of approach would be crucial in determining the relative amounts of SDRs relinquished by various countries.

The real-resource and international-reserve implications of the link depend upon its precise configuration. Let us compare two extreme systems of SDR allocation. At one extreme, where no link exists and SDRs are allocated to individual countries, which then hold all the SDRs received, the implications will be that *all* participants will experience an increase in their reserves, and *no* participant will experience a loss or gain of real resources. At the other extreme, where the total SDR allocation is distributed to LDCs through the link, the outcome is less predictable. If LDCs do not spend the SDRs, their reserve holdings will rise to the full extent of the SDR allocation, whilst in developed countries neither reserves nor real-resource levels will change. It is in the nature of the link, however, that linked SDRs should be spent. If LDCs spend all the linked SDRs that they receive, they will lose the opportunity to increase their reserves but will gain real resources in exchange. Assuming that LDCs spend the SDRs on imports purchased from developed countries, the developed countries' reserves will increase, but at a cost in terms of the real resources exported to LDCs.

The manner in which this impact is spread between developed countries depends, in the first instance, on where LDCs spend SDRs. If the SDR expenditure of LDCs is concentrated in a few surplus developed countries, then these countries will experience the whole of the reserve gain, but also the entire real-resource loss. In these circumstances, deficit developed countries will experience no change in either reserves or real resources unless there occurs a secondary redistribution whereby the surplus developed countries spend part of their acquired SDRs on imports from them. If such second-round spending does occur, then the reserve and real-resource effects of the allocation of linked SDRs will be more evenly distributed among all developed countries.

Under a linked system of SDR allocation such as that elaborated in the preceding paragraph, it is quite possible that, where a developed country has a low IMF quota and thus a low SDR allocation, but wins a large share of aid-induced exports and has a high propensity to earn reserves, it will finish up with more reserves under a linked scheme than under an unlinked one.[17]

Arguments For and Against the Link

The relevance of particular arguments for or against the SDR – aid link tend to vary with the type of link being discussed. Thus, for instance, some arguments relevant to a link which allocates SDRs directly to LDCs might not apply, or would apply with less force, to a link which allocates SDRs indirectly to LDCs through the intermediation of a development agency. Having acknowledged this factor, however, it is possible to draw up a list of facets of the link which have generally been suggested as being either favourable or unfavourable. First we shall present these arguments, and then we shall discuss them.

Arguments in favour of the link

First, the link provides a mechanism through which the international community can organise an increase in the flow of real resources to LDCs. The growth of aid through conventional channels has failed to keep up with the growth of world output and trade, and what aid has been provided has frequently been tied. The link could be so arranged as to supply untied, and perhaps concessionary, multilateral aid, which would tend to expand automatically with world economic growth. An often-stated constraint on the granting of aid by developed countries has been its implications for the balance of payments.

Second, the link could have favourable implications for the balance of payments of developed countries. These countries would earn SDRs through exporting goods and services to LDCs. The cost of the scheme to developed countries would be a real-resource one rather than a balance-of-payments one. Indeed, where developed countries show a preference for *earning* reserves through surpluses and LDCs show a preference for real resources, the link would indeed be Pareto efficient. The desire of developed countries to run surpluses will tend to be frustrated if no country or group of countries is prepared to run the implied deficits. If LDCs are prepared to run deficits and an SDR link enables them to finance these deficits, surpluses may be achieved by developed countries without incurring a cost in terms of unemployment. In a situation where the choice is between a linked and an unlinked SDR system, the linked system may have an equivalent beneficial impact on price stability, since with a link in operation developed countries will be forced to earn SDRs. Developed countries wanting extra reserves will thus have to adjust their economies in order to maintain competitiveness.[18]

Third, SDRs are a fiat money, and fiat money gives rise to a social saving. Although Pareto efficiency in the international monetary system does not dictate a particular distribution of SDRs, considerations of equity suggest that the social saving should be directed towards poor rather than rich countries.

It is probably fair to conclude that the case in favour of the link hinges fundamentally on the three points raised above: namely, the quantity and quality of aid, the reconciliation of developed countries' trading targets, and the equitable distribution of the social saving. However, the compulsion of the case for an SDR – aid link is not independent of world economic conditions, and is likely to be strongest where developed countries are experiencing difficulties in avoiding both unemployment and balance-of-trade deficits. Deflationary actions taken by individual developed countries in order to improve their balance of payments at the balance-of-payments cost of other developed countries may lead to competitive deflations and a rise in the level of unemployment in the developed world as a whole, with little or no change in relative balance-of-payments positions. The problem facing developed countries combines two elements: an inadequate level of aggregate demand and an inadequate level of exports relative to imports. In these circumstances the SDR – aid link may provide the solution. Exports represent a component of aggregate demand. An increase in the exports of developed countries would then not only serve to improve the balance-of-payments positions of these countries but would also absorb unutilised capacity. An increase in the exports of developed countries could be brought about by an SDR—aid link, since LDCs with excess SDRs would tend to spend them on imports from developed countries. By means of the link the notional demand in LDCs for the products of developed countries could be made effective, and the unemployment caused in the developed countries by inadequate aggregate demand could thereby be removed. In conditions of unemployment, the real-resource cost of the link to developed countries is less apparent; indeed, the opportunity cost of the link to these countries becomes zero. This is because the link itself serves to create an incentive to produce the extra real resources which are exported. As compared with a situation in which there is no link, developed countries experience a net gain in terms of the employment generated, and may even experience a resource gain through the multiplied increase in aggregate output.[19] In conditions of unemployment, then, there appears to be a fourth argument in favour of the link.

Arguments against the link

It is suggested by opponents of the link, first, that the link would generate additional inflation. Effectively this argument is based on an international version of the quantity theory of money. A net increase in world aggregate monetary demand with no matching increase in real supply will be reflected in an upward movement in prices. Where aid is expressed in money terms, and the inflation is such that the terms of trade move against the LDCs, then LDCs least of all will benefit from the link.

A second argument is that any aid equivalent gained by LDCs as a result of the link will be offset by reductions in other forms of aid. Third, the allocation of aid would tend to be rather random if SDR creation is related solely to the needs of the international monetary system. This point involves the belief that international money creation and development assistance are independent activities, motivated and determined by different factors, that should not be pursued through the use of one common instrument. The fear appears to be that (from the point of view of the international monetary system) too many or (from the point of view of development) too few SDRs would be created.

Fourth, but leading on from this, it is maintained by critics that the link distributes the aid burden in a rather inappropriate way. The basis of this argument is that quotas do not provide a suitable criterion for determining the allocation of the aid burden.

A fifth often-voiced argument against the link is that it would tend to reduce confidence in the SDR as a reserve asset. Other arguments are: sixth, that the link scheme would somehow reduce or remove parliamentary control over the provision of aid, with this exacerbating the threat of inflation; seventh, that balance-of-payments disequilibria between developed countries would be enhanced, as surplus countries would tend to win most of the LDCs' SDR-financed export orders; and, eighth, that the link represents inefficient international monetary reform, inasmuch as the SDR system could be organised in a way which would generate no permanent real-resource transfers. By distributing SDRs in line with countries' long-run demand for reserves to hold, or by charging a competitive rate of interest on SDR use equivalent to the rate of return on real resources, it would be possible to make all countries better off in terms of the liquidity yield from SDRs, and no country worse off in terms of the loss of real resources.

An assessment of the arguments for and against the link

Space does not permit a full evaluation of all the arguments and counter-arguments which have been raised in discussions over the link. Instead of attempting to present an all-embracing appraisal therefore, this section concentrates on certain broad areas of concern.

(a) *Aid.* There are a number of aspects of aid over which the SDR link might exert an influence. Crucial amongst these are (i) the total quantity of aid, (ii) the quality of aid, and (iii) the distribution of the benefits and burdens of aid.

Although an *ex ante* answer to the question of whether *additional* aid will be generated by the link is impossible, it seems probable that extra aid *would* result, since linked aid would be multilateral and the reserve cost would be more evenly spread among donors than is the case with unilateral aid. Additional aid may be particularly likely if the link adopted takes the form of direct country allocations. Allocations to a development agency may be associated to a greater degree with conventional aid, and may encourage the view amongst aid donors that agency finance is provided through the international monetary system. Even so, there may be something to be said from the LDCs' point of view for getting aid provision based on more formal arrangements.

The magnitude of the aid provided through the link, additional or not, is likely to be relatively small. Over the first basic period of SDR allocation, the overall increase in concessional aid, even if developed countries had contributed 50 per cent of their allocated SDRs to aid, *ceteris paribus*, would have been little more than 10 per cent. Part of the benefit to LDCs from the link may of course come from the improved quality of aid rather than from an increase in its quantity. The quality of aid generated through the link depends essentially on two factors, namely (i) whether the aid comes through an agency, and, if so, which agency, and (ii) the rate of interest on SDR net use. Individual LDCs will tend to value direct allocations more highly than indirect agency allocations. Again, as the rate of interest on SDRs rises in relation to rates on other loans, from the point of view of LDCs the relative quality of SDRs falls. With an interest rate of 5 per cent on SDRs, the grant component is about 33 per cent, whilst the grant element on Development Assistance Committee aid is approximately 80 per cent.

With regard to the distribution of the benefits, the type of link adopted is very significant. With a system of direct allocations based on IMF quotas, a high percentage of the development assistance associated with the link would go to the relatively well-off LDCs. If conventional aid fell as a result of the implementation of a link, then the link could turn out to have a regressive impact on aid. It might be anticipated that the least-developed countries will favour a link which embodies agency allocation and concessional interest rates. Richer LDCs, on the other hand, will, if they are substantial holders of SDRs, tend to favour a direct link, which incorporates a higher interest rate.

It emerges from this analysis that the implications of the link for aid depend very much on the *type* of link adopted. Although most forms of the link would probably have a beneficial influence on aid, enough doubts exist, concerning the size of the aid provision, the quality of the assistance and the distribution of the aid, to question whether the aid gain would be as large as some of the more outspoken advocates of the link suggest. However, evidence would seem to suggest that there is little reason to hope that, without the link, aid will increase markedly. If it may be assumed that developed countries would be unlikely to cut current aid levels, the link may still present the best available means by which to effect a more equitable distribution of world income.

(b) *Inflation.*[20]   The real value of aid could, of course, fall if the link were to cause inflation. Assuming the existence of certain conditions, the theoretical logic of the argument that the SDR–aid link is inflationary cannot be challenged. The necessary conditions are, first, that the linked

SDRs which are allocated to LDCs are spent; second, that aggregate real supply does not expand sufficiently to offset the increase in aggregate monetary demand which is financed by the allocation of SDRs; third, that compensatory expenditure-reducing policies which would serve to free the real resources to be transferred to LDCs are not undertaken; and, fourth, that the world economy does not possess spare capacity which may be used to increase real output. The smaller the extent to which these conditions are met, the less likely it is that the link will be inflationary. But, even assuming that the conditions are met, this does not herald the end of the discussion on the inflationary impact of the link. Three key issues now arise.

The first of these concerns aid. If the international community agrees that its richer members should provide development assistance to its poorer members, the inflation case against the link rests on the assumption that SDR linked aid is *more* inflationary than other forms of aid. The crux of the argument that this is indeed the case relies on the view that conventional aid is visible and is matched at a national level by compensating fiscal actions, whilst SDR linked aid is less visible and will not be so compensated. The strength of this argument is, however, by no means self evident.

The second issue concerns the desire to increase the quantity of international liquidity. If it is felt appropriate that liquidity should be expanded, then the significant question is whether the SDR–aid link is a more inflationary mechanism for bringing this expansion about than alternative mechanisms. Three alternative mechanisms may be mentioned: increasing the price of gold; expanding the reserve-currency system; and increasing the allocation of unlinked SDRs. Each of these mechanisms might also be inflationary. Indeed, it may be suggested that the SDR–aid link is the *least* inflationary method of creating extra international reserves. Compared, for instance, with the unlinked SDR scheme, the linked scheme forces developed countries to earn reserves and thus encourages the competitive pursuit of low rates of inflation. Direct, unearned SDR allocations are initially distributed to all participants, irrespective of the state of their domestic economies. The unlinked method of SDR distribution thereby forgoes the opportunity to incorporate an anti-inflationary bias in the initial allocation of reserves.[21] Furthermore, if, in terms of real resources, reserves are more productive in LDCs than in developed countries, from a supply point of view the linked method of SDR allocation may be less inflationary.

The third issue concerns the *size* of the inflationary threat. This in turn depends on a number of factors, including the size of the SDR emission;

the proportion of SDRs that are linked; the propensity of LDCs to spend SDRs; the geographical location of SDR-financed expenditure; the level of employment and capacity utilisation in the countries receiving SDR-financed export orders; and the saving and trading propensities and patterns in these export-order receiving countries, along with the desire of these countries to increase their holdings of international reserves.

To some extent it is possible to estimate the size of the inflationary impetus emanating from the link. This is conventionally done in an *ex post* fashion by calculating the percentage addition to aggregate demand through extra export demand that would have resulted if various forms of the link had been in operation. Every estimation that has been made shares the common conclusion that the size of the increased demand generated by the link, whatever its precise form, would be very small. Dell (1969), for instance, calculates that, even with an SDR allocation of SDR 5000 million, the addition to demand for output in the OECD countries would be less than 0.3 per cent.[22] Such calculations view the inflationary impact of the link in global terms. For individual surplus developed countries, which, because of their greater competitiveness, might expect to receive most of the extra export demand, the threat of inflation may, at first sight, seem more severe. Once again, however, estimation of the inflationary impact, even allowing for the concentration of expenditure on the exports of these countries, reveals that the threat is insignificant. Cline (1976) estimates that the first-round net impact of an SDR – aid link on export demand (with an SDR emission of SDR 3000 million) would be no more than 0·70 per cent, even in the most competitive economies. It is difficult to see how such a small increase in aggregate demand could generate significant additional inflationary pressure, even assuming that aggregate supply is inelastic. Given the generally small import propensities of the major surplus developed countries, the second-round inflationary impact in other developed countries would be even smaller.

What evidence is available, then, unanimously demonstrates that, although the inflation argument against the link is qualitatively correct, it is quantitatively unimportant.

The evidence is, however, not comprehensive. One concern that has been expressed by opponents of the link is that, once it has been adopted, considerable pressure would be exerted by LDCs to increase the allocation of SDRs beyond the amount required for global liquidity purposes. It may be countered, of course, that developed countries, which bear the real-resource cost of the link, may be reluctant to increase SDR allocations at anything but a fairly moderate rate. The voting requirements of the SDR scheme would seem to ensure that a substantial degree of consensus over the appropriate allocation of SDRs is required before allocations are made. The inflationary threat from this aspect of the link would therefore appear to be somewhat overstated.

(c) *Relevance to current economic conditions.*   In conditions where developed countries are experiencing unemployment, the inflation argument against the link reappears as an expansion argument in its favour. Similarly, however, many of the arguments mustered to challenge the claim that the link would be inflationary in conditions of full employment may be used to question the view that it would induce expansion in conditions of unemployment. Perhaps the most significant of these is the argument that the actual *size* of the link would be relatively small. Whilst this point may be valid, the argument that unemployment is temporary whilst the link is permanent is less well founded, since there is no reason why the SDR–aid link should not incorporate a facility to be used as a counter-cyclical device.[23] All participants would gain from such a modification: LDCs in terms of extra real resources, and developed countries in terms of fuller employment and a less unsatisfactory balance-of-payments position.

(d) *Efficiency and equity.*   Issues of efficiency and equity are usually contentious. Little point will be served by becoming too deeply embroiled in them. A number of factors are, however, reasonably clear cut. The SDR scheme does give rise to social saving and seigniorage. This social saving and seigniorage may be distributed in various ways and to various recipients. The gold-exchange standard (GES) also involves a measure of social saving and seigniorage. Seigniorage under the GES is distributed to gold producers and reserve-currency countries. The only new question raised by the SDR–aid link is that of the optimal distribution of seigniorage. It cannot be denied that distributing financial claims on real resources to LDCs, at a cost lower than the value of the real resources to LDCs, would help to bring about a more equal distribution of world income. As compared with the GES, LDCs would gain in terms of extra real resources, non reserve-currency countries would neither gain nor lose from the link, (although, as compared with the unlinked SDR scheme, they would forgo the opportunity of deriving an unearned increase in reserves), and reserve-currency countries would lose real resources, having to earn reserves instead of gaining real resources by spending internationally acceptable but domestically produced reserves, (of course, they would gain to the extent that there are costs as well as benefits associated with being the world's banker[24]). The SDR scheme as currently constituted is in many ways quite efficient. SDRs are relatively costless to produce; are generally accepted although not backed; are purposefully created by international agreement rather than indirectly created as a result of deficits in reserve-currency countries; and yield liquidity benefits to holders. Although a social saving could be derived by alternative methods of reserve growth, such as increasing the price of gold or expanding the supply of foreign exchange, the distribution of seigniorage associated with these methods would be different from that under a link. Although the link implies inefficiency in terms of the optimal supply of international money, the Pareto optimality of the international money supply in turn rests on the *existing* international distribution of wealth. If the existing distribution of wealth is considered unsatisfactory, arguments which imply its retention immediately become less compelling.

A Summary Assessment of the SDR–Aid Link

The idea of a link between liquidity creation and development assistance has generated a great deal of attention over recent years, in both academic and official circles. The official discussion has yet to culminate in the establishment of a link. LDCs did succeed in getting established a Joint Ministerial Committee of the IBRD and IMF which concerns itself with the transfer of real resources from rich to poor countries, but more recently the link has been dropped from the agenda of the Committee. Prior to the establishment of this Committee, the Committee of Twenty discussed the concept of an SDR–aid link fairly extensively, and in its 'Outline of Reform' declared that 'the reformed monetary system will contain arrangements to promote an increasing net flow of real resources to developing countries' – IMF, Committee on Reform (1974), p. 17.

The main strength of the linkage proposed lies in its stated objective of assisting LDCs. The rationale of the link is as a wealth-redistributive measure. Many of the economic arguments for and against the link are, however, difficult to verify *ex ante*. Examples include the argument that the implementation of a link will result in compensating reductions in other forms of aid, and that the link will sabotage confidence in the SDR as an asset. Where quantification is possible, the implications of the SDR–aid link appear uniformly to be fairly minor, whether in terms of generating aid (assuming that LDCs pay a market-related interest rate), of causing additional inflation, or of exacerbating disequalibria between countries. It might seem from the estimated size of the link's impact that it hardly merits the discussion devoted to it.

The exact impact of the link significantly depends on its precise nature. A high interest rate, for instance, implies a lower grant element. Direct country allocation implies that relatively rich LDCs will gain, instead of the gain being concentrated on the least-developed countries, as would tend to be the case if the link were channelled through a development agency.

In fact LDCs have reached a compromise on this issue, as reflected by their common position during the Committee of Twenty negotiations. As a group, LDCs favour a system whereby SDRs are allocated on the basis of IMF quotas, which are for this purpose weighted to their advantage. LDCs have further proposed that the weighting factor be rather higher for the least-developed than for the other LDCs. Developed countries, in contrast to LDCs, favour a form of link which ensures both a greater degree of outside control over the uses to which linked SDRs are put, and that the maximum degree of progressive income re-distribution is achieved.

It is not a new feature of the international monetary system that it should distribute the seigniorage associated with reserve creation in an unequal way. Under the Bretton Woods system the United States enjoyed the seigniorage which resulted from being a major supplier of international money. The link proposal rests on the assumption that a more egalitarian distribution of seigniorage could be achieved in any reformed system. The recent increases in the amount of non-SDR international liquidity, and the introduction of more flexible exchange rates, which tend to reduce the global need for liquidity, have, to a certain extent, served to upstage the link. However, not all versions of the link rely on there being net additions to international reserves. One which does not integrates the link with reserve-currency amortisation. By creating SDRs equivalent to the amortisation obligations of the reserve-currency countries, the IMF could both prevent the decline in international liquidity that would otherwise take place, and ensure that the link would be operative even in years when there were no general allocation of SDRs. Since the establishment of the SDR as the principal reserve asset in a reformed international monetary system is embodied in the Second Amendment to the Articles of Agreement of the IMF, a version of the link which associates it with reserve-currency amort-isation may stand relatively more chance of being adopted than one which involves a competitive interest rate for holders of SDRs and a subsidised concessionary rate for LDC users. Though the latter version of the link would be more beneficial to LDCs, it involves richer countries in the extra cost associated with interest-rate subsidisation.

Looking to the future, if SDRs become the sole reserve asset in the international monetary system, and international reserves are required to grow at a continuous positive rate, then the SDR–aid link could provide substantial assistance to LDCs. If SDR-linked allocations are concentrated on the least-developed countries, and the interest rate on SDR use is subsidised for these countries, then the link could make a major contribution to improving the standard of living of many millions of people.

12 Exchange-Rate Policy and LDCs[1]

Since the early 1970s the international monetary system has been characterised by the existence of flexible exchange rates – a state of affairs which has been condoned by the IMF.[2] Exchange-rate flexibility has raised two questions for LDCs: first, should they lend support to a system based on flexible rates?; and, second, what should their own exchange-rate policy be, in an environment of flexible rates? Both these questions will be examined in this chapter.

LDCs' Attitude to Generalised Floating

LDCs have, in general, been rather sceptical of an international monetary system which is based on floating rates. Their scepticism hinges on a number of areas of concern. First, it is felt that floating rates produce uncertainty, and that uncertainty, in turn, discourages international trade and investment. It may be countered that a flexible exchange-rate system may be more stable and may involve less uncertainty than an adjustable-peg system which operates imperfectly. The Bretton Woods system, which, especially in the 1960s, fitted into this latter category, incorporated features which acted against the interests of LDCs. Amongst these, the system tended to put asymmetrical pressure to adjust on deficit countries. Adjustment often involved deflation and trade restriction, with devaluation constituting a last resort to be used only when disequilibrium rates could no longer be supported by other measures. As a result, the size of exchange-rate adjustments was often large. Furthermore, since adjustments were widely anticipated, disruptive speculative capital flows were usually associated with devaluation. The use of non exchange-rate policies to protect disequilibrium rates, the size and infrequency of exchange-rate adjustments, and the existence and implications of hot-money movements combine to suggest that the uncertainties facing traders under an

imperfect adjustable-peg system are considerable. Indeed the uncertainties associated with a so-called fixed exchange-rate system, which
in fact involves large but infrequent exchange-rate adjustments, may be
greater than those under a system of flexible rates, where the adjustments are smaller but more frequent.

One standard way of compensating for the uncertainty caused by
prospective movements in exchange rates and the risk of receiving a
devalued currency or having to buy an appreciated currency is by
making use of forward exchange markets. With forward exchange
cover, the parameters of any trading transaction may be fixed in advance
and uncertainty may be removed. Indeed, it is the purpose of the
forward exchange market to buy and sell uncertainty. Traders may thus
eliminate exchange risk and buy certainty. A reservation held by LDCs
about flexible rates relates to the worry that they have inadequate access
to forward exchange markets. For dealings which employ foreign
currencies, forward exchange facilities in developed countries might be
used, but, for dealings involving domestic currency, domestic facilities
are required.[3] Although certain LDCs have been able to establish some
form of forward exchange facility, the level of financial sophistication in
many LDCs is such that there may be cause for concern over the
exchange risk and the competitive disadvantage associated with the
absence of forward cover.[4] At the same time, it should be emphasised
that exchange risk is not absent in an adjustable-peg system. Furthermore, since trading uncertainty may arise not only through exchange
risk but also through inflation, to the extent that it is differential
inflation which generates exchange-rate movements, this source of
uncertainty may be neutralised.

A second concern of LDCs with regard to a flexible exchange-rate
system is the fear that flexibility will result in additional fluctuations in
commodity prices. More precisely, the fear is that, since the prices of
many of the primary-product exports of LDCs are normally quoted in
dollars or sterling, and since it may be just these currencies that are the
ones most likely to depreciate, it is probable that flexibility will imply a
fall in the price of LDC exports expressed in terms of other foreign
currencies. There in fact appears to be little substance to this argument,
since, especially in circumstances where producers co-operate over
pricing policy, the relevant foreign-currency price may be increased to
compensate for the depreciation in the value of the foreign currency.
Indeed, devaluation in developed countries may be used as an opportunity to increase the price of the good in terms of foreign currencies.

Perhaps of more legitimate concern is the argument that the real opportunity cost of certain imports may rise under a flexible-rate system. This may be the outcome either of a devaluation in the currency of export quotation, or of a revaluation in the currency of import quotation. Where LDC exports and imports are sold and bought from different markets and using different currencies, it is possible that, in the absence of offsetting foreign-currency price changes, the LDCs' terms of trade will deteriorate as a result of exchange-rate flexibility. The impact of floating amongst foreign currencies on any particular LDC's terms of trade will clearly depend on the pattern of that LDC's trade. Where, for instance, trade is concentrated in one currency bloc, depreciation of that currency will exert no adverse effect: the real relative price of exports and imports will remain unchanged.

The third area for concern moves the discussion away from the direct treatment of trade flows and focuses attention on the problem that a flexible exchange-rate system creates for reserve management. There are two dimensions to the problem: one relates to the appropriate *level* of reserves, whilst the second relates to the *composition* of reserves. Where LDCs themselves adopt a flexible exchange rate, the need for reserves to finance balance-of-payments deficits will, in theory, fall. If, on the other hand, LDCs do not join developed countries in allowing their exchange rates to move in response to shifts in demand and supply, then it is possible that they may need a higher level of reserves to compensate for any fall in export earnings, rise in import payments, or general increase in the incidence of balance-of-payments deficits which might be generated by flexible exchange rates elsewhere.

With regard to the optimal composition of the reserve portfolio, a flexible exchange-rate system as compared with a fixed-rate system introduces the extra risk of exchange loss resulting from depreciation, and the extra opportunity for exchange gain resulting from appreciation. LDCs which hold a high proportion of their reserves in currencies which depreciate will suffer a reduction in the real value of their reserves. The same type of reserve risk will of course be associated with an adjustable-peg system. To some extent LDCs might neutralise the implications of a flexible exchange-rate system for the value of reserves by holding a diversified portfolio of reserve assets. The portfolio could be apportioned on the basis of the shares of various developed countries in the LDC's imports, or on the basis of expected deficits with certain currency areas. In any case, under a flexible exchange-rate system it is likely that interest-rate differentials between developed countries will be adjusted to compensate for differential exchange-rate movements. Furthermore, if the international monetary system moves in the direction of having the SDR as its central reserve asset, the composition problem will largely disappear. It is only whilst the system is based on multiple reserve assets that currency flexibility produces problems for reserve management. The opposition of LDCs to flexible rates reflects the risk aversion of LDCs as well as the existence of various, not necessarily economic, constraints on efficient portfolio management.

A fourth reason why LDCs have been opposed to a flexible exchange-rate system is the risk that their debt may be denominated in currencies which appreciate, thus causing the real value of such debt to rise. Since the real value of debt denominated in depreciating currencies will fall, the structure of an LDC's debt burden is likely to be a major determinant of its attitude toward the adoption of exchange-rate flexibility by developed countries. LDCs might attempt to offset the effect of appreciation on their real debt burden by distributing their debt amongst developed countries in proportions similar to their export trade shares; this would tend to ensure that export earnings would rise to offset any rise in debt payments.

A fifth reason for concern amongst LDCs over generalised floating is the belief that a permanent move towards a system of fairly freely floating exchange rates would represent a decisive move away from a centrally managed monetary and trading system, which could be designed to provide substantial benefits to LDCs in the form of resource transfers and easier access to the markets of developed countries. To the extent that greater exchange-rate flexibility reduces the international monetary system's need for reserve assets, there would be less reason for further SDR emissions, as a result LDCs clearly might forgo actual and potential benefits. Paradoxically, at the same time as reducing the likelihood of future SDR emissions, exchange-rate flexibility amongst developed countries could also increase the LDCs' need for reserves.

The period of generalised floating amongst developed countries since 1973 provides some opportunity to assess the impact of floating on LDCs. The evidence is far from perfect, since other economic developments, such as the rise in the oil price, have also exerted a significant influence. Even bearing this in mind, however, the evidence reveals no clear empirical case that floating necessarily inhibits export growth in LDCs or causes adverse movements in their terms of trade. Furthermore, calculations made by the IMF suggest that LDCs have gained roughly as much from dollar devaluation, through the reduction in the real value of their debt burden, as they have lost through the reduction in the real value of their reserves.[5] Furthermore, Williamson (1976) estimates that the quantitative significance of the LDCs' increased need for reserves under a generalised floating system is 'trivial'.

Such evidence as is available seems to suggest that many of the LDCs' worst fears concerning the implications of a flexible exchange-rate system have little foundation. Any injuries which might be caused in the ways outlined above are, in any case, likely to be offset, inasmuch as flexibility represents a general improvement in the operation of the international monetary system as a whole. To the extent that exchange-rate flexibility enables developed countries to avoid contractionary domestic policies and restrictive trading and financial policies, LDCs will gain indirectly; and the size of this gain may easily outweigh any losses incurred. A system of fixed exchange rates which superficially appears to eliminate a number of problems for LDCs may be against their interests if it is maintained only by the pursuit of complementary measures of trade and financial illiberalisation.[6] Although LDCs might ideally prefer a stable system of fixed exchange rates amongst developed countries, combined with liberal trade and financial arrangements and expansionary demand policies, this may not represent a realistic option. The second-best system from the LDCs' point of view may be a system of flexible exchange rates rather than a feasible but unstable fixed-rate system.

LDCs' Own Exchange-Rate Policy

We now come to the question of how LDCs should conduct their own exchange-rate policy in an environment of floating exchange rates amongst developed countries. Fundamentally, LDCs have to choose whether to float or peg their exchange rates. Where it is decided to float, a further decision has to be made concerning the precise nature of the float: basically, whether it is to be free or managed. Where it is decided to peg the exchange rate, the question arises of what it should be pegged against: one currency or a basket of currencies? If a basket is to be used, what currencies should be included in the basket, and in what proportions? In choosing exchange-rate policy, LDCs implicitly assess the costs and benefits associated with each option and endeavour to adopt the one which maximises benefits and minimises costs; of course, in many instances the costs of one option are the forgone benefits of another option.

Flexible exchange rates: the decision whether to float

Theory provides us with a number of guidelines for assessing the suitability of flexible exchange rates in particular countries. These guidelines include: the relative importance of internal and external disturbances; the size of the trading sector relative to the size of national income, or the degree of openness of the economy; the extent of commodity diversification; the extent of geographical trade diversification; the degree of financial integration with the rest of the world; the relative rate of inflation; the values of certain strategic elasticities; the response of key domestic variables to exchange-rate changes; the feasibility of alternative demand and cost management policies; the level of international reserves; and the community's preferences as between the level and stability of income. Let us examine these country characteristics more carefully.

(a) *The source of disturbances.* Where disturbances are, in the main, generated externally, a flexible exchange rate may be used to insulate the domestic economy from the effects of such disturbances. The internal effects of domestic disturbances may, on the other hand, be softened by permitting them to filter abroad. The filtering process is facilitated by a fixed exchange-rate system. Thus, for instance, the implications of excess domestic aggregate demand under a flexible exchange rate will be felt fully in terms of domestic inflation, while, under a fixed-rate system, some of the excess demand will spread abroad through the trade sector.

(b) *The degree of openness.* For economies with relatively large traded-goods sectors, a flexible exchange rate need not constitute the lowest-cost-adjustment policy. Under a fixed-rate system, a balance-of-trade deficit may be eliminated by domestic demand deflation. The extent of the deflation that is necessary will be inversely related to the size of the marginal propensity to import. For closed economies with low propensities to import, the cost of deflation in terms of reduced national income will be relatively higher than for open economies with larger import propensities. In open economies, therefore, there may be less incentive to adopt a flexible exchange rate. [7]

A further reason why a fixed exchange rate may be preferred amongst open economies is that openness will tend to exacerbate the short-run effect of exchange-rate changes on the domestic price level. Alternatively however, inasmuch as open economies with fixed exchange rates are more vulnerable to external disturbances, and are likely to have less control over the domestic money supply, a flexible exchange rate may be preferred.

(c) *Commodity diversification.* The more diversified is an economy in terms of its production, exports and imports, the less likely it is to encounter balance-of-payments difficulties (because, for instance, short-falls in certain exports may be compensated by excesses in others), and therefore the less likely it is to have to adjust. If adjustment is not required, a flexible exchange rate will not be needed. On the basis of this argument, non-diversified economies seem likely to favour flexible exchange rates. Since economies with a high degree of product concentration are also likely to be fairly open, the diversification argument to some extent contradicts the openness argument discussed earlier. Although it would seem that non-diversified economies would tend to favour flexible rates, exchange-rate movements in such econ-omies may be rather large and frequent if the principal export product is subject to sudden shifts in demand and supply. Where an objective of economic policy is to avoid sudden fluctuations in the exchange rate, the combination of a fixed rate and financing may be preferred to floating.

(d) *Geographical concentration.* In the same way that the law of large numbers operates to reduce the incidence of balance-of-payments difficulties in an export-diversified country, so also it will work in the case of geographically diversified trade to protect the economy from external shocks emanating from trading partners. Where, however, trade is heavily concentrated with one or a few partners, disturbances in these countries will tend to be transmitted to a significant extent. It may then be in the interests of a small country to peg to the currency of its principal trading partner, thus ensuring domestic-currency price stabi-lity for a large proportion of trade.

(e) *The degree of capital-market integration.* It has been established in the theory of optimum currency areas that factor mobility (of both labour and capital) may substitute for exchange-rate flexibility. The higher the degree of factor mobility, the greater the extent to which adjustment may be engineered through factor movements, and the less the extent to which exchange-rate variation is required. For instance, with well developed and integrated capital markets, balance-of-trade deficits may effectively be financed over the short-to medium term; in these circumstances it is capital that moves rather than the exchange rate. On the other hand, a high degree of capital-market integration may imply a loss of control over domestic monetary policy, and this may encourage the adoption of a flexible exchange rate.

(f) *The relative rate of inflation.* Where the rate of inflation in one country is approximately similar to the rate of inflation in that country's trading partners, a fixed exchange rate will be more viable than it will be if the inflation rates are dissimilar. Dissimilarity in inflation trends will tend to encourage the use of flexible exchange rates. In particular, currency depreciation may be used to offset the effect of excessive domestic inflation on the foreign-currency price of exports.[8]

(g) *Trade elasticities.* Where the price elasticity of demand for exports and imports is low, and the price elasticity of supply of exports is also low, a flexible exchange rate will tend to be ineffective in improving the balance of payments.[9]

(h) *The effect of exchange-rate changes on real domestic absorption and the domestic money supply.*[10] Where exchange-rate variations induce equilibrating changes in the level of real domestic absorption and money supply, a flexible exchange rate system will be more appropriate than where these effects are not forthcoming. Inasmuch as a balance-of-payments deficit may be seen as reflecting excess absorption relative to capacity, or excess supply of money, it is these disequilibria that have to be corrected if the balance-of-payments problem is to be solved.

(i) *Demand- and cost-management policies.* Exchange-rate variations in influencing the balance of payments work through certain monetary channels. Effectively, currency depreciation tends to reduce the real supply of money. Although results similar to those achieved through exchange-rate flexibility could also be achieved directly through monetary policy, a flexible exchange rate may, if the appropriate independent monetary policy is infeasible for some reason, offer a feasible alternative.

(j) *The level of international reserves.* The extent of choice available to an economy with respect to exchange-rate policy will be influenced by the level of international reserves. Other things remaining constant, the larger the reserves the less immediate will be the problem of correcting a balance-of-trade deficit, since the deficit may be financed. As holdings of reserves fall, the degree to which a deficit may be financed also tends to fall, and adjustment becomes necessary more rapidly. Thus, exchange-rate flexibility is perhaps more likely to be countenanced by countries which have low levels of reserves, and little access to international borrowing.

(k) *The community's preferences for income stability as opposed to income level.* Where a community, as represented by its monetary authorities, has a preference for stable income, it will tend to favour financing policies as opposed to adjustment policies with respect to the balance of payments, and may initially therefore tend to favour a fixed rather than a flexible exchange rate.

Unfortunately, LDCs do not constitute an homogeneous group in terms of the country characteristics that we have just identified, and it is therefore perhaps unwise to treat LDCs as a group in the context of appropriate exchange-rate policy. Even in the case of individual LDCs, the position with respect to the most desirable exchange-rate policy may be ambiguous, since while an LDC may have certain characteristics which suggest that a flexible exchange rate would be appropriate, it may simultaneously display characteristics which support a fixed rate. What can be said is that, in theory, if LDCs could legitimately be typified as being open, non-diversified economies which possess low foreign-trade elasticities and generate most economic disturbances internally, a fixed exchange rate may seem preferable to a floating rate. For closed, diversified economies which have high trading elasticities and low levels of reserves, a flexible exchange rate may generally be advocated.

Other considerations relevant to an LDC's decision about whether to float or to peg are as follows. First, if floating results in unstable exchange rates between LDCs and developed countries, LDCs may lose through lower trade growth and foreign investment. Second, flexible rates can generate uncertainty, and it may not be possible to cover this given the lack of forward facilities in many LDCs. Third, the short-run equilibrium exchange rate which would result from free floating may be inappropriate in terms of the long-run objectives of the economy, and may even impede the realisation of such objectives. Fourth, floating may encourage foreign investors to suspect that internal monetary and fiscal discipline will be abandoned, and may therefore initially serve to reduce the inflow of capital. Finally, exchange-rate variation exerts fairly non-selective effects, and it may be selectivity that is required, in terms of both products and markets.

Clearly, the decision with respect to floating is an involved one. Given the range of relevant considerations, and the non-homogeneity of LDCs with respect to the vital factors, it might be anticipated that no universal truth would emerge for LDCs as a group. This is confirmed by the empirical evidence examined later in this chapter.

Pegged exchange rates

Assuming that, for some of the reasons examined in the previous section, an LDC decides to peg its currency, the question arises of what type of currency peg should be adopted.

(a) *Pegging to a single currency.* Where trade and financial relations are highly concentrated with one developed country, the problem of choosing the appropriate exchange-rate peg is fairly easily solved, since, by pegging its rate to that of the developed country in question, the LDC ensures the stability of its own domestic currency in terms of the wide range of goods and services traded with the developed country. Pegging to a major currency in a world of floating rates may yield other advantages, such as access to forward-exchange facilities, but it may also involve potential disadvantages. These are particularly apparent when the LDC's trading and financial arrangements are more diversified, since, in these circumstances, pegging to the currency of one developed country which is itself floating against the currencies of other developed countries will have an indirect impact on the *effective* exchange rate of the LDC. Exchange-rate movements which may be appropriate with respect to one trading partner may be inappropriate with respect to others, and the result may be that LDCs will experience variations in their effective exchange rates which have little to do with their own balance-of-payments positions, but instead reflect disequilibria between trading partners.[11] In the case of LDCs which are pursuing a policy of trade and financial diversification, the option of pegging to one currency therefore tends to become less attractive.

Single-currency pegging could thus imply a need for larger reserves in the LDC involved, if movements in the intervention currency relative to other major currencies are inappropriate from the viewpoint of the LDC. Furthermore, if different LDCs peg to different intervention currencies, exchange-rate variations between LDCs will occur indirectly as a result of variations in the exchange rates between the intervention currencies. This will be particularly unfortunate where LDCs are endeavouring to encourage intra-LDC trade.

(b) *Pegging to a basket of currencies.* Where for the reasons listed above pegging to a single currency is deemed unsuitable, an alternative is to peg to a group or basket of currencies, the currencies being the ones in which the LDC conducts most of its dealings. The basket may be weighted to reflect not only the significance of particular currencies with regard to trade and financial flows but also particular elasticities of demand and supply. An LDC's exchange rate would not, then, move exactly in line with one currency, but would move in relation to a weighted average of movements in a number of currencies. The idea behind the adoption of a weighted basket is to minimise the detrimental effects of exogenous exchange-rate variations on the balance of payments of the LDC concerned. It has normally been suggested that the basket of currencies should be weighted in terms of import share, since this weighting scheme serves to offset the impact of exchange-rate changes in developed countries on the average level of LDC currency prices.[12]

More conveniently, if less precisely, LDCs might attempt to ensure the appropriateness of their own exchange rate by pegging to the SDR, the value of which, since July 1974, is determined by a representative trade-weighted basket of sixteen major currencies. Precision would, of course, be lost only if the currencies and weights used in the SDR basket were different from those which would have been chosen independently by individual LDCs on the basis of an import-weighted basket. The greater the discrepancy between the SDR basket and the import-weighted basket the less appropriate will the SDR be. Use of the SDR, however, could act as a common point of reference for all LDCs and thus might facilitate intra-LDC trade. Interestingly, Crockett and Nsouli (1977) have shown that, on the basis of the period January 1970 to March 1975, and for the clear majority of LDCs, the SDR peg does not significantly deviate from the import-weighted basket peg. Indeed, for LDCs as diverse as Argentina, Costa Rica, Guatemala, Peru, Israel, India and Ghana, the SDR peg coincides almost exactly with the import-weighted peg. Only in certain LDCs that are heavily reliant on trade with one currency bloc does it seem that single-currency pegging represents a superior alternative to SDR pegging, and even in these circumstances it is only in the case of the group of LDCs whose currencies are pegged to the French franc that the superiority of single-currency pegging is clear cut.[13] For many LDCs whose currencies are actually pegged to the US dollar, the SDR peg would appear to come much closer to the import-weighted peg;[14] and, whereas for Zambia and Sierra Leone a sterling peg appears to be more appropriate than an SDR peg, for some other LDCs whose currencies are pegged to sterling the SDR peg would seem better. Generally, where LDCs have a fairly diversified import pattern, the SDR peg approaches the import-weighted peg much more closely than does a single-currency peg, and only LDCs with highly concentrated import structures stand to offset exogenous exchange-rate variations effectively by means of pegging to just one currency.

Whatever the way in which the peg is determined, many of the points for or against pegging as opposed to floating remain the same. Pegging has advantages in terms of imposed discipline and the related potential generation of confidence in the minds of foreign investors; and disadvantages in terms of the need for larger reserves, and the greater and more rapid degree of internal adjustment that has to be countenanced.

Exchange-Rate Behaviour in LDCs: Empirical Evidence

During the period preceding the collapse of the Bretton Woods system, almost all LDCs maintained a par value against an intervention currency, such as the US dollar, the UK pound, or the French franc. However, Lebanon, since 1947, and the Philippines, since 1970, have floated their currencies, whilst Brazil, Chile, Colombia and Uruguay have made frequent adjustments to their peg. Most notoriously, in Brazil, managed flexibility in the form of a crawling or trotting peg has been used to compensate for the effects of excessive domestic inflation on the trade sector.

Following the move amongst industrial countries towards a system of generalised floating, some LDCs have made modifications to their exchange-rate practices. Initially, few changes were in fact made, and LDCs remained fairly firmly pegged to intervention currencies, but, as it became clear that the introduction of generalised floating was not merely a temporary measure, certain LDCs began to alter their exchange-rate policies. Some LDCs have moved away from single-currency pegs to their own weighted baskets or to the SDR (by the end of 1975, twenty-one LDCs were pegged to some form of currency basket), whilst others have introduced some measure of exchange-rate flexibility (although by the end of 1975 only Afghanistan, Lebanon, Nigeria and the Philippines had completely unpegged exchange rates). The clear majority of LDCs, however, remain pegged to a single currency, and almost 50 per cent of LDCs are pegged to the US dollar.

A summary of the history and current status of LDC exchange-rate behaviour is presented in Table 12.1. A number of notable features emerge from a study of the pegging behaviour of LDCs during the

Table 12.1
LDC's Exchange-Rate Policies

Country	1973 Pegged to	1975 Pegged to	1976 Pegged to
Afghanistan	US dollar	Unpegged	Unpegged
Algeria	SDR basket	Own weighted basket	Own weighted basket
Argentina	US dollar	US dollar	US dollar
Bahrain	US dollar	US dollar	US dollar
Bangladesh	£ sterling	£ sterling	£ sterling
Barbados	£ sterling	US dollar	US dollar
Bolivia	US dollar	US dollar	US dollar
Botswana	US dollar/ South African rand	US dollar/ South African rand	South African rand
Brazil	US dollar	US dollar	US dollar – unpegged
Burma	US dollar	SDR basket	SDR basket
Burundi	US dollar	US dollar	US dollar
Cambodia	US dollar	US dollar	–
Cameroon	French franc	French franc	French franc
Central African Empire	French franc	French franc	French franc
Chad	French franc	French franc	French franc
Chile	US dollar	US dollar	US dollar – unpegged
China Rep. of	US dollar	US dollar	US dollar
Colombia	US dollar	US dollar	US dollar – unpegged
Congo, People's Rep.	French franc	French franc	French franc
Costa Rica	US dollar	US dollar	US dollar
Cyprus	Unpegged	Own weighted basket	Own weighted basket
Dahomey (Benin)	French franc	French franc	French franc
Dominican Rep.	US dollar	US dollar	US dollar
Ecuador	US dollar	US dollar	US dollar
Egypt	US dollar	US dollar	US dollar
El Salvador	US dollar	US dollar	US dollar
Equatorial Guinea	Spanish peseta	Spanish peseta	Spanish peseta
Ethiopia	US dollar	US dollar	US dollar
Fiji	£ sterling	Own weighted basket	Own weighted basket
Gabon	French franc	French franc	French franc
Gambia	£ sterling	£ sterling	£ sterling
Ghana	US dollar	US dollar	US dollar
Guatemala	US dollar	US dollar	US dollar
Guinea	Gold	Own weighted basket	SDR basket
Guyana	£ sterling	US dollar	US dollar
Haiti	US dollar	US dollar	US dollar
Honduras	US dollar	US dollar	US dollar
India	£ sterling	Own weighted basket	Own weighted basket
Indonesia	US dollar	US dollar	US dollar
Iran	US dollar	SDR basket	SDR basket
Iraq	US dollar	US dollar	US dollar
Israel	US dollar	US dollar	US dollar – unpegged
Ivory Coast	French franc	French franc	French franc
Jamaica	US dollar	US dollar	US dollar
Jordan	US dollar	SDR basket	SDR basket
Kenya	US dollar	SDR basket	SDR basket
Korea	US dollar	US dollar	US dollar
Kuwait	US dollar	Own weighted basket	Own weighted basket
Laos	US dollar	US dollar	US dollar
Lebanon	Unpegged	Unpegged	–
Lesotho	US dollar/ South African rand	US dollar/ South African rand	US dollar/ South African rand
Liberia	US dollar	US dollar	US dollar
Libya	US dollar	US dollar	US dollar

Table 12.1 cont.

Country	1973 Pegged to	1975 Pegged to	1976 Pegged to
Malagasy Rep.	French franc	French franc	French franc
Malawi	£ sterling	SDR basket	SDR basket
Malaysia	US dollar – unpegged	Own weighted basket	Own weighted basket
Mali	French franc	French franc	French franc
Mauritania	French franc	Own weighted basket	Own weighted basket
Mauritius	£ sterling	£ sterling	SDR basket
Mexico	US dollar	US dollar	US dollar – unpegged
Morocco	French franc – unpegged	Own weighted basket	Own weighted basket
Nepal	US dollar/ own weighted basket	US dollar/ own weighted basket	US dollar/ own weighted basket
Nicaragua	US dollar	US dollar	US dollar
Niger	French franc	French franc	French franc
Nigeria	US dollar	Unpegged	Unpegged
Oman	US dollar	US dollar	US dollar
Pakistan	US dollar	US dollar	US dollar
Panama	US dollar	US dollar	US dollar
Paraguay	US dollar	US dollar	US dollar
Peru	US dollar	US dollar	US dollar
Philippines	Unpegged	Unpegged	Unpegged
Qatar	US dollar	SDR basket	SDR basket
Rwanda	US dollar	US dollar	US dollar
Saudi Arabia	US dollar	SDR basket – unpegged	SDR basket – unpegged
Senegal	French franc	French franc	French franc
Sierra Leone	£ sterling	£ sterling	£ sterling
Singapore	US dollar – unpegged	Own weighted basket	Own weighted basket
Somalia	US dollar	US dollar	US dollar
Sri Lanka	£ sterling	£ sterling	Own weighted basket
Sudan	US dollar	US dollar	US dollar
Swaziland	US dollar/ South African rand	US dollar/ South African rand	South African rand
Syria	US dollar	US dollar	US dollar
Tanzania	US dollar	SDR basket	SDR basket
Thailand	US dollar	US dollar	US dollar
Togo	French franc	French franc	French franc
Trinidad and Tobago	£ sterling	£ sterling	US dollar
Tunisia	French franc	Own weighted basket	Own weighted basket
Uganda	US dollar	SDR basket	SDR basket
Upper Volta	French franc	French franc	French franc
Uruguay	US dollar	US dollar	US dollar
Venezuela	US dollar	US dollar	US dollar
Vietnam	US dollar	US dollar	US dollar
Western Samoa	US dollar	Own weighted basket	Own weighted basket
Yemen Arab Rep.	US dollar	US dollar	US dollar
Yemen, People's Dem. Rep.	US dollar	US dollar	US dollar
Zaire	US dollar	US dollar	SDR basket
Zambia	US dollar	US dollar	SDR basket

Source. International Monetary Fund.

period of generalised floating. First, there is the strong preference for pegging: LDCs have in general shown some reluctance to experiment with independently floating rates. Second, many LDCs which do not appear to possess particularly close financial ties with the US have nonetheless pegged to the dollar, though a policy of pegging to the SDR or some other basket of currencies would seem more appropriate. Third, excepting the continuing significance of the dollar, the period of generalised floating has not witnessed a polarisation of LDCs into currency blocs.

An interesting empirical question is whether the observed exchange-rate behaviour of LDCs is consistent with the theoretical analysis outlined earlier. Is it the case that those LDCs most suited to floating have floated, whilst those most suited to fixed exchange rates have pegged? Broadly speaking, are LDCs behaving rationally in terms of their exchange-rate policy? This question has been examined by Heller, (1977). By comparing various country characteristics with exchange-rate policy, Heller discovers that floating tends to be significantly associated with a low ratio of imports to GNP (a low degree of openness); a high degree of both commodity and geographical diversification in foreign trade; large size, measured by GDP; a relatively high rate of inflation; and a high degree of financial integration. The opposite characteristics are associated with pegging. Certain other characteristics which are identified by Heller, such as the existence of trade restrictions, do not appear significantly to affect the choice of exchange-rate policy. Of those characteristics that do, the most important (in terms of making the greatest contribution to explaining exchange-rate behaviour) are the degree of export concentration and openness; in fact, these two factors together accounted for more than 50 per cent of the explanatory power of the discriminant function which predicts exchange-rate choice. The results achieved by Heller do not perfectly match what might have been expected on the basis of theory. For instance, it might have been anticipated that the degree of commodity diversification would be positively associated with a preference for pegging. However, it does seem valid to conclude that the basic choice of exchange-rate systems by LDCs, i.e. the choice betweeen fixed and flexible rates, has been guided by certain identifiable principles which are broadly consistent with theory. Heller suggests, however, that certain LDCs that have floated their currencies should, on the basis of the characteristics of their economies, have pegged them, and that the choice of peg, in cases where LDCs have decided to peg their currencies, has not always been optimal.

Concluding Remarks

The exchange rate can be an influential instrument of economic policy.

Evidence exists to support the view that, where this instrument has been used by LDCs, an improvement in the balance of payments has normally been achieved.[15] This finding, of course, need not necessarily mean that all LDCs would be advised to adopt flexible exchange rates.[16] Indeed, given the economic characteristics of many LDCs, a flexible exchange rate would, in theory, seem to be inappropriate; and, in practice, the clear majority of LDCs have pegged their currencies, even though the actual type of peg used has not always been optimal. LDCs would be wise, however, to keep their exchange-rate policies under review, and to contemplate a more aggressive use of the exchange-rate instrument where this might yield economic benefits.

More broadly, the opposition of LDCs to an international monetary system which is based on generalised floating has some degree of rationality. Even though it seems that much of the concern exhibited by LDCs over the detrimental effects on them of floating is unfounded, an international monetary system based on floating will require fewer additions to the quantity of international reserves, and LDCs have been very close to persuading the international community to bias the allocation of new reserves in their favour. The eventual adoption of such a modification would be more likely in an international environment of fixed, rather than of flexible, exchange rates.

13 Postscript to the Second Edition

In the process of producing a second edition of this book, a number of alternatives were available. The first was to make no changes whatsoever, the second was to undertake a complete updating of all the chapters, and the third was to write a brief postscript that attempted to bring certain key issues up to date. It is the third option which has been adopted. Certainly since the book was initially written a number of significant developments have taken place. Not least amongst these has been the publication of the Brandt Report in 1980 which has served to bring many aspects of the so-called New International Economic Order into more general public debate.

Following the layout of the preceding chapters this postscript concentrates on:

(i) the continuing evolution of relations between the IMF and developing countries;
(ii) the use of Fund resources by developing countries;
(iii) the role of the private sector in financing LDC payments deficits; and
(iv) the interests of developing countries in international financial reform particularly with respect to the role of the SDR.

(i) Relations between the IMF and the developing countries, and the debate over conditionality

Up until the mid 1970s the IMF tended to respond to pressures from developing countries by enlarging the range of its facilities rather than by changing its policy conditions. In the late 1970s and early 1980s, however, potentially significant changes have taken place in the form of lengthening the possible period of repayment for both stand-bys and extended facility drawings, and in the form of the *1979 Review of the*

Guidelines on Conditionality. These changes could turn out to be strategic. The lengthening of the repayment period may enable countries to pursue rather longer-term balance of payments policies and this may allow the Fund to put greater emphasis on structurally oriented policies, and on supply, as opposed to demand management. The nature of the relationship between stability and development will therefore become an issue of great significance for the Fund as the movement towards longer term credits continues.

While the *1979 Review of Guidelines on Conditionality* endorses the Fund's belief in conditionality, it includes changes from the previous position.[1] First, the Review encourages countries to turn to the Fund 'at an early stage of their balance of payments difficulties or as a precaution against the emergence of such difficulties'. Second, there is a cautious move towards extending the time over which stand-by drawings may be made, though the normal period remains twelve months. Significantly Gold maintains that, 'a reason for caution about longer periods as a more normal practice is the undesirability of blurring the distinction between balance of payments assistance and development financing'. Third, the Review states that, 'the Fund will pay due regard to the domestic social and political objectives, the economic priorities, and the circumstances of members, including the causes of their balance of payments problems'. It seems to have been accepted then that certain policies may be necessary to maintain political and social stability and that this should be taken into account in devising an economic programme. However, an elucidation of the phrase 'economic priorities' by Gold makes it clear that, while the Fund is aware of the potentially adverse effects which policies directed primarily towards short-term macroeconomic stability may have on long term development, and is anxious to avoid these, it rules out the use of Fund resources to help structural change. The Fund still feels unable to provide assistance unless adjustment can be achieved with only the *temporary* use of its resources. The emphasis remains on what are essentially short-term policies. Although the reference to the causes of payments problems represents some recognition that payments difficulties in developing countries may result from factors beyond their control, the Fund retains the view that 'members must adjust their balance of payments whatever may be the origin of their problems'. There is no formal recognition that different causes require different policies even though informally the Fund does claim to take account of the sources of balance of payments difficulties and to be somewhat less strict where these are externally generated. Fourth, the Review suggests that the Fund continues to want to avoid becoming heavily involved in a country's economic, and by implication political and social life, concentrating on aggregate macroeconomic variables rather than the mechanisms by which targets are achieved. Finally the Review states that the Fund intends to keep all aspects of stand-bys and their related conditionality under scrutiny. Some research on conditionality has already been undertaken both within the Fund and elsewhere (Reichmann (1978), Reichmann and Stillson (1978), Connors (1979)), and it would seem likely that, in part, it was as a result of this that the 1979 reappraisal was made. The evidence suggests that while Fund policies have caused economies to move in the directions intended there has been relatively little success in realising specific ultimate targets. Thus although in the clear majority of cases intermediate targets on credit expansion, for instance, have been realised and the principal purpose of the stand-by achieved, in terms of trade liberalisation for example the effect of stand-by programmes on ultimate targets such as economic growth, inflation and the balance of payments has been much less marked. The apparent general failure of precise macroeconomic targeting suggests that the Fund is becoming increasingly sceptical of the scope for fine tuning in developing countries and it is beginning to favour a broadly based and longer term macroeconomic policy approach.

While the new guidelines on conditionality permit a significant alteration in the nature of the Fund involvement in economic management, their effect will depend crucially on how they are interpreted in *practice*. Statements by Fund personnel fail to clarify just how significant a change there has been in the Fund's adjustment policy. Monetary stability still seems to be viewed as a prerequisite for economic development. In a speech delivered in 1980 the Managing Director maintained that, 'sound adjustment means, above all, implementation of fiscal and monetary policies designed to avoid overconsumption in relation to available resources and to prevent waste or mismanagement of those resources. In this connection, there is one simple truth which must be recognised: when demand is stimulated by measures which are rapidly dissipated in higher prices, this stimulus is fruitless, or counterproductive, from the standpoint of inflation and balance of payments stability. A more positive consideration is that the adoption and pursuit of suitable adjustment programmes in cooperation with the Fund generally tends, through enhancement of the creditworthiness of borrowing countries, to facilitate the attraction of private capital. The resources of the Fund and adjustment programmes of the type that it sponsors thus seem to me to be indispensable elements in the fostering of investment and economic growth.' However he did go on to point out that, 'they clearly do not represent comprehensive solutions for the difficulties now confronted'. Such remarks make it plain that the shift from demand management towards supply management is easily exaggerated. The Fund remains primarily committed to what it sees as sound internal financial policy. If there has been a change in emphasis it seems to be that the Fund now recognises that sound financial policy may not be sufficient to ensure development, that the short term costs of some of the policies it has supported may have been underestimated and that the policies may have concentrated too much on the sole objective of bringing about a short-run improvement in the balance of payments. If this is an accurate interpretation the change could indeed be significant.

From being viewed in its early years as an institution which had no special concern for the problem of developing countries, more recent reviews see the Fund as having become, or at least as being well on the way to becoming, an instituion whose *only* role is that of assisting the poorer countries for whom the private financial markets do not provide a feasible alternative (Southard (1979), Williamson (1979)).

A major problem with this apparent transition is, however, that the Articles of Agreement define the Fund's responsibilities as providing short-run balance of payments finance, not longer run development assistance. Although this distinction is not always clear in practice the Articles do constrain the Fund's involvement with countries where balance of payments adjustment is seen as a long term process. It is therefore not clear exactly how far the transition will be able to proceed under the IMF's existing Articles and rules. Currently the Fund is caught in the awkward position of helping to deal with problems for which its own rules and procedures may not ideally equip it.

(ii)   The use of IMF resources by developing countries

1976 turned out to be a peak year for drawings on the Fund. These fell quite dramatically in 1977 and 1978, indeed in 1978 LDCs actually made a net repayment to the Fund. Drawings picked up in 1979 and expanded considerably in 1980 (see Bird (1981a) for fuller details).

While the current account deficit of non-oil LDCs amounted to $233 billion in 1974–79 net Fund credit financed less than $10 billion of this. Although such evidence seems to confirm that the direct importance of the Fund as a source of finance is small, at least three riders to this statement are appropriate. First, the IMF may provide a directly significant quantity of assistance in particular cases. Thus, while drawings on the Fund covered only 3.2 per cent of the combined balance of trade deficit of all non-oil LDCs taken together in 1978 drawings covered more than 40 per cent of the deficits of Peru, Jamaica, Burma and Sri Lanka. Second, even where only a small proportion of the deficit has been covered, the availability of Fund resources is such that a much larger proportion might have been covered. Further increases in quotas, along with the 1980 decision by the Executive Board to permit drawings on the Fund to expand to 600 per cent of quota mean that a potentially significant proportion of LDCs' financing needs may in principle be met by the IMF. Third, even though the absolute amounts of finance provided by the IMF may be small they may result in much larger inflows from other sources, particularly the Eurocurrency market. There is some, not unambiguous, evidence to support this view.[2]

(iii)   The role of the private sector in financing LDC payments deficits

There is some debate over just how important the private sector has been in financing LDC payments deficits in the past and over how important it will be in the future. Figures on net flows certainly suggest that the overall contribution of the Eurocurrency market to recycling to developing countries has been rather less than half the figure suggested by gross flows, with the finance being very heavily concentrated in a very few countries. Developing countries have significant assets with the Eurocurrency market, and some have been in a net creditor position (Killick (1981)). There are a number of reasons to believe that the private sector will make a relatively smaller contribution towards meeting the developing countries' financing gap in the 1980s than in the past. On the supply side, evidence suggests that the flow of Eurocurrency credits to developing countries is related to the size of debt service ratios and exposure levels. As already noted, bank lending to developing countries is heavily concentrated in a small number of countries. Debt service ratios rose rapidly during the 1970s and are projected to rise still further during the first half of the 1980s. The World Bank has projected a debt service ratio for middle income developing countries of 28.6 per cent in 1985 as compared with 19.8 per cent in 1977. It also seems probable that a fall in the private banks' capital base, relative to their lending, along with the rising proportion of foreign to domestic assets in the balance sheets of commercial banks, will constrain their willingness to lend to developing countries.[3] New banks not experiencing these particular constraints may even so be fairly risk averse and may, therefore, wish to minimise their lending to developing countries, while the risk aversion of those banks with experience of lending to developing countries may increase with increasing political uncertainties that may affect banks' ability to raise capital. Furthermore, there is evidence of a declining price incentive to lend to developing countries. Spreads have narrowed considerably since 1976, as has the additional spread associated with lending to developing countries as compared with industrial countries.

While all the above factors might be expected to affect the banks' *willingness* to lend to developing countries, the introduction of a greater degree of multilateral regulation of international banking, should this materialise, could impose additional constraints on their *ability* to lend. In addition, it seems probable that further increases in the price of oil will strengthen the demand for credits by industrial countries, and the World Bank anticipates an increase in demand from European centrally-planned economies as well as from China.[4] Such widening opportunities for banks that are already concerned about the narrowness of their lending portfolio may have a relatively detrimental influence on their lending to developing countries.[5] Having said this, any increase in the price of oil will also tend to raise the funds that banks have available to lend.[6]

On the demand side, it is possible that those developing countries that have the option of borrowing from the private sector may themselves become less inclined to use it. Concern over their capacity to service the related debt, given uncertain export prospects, and over maintaining their long term credit-worthiness may encourage them to opt for a higher degree of adjustment, and a lower degree of financing. Furthermore, with hardening terms they would be under an incentive to economise on private borrowing.

For these reasons, it might be expected that the growth in commercial lending to developing countries will diminish and may fail to keep pace with the increasing financing requirements of these countries. Towards the end of the 1970s there was evidence to suggest such a slowdown, with the year on year growth in Eurocurrency lending to developing countries falling from about 90 per cent in 1978 to 10 per cent in 1979. In 1980 there seems to have been no growth at all and perhaps even a decline.[7] Meanwhile, the share of developing countries in Eurocurrency borrowing fell from 61.5 per cent in 1979 to 54.6 per cent in the first half of 1980.[8] Given the increasing debt payments to which developing countries are committed as a result of their past borrowing, a decline in the growth of new lending has important ramifications for the net transfer to developing countries, which seems likely to fall to quite low levels and may become negative in certain cases.

In principle any shortfall in terms of financial inflow may in the short run be made good by a decumulation of international reserves. However, for the majority of developing countries reserves are already at a low level in relation to their need for reserves to hold and this option is, therefore, not widely available. For them, and in the longer run even for those countries with excess reserves, the only alternative is to adjust the balance of payments to be consistent with the available financial inflow. This will generally imply a reduction in the volume of imports and an inter-related reduction in the rate of economic growth. Evidence presented by Dell and Lawrence (1980) for the mid-1970s clearly supports the argument that, where developing countries were forced to adjust because of the non-availability of finance, economic growth and living standards suffered.

Of course, in assessing the significance of the prospective financing gap that developing countries seem likely to encounter, much depends on the view taken concerning their target growth rate. If an inappropriately high growth rate is assumed, then the financing gap associated with it becomes of only academic interest. Furthermore, a reduction in a country's rate of economic growth may not in itself be a bad thing if one accepts the argument that there are considerable external costs associated with growth and that these may exceed the benefits. However, in the context of developing countries, neither of these arguments seems valid. Even with a very modest rate of economic growth, sufficient to generate only a small annual increase in per capita GNP, a significant financing gap seems certain to occur; whilst the debate over the costs of economic growth is more legitimately conducted in the context of countries that are already developed and have already achieved a satisfactory level of material well being.

Furthermore, the argument that developing countries will only have to make sacrifices in terms of economic welfare similar to those that will have to be made in other countries also seems to be largely invalid. Because of the structural rigidities of their economies in the short run the costs, in terms of lost national income, associated with any given improvement in the balance of payments, are likely to be higher in developing than in developed countries. When it is remembered that adjustment in developing countries commences from an already relatively low level of income, and assuming a diminishing marginal rate of utility, it may further be suggested that the welfare costs associated with any given reduction in national income will be higher in developing countries than in developed countries. In addition, for developing countries with relatively high rates of population growth, it is more probable that any given reduction in the rate of economic growth will lead to an absolute fall in per capita GNP. In any case, the distribution of financing is such that developed countries will be in a stronger position to avoid short-run adjustment by financing their payments deficits. However, in appraising the implications of a financing gap for developing countries, it is again important to distinguish between those middle and high income developing countries that have had considerable access to private finance and the other, in the main low income, developing countries that have not. In the former group of countries there seems likely to be a significant fall in the relatively rapid rate of growth that was achieved by them during the 1970s, though they will probably be able to maintain a positive annual increase in per capita GNP. The structure of their economies is such that they may be able to achieve the necessary degree of correction to their balance of payments at a lower welfare cost than can the least developed countries. A major financing problem that they do seem likely to encounter arises from their growing debt payments and debt service ratios. The way in which this problem is handled will have an important bearing on the extent to which economic growth may be maintained. For many of the low income countries, however, a decline in the real standard of living would seem to be a definite probability.

(iv)   The interests of developing countries in international financial reform: the future of the SDR and the link

Attention here is focused on the role of the SDR and in particular on the idea of introducing a link. However this should not be interpreted as implying that there are not other mechanisms for transferring resources to developing countries nor that there are not other financial reforms, such as altering the form of IMF conditionality, that would not be of significance to LDCs.[9]

Since the first edition was written perhaps the most significant development with respect to the introduction of a link has been the increase in the rate of interest on SDRs to a competitive level. Although a competitive SDR rate certainly reduces the benefits of the link to net users it is invalid to conclude that as a result these fall to zero. First, most of the developing countries that are able to raise commercial credit have to pay a rate above the combined market rate used for calculating the rate of interest on SDRs. Furthermore the rate on SDRs represents a weighted average of rates across countries and these may be subject to a considerable measure of dispersion. To a certain extent then the grant element on SDRs will depend on the currency in which commercial borrowing would otherwise have been undertaken.[10] These two factors combine to suggest that SDRs may continue to incorporate a significant grant element for LDCs even with a so-called market equivalent interest rate. Comparing the interest rate on SDRs with the Eurocurrency rate in early 1981 gives a grant element of about 23 per cent, while comparing it with short-term US rates gives a grant element of approaching 35 per cent. While these are clearly below the grant elements that used to be associated with SDRs when the interest rate was significantly below the market rate they are still significant. Second, some LDCs find it impossible to borrow even at commercial interest rates; what these countries face is an *availability* constraint. The allocation of SDRs to them even at a commercial interest rate will help to overcome this. Indeed to the extent that there are capital market imperfections which prevent resources from moving to where their marginal productivity is highest (in LDCs?), the link will serve to raise international economic efficiency by encouraging world output to rise. Third, from a theoretical point of view, it is the interest rate on the marginal acquisition of SDRs that needs to be at a commercial level. In terms of efficiency there is no reason why the rate paid by LDC users should not be subsidised thereby raising the grant element. The problem here is the practical one of how the subsidy would be financed. In principle this could be arranged by developed countries transferring SDRs to LDCs whilst retaining the interest obligations, or by additional SDRs being allocated to LDCs in perpetuity or by the Special Drawing Account simply charging LDCs a lower rate on their net use than is paid to those countries acquiring SDRs.[11] Finally, aside from the interest rate on them, SDRs are a form of unconditional credit; they involve no fixed repayment schedule and require no statement of need by users. LDCs, wary of borrowing from the IMF because of the nature of the conditionality associated with some types of Fund drawings and seeing commercial borrowing as also involving a form of conditionality may find SDRs very attractive. Furthermore since net users only have to pay interest and do not have to repay capital in the short run payments on SDR net use will therefore tend to be lower than they would be for an equivalent commercial loan.[12] On the other hand LDCs have shown concern that an increasing interest rate on SDRs brings with it an increase in general IMF charges.

There is also the possibility that a higher rate may induce a greater reluctance on the part of surplus countries to adjust by spending reserves. In each of these cases a higher interest rate on SDRs imposes costs on LDCs.

In addition to the versions discussed in Chapter 10, more recently two further types of link have been proposed and discussed within the IMF; each of these would have the effect of integrating the link with the activities of the Fund. The first would involve SDRs being used to provide the finance for some form of Subsidy Account. Under this version SDRs could either be directly allocated to such an Account, or contributions could be made by initial recipients voluntarily or according to a pre-arranged format. The Account would then redirect the SDRs at its command to LDCs or exclusively to low-income countries either as grants, in which case contributors would themselves have to retain the obligations associated with the SDRs contributed or as a line of interest bearing credit in which case the LDCs receiving the SDRs would be asked to meet the related interest obligations. In this last case there would be no 'subsidy' as such, though LDCs would still receive more SDRs than they would under a distribution based on quotas. In many ways this version differs little from other versions. One significant difference, however, is that, as proposed, the SDRs would be used by LDCs to help meet IMF charges. In this way this version of the link is, to an extent, tied to Fund conditionality and may therefore be less attractive to LDCs though clearly the idea of subsidised interest rates would be appealing to them.

Under the second version SDRs would either be directly allocated to or contributed to a Special Account which would use them to support stabilisation programmes approved by the Fund. In effect LDCs able to agree a programme with the Fund would gain access to more resources than was previously the case. The SDRs could be used either to expand drawings under existing tranches and facilities, or to finance a new IMF lending facility. In one sense LDCs might find such a scheme attractive since they would receive more finance for accepting a programme that they had already agreed to in order to secure a Fund standby of EFF drawing. This version would therefore provide an extra incentive for LDCs to turn to the Fund. However, there is little doubt that they would prefer a scheme of direct and unconditional allocation to one that involves the intermediation of the Fund, the appropriateness of whose conditionality for LDCs is in some debate. Given the market equivalent interest rate on SDRs creditworthy LDCs might be expected to prefer to borrow from the Eurocurrency market since such borrowing is to some extent independent of IMF conditionality.[13] This version would become more attractive to LDCs if the SDRs allocated to them by the Special Account did not have to be repaid, and if the interest rate on their use of the SDRs was subsidised by, for instance, contributors retaining all or part of the related obligations.

Although there is no doubt that an increase in the rate of interest on SDRs relative to commercial interest rates reduces the grant element associated with their allocation it is not accurate to assume from this that developing countries will gain nothing from the introduction of a link. LDCs may still find a link attractive if it offers them unconditional finance at a rate of interest below that which they would have to pay for private finance and if it makes finance available to them that would simply not have been made available by private banks. If, at the same time, measures can be taken to establish the SDR as the principal reserve asset in the international financial system and therefore the principal source of reserve growth then the link could still make a significant contribution to improving the economic welfare of the third world. If recent modifications to the SDR encourage such a development it may well turn out that, on balance, they have been in the interests of developing countries.[14]

Notes

Chapter 1

1. International Monetary Fund Committee on Reform of the International Monetary System and Related Issues.
2. It is also true, of course, that developed countries may benefit from economic stability among LDCs (see Chapter 10).
3. Even the cancellation of the reconstitution provision would increase the potential real-resource transfer equivalent of SDR allocation.
4. On the other hand, however, monetary problems may give rise to trading problems, or at least inhibit their solution. The trading position of LDCs could perhaps be improved by means of an increase in their trade with each other. There is some evidence to suggest that the balance-of-payments difficulties which LDCs faced in the early to mid 1970s caused them to impose trading restrictions on each other, thus slowing down progress towards the establishment of regional trade arrangements. For a discussion of the trading problems of LDCs, see *IMF Survey*, 4 July 1977 (issue on trade).

Chapter 2

1. As such, the IMF may be viewed as reflecting the ideas of White rather than of Keynes. Keynes envisaged much greater use of the exchange rate in order to protect domestic policies (see the Keynes Plan and the White Plan reprinted in Horsefield, 1969). Under the Bretton Woods system which the IMF embodied, exchange-rate alteration was deemed acceptable only in conditions of 'fundamental disequilibrium'.
2. In a speech to the Washington Chapter of the Society for International Development, reported in *IMF Survey*, 1 March 1976.
3. In the past the IMF has actively sought assurances that the financial assistance granted by it would be used only for the purpose of short-run stabilisation and not for reconstruction and development.
4. An expression of this may be found in, for instance, Gold (1970, 1971). The Report on the First Ten Years of the IMF (1956) viewed inflation and not lack of capital as the main impediment to development. Rooth (1955), a former Managing Director of the IMF, explained the Fund view succinctly, as follows: 'the proper objective of economic policy [in LDCs] is development with stability. Without stability the objective of development will not be achieved. There may be some temporary stimulus to investment through inflationary measures, but investment will be distorted and

misdirected and it will decline to lower levels than would have prevailed without inflation. That is why the best hope of sound and sustained development must be in conjunction with measures to maintain domestic stability in a country's finances and international balance of payments.'

5. Versions of the critics' view may be found in Krasner (1968) Scott (1967), Colloquium on the Interests of Developing Countries in International Monetary Reform (1970), Corea (1971), Konig (1973) and Payer (1974).
6. In Ch. 6 the issue of balance-of-payments adjustment in LDCs is discussed more fully. A thorough investigation of the Fund's policy in allocating its resources to developing members is made in Ch. 8.
7. Scott (1967) argues that LDCs have been, 'almost universally hostile, suspicious and resentful of the Fund's intervention in their domestic policies with recommendations which would create severe hardship, and which, in the opinion of many economists would have a deflationary, stagnating effect on their economies'.
8. For an expression of this view see Colloquium on the Interests of Developing Countries in International Monetary Reform (1970). Schleiminger (1970), on the other hand, argues, that it would have been most harmful to international monetary co-operation had the Fund differentiated between different classes of countries.
9. Facilities such as the stand-by are explained in Chapter 7.
10. Evidence to support this contention is contained in Scott (1967), Horsefield (1970) and Mookerjee (1966).
11. See Scott (1967).
12. Mookerjee (1966) confirms the existence of such constraints when he argues that the evolution of Fund policies has been dominated by the desire to assist members to adjust to payments imbalance, in a manner compatible with the Fund's objectives.
13. See Chapter 5.
14. This is illustrated in Machlup (1964).
15. A view expressed in Mundell (1969).
16. This was a committee of the Board of Governors of the IMF and was established by a resolution adopted by the Board on 26 July 1972.
17. See Annex 10 of 'Outline of Reform', IMF, Committee on Reform of the International Monetary System and Related Issues (1974).
18. The share oil-exporting countries in world exports rose from about 6 or 7 per cent in the 1950s and 1960s to almost 14 per cent by 1975. More generally, the increasing involvement of LDCs in international monetary reform has occurred against a trade backdrop which shows LDCs failing to increase their percentage of world trade.

Chapter 3

1. The time trend may of course equal zero.
2. We shall examine some of these variables in Chapter 4.
3. A problem may arise in comparing two export-earnings series, since one series may be less stable than the other when evaluation is carried out on the basis of the mean amplitude of deviations, and simultaneously more stable

when evaluation is made on the basis of the sporadicity of deviations.

4. The statistical aspects of instability are discussed later in this chapter.

5. It should be noted that the price elasticity of demand for individual commodities is likely to be higher than the elasticity of demand for a category of commodities. Thus the demand for food will be less elastic than the demand for individual foodstuffs.

6. However, in the case of certain commodities, primarily of an agricultural nature, supply factors, such as drought in certain parts of Africa, no doubt contributed to the rise in price that occurred.

7. The distribution of instability between price and quantity may be of some assistance in identifying the causes of instability. The distinction between price and volume instability is something to which we shall return in a moment.

8. Unfortunately, since both demand and supply curves are likely to be shifting at the same time, it becomes difficult to derive anything about elasticities from data on relative price and volume instability.

9. See Katrak (1973) for an elaboration of this argument.

10. The results of such studies fundamentally rest on the way in which instability is measured.

11. This assumption seems to be consistent with the empirical evidence. The IMF–IBRD Joint Staff Study (1969) states that, 'Fluctuations in the prices of most metals and agricultural raw materials exported by the less developed countries continue to show a significant relationship with short term changes in the pressure of world demand, as broadly indicated by changes in the level of world industrial production. The price movements associated with changes in the level of world industrial production appear to be more than proportional to those changes in the case of non-ferrous metals as a group and roughly proportional for agricultural raw materials. A similar relationship has not been found between short run changes in the level of economic activity and the prices of the other group of agricultural products exported by less developed countries – food and beverages – which account for about half of the developing countries' exports of primary products other than petroleum. Fluctuations in the prices of these products since World War II – as distinct from trend factors related to structural shifts in demand or supply – appear attributable in large part to instability originating on the supply side.'

12. Evidence on elasticities is presented in the Chapter 4.

13. Massell (1970), on the other hand, found a positive relationship between these two variables.

14. See Tables 3.2 and 3.3.

15. See Erb and Schiavo-Campo (1969) and Lawson (1974).

16. On the other hand, a high marginal propensity to import or a high marginal tax rate will serve to reduce the size of the multiplier, which depends inversely on the size of leakages from the circular flow of income. Empirical evidence presented by Rangarajan and Sundararajan (1976) does, however, support the view that the export–income multiplier is, as a rule, larger in LDCs than in developed countries.

17. Assuming that growth is desirable.

18. See, for example, Erb and Schiavo-Campo (1969).

19. To some extent, export instability may have a ratchet effect on the balance of trade. During an export boom, imports may rise but then fail to fall back to their old level when export earnings decline. Export cycles will then be associated with a progressively deteriorating balance of trade. In LDCs, however, the use of import controls may prevent this import ratchet effect.
20. The theory behind this is explained in Chapter 4.
21. This remains true even though reserve gains resulting from falling import prices may in theory be used to compensate for reserve losses resulting from rising import prices.
22. Long-term redistribution may occur if a country responds to short-run high import prices by reducing demand in the long run. The reduction in demand may be achieved just at the time when import prices fall, with the result that the importing country, having borne the costs of high import prices, fails to derive the benefits from low import prices.
23. Whether a rise in import prices results in a rise in import payments depends on the price elasticity of demand for imports. Where the price elasticity is low, as it may be for LDCs, import payments will be positively related to import prices.
24. Though on the one hand these variables will be relatively stable, because of the relative stability of income, on the other hand the high values of the marginal propensities to save, tax and import will imply that any given variation in income will exert a relatively greater impact on savings, tax receipts and imports than would have been the case had the marginal propensities been lower.
25. The effects of currency depreciation are discussed more generally in Chapter 6. It may be noted, however, that, even ignoring the effects of exchange-rate movements on the economy as a whole, the efficacy of exchange-rate variation as a means of stabilising the export sector will depend on other factors, such as the import content of exports.
26. For a discussion of this see Chapter 7.
27. Although all researchers studying export instability are trying to derive information concerning the incidence and size of export fluctuations, a choice of statistical measures of instability does exist. Coppock (1962), for instance, used the anti-log of the log variance of the yearly rates of change of the time series. MacBean (1966) endeavoured to estimate the trend in export earnings by using a five-year moving average. He then proceeded to construct an instability index by measuring the average percentage deviation from this trend. Massell (1964) attempted to find the time trend of export earnings by using ordinary-least-squares regression analysis. He fitted a regression line expressing export earnings as a function of time, and then derived an instability index by measuring the standard deviations of the series from this trend. Other researchers have used a similar technique for estimating trend, but slightly different techniques for measuring deviations from this trend: Glezakos (1973), for instance, used the mean percentage deviation from trend; Stern (1976), in deriving a price instability index, divided the standard error of the log-linear time-trend equation by the mean value of the series. In reaching conclusions concerning relative instability as between groups of countries, Lawson (1974) shows that some weighting scheme, such as export share, is required.

28. Precise differences depend on the instability index used.
29. In fact, using a weighted (by export share) instability index based on a linear trend, the percentage increase in export instability was no greater in oil-importing LDCs than it was in developed countries.

Chapter 4

1. For this to be possible, however, the income elasticity of demand for primary commodities would have to be positive.
2. Where the prices of internationally traded goods are determined on world markets, LDCs will not even be able to influence the real price of exports expressed in terms of imports by exchange-rate variation, since the foreign price of exports and imports will remain unchanged, and the real domestic opportunity cost of imports in terms of exports will stay the same. For a fuller discussion of the matter, see Chapter 6.
3. Indeed, the first and second conditions noted above are sufficient to ensure falling LDC terms of trade.
4. As expressed by the Club of Rome (1972), for instance.
5. Similarly, the terms of trade of individual LDCs will tend to depend on the commodity composition of their imports.
6. Whether export earnings rise depends on the price elasticity of demand for the export: where this exceeds one, export earnings will rise.
7. Later in this chapter we shall discuss in more depth the elasticities which face LDCs. It will be seen there that there exists some empirical evidence to suggest that a general statement that LDCs face inelastic demand curves may be rather misleading.
8. The extent to which there is a conflict between the objectives of balance-of-payments equilibrium and development is discussed in Chapter 2.
9. The increase in efficiency may occur within one country or apply to all producing countries. In the former case, the price may not fall but the profits of producers, expressed in domestic currency, will rise, and this will serve to expand money, and perhaps real national income.
10. Except perhaps where a major export is also heavily consumed domestically.
11. The rise in the price of coffee had been largely caused by a major shortfall in Brazilian production, because of a frost-affected crop. Thus, while in Brazil the price of coffee increased, and the quantity exported fell, in other coffee-producing countries the rise in price was not accompanied by a fall in quantity exported and export earnings therefore rose.
12. The research used by Andic, Andic and Dosser in forming their elasticity estimates is that by Tinbergen (1962), Ball and Marwah (1962) and Kreinin (1961).
13. Balassa (1964) shows, however, that substantial differences exist between different areas because of the differences in the commodity and geographic composition of trade. For instance, LDCs which produce commodities which have high income elasticities of demand and export these to areas which are growing relatively rapidly might clearly be expected to have better trade prospects than those LDCs producing goods with low income

elasticities and exporting them to areas that are growing only slowly. On the other hand, LDCs with low income elasticities of demand for imports might be expected, *ceteris paribus,* to have fewer balance of payments problems than LDCs with high income elasticities. For reasons such as these , Balassa, in 1964, predicted a major deterioration in the trade position of Asian LDCs, reflecting the slow growth of exports and a rapid increase in import requirements; an improvement in the balance-of-trade position of African LDCs, reflecting the expansion of metal and mineral exports; no change in the balance-of-payments position of Middle East LDCs; and a slight deterioration in the balance of trade for Latin American LDCs, reflecting an even slower growth in exports than the relatively slow growth of imports into this area.

14. In Chapter 6 the issue of optimal adjustment behaviour in LDCs is discussed.

Chapter 5

1. In fact, during the 1970s certain middle-income LDCs have borrowed fairly heavily from the Eurocurrency market (see Chapter 9).
2. Again we shall not delve into these semantic problems, except incidentally. Those interested may consult Machlup (1966).
3. The speed of adjustment represents the proportion of any discrepancy, between the target level of reserves and the actual level of reserves inherited from the previous period, that it is planned to eliminate during the current period.
4. For a discussion of the limitations of the analysis underlying Figure 5.1, which is taken from Clark (1970a), see Williamson (1973).
5. The literature includes the following important contributions: Kenen and Yudin (1965), Archibald and Richmond (1971), Heller (1966), Clark (1970a, 1970b) and Kelly (1970). The literature has been surveyed by Clower and Lipsey (1968), Grubel (1971), Williamson (1973), and Maynard and Bird (1975).
6. Flanders (1971) maintains, however, that adjustment may be easier in LDCs, because of the use of direct controls over trade. It may be easier but it will still be costly in terms of income.
7. Unfortunately, it is rather difficult to capture in an empirical fashion the expectations and indeed the preferences of monetary authorities.
8. I am grateful to Danny Leipziger for suggesting to me certain ways in which Clark's model and diagram might be modified in order to compare the reserve policies of LDCs with those of developed countries.
9. For a discussion of this evidence see Chapter 3.
10. For a fuller discussion, and diagrammatic representation, of this analysis, see Chapter 6.
11. Clark omits the opportunity cost of reserves from his cross-country regressions, because of the difficulties encountered in giving it operational significance, and because capital inflows may be positively associated with interest-rate movements so that a rise in the interest rate may cause an increase in the supply of reserves. This clearly creates problems when

endeavouring to relate changes in the demand for reserves to changes in the rate of interest.

Incidentally, in regressing the speed of adjustment on the independent variables, Clark discovers that on average the adjustment behaviour of LDCs is significantly different from that of developed countries. The speed of adjustment appears to be negatively related to per capita income. Richer countries are apparently more reluctant than poorer countries are to adjust their economies in order to restore balance-of-payments equilibrium. This could imply either that LDCs require relatively smaller reserves, or that reserve inadequacy has forced LDCs to adjust their economies promptly when deficits have occurred.

12. Kelly further finds that the signs of the coefficients are similar for both developed countries and LDCs, except in the case of the coefficient on per capita income, which has a negative sign in the case of LDCs. This, however, is difficult to accept, since it suggests either a negative income effect or, since Kelly uses per capita income as a proxy for the opportunity cost of holding reserves, a positive relationship between reserve holding and opportunity cost.

13. Flanders also investigates the possibility that the determination of reserve holdings is a non-economic phenomenon, but rejects this by arguing that 'it is possible that all (or most) of the central bankers and monetary authorities have in mind considerations such as those implied by the model, but that individual differences may be great enough to rob the functions of any discernible shape. Such differences could inhere in the weight given by various central bankers to the several variables; in the time horizon for balance of payments adjustment; in legal and political constraints (not to mention changes in those constraints, or changes in the persons of the central bankers, within the period studied); in the choice of different measures of export variability; and in levels of success in carrying out intended policies.'

14. In any case, central banks' reserves do not necessarily represent the medium of exchange for a country's international transactions (Niehans, 1970).

15. It may be noted that the rise in the R/M ratio in LDCs after 1964 and before 1970 has been interpreted by the IMF (1970) as reflecting a rightward shift in the LDCs' demand for reserves. In a number of LDCs in this period, the balance of payments and the growth of reserves constituted a focal point of economic policy. Domestic policies and exchange-rate policies were formulated with the purpose of acquiring reserves. The availability of stand-by agreements was often made conditional upon the adoption of such policies.

16.
$$R \text{ opt} = h\frac{\log (r.m)}{\log 0.5}$$

where R opt represents the optimal level of international reserves for any particular country. h is the average absolute change in reserves, r is the marginal cost of holding reserves representing the difference between the social rate of return on capital and return on reserves, m is the propensity to import, and 0.5 represents the probability of a deficit. The theory underlying this formula should be clear from the preceding discussion.

17. This formula may be derived in the following way. With $Y = $ GDP, $K = $ capital stock and $M = $ imports of production goods,

$$Y^2 = R.\frac{m^1}{q^1}; \ m^1 = \frac{Y}{K}; \ q^1 = \frac{M}{K} \ \therefore \ Y_2 = R.\frac{Y/K}{M/K} = R.\frac{Y}{M}$$

since

$$\frac{Y}{M} = \frac{1}{q^2}; \ Y_2 = \frac{R}{q_2}$$

18. The rise in the price of oil served to exacerbate intra-LDC group variations in the optimality of reserves. The reserve problems of oil-exporting LDCs became very different from those of oil-importing LDCs. Reserve inadequcy is hardly a problem facing the major oil exporters.

19. The empirical evidence of this proliferation is presented in the IMF's twenty-seventh and twenty-eighth *Annual Reports on Exchange Restrictions*. Among the LDCs which introduced or extended some form of import control during 1976–77 are Argentina, Bangladesh, Bolivia, Brazil, Cameroon, Chile, Colombia, Costa Rica, the Dominican Republic, Ethiopia, Ghana, Guyana, Indonesia, Israel, Jamaica, Malawi, Mauritius, Mexico, Nigeria, Pakistan, Panama, Peru, the Philippines, Sierra Leone, Tanzania, Uganda and Zaire.

20. However, on the basis of a study which examines the extrapolated and actual payments variability of five LDCs, Williamson (1976) has argued that, in practice, generalised floating has had little impact on the payments variability of LDCs, and that the welfare effect of what increased variability there has been could have been neutralised by an increase in the reserves of LDCs by less than one half of one per cent. Williamson's findings are based on a model which estimates the increase in the reserve holdings of LDCs that would be necessary to maintain a constant probability of reserve depletion over a given period of time under a generalised floating as opposed to fixed-rate system. Even allowing for the fact that Williamson's methodology may be criticised (see for instance, Leipziger, 1976), his conclusion that the reserve needs of LDCs are, in a quantitative sense, insignificantly augmented by floating rates amongst developed countries remains rather surprising.

21. See Chapter 11 for empirical support of this.

22. A proposal of this kind has been put forward by Frances and Michael Stewart (1972). At the third UNCTAD conference it was suggested that the IMF might establish a special facility to support trade expansion amongst LDCs.

23. Examples are the Central American Common Market, the Latin American Free Trade Area, the Regional Co-operation for Development Group, the West African Monetary Union and the Equatorial and Central African Monetary Union. For a discussion of these arrangements and of the role of outside financing, see Michalopoulos (1973).

24. The Fund's position on adjustment policy is discussed in Chapter 2.

Chapter 6

1. Evidence on the elasticities which confront LDCs is presented in Chapter 4.
2. LDCs may, however, have a comparative advantage in the production of labour-intensive manufactures.
3. Although, no. doubt, these factors could be given broadly monetary explanations, the balance-of-payments deficits facing oil-importing LDCs did not reflect, in any direct sense, specific internal monetary mismanagement. The deficits rather more reflected the particular structural characteristics of these countries and the vulnerability of their balances of payments to discrete increases in prices of strategic imports.
4. A practical problem emerges in distinguishing *ex ante* between transitory deficits which do not require adjustment and non-transitory deficits which do.
5. Indeed, distributional considerations may be particularly relevant in LDCs, where there are wide dispersions of economic power and influence.
6. In the early 1970s, however, LDCs began to make more use of commercial borrowing than they had previously (see Chapter 9).
7. For a detailed presentation of the monetary approach to the balance of payments see Frenkel and Johnson (1976). A good textbook treatment of balance-of-payments theory may be found in Scammell (1974) and Stern (1973)
8. Equilibrium between the demand for and supply of money may be restored not only by changes in the price level but also by changes in the rate of interest; thus excess money supply will, in the short run at least, tend to cause interest rates to fall and the demand for money to rise.
9. Interestingly, the impetus for much of the work on the monetary approach to the balance of payments (especially for that conducted in the IMF) has come from studying the monetary problems of LDCs. Developing countries are perhaps particularly suitable for reasonably straightforward monetary analysis because of their relatively uncomplicated financial structures. Rhomberg and Heller (1977) maintain that, 'in the absence of well developed asset markets and financial instruments, the developing countries generally had either to hold reserves in monetary assets or to make expenditures on goods and services. Thus the implication for the external balance of payments in developing countries of a difference between the amount of money newly supplied through domestic credit creation and the additional amount that residents wish to hold is more obvious that it is in countries with more complex economies.' Monetary analysis relating to LDCs may be rendered even more appealing because of the relatively greater availability of monetary than of other statistics for those countries, and by the significance which is often attached to monetary policy (frequently at the insistence of the IMF).
10. For a full catalogue of the import controls used by LDCs, see the IMF's *Annual Report on Exchange Restrictions*. Over recent years, quantitative import controls have been used by, *inter alia*, Argentina, Bangladesh, Chile, Colombia, Jamaica, India, Mexico, Nigeria, Peru and Pakistan; import surcharges and taxes by Bolivia, Brazil, Cameroon, Costa Rica, Ecuador,

Ghana, Israel, Jordan, Malawi, Mexico, Pakistan, Panama and Uruguay; systems of advance import deposits by Bolivia, Brazil, Chile, Colombia, Greece, Korea, Mauritius and Zaire; controls over import payments by Argentina, Chile, the Dominican Republic, Ethiopia, Indonesia, Peru, Sierra Leone and Zaire; restrictions on current invisibles by Afghanistan, Argentina, Bangladesh, Brazil, Chile, Colombia, Cyprus, Egypt, Ghana, Guyana, Israel, Jamaica, Lesotho, Malta, Pakistan, Peru, the Philippines, Sierra Leone, Tanzania and Zaire; and some form of multiple-currency practice by Argentina, Afghanistan, Brazil, Burma, Colombia, Ghana, Indonesia and Nepal.

11. For example, during 1976–7 Burma established an export-price equalisation fund into which is paid the revenue from taxes levied on the surplus of export earnings over domestic export costs. The fund is used to finance losses on unprofitable exports.

12. Where LDC exporters use the opportunity afforded by devaluation to undercut the world price, the substitution effect may be larger, since it implies a switch away from other sources of supply of the same good.

13. The absence of a foreign-price effect need not preclude an expansion in export demand where the increased profits of domestic suppliers finance an improvement in the quality of the export good. Such quality effects are, however, unlikely to be relevant to many of the primary-product exports of LDCs.

14. Some observers also maintain that multiple exchange rates are less likely to generate inflation than is devaluation: see, for instance, Streeten (1971), Konig (1968) and Jayarajah (1969). This, however, may be a mixed blessing if it is the inflation that devaluation generates that acts to restore equilibrium. We discuss this issue later.

15. The arguments in favour of a system of dual exchange rates have been presented by Streeten (1971).

16. Although in the traditional analysis of devaluation much play is made of the relevance of the price elasticity of demand for exports, in the case of a small LDC devaluation will have little or no effect on the foreign-currency price of exports, and therefore the price elasticity of demand for exports will be irrelevant.

17. For a full discussion of the income redistributive effects of devaluation in LDCs, see Knight (1976). Knight argues that an approach which emphasises sectoral income differences and 'non-market pressures by socioeconomic groups' is appropriate to LDCs.

18. These preferences may be inter-temporal in the case of a zero long-term trade-off.

19. Politicians are, of course, likely to attempt to maximise their own utility function rather than some social-welfare function, which, in any case, it is very difficult to construct. The political costs of individual economic policies are important influences on the actual choice of policy. Since the costs of devaluation in terms of reduced living standards are in some ways concealed, and may take some time to work themselves out, certainly as compared with the alternative of monetary contraction, there may be political reasons for a devaluation-bias in the choice of adjustment strategy.

20. McKinnon (1973) and Kapur (1976) have suggested that in LDCs, and

314 The International Monetary System and the LDCs

especially during the initial stages of a stabilisation programme, a policy of increasing the interest rate paid on money holdings might be a better way of creating monetary equilibrium than would be a policy of reducing the rate of growth of the money supply. The reason they give is that, whilst a reduction in the money supply (or rate of growth of the money supply) will adversely affect real output, through its impact on firms which rely on the availability of bank credit, a rise in the interest rate on money holdings will induce an increase in the demand for real money balances, a related increase in the supply of real bank credit available to firms, and hence an increase in real output. This argument in fact begs a series of questions. For example, whilst an administered increase in the rate of interest on money holdings may induce an increase in the real supply of bank credit, it may also, if reflected in an increase in the cost of bank credit, lead to a reduction in the demand for bank credit. Furthermore, since an increase in money holding implies a reduction in domestic consumption, the demand schedule for bank credit may shift to the left.

21. It may be that devaluation is part of a package which incorporates import liberalisation. In this case the impact of devaluation on import prices may be neutralised, or even overwhelmed such that the volume of imports rises following a devaluation.

22. For details of exchange-rate changes, see IMF, *International Financial Statistics*.

23. The impact of devaluation on the prices of domestically consumed export goods may have a particularly telling effect on the cost of living where the goods are staple consumption goods. Beef in Argentina and rice in South-East Asia are examples.

24. More properly, provided all factor rewards are not maintained in real terms.

25. For a thorough exposition of this, see Diaz-Alejandro (1965).

26. The inflow of capital might be responsive to devaluation where devaluation serves to improve confidence, expand opportunities for investment, and reduce the level of import and related controls. An expansion in investment might however also tend to increase the import of capital goods, whilst a lifting of import controls would tend to have a generally expansive impact on importation.

27. Or more accurately the regression results would lead us to reject the hypothesis that devaluation has no effect in improving the balance of payments, (for details of the regression analysis, see Connolly and Taylor, (1976b).

28. There might, however, be some debate over the methodology used by Connolly and Taylor as well as their choice of LDCs, and time periods.

29. Khan (1976) admits that, for various reasons, his results may exaggerate the explanatory powers of the monetary model.

30. To the extent that living standards depend on the level of employment and output rather than on the level of domestic absorption, devaluation may be preferred to monetary contraction.

31. For a fuller discussion of the relationship between the IMF and balance-of-payments policy in LDCs, see Chapter 2.

Chapter 7

1. Pending ratification of a decision to increase quotas and to amend the Articles of Agreement, the credit tranche was temporarily extended by 45 per cent, to 145 per cent of quota, at the beginning of 1976. Individual credit tranches became equal to 36·25 per cent of quota. The conditions applying to credit tranche drawings remain the same under this temporary extension as they were before it took effect.
2. These overall constraints on drawings, and the conditions under which waivers are required remain the same even under the temporary extension of the credit tranches.
3. The granting of a stand-by arrangement, according to Scott (1967), 'indicates to all whom it may concern that the Fund regards the country as credit worthy – an indication that often helps the country to tap other sources of credit – but also relieves the country of the necessity of tying up large amounts of resources in the form of reserves, thereby releasing them for use in development programmes.'
4. See, for example, Polak (1967, 1971); HMSO, Cmnd 3662 (1968); Machlup (1968); Tew (1977); Gold (1970b).
5. For an explanation of this method of valuation see for instance Cutler and Gupta (1974).
6. See Fleming, Rhomberg and Boissonreault (1963).
7. See *Compensatory Financing of Export Fluctuations: A Report by the International Monetary Fund.* IMF Washington, 1963.
8. The growth factor is represented by the ratio of the sum of export earnings in the last three years to that in the three years before that. In determining the medium-term trend of export earnings, the Fund has made use of lower and upper forecasting limits. The estimated value of export earnings in the two years following the shortfall year may not be valued at less than export earnings in the shortfall year itself, and not at more than 10 per cent above the average value of the export earnings in the two years preceding the shortfall year. These limits themselves clearly constrain the estimated shortfall in any particular year.
9. In circumstances where available data does not as yet relate to the twelve months preceding a drawing request, the latest period for which sufficient statistical evidence is available is used; the Fund may allow a member to draw in respect of a shortfall for a twelve-month period ending not later than six months after the latest month for which the Fund has sufficient statistical data.
10. See *Compensatory Financing of Export Fluctuations: A Second Report by the International Monetary Fund.* IMF Washington, 1966.
11. The granting of requests for drawings which would imply an outstanding drawing of over 50 per cent of the member's quota (25 per cent before 1975) is subject to the member's previous co-operation with the Fund.
12. There is no separate limit on the amount which may be drawn under the BSFF in any twelve-month period.
13. However, it seems that the BSFF may soon be made completely separate from the gold and credit tranches, as the CFF already is.

14. The Oil Facility will be explained below.
15. Following the temporary increase in the size of the credit tranches at the beginning of 1976, the overall ceiling on use of the EFF was raised to 276·25 per cent of quota.
16. Or before, if there is a marked improvement in the balance of payments.
17. The increase in the oil-import cost was calculated by multiplying the volume of net oil imports in 1972 or 1973 (whichever was the higher) by $7·50 per barrel. The Fund could at its discretion change a member's total access to the OF if it felt that imports of petrol and petroleum products were abnormally low in 1972 and 1973.
18. The formula used for the 1974 OF was based on 100 per cent of the calculated rise in the cost of oil imports and only 75 per cent of quota.
19. $7\frac{5}{8}$ per cent per annum for the first three years, rising to $7\frac{3}{4}$ per cent for the fourth year and $7\frac{7}{8}$ per cent for remaining years.
20. See Corden (1977).
21. Import projections take into account developmental needs.
22. The interest rate is 0·5 per cent on the outstanding balance of any loan.
23. A further, rather less direct source of finance may come from the gold-restitution programme of the IMF. Under this scheme, members whose currency the IMF wishes to replenish may buy gold from the IMF at the official price, SDR 35 per ounce, in exchange for their currency. Additional finance may be provided for the Trust Fund by these members selling the gold at the same price that they paid for it to the Trust Fund in exchange for foreign currency, thus enabling the Trust Fund to make a profit by selling the gold at auction at market price. The main part of the IMF's restitution scheme is to sell one-sixth of its gold holdings to members. Under the old Articles of Agreement, this may be done only through replenishment, by selling gold to those members whose currency is in demand by the IMF, allowing those members to channel the gold to other members in exchange for acceptable currency. After amendment to the Articles of Agreement, the IMF will be permitted to sell gold directly to all members.

Chapter 8

1. Over the period 1951–75, drawings by LDCs exceeded those by industrial countries in 1951, 1952, 1954, 1955, 1959, 1960, 1963, 1967, 1972 and 1975.
2. Many of these ordinary tranche drawings have been under stand-by arrangements.
3. It may be noted at this stage that the evidence is consistent with the hypothesis that LDCs are rather reluctant to use the credit tranches, certainly beyond the first tranche, and prefer to use other facilities.
4. See Marquez (1970) and Horsefield (1970).
5. Horsefield (1970) stresses that 'the Fund did not then, nor does it now, rely on any formula for determining quotas'.
6. Certainly Scott (1967) has maintained that 'the fact that all the waivers in the mid-1950s were given in connection with transactions with these nations (LDCs) merely reflects the fact that their quotas as compared to those of developed nations were very small in relation to the volume of their trade'.

7. See Williams (1970).
8. It was also agreed by the Governors that the next general review should be completed by 9 February 1978 and that quotas should be reviewed every three rather than every five years.
9. Quotas largely reflect conditional liquidity and an increase in quotas causes an expansion in conditional liquidity. When quotas were increased, each member was supposed to pay 25 per cent of the increase in gold (although there were modifications to this requirement, as we shall see); as a result the member gained *conditional* access to liquidity some four times larger than the amount of gold paid to the Fund. For those countries whose currencies were held by the Fund in amounts equal to less than 100 per cent of the quota, it has been argued by Williams (1970) that the member lost nothing in terms of unconditional liquidity, since the gold payment was matched by an unconditional Reserve Position in the Fund which represented access to foreign exchange. For members whose currency was held by the Fund in excess of 100 per cent of the relevant quota, however, the gold tranche was unavailable, and, although the size of the gold tranche and credit tranches was expanded by the quota increase, and the size of the member's indebtedness to the Fund was reduced, the short-term implication of the gold payment was a fall in the size of the country's 'owned' or unconditional reserves. It may be the case that an increase of more than one unit of conditional liquidity is required to compensate a country for the loss of one unit of unconditional liquidity.

The gold payment by members and the nature of liquidity may be particularly relevant to LDCs. Some authors, as we shall see, have suggested that LDCs may require unconditional and not conditional liquidity. Furthermore, LDCs have relatively low holdings of gold. LDCs may, then, put an increasing marginal value on the intramarginal units of gold which they do own. There may exist a diminishing marginal rate of substitution between gold and other international reserves. Apparently in contradiction Flanders (1971) has stressed that LDCs may not *wish* to hold their reserves in gold but may wish to hold them in assets which yield a financial return in terms of interest, and which thus reduce the cost of holding reserves. This in fact would influence an LDC's choice as between gold and foreign exchange, but probably not its choice as between gold and a Reserve Position in the Fund. It remains quite tenable that LDCs would rather have gold than drawing rights in the Fund. The quota system has acted to reduce LDCs' already low holdings of gold.

To some extent the gold-holding 'burden' of the IMF quota system had been alleviated by modifications introduced by the Fund in 1959 and subsequently. First, members could accept approved quota increases in instalments. Second, members were permitted to make special drawings on the Fund in order to raise the foreign exchange required to replace or buy the gold needed to meet gold subscriptions. Third, and since 1970, the Fund, at its discretion, could reduce the proportion of a quota increase which had to be paid in gold. Under Article 3 Section (iv)(a), it was allowed that the part of a quota increase that a member had to pay in gold could be less than 25 per cent. The part that had to be paid in gold was related to the ratio between a member's monetary reserves and the new quota. The balance of the subscription was paid in the member's own currency. A member making use of this provision was, however, obliged to repurchase its own currency to the extent of the difference between the gold payment actually made and the 25 per cent gold payment required, within five years – unless, that is, the Fund's holdings of that member's currency fell below 75 per cent of its quota. For repurchasing, gold, SDRs, or any currency acceptable to the Fund could be used. As Williams (1970) recognises, the techniques described above concern 'the distribution of the burden of paying for quota increases over a number of years. The effects on members' reserves would be minimised in any one year, though, over time, the total amount of the increase in quota would be paid in the proportion of 75 per cent currency and 25 per cent gold (or convertible currencies or special drawings rights).' It might still be maintained that members, and particularly LDCs, lost something in terms of 'owned' reserves as a result of the quota system.

10. This is certainly a view taken by Corea, (1971).
11. A system of interest-rate subsidisation for certain LDCs already exists under the Oil Facility Subsidy Account (see Chapter 7).
12. Readers are advised to reread (or read) the first two sections of Chapter 2, which complement the discussion that follows.
13. For an elaboration of this notion and its empirical testing see Thirlwall and Barton (1970).
14. Mookerjee (1966) notes that 'in the evolution of IMF policies and practices one consideration predominated. This has been the Fund's desire to assist . . . in a manner compatible with the Fund's objectives.' Payer (1974) views the liberalisation of exchange and import controls as lying at the heart of IMF stabilisation programmes. She has argued strongly that the trade liberalisation cost of IMF assistance outweighs the benefits.
15. Santapillai (1970) has emphasised how export expansion in LDCs has been constrained by the lack of access to the markets of the developed countries. He also, however, points to the lack of assistance for export promotion in LDCs. For a discussion of the use of export subsidies in LDCs, see Perez (1976).
16. See Corea (1971).
17. For an elaboration of these views, see Corea (1971), Marquez (1970) and Krasner (1968).
18. The Fund selected the formula $X_t^N = 0{\cdot}5 X_t^A + 0{\cdot}25 X_{t-1} + 0{\cdot}25 X_{t-2}$, where X_t^N is the estimated normal value of exports in year t, and X_t^A is the actual export earnings in year t, after testing 137 variants of it against actual export earnings in forty-eight countries over a period of thirteen years.
19. IMF (1975).
20. For a full discussion of the quantitative aspects of compensatory financing, see de Vries (1975). De Vries shows that, whilst commodity earnings have increased by constant absolute amounts (for which the CFF estimation method would be appropriate), total earnings have grown at a constant rate. The CFF scheme, of course, relates to total earnings and not to commodity earnings. De Vries also shows that the degree of inaccuracy in the estimation of trend increases as growth of earnings rises: with export earnings growing

at a constant rate of 10 per cent per annum and with a standard deviation of earnings equal to 10 per cent of trend value, de Vries calculates that the CFF will overestimate total shortfalls by 12 per cent. He notes that the way in which total shortfalls are affected by a biased estimate of trend depends on the distribution of earnings around their trend value. If deviations are small, then a relatively minor degree of underestimation can be quite serious in terms of its influence on disbursements. For further compensatory financing simulations, see Morrison and Perez (1975). They show that schemes for compensatory financing provide considerable scope for assisting LDCs, though it is also pointed out that, 'the extent to which a compensatory financing scheme can help developing countries with the problems associated with instability of export earnings depends in the end on how the funds are used by the beneficiary governments'.

21. In fact, under the 1966 decision, the twenty four month projection of export earnings following a shortfall was constrained inasmuch as average earnings in the two years after the shortfall year could not be taken at more than 10 per cent above average earnings in the two years before the shortfall year. Without a 10 per cent forecast restriction, inflation tends to increase the size of nominal access to the CFF, since it serves to increase the estimated trend value.
22. See Goreux (1977).
23. The world recession was, of course, also a major contributory factor to the sharp rise in drawings under the CFF in 1976.
24. Corea (1971) maintains that the size and limitations of the use of the CFF, which are of course determined by the size of the relevant quota as well as by the provisions of the CFF itself, could mean that the facility would be quantitatively insignificant in the face of major downswings in export receipts.
25. For confirmation of this, see de Vries (1975).
26. Goreux (1977) shows that price movements in only eleven commodities accounted for over half the export shortfalls experienced in 1976. Goreux notes that of fifty two members that had used the CFF since the 1975 liberalisation, forty eight had experienced export shortfalls for one or several of twelve commodites: copper, wool, beef and veal, cotton, rubber, timber, sugar, tin, alumina and bauxite, phosphates, jute, and coconut products. Export earnings from these commodities experienced an average shortfall of 17 per cent below trend. Of the total export shortfall for these commodities (SDR 3183 million), almost two-thirds (SDR 2067 million) was covered by CFF drawings. The fact remains, however, that a shortfall of over SDR 1000 million was not covered by the CFF, and that in certain LDCs, such as Tanzania, Cameroon and Jamaica, a relatively small proportion of the export shortfall and related balance-of-payments deficit was covered by the CFF. In the clear majority of cases, drawings under the liberalised CFF have been effectively constrained by the quantitative provisions of the facility.
27. UNCTAD (1967).
28. See, for instance, Scott (1967), Marquez (1970) and Corea (1971). Scott envisages, 'the IMF and the IBRD acting jointly to approve long term development projects and plans, with the IBRD providing the bulk of the

financing and the IMF pledging a use of its resources as a guarantee of the fulfilment of the plan'.

29. This is confirmed by Goreux (1977).

30. These difficulties are discussed in Chapter 10, which deals with the commodities problem that faces LDCs.

31. It is those LDCs which are 'suffering serious payments imbalance relating to structural maladjustments in production and trade', and those in which 'prices and cost distortions have been widespread', as well as those 'characterized by slow growth and an inherently weak balance of payments position which prevents pursuit of an active development policy' that are the ones most likely to receive assistance under the EFF.

32. The IMF views as acceptable policies those which will serve to correct 'structural imbalances in production, trade and prices'. The Fund has, however, stated that particular attention will be given to 'policy measures that the member intends to implement in order to mobilize resources and improve the utilization of them and to reduce reliance on external restrictions'.

33. This statistic hides the fact that there is considerable intra-group variation amongst industrial countries. Whilst the UK, the US, France and Italy have made a net use of SDRs, Germany holds more than three times and the Netherlands more than twice the relevant cumulative allocation.

34. The more LDCs that opt to spend their reserves, the lower, in theory, will be the real resources acquired per unit of SDRs, because of induced demand inflation. This point is, however, unlikely to be quantitatively significant.

35. Machlup (1968) concludes that 'the benefits which the LDCs may obtain through additional trade and additional aid made possible through SDR allocations to developed countries may be much greater than any direct benefits through SDR allocations to them'.

36. Spending may in fact precede the transfer of SDRs.

37. For ease of exposition, the resource-flow patterns are discussed in the context of a system void of interest charges. The inclusion of interest charges on net use of SDRs, and, indeed, interest payments on net acquisition of SDRs, would alter the details of the picture somewhat. Net-use data will, for instance, incorporate an element of interest, with the result that real-resource acquisition will never precisely equal the value of SDR net use. The figures quoted in the text should therefore be interpreted with this in mind.

38. Leipziger finds that, taking all LDCs together, the elasticities of SDR use with respect to changes in the determining variables are such that a 1 per cent deterioration in the balance of payments leads to an increase in SDR use by 0·16 per cent, whilst a 1 per cent increase in non-SDR reserves leads to a decrease in SDR use by 0·23 per cent. The response elasticities are considerably greater for Latin American LDCs alone.

39. Leipziger discovered that the aggregate marginal propensity to use SDRs out of new allocations is 0·44.

40. Though, of course, there is the 30 per cent reconstitution clause.

41. This point has been argued strongly by Triffin (1971).

42. This issue has already been discussed at some length in Chapter 6.

43. For empirical support of this proposition, see Hawkins and Rangarajan (1970).

44. Loans under the first two Trust Fund disbursements represented just under 30 per cent of total drawings on the IMF in 1975 by those countries receiving the Trust Fund loans. There was considerable intra-group variation in the relative significance of Trust Fund assistance, as examination of Tables 8.1, 8.4, 8.5 and 8.10 will show.

Chapter 9

1. This pattern remains essentially the same irrespective of whether oil-exporting LDCs are included or excluded from the LDC category.
2. In some cases, however, new loans to LDCs which already possess high debt-service ratios may be granted on a 'roll-over' basis, with a view to preventing default. At the extreme, some LDCs have reached a position where debt-service payments represent more than 100 per cent of annual disbursements. For non-oil LDCs as a group, the roll-over ratio, which measures the proportion of disbursements used to service existing debt, rose substantially in the late 1960s and early 1970s, implying that LDCs will need to increase their borrowings if they are to maintain the net inflow or transfer of capital for the purpose of development and balance-of-payment financing.
3. Amongst LDCs, bond issues by Mexico and Brazil have again predominated.
4. Certain industrial countries have also gained from the invisible earnings generated by the growth of Euromarket activity in LDCs.
5. Indeed, the availability of IMF assistance depends to a significant extent on the willingness of the borrowing country to undertake adjustment policies. Clearly, a switch of resources into the export sector tends, in the short run at least, to reduce domestic absorption.
6. The exact distribution of the benefits depends on the particular version of the link that is introduced (see Chapter 11).
7. This is a line of argument that has often been put forward by the IMF.
8. Eurorates are very sensitive to market conditions and do fluctuate considerably. The Eurocurrency transactions involving LDCs have usually been based on the six-month London interbank offer rate, as a result of which the loan rate has been adjusted every six months until final maturity.
9. Already private loans to Zaire have been made conditional on the realisation of policies stipulated by the IMF. Generally, IMF supervision has seemed to facilitate commercial borrowing.
10. The repayment problem will be cushioned if refinancing of debts is available through further Eurocredits; but there is no guarantee of such availability. If refinancing is not possible, reserves will have to be used, although in many cases these may already be inadequate, as is suggested by the reluctance of LDCs to reduce them, and the preference for borrowing that has been shown.
11. In real terms, however, LDCs' external debt rose by only about 25 per cent over this period.
12. This problem will evaporate where the exchange rate is pegged to the dollar and it is Eurodollars that are borrowed.

13. For a full discussion of these proposals, see Michalopoulos (1975).
14. The Development Committee, on the basis of a report by its Working Group on Access to Capital Markets, has called for preferential treatment to be given to LDC borrowers by the governments of capital-market countries. For a summary of the Working Group's report, see *IMF Survey*, 6 Dec 1976.

Chapter 10

1. The UNCTAD envisages that more general commodity agreements could be concluded, for a longer list of commodities. These would include the ten core commodities, plus bananas, bauxite, hard fibres and related products, iron ore, manganese, meat, phosphates, tropical timber, vegetable oils and oilseeds.
2. The CFF has already been evaluated in Chapter 8 and readers are referred to that chapter for a fuller discussion. In summary, the CFF may be criticised for a number of reasons. First, uncertainty may be generated by the fact that assistance is not automatically available: second, assistance may be delayed; and, third, assistance even if granted, is subject to conditions which the borrowing country may consider inappropriate. Fourth, the CFF implicitly assumes that the duration of any cycle in commodity prices is such that a shortfall in export receipts will be reversed and offset within a relatively short period of time. Fifth, the CFF has concentrated exclusively on shortfalls in export receipts and has ignored increases in import expenditure. The EEC Stabex scheme may be similarly criticised. This scheme formed a component of the Lomé Convention, signed in 1975 between the EEC and forty-six African, Caribbean and Pacific LDCs. Under the scheme, these LDCs are reimbursed for the difference between their actual export earnings and the average of their export earnings over the previous four years, subject to the restrictions that (1) only earnings from exports to the EEC are taken into account; (ii) only earnings from twelve commodity groups (groundnut products, cocoa products, coffee products, cotton products, coconut products, palm, palmnut and kernel products, rawhides skins and leather, wood products, fresh bananas, tea, raw sisal and iron ore) are covered; (iii) the earnings of the exports of the commodity to all destinations during the year preceding that of the application must have exceeded 7·5 per cent of the total merchandise exports of the country concerned (5 per cent for sisal, and 2·5 for exports from the group of least-developed, landlocked and island (LLI) states); and (iv) the export shortfall must be at least 7·5 per cent, or 2·5 per cent for LLI countries. Compensatory payments, which are limited in total to 375 million units of account, take the form of grants for the least-developed ACP countries, and free loans for the other countries. The main criticism that can be made of the Stabex scheme concerns the way in which the trend is measured. By estimating the trend value of exports on the basis of past years, underestimation will be made wherever export earnings are growing, and, of course, the compensatory aspects of the Stabex scheme are particularly subject to erosion during a period of inflation. See de Vries (1975) for quantitative confirmation of this.

3. Supply might also be more assured if price stability encouraged producers to expand output.

4. The analysis of the gains from price stabilisation may be conducted in terms of the size and distribution of the producer and consumer surpluses. Massell (1970) concludes that price stabilisation with costless storage will generate net gains for producers and consumers and that producers will gain more than consumers where stochastic supply variations are more significant than stochastic demand variations, and where the price elasticity of supply is less than that of demand. Such static analysis, however, ignores the dynamic gains from price stabilisation; and these may be more important.

5. This has been a consistent theme of Kaldor: see Hart, Kaldor and Tinbergen (1964) and Kaldor (1976). We return to examine this notion in more detail in a later section of this chapter. World economic stability may be defined to cover variations not only in prices but also in output, income and employment.

6. Alterations in the incidence of earnings gains and losses may clearly have consequences for the world distribution of income as between primary-product producing and consuming countries. Depending on the particular configuration of demand and supply shifts and price elasticities, buffer-stock intervention in commodity markets may either redistribute income away from consumers and towards producers or away from producers and towards consumers. There is certainly no *a priori* universal rule which states that buffer-stock intervention will benefit producing countries at the cost of consuming ones.

7. We return to this issue in a moment.

8. Where future prices could be foreseen with some degree of certainty arbitrage would tend to stabilise the price around its long-term trend level.

9. Again we may note that the belief by producers that the agency will act to prevent price reductions may encourage them to increase supply at any given price, and thus lower the long-run equilibrium price.

10. If private speculators expect the price of a commodity to rise and act accordingly by buying the commodity, this in itself will cause the price to rise. If speculators have elastic expectations, they may take a movement in price as an indication that there will be a further movement in price in the same direction. Action based upon such expectations would tend to be self-fulfilling. Intervention by an agency with accurate information would not only be price-stabilising but also profitable for the agency concerned.

11. See, for instance, Henderson and Lal (1976).

12. In theory and in the right circumstances there is no reason why price stabilisation could not be brought about through the activities of private speculation. All that is necessary is that speculators sell when price rises above its equilibirium level, and buy when it falls below it.

13. For a definition of these terms and for a fuller discussion see IMF–IBRD, Joint Staff (1969) and UNCTAD (1969). In some cases a certain amount of product deterioration may be acceptable.

14. Where a commodity is subject to fairly rapid deterioration, the stock may, of course be frequently turned over. However, the economics of the matter may preclude such a policy even where the physical characteristics of the commodity do not.

15. Details of this agreement, and of others that have relied on some alternative means of commodity regulation, may be found in IMF—IBRD, Joint Staff Study (1969). More specific investigations of the Tin Agreement have been conducted by Fox (1974) and Smith and Schink (1976).

16. Where it is large, sudden and abnormal deviations from trend prices that cause the major economic problems, the size of the buffer stock will have to be correspondingly large; see Kaldor (1976) and Johnson (1976). Smith and Schink (1976) maintain that, in order to have achieved some moderate degree of price stability independently of other factors, the tin buffer stock would have had to have been considerably larger than it was. The example of tin illustrates that small buffer stocks are likely to suffer from one or more of three limitations: first, the band of prices that is defended will have to be fairly wide; second, the band will have to follow short-term market trends quite closely; and, third, it will have to be accepted that market prices may frequently move outside the band. In each of these three cases the degree of stabilising influence exerted by the buffer stock will be reduced. Smith and Schink argue further that, in the absence of the US stockpile, conflict between producers and consumers on the International Tin Council (which would then to a larger extent have become a price maker), as well as the problem of financing the larger buffer stock that would have been needed, would have resulted in the collapse of the ITA

17. Since many primary products are sold in competitive markets, producers tend to be price takers rather than price makers. Action taken by one producer in isolation to increase his revenue may not be appropriate from the point of view of maximising the revenue of producers as a group. Maximisation of producer-group revenue might be achieved through cartelisation.

18. This topic is discussed in Chapter 4.

19. This is not to argue that other solutions, such as an increase in aid, are not superior to 'tinkering with the price mechanism'. There may indeed be a conflict between equity and economic efficiency. But if first-best solutions are not forthcoming, feasible second-best solutions should perhaps be examined. For a critical discussion of this notion, see Johnson (1976). Johnson further criticises the UNCTAD for confusing protection against unanticipated inflation through indexation, which is legitimate, with protection against and prevention of changes in relative prices, which he maintains is neither legitimate nor desirable.

20. The use of commodity arrangements to stabilise or raise prices involves questions both of efficiency and of equity. Generally, since LDCs export more primary commodities than they import, it might be anticipated that they would gain from a relative increase in the price of primary products. However, with any buffer-stocking scheme, the extent to which they would benefit, if at all, would depend on the particular commodities included in the scheme. Schemes for tea, jute and cocoa would tend to favour low-income LDCs most, since exports of these commodities are concentrated in the low-income LDCs, whilst schemes for coffee, copper and sugar would favour middle-income LDCs. Export shares for tin, rubber, sisal and cotton are fairly evenly distributed among low- and middle-income LDCs. The distribution of the costs associated with buffer stocks depends, again, on the

commodities covered, the extent to which increased raw-material prices are reflected in higher manufactured good prices, and the import pattern for particular manufactured goods. It is quite possible that a non-exporting LDC will lose as a result of an increase in the price of a particular commodity, not only directly, because of the higher commodity price, but also indirectly, because of the higher price of imported manufactures which use the primary commodity as an input. The pattern of costs and benefits associated with buffer-stock schemes will also depend on whether the objective of the buffer stock is to raise or merely stabilise price; clearly, the stabilisation of a price which might otherwise have risen may impose costs on exporting countries. For a full discussion of the distributional aspects of buffer-stock schemes, see Michalopoulos and Perez (1977).

21. Kaldor (1964) has advocated a variable export duty or levy the level of which would be positively related to the level of stocks held. 'The external price would be stabilized by the operation of the export restriction agreement itself, and the purpose of the variable export duty would be to regulate internal supplies so as to keep pace with external requirements, and thus assist in the necessary structural readjustment of the economy.'

22. Of course, the international monetary system as currently constituted provides some financial assistance to such schemes, (see Chapter 7).

23. See Hart (1976).

24. For an elaboration of this argument, see Grubel (1965). The argument has been challenged; see Hart (1966, 1976). See also Williamson (1973).

25. Kaldor (1976) and Hart (1976) still maintain however, that a link between the international monetary sector and the real sector which would result from commodity backing would yield benefits in terms of stability which are not generated by fiat systems.

26. With international fiat monetary expansion, LDCs may of course gain indirectly from the expansionist policies thereby encouraged in developed countries; see Grubel (1965).

27. The following section draws heavily on Bird (1976). The notion of financing buffer stocks through the creation of international money follows the tradition of Keynes (1942).

28. These schemes are discussed more fully in Chapter 11.

29. Where unutilised existing warehousing facilities are brought into use, both the private and social costs of the buffer-stock scheme will be reduced. Indeed, the social opportunity cost will fall to zero.

30. Indeed, the strength of the case for buffer stocks lies in the belief that, because of the benefits, the net social costs of buffer-stock schemes are negative. An interesting question touched on earlier in this chapter relates to the distribution of the costs and benefits. Much depends here on whether a short-term or long-term view is taken.

31. Commodity coverage may of course also affect storage costs, since some commodities are more cheaply stored than others.

32. This constitutes a financial economy associated with centrally financed buffer stocks. Where individual buffer stocks operate separately, such financial economies are less likely to be forthcoming.

33. See UNCTAD (1977), and Behrman (1976).

34. The cost of operating buffer-stocks varies significantly according to

commodity: out of the ten core commodities, those for which stocking arrangements would appear to be the most expensive are copper and sugar (see Michalopoulos and Perez, 1977).

35. See Keynes (1942), Hart, Kaldor and Tinbergen (1964), Bird (1975), Hart (1976) and Kaldor (1976).

36. Hart, Kaldor and Tinbergen (1964) maintain that 'for the world economy as a whole each unit of income so generated would probably be amplified by a "super-multiplier" (allowing for induced investment) of at least four or five (indeed, the figure may be much larger)'. Where developed economies have no spare capacity, the expansionary industrial implications of the buffer-stock scheme will, HKT maintain, be diffused to less developed economies. 'Since the world as a whole is a vast under-developed economy – with vast reserves of underutilised and unemployed labour which can be drawn on for employment in industry so long as raw material supplies are available and demand is expanding – it cannot be denied that it is possible to step up the growth of world manufacturing production sufficiently so as to match any likely increase in the supply of primary products.'

Chapter 11

1. It is not intended to discuss in this chapter the theory of the optimum quantity of international money. Those interested are referred to Johnson (1970), Mundell (1971), Clark (1972) and Grubel (1973).

2. The SDR scheme has already been discussed at some length in Chapters 7 and 8, to which readers should refer for technical details of the scheme.

3. For a fuller discussion of this, see Chapter 8.

4. The following analysis has been discussed more rigorously by a number of authors; see, for instance, Grubel (1972).

5. The nature of the relationship between the grant element in SDR allocation and the rate of interest may be expressed as

$$G = 100 \left(1 - \frac{i}{r}\right)$$

where G is the grant content of SDRs (as a percentage), i is the interest rate on SDRs and r is the market-related reference interest rate. Given a reference rate of, say, 7·5 per cent, a rise in the interest rate on SDRs from 1·5 per cent to 5 per cent, as occurred in July 1974, implies a fall in the grant element on SDRs from about 80 per cent to $33\frac{1}{3}$ per cent. Since, however, the rate of interest on SDRs is approximately tied to the commercial market interest rate, the differential between the two rates which determines the grant element is likely to remain more constant.

6. A fairly detailed examination of the distribution formula is conducted in Chapter 8.

7. A brief but useful summary of the link concept may be found in Park (1973), Maynard and Bird (1975), Bird (1977) and Williamson (1976).

8. This question is discussed in Chapter 5.

9. For a more detailed explanation of the scheme, see Maynard (1973).
10. It is unlikely, however, that a 'competitive' rate means a rate equal to that offered on reserve currencies, since the *value* of SDRs is more firmly guaranteed in terms of a standard 'basket' of major currencies.
11. A rigorous substantiation of this claim may be found in Isard and Truman (1974). They calculate that with a constant annual rate of SDR-link allocations of 1000 million and a rate of interest on SDR use of 5 per cent, the interest due on previous link allocations will begin to exceed the volume of new allocations after twenty-one years.
12. See Williamson (1972, 1976).
13. See Helleiner (1974).
14. See Chapter 10 for a fuller discussion of this issue.
15. Although reference is made to *the* link, it has been seen that there are in fact many variants. The implications of the various schemes differ in certain ways, and this section is therefore designed to be fairly general rather than specific. A more explicit examination of the implications of various link proposals has been presented by Maynard (1973).
16. Under certain tied versions of the link, contributions might be determined by the ability or willingness of individual donors to absorb the extra demand associated with the link.
17. More generally, it may be shown that the short-term real-resource cost incurred by a donor country *per unit* of extra reserves gained, allowing for both allocated and earned SDRs, depends on (i) the size of the country's IMF quota, (ii) the proportion of total SDRs created in the allocation period that are devoted to the link, (iii) the country's assigned share in the amount of SDRs forgone in favour of the link, assuming that only developed countries and not LDCs forgo SDRs in this way, and (iv) the country's earning share in meeting the LDCs' link-financed orders for development goods. The resource cost per unit of reserves gained will be greater the smaller is (i) and the larger are (ii), (iii) and (iv).

On the basis of various assumptions concerning quota size, export procurement, proportion of SDR allocation linked, and distribution of link contributions, Maynard (1973) calculates that *on average* Development Assistance Committee countries would be involved in a real-resource cost of about $0·50 for every $1 of reserves received, although there is considerable inter-country dispersion.
18. This analysis of the impact of the link on employment and inflation is crucially dependent on our assumptions concerning the objectives of macroeconomic policy in developed countries. The implications of an SDR linked as opposed to a non-SDR or un-linked SDR system depend on whether developed countries possess a target level of international reserves, or pursue surpluses irrespective of the level of reserves, in order to achieve reserve growth. Mercantilist modes of thought, which appear reasonably durable, suggest that developed countries will wish to earn extra reserves year upon year. If this is the case, under a fixed exchange-rate system the benefit of the link to these countries will be felt primarily in terms of reduced unemployment. The reduced inflation argument applies when comparing a linked with an unlinked SDR system only if allocated SDRs are spent by developed countries, or encourage expansionary domestic policies.

19. Bird (1974) discusses in more detail the relevance of the link to economic conditions existing in 1974 and 1975. He shows how the link could compensate to a certain extent for the demand-deflationary effects of the oil-price rise.
20. The debate over the inflation 'cost' of the link has been well documented. See, for instance, Bauer (1973), Kessler (1971), Kahn (1973), Abbott (1975), Maynard (1973), UNCTAD (1965), Dell (1969) and Cline (1976).
21. This, of course, ignores the fact that unlinked SDRs may be held and not spent.
22. Similar calculations are to be found in Group of Countries Participating in the GAB (1965), UNCTAD (1965), Triffin (1969), Kahn (1973) and Maynard (1973).
23. Counter-cyclical international monetary policy might, however, share some of the problems encountered in the pursuit of counter-cyclical domestic monetary policy.
24. For a discussion of these costs and benefits see for example Aliber (1964, 1965), Salant (1964), Grubel (1964), Goldstein (1965), Kareken (1965), Kirman and Schmidt (1965) and Cohen (1971a, 1971b).

Chapter 12

1. It may be useful to reread (or read) Chapter 6 before reading this chapter.
2. Under the Second Amendment to the Articles of Agreement of the IMF, each member country may adopt the exchange-rate system which it considers most appropriate to its own circumstances.
3. Leipziger (1977) quotes evidence which suggests that the cost of forward cover has risen quite significantly since the introduction of generalised floating. Thus, even when LDCs can gain access to forward cover, they are likely to find it expensive.
4. For a good discussion of the problems involved with forward-exchange facilities in LDCs, see Miller (1975). A form of forward facility administered by the central bank and operating not unlike an insurance scheme does exist in some LDCs, but only in a very small number of LDCs do commercial banks engage in forward foreign-exchange transactions.
5. For a discussion of this evidence, see Cline (1976).
6. Disequilibrium exchange rates amongst developed countries may cause LDCs to pursue a pattern of industrialisation that is inappropriate when equilibrium rates are attained. Exchange-rate overvaluation amongst developed countries may, for instance, give LDCs a largely artificial, spurious, and short-term advantage in the production and export of certain goods in world markets; an advantage which disappears when devaluation eventually takes place in developed countries. Given that the postponement of adjustment in developed countries will not be infinite, the longer it is postponed the more difficult it is for LDCs to plan their development in a way which makes the most efficient use of their resources.
7. The strength of the argument just outlined depends on the level of employment: basically it assumes full employment. In conditions of over full employment, for instance, the deflationary aspect of demand management

may be regarded as an external benefit of the policy, and the size of this benefit will tend to be inversely related to the degree of openness. A similar argument also holds for a balance-of-payments surplus situation and demand expansion. In any case, as was seen in Chapter 6, exchange-rate depreciation may be deflationary. The deflationary aspects of exchange-rate changes are, however, concealed in comparison with demand-management policy.

8. It may be noted that in some ways the inflation factor is inconsistent with the factor relating to the source of generation of disturbance. One argument says that an excessive domestic rate of inflation will encourage fixed exchange rates, whilst the other says that it may require exchange-rate flexibility.
9. The relevance of elasticities to the efficacy of floating exchange rates is more fully discussed in Chapter 6.
10. For a fuller discussion of this issue, see Chapter 6.
11. Whilst it may forestall the destruction that foreign-exchange risk would have caused to the LDCs export trade, pegging to the currency of a major trading partner in an environment of floating rates will introduce a trade-diverting bias against the rest of the world (see Diaz-Alejandro, 1976).
12. For a discussion of the choice of exchange-rate peg, see Black (1976) and Crockett and Nsouli (1977).
13. Mali was the only case where the franc peg was inferior to an SDR peg.
14. Examples are Argentina, Bolivia, Brazil, Chile, Syria, Yemen and Thailand.
15. See, for instance, Cooper (1971) and Connolly and Taylor (1976).
16. It may simply mean that exchange-rate flexibility is suitable for a limited number of LDCs, and the LDCs have efficiently identified the suitability and unsuitability of floating.

Chapter 13

1. Thus Gold (1979) points out that while 'most of the decision is declaratory of the practice that has emerged in the years since 1968 . . . the decision includes certain new or clarified elements, largely in deference to the views of developing members, who feel that the Fund's conditionality has been, 'too severe in relation to them'. Subsequent quotations in this section are also from Gold (1979) unless otherwise stipulated.
2. For a fuller discussion see Bird (1981a), Bird and Orme (1981) and Bird (1981b). It may be noted that the IMF may in certain cases impose restrictions on a country's external borrowing as a condition of Fund assistance.
3. It may be noted, however, that the exposure of the international banking system as a whole is still low; no individual developing country accounts for more than 3 per cent of total international banking assets. The problem of exposure levels therefore relates only to individual banks. Of course, it is possible that some developing countries may benefit from the desire of banks to limit exposure and diversify their lending.
4. Increasing monetary stringency in the US could also increase the demand for Eurodollars by US firms.

5. Larger deficits in OECD countries need not necessarily crowd out developing country borrowers, since the former group of countries may be in a position to tap the bond market which has been relatively insignificant for developing countries.

6. There remain, of course, the problems associated with matching the distribution of additional finance with that of the deficits.

7. Given the concentration of Eurocurrency lending to developing countries, it may be noted that changes in the aggregate value of credits reflects very closely the situation in the major borrowing countries. Thus the low level of borrowing in 1980 can to a large extent be explained by specific events in Brazil, where there has been a conscious attempt to reduce the reliance on commercial credit; in Korea, where political uncertainties have had an adverse effect on the willingness of private banks to lend; in Mexico, where increasing oil receipts have reduced the size of the external financing requirement; and in the Philippines, where conditions attached to IMF loans have limited the country's recourse to commercial borrowing.

8. In principle, the international bond market could offer developing countries an alternative source of finance. Bond issues increased quite quickly after 1975, reaching $6.0 billion in 1978, but falling back to only $3.9 billion in 1979. Again, however, bond finance has only been a practical option for a very small number of middle-income developing countries. As the World Bank points out, 'the bond market is a very conservative area in which investor acceptance is acquired only slowly; borrowers must approach the market cautiously until they establish sound reputations. This suggests that in the foreseeable future bonds will not substitute to any great extent for commercial bank lending.' (World Development Report, 1980).

9. For a fuller appraisal of IMF conditionality including analysis of case studies see Killick *et al.* (1982).

10. Care has to be exercised here, however, since to an extent the interest rate dispersion reflects the likelihood and expected direction of interest rate variation in a particular currency.

11. However this would still leave the problem of dealing with a deficit in the Special Drawing Account.

12. Other forms of lending to LDCs may involve grace periods which duplicate this SDR effect.

13. The relationship between the IMF and commercial banks is complex, and in a significant number of cases the availability of private finance rests on the conclusion of an IMF stand-by arrangement by the borrower. For further analysis of the relationship between the official and private sectors in international lending see Bird (1981a) and (1981b).

14. For a fuller discussion of the interests of developing countries in international financial reform see Bird (1981c).

Chapter Bibliographies

Chapter 1

Bird, G. R. 'Less Developed Countries and the Reform of the International Monetary System', *ODI Review*, no. 1, 1977.
Colloquium on the Interests of Developing Countries in International Monetary Reform, *Money in a Village World* (Geneva: Committee on Society, Development and Peace, 1970).
Cline, W. R., *International Monetary Reform and the Developing Countries* (Washington, DC: Brookings Institution, 1976).
Diaz-Alejandro, C., 'The Post 1971 International Financial System and the Less Developed Countries', in *A World Divided*, ed. G. K. Helleiner (Cambridge University Press, 1976).
Helleiner, G. K., 'The Less Developed Countries and the International Monetary System', *Journal of Development Studies*, Apr–July 1974.
Holsen, J. A., and Waelbroeck, J. L., 'The Less Developed Countries and the International Monetary Mechanism', *American Economic Review*, May 1976.
IMF, *IMF Survey*, various issues.
Leipziger, D. M. (ed.), *The International Monetary System and the Developing Nations* (Washington, DC: US Agency for International Development.
Maynard, G. W., and Bird, G. R., 'International Monetary Issues and the Developing Countries: A Survey', *World Development*, Sep 1975.

Chapter 2

Belsare, S. K., 'International Liquidity Problem and the Developing Countries', in *Indian Economic Thought and Development*, ed. A. V. Bhuleshkhar (New York: Humanities Press, 1969).
Bird, G.R., 'The Dollar Crisis and Settlement in Perspective', *Economics*, Summer 1972:
Colloquium on the Interests of the Developing Countries in International Monetary Reform, *Money in a Village World* (1970).

332   *The International Monetary System and the LDCs*

Corea, G., 'The International Monetary System and the Developing Countries', *Staff Studies, Central Bank of Ceylon*, Sep 1971.

Gold, J., ' " . . . to contribute thereby to . . . development . . .": Aspects of the Relations of the IMF with its Developing Members', *Columbia Journal of Transnational Law*, Fall 1971.

Horsefield, J. K., *The International Monetary Fund 1945–1965* (Washington, DC: IMF, 1969).

IMF, Committee on Reform of the International Monetary System and Related Issues, *International Monetary Reform: Documents of the Committee of Twenty*, (Washington, DC, 1974).

IMF, *IMF Survey*, various issues.

IMF, *Finance and Development*, various issues.

Kenen, P., *Giant Among Nations* (Chicago: Rand-McNally, 1963).

Konig, W., 'International Financial Institutions and Latin American Development', in *Latin America in the International Economy*, ed. V. L. Urquidi and R. Thorp (London: Macmillan, 1973).

Krasner, S. D., 'The IMF and the Third World', *International Organization*, Summer 1968.

Machlup, F., *Plans for the Reform of the International Monetary System*, Special Papers in International Economics no. 3, International Finance Section, Princeton University, (Princeton, NJ, 1964).

Mookerjee, S., 'Policies on the Use of Fund Resources', *IMF Staff Papers*, Nov 1966.

Mundell, R. A., 'The International Monetary Fund', *Journal of World Trade Law*, III (1969).

Payer, C., *The Debt Trap* (Harmondsworth, Middx: Penguin, 1974).

Schleiminger, G., 'Developed and Developing Countries in the IMF: Co-operation or Confrontation', *Intereconomics*, Dec 1970.

Scott, A. D., 'The Role of the International Monetary Fund in Economic Development', in *Columbia Essays in International Affairs: The Deans Papers* (New York: Columbia University Press, 1967).

Seers, D., quoted in *Inflation and Growth in Latin America*, ed. W. Baer and I. Kerstenetsky (Homewood, Ill.: Irwin, 1964).

UNCTAD, *International Monetary Issues and the Developing Countries*, Report of the Group of Experts (New York: United Nations, 1965).

UNCTAD, *Commodity Trade*, (New York: United Nations, 1965).

Chapter 3

Askari, H., and Weil, G., 'Stability of Export Earnings of Developing

Nations', *Journal of Development Studies*, Oct 1974.

Coppock, J. D., *International Economic Instability* (New York: McGraw Hill, 1962).

Erb, G. R., and Schiavo-Campo, S., 'Export Instability, Level of Development, and Economic Size of Less Developed Countries', *Oxford Bulletin of Economics and Statistics*, Nov 1969.

Erb, G. R. and Schiavo-Campo, S., 'The Decline in World Export Instability: A Reply', *Oxford Bulletin of Economics and Statistics*, Aug 1971.

Flanders, J. M., 'Prebisch on Protectionism: an Evaluation', *Economic Journal*, 1964.

Glezakos, G., 'Export Instability and Economic Growth: A Statistical Verification', *Economic Development and Cultural Change*, July 1973.

Hambulu, W., 'Export Instability', M. Sc. Dissertation, University of Surrey, 1976.

IMF–IBRD, *The Problem of Stabilization of Prices of Primary Products*, Joint Staff Study (Washington, DC, 1969).

Katrak, H., 'Commodity Concentration and Export Fluctuations: A Probability Analysis', *Journal of Development Studies*, July 1973.

Kenen, P. B., and Voivodas, C. S., 'Export Instability and Economic Growth', *Kyklos*, 1972.

Khalaf, N. G., 'Country Size and Economic Instability', *Journal of Development Studies*, July 1976.

Kingston, J. L., 'Export Concentration and Export Performance in Developing Countries, 1954–67', *Journal of Development Studies*, July 1976.

Lawson, C. W., 'The Decline in World Export Instability: A Reappraisal', *Oxford Bulletin of Economics and Statistics*, Mar 1974.

Leith, J. C., 'The Decline in World Export Instability: A Comment', *Oxford Bulletin of Economics and Statistics*, Aug 1970.

Lim, D., 'Export Instability and Economic Growth: A Return to Fundamentals', *Oxford Bulletin of Economics and Statistics*, Nov 1976.

MacBean, A., *Export Instability and Economic Development* (Cambridge, Mass.: Harvard University Press, 1966).

Maizels, A., *Exports and Economic Growth of Developing Countries* (London: Allen and Unwin, 1968).

Massell, B. F., 'Export Concentration and Fluctuations in Export Earnings: A Cross Section Analysis', *American Economic Review*, Mar 1964.

Massell, B. F., 'Export Instability and Economic Structure', *American*

Economic Review, Sep 1970.

Massell, B. F., Pearson, S. R., and Fitch, J., 'Foreign Exchange and Economic Development: An Empirical Study of Selected Latin American Countries', *Review of Economics and Statistics*, 1972.

Michaely, M., *Concentration in International Trade* (Amsterdam: North-Holland, 1962).

Naya, S., 'Fluctuations in Export Earnings and Economic Patterns of Asian Countries', *Economic Development and Cultural Change*, July 1973.

Pearson, L., *Partners in Development*, (New York: Praeger, 1969).

Porter, R. C., 'Who Destabilizes Primary Product Prices?', *Indian Economic Journal*, 1969.

Prebisch, R., *Towards a New Trade Policy for Development* (1964).

Rangarajan, C., and Sundararajan, V., 'Impact of Export Fluctuations on Income – A Cross Country Analysis', *Review of Economics and Statistics*, Aug 1976.

Schiavo-Campo, S., and Singer, H., *Perspectives of Economic Development* (Boston: Houghton Mifflin, 1970).

Stern, R., 'World Market Instability in Primary Commodities', *Banca Nazionale del Lavoro Quarterly Review*, June 1976.

Voivodas, C. S., 'The Effect of Foreign Exchange Instability on Growth', *Review of Economics and Statistics*, Aug 1974.

Chapter 4

Andic, F., Andic, S., and Dosser, D., *A Theory of Economic Integration for Developing Countries* (London: Allen and Unwin, 1971).

Balassa, B. A., *Trade Liberalization among Industrial Countries* (New York: McGraw-Hill, 1967).

Balassa, B. A. *Trade Prospects for Developing Countries* (Homewood, Ill.: Irwin, 1964).

Balassa, B. A., 'The First Half of the Development Decade: Growth, Trade and the Balance of Payments of the Developing Countries, 1960–1965'; *Banca Nazionale del Lavoro Quarterly Review*, Dec 1968.

Ball, R., and Marwah, K., 'The US Demand for Imports 1948–1958', *Review of Economics and Statistics*, Nov 1962.

Club of Rome, *The Limits to Growth* (1972).

Flanders, *Economic Journal*, 1964.

Houthakker, H. S. and Magee, S. P., 'Income and Price Elasticities in World Trade', *Review of Economics and Statistics*, May 1969.

Khan, M. S., 'Import and Export Demand in Developing Countries', *IMF Staff Papers*, 1975.

Kreinin, M., 'Effect of Tariff Changes on the Prices and Volume of Imports', *American Economic Review*, June 1961.

Pearson, *Partners in Development* (1969).

Prebisch, *Towards a New Trade Policy for Development* (1964).

Schiavo-Campo and Singer, *Perspectives of Economic Development* (1970).

Stern, R. M., Francis, J., and Schumacher, B., *Price Elasticities in International Trade: An Annotated Bibliography* (London: Macmillan, 1976).

Tinbergen, J., *Shaping the World Economy* (New York: Twentieth Century Press, 1962).

Wilson, T., Sinha, R. P., and Castree, J. R. (1969), 'The Income Terms of Trade of Developed and Developing Countries', *Economic Journal*, Dec 1969.

Chapter 5

Agarwal, J. P., 'Optimal Monetary Reserves for Developing Countries', *Weltwirtschaftliches Archiv*, cvii (1971).

Archibald, G. C., and Richmond, J., 'On the Theory of Foreign Exchange Reserve Requirements', *Review of Economic Studies*, Apr 1971.

Bird, G. R., *Some General Considerations Relevant to Evaluating the Performance of the International Monetary System*, Kingston Polytechnic, School of Economics and Politics, Occasional Paper No. I (1973).

Bird, G. R., 'International Liquidity and the Developing Countries', *Economic Notes*, vi (1977).

Brown, W. M. *The External Liquidity of an Advanced Country*, Studies in International Finance (Princeton, NJ, 1964).

Clark, P. B., 'Optimum International Reserves and the Speed of Adjustment', *Journal of Political Economy*, lxxviii (1970).

Clark, P. B., 'The Demand for International Reserves: A Cross-Country Analysis', *Canadian Journal of Economics*, Nov 1970.

Clower, R. W., and Lipsey, R. G., 'The Present State of International Liquidity Theory', *American Economic Review, Papers and Proceedings*, May 1968.

Flanders, M. J., *The Demand for International Reserves*, Princeton

Studies in International Finance, no. 27 (Princeton, NJ, 1971).

Frenkel, J. A., 'The Demand for International Reserves by Developed and Less Developed Countries', *Economica*, Feb 1974.

Group of Ten, *Ministerial Statement*, 1 Aug 1964.

Grubel, H. G., 'The Demand for International Reserves: A Critical Review of the Literature', *Journal of Economic Literature*, Dec 1971.

Heller, H. R., 'Optimal International Reserves', *Economic Journal*, June 1966.

Heller, H. R., 'The Transactions Demand for International Means of Payment', *Journal of Political Economy*, LXXVI (1968).

Iyoha, M. A., 'Demand for International Reserves in Less Developed Countries: A Distributed Lag Specification', *Review of Economics and Statistics*, Aug 1976.

IMF, *International Reserves: Needs and Availability* (Washington, DC, 1970).

Johnson, H. G., *International Trade and Economic Growth* (London: Allen and Unwin, 1958).

Kane, E. J., 'International Liquidity: A Probabilistic Approach', *Kyklos*, 1965.

Kafka, A., 'International Liquidity: Its Present Relevance to the Less Developed Countries', *American Economic Review, Papers and Proceedings*, May 1968.

Kelly, M. G., 'The Demand for International Reserves', *American Economic Review*, Sep 1970.

Kenen, P. B., and Yudin, E., 'The Demand for International Reserves', *Review of Economics and Statistics*, Aug 1965.

Lamfalussy, A., *The Role of Monetary Gold over the Next Ten Years*, (Washington, DC: IMF, 1969).

Leipziger, D. M., 'A Comment on Williamson's "Generalized Floating and the Reserve Needs of Developing Nations" ', in *The International Monetary System and the Developing Nations*, ed. Leipziger (1976).

Machlup, F., 'The Need for Monetary Reserves', *Banca Nazionale del Lavoro Quarterly Review*, Sep 1966.

Maynard and Bird, in *World Development*, 1975.

Michalopoulos, C., *Payments Arrangements for Less Developed Countries: The Role of Foreign Assistance*, Agency for International Development Discussion Paper no. 26 (Washington, DC, Feb 1973).

Niehans, J.,'The Need for Reserves of a Single Country', in IMF, *International Reserves: Needs and Availability* (1970).

Olivera, J. H. G., 'A Note on the Optimal Rate of Growth of

International Reserves', *Journal of Political Economy*, LXXVII (1969).

Salant, W. S., 'Practical Techniques for Assessing the Need for World Reserves', in IMF, *International Reserves: Needs and Availability* (1970).

Scitovsky, T., *Economic Theory and Western European Integration* (London: Allen and Unwin, 1958).

Stewart, F., and Stewart, M., 'Developing Countries, Trade and Liquidity: A New Approach', *The Banker*, Mar 1972.

Williamson, J., 'Surveys in Applied Economics: International Liquidity', *Economic Journal*, Sep 1973.

Williamson, J., 'Generalized Floating and the Reserve Needs of Developing Countries', in *The International Monetary System and the Developing Nations*, ed. Leipziger (1976).

Chapter 6

Aghevli, B. B., and Khan, M. S., 'The Monetary Approach to Balance of Payments Determination: An Empirical Test', in *The Monetary Approach to the Balance of Payments*, ed. Rhomberg and Heller (1977).

Bhagwat, A., and Onitsuka, Y., 'Export-Import Responses to Devaluation: Experience of Non-Industrial Countries in the 1960s', *IMF Staff Papers*, July 1974.

Bhagwati, J. N., 'The International Monetary System: Issues in the Symposium', *Journal of International Economics*, II (1972).

Colloquium on the Interests of the Developing Countries in International Monetary Reform, *Money in a Village World* (1970).

Connolly, M., and Taylor, D., 'Adjustment to Devaluation with Money and Non-traded Goods', *Journal of International Economics*, VI (1976).

Connolly, M., and Taylor, D., 'Testing the Monetary Approach to Devaluation in Developing Countries', *Journal of Political Economy*, LXXXIV (1976).

Cooper, R. N., *Currency Depreciation in Developing Countries*, Essays in International Finance no. 86 (Princeton, NJ, June 1971).

Cooper, R. N., 'Currency Devaluation in Developing Countries', in *Government and Economic Development*, ed. Ranis (1971).

Cooper, R. N., 'An Analysis of Currency Devaluation in Developing Countries', in *International Trade and Money*, ed. M. B. Connolly and A. K. Swoboda (London: Allen and Unwin, 1973).

de Vries, M. G., 'Multiple Exchange Rates, Expectations and Experiences', *IMF Staff Papers*, 1965.

de Vries, M. G., 'The Decline of Multiple Exchange Rates, *Finance and Development*, Dec 1967.

de Vries, M. G., 'Exchange Restrictions: Progress towards Liberalization', *Finance and Development*, Sept 1969.

de Vries, M. G., 'Multiple Exchange Rates', in Horsefield *The International Monetary Fund 1945–1965* (1969).

Diaz-Alejandro, C., *Exchange Rate Devaluation in a Semi-Industrialized Country: The Experience of Argentina, 1955–1961* (Cambridge, Mass.: MIT Press, 1965).

Diaz-Alejandro, C., 'Comment on Cooper', in *Government and Economic Development*, ed. Ranis (1971).

Diaz-Alejandro, C., in *A World Divided*, ed. Helleiner (1976).

Frenkel, J. A., and Johnson, H. G. (eds), *The Monetary Approach to the Balance of Payments* (London: Allen and Unwin, 1976).

Helleiner, in *Journal of Development Studies*, 1974.

Hinshaw, R., 'Elasticity Pessimism, Absorption and Flexible Exchange Rates', in *International Trade and Finance*, ed. W. Sellekaerts (London: Macmillan, 1974).

IMF, Committee on Reform of the International Monetary System and Related Issues, *International Monetary Reform: Documents of the Committee of Twenty* (1974).

Jayarajah, C. A. B. N., 'Problems and Prospects with Respect to the International Monetary System, Implications of Alternative Exchange Rate Systems for Developing Countries', *Bulletin, Central Bank of Ceylon*, Dec 1969.

Johnson, H. G., 'Towards a General Theory of the Balance of Payments', in Johnson, *International Trade and Economic Growth* (1958).

Johnson, H. G., 'The Monetary Approach to Balance of Payments Theory', in *International Trade and Money*, ed. M. B. Connolly and A. K. Swoboda (London: Allen and Unwin, 1973), and in *The Monetary Approach to the Balance of Payments, ed. Frenkel and Johnson (1976)*.

Johnson, O. E. G., 'The Exchange Rate as an Instrument of Policy in a Developing Country', *IMF Staff Papers*, July 1976.

Kafka, A., 'Adjustment Under the Bretton Woods Code with Special Reference to the Less Developed Countries', in *Development and Planning*, ed. J. N. Bhagwati and R. S. Eckaus (London: Allen and Unwin, 1972).

Kapur, B. K., 'Alternative Stabilization Policies for Less Developed Economies', *Journal of Political Economy*, LXXIV (1976).

Khan, M. S., in *IMF Staff Papers*, 1974.

Khan, M. S., 'A Monetary Model of the Balance of Payments: The Case of Venezuela', *Journal of Monetary Economics*, July 1976.

Khan, M. S., 'The Determination of the Balance of Payments and Income in Developing Countries', in *The Monetary Approach to the Balance of Payments*, ed. Rhomberg and Heller (1977).

Konig, W., 'Multiple Exchange Rate Policies in Latin America', *Journal of Inter-American Studies*, Jan 1968.

Knight, J. B., 'Devaluation and Income Distribution in Less Developed Economies' *Oxford Economic Papers*, July 1976.

McKinnon, R. I., *Money and Capital in Economic Development* (Washington, DC: Brookings Institution, 1973).

McLeod, A. N., 'Reform of the International Monetary System and the Interests of the Developing Countries', in Colloquium on the Interests of Developing Countries in International Monetary Reform, *Money in a Village World* (1970).

Maynard and Bird, in *World Development*, 1975.

Ranis, G., *Government and Economic Development* (New Haven, Conn.: Yale University Press, 1971).

Rhomberg, R. R., and Heller, H. R. (eds) *The Monetary Approach to The Balance of Payments* (Washington, DC: IMF, 1977).

Scammell, W. M., *International Trade and Payments* (London: Macmillan, 1974).

Stern, R. M., *The Balance of Payments Theory and Economic Policy* (London: Macmillan, 1973).

Streeten, P., 'The Developing Countries in a World of Flexible Exchange Rates,' *International Currency Review*, Jan–Feb 1971.

Zulu, J. B., 'The Interests of Developing Countries in the Current Reform of the International Monetary System – A Review', in Colloquium on the Interests of Developing Countries in International Monetary Reform, *Money in a Village World* (1970).

Chapter 7

Corea, in *Staff Studies, Central Bank of Ceylon*, 1971.

Corden, W. M., *Inflation, Exchange Rates and the World Economy* (London: Oxford University Press, 1977).

Cutler, D. S. and Gupta, D., 'SDRs: Valuation and Interest Rate',

Finance and Development, Dec 1974.

Fleming, M., Rhomberg, R., and Boissoneault, L., 'Export Norms and their Role in Compensatory Financing', *IMF Staff Papers*, 1963.

Gold, J., *The Stand-by Arrangements of the International Monetary Fund* (Washington, DC: IMF, 1970).

Gold, J., *Special Drawing Rights: Character and Use*, IMF Pamphlet Series no. 13 (Washington, DC, 1970).

Gold, J., *Columbia Journal of Transnational Law*, 1971.

Her Majesty's Stationery Office, *Special Drawings Rights*, Cmnd 3662 (London, 1968).

Horsefield (ed.), *The International Monetary Fund 1945–1965* (1969).

Horsefield, J. K., 'The Fund's Compensatory Financing', *Finance and Development*, Dec 1969.

Horsefield, J. K., and Lovasy, G., 'Evolutions of the Fund's Policy on Drawings', in *The International Monetary Fund 1945–1965*, ed. Horsefield (1969).

IMF, *Finance and Development*, various issues.

IMF, *IMF Survey*, various issues.

Krasner, in *International Organization*, 1968.

Lovasy, G., 'Survey and Appraisal of Proposed Schemes of Compensatory Financing', *IMF Staff Papers*, 1965.

Machlup, F., *Remaking the International Monetary System* (Baltimore, Md: Johns Hopkins University Press, 1968).

Polak, J. J., 'The Outline of a New Facility in the Fund', *Finance and Development*, Dec 1967.

Polak, J. J., *Some Reflections on the Nature of Special Drawing Rights*, IMF Pamphlet Series, no. 16 (Washington, DC, 1971).

Schiavo-Campo and Singer, *Perspectives of Economic Development*, (1970).

Scott, in *Colombia Essays in International Affairs: The Dean's Papers* (1967).

Tew, B., *The Evolution of the International Monetary System 1949–77* (London: Hutchinson, 1977).

Thornton, J. C., 'Compensatory and Supplementary Financing as Aid for Development', *Journal of Law and Economic Development*, 1969.

Chapter 8

Bhatia, R. J., and Rothman, S. L., 'Introducing the Extended Fund Facility: The Kenyan Case', *Finance and Development*, Dec 1975.

Corea, in *Staff Studies, Central Bank of Ceylon*, 1971.

de Vries, J., *Compensatory Financing: A Quantitative Analysis*, World Bank Staff Working Paper no. 228 (Dec 1975).

Flanders, *The Demand for International Reserves* (1971).

Goreux, L. M., 'Report on Compensatory Financing', *IMF Survey*, 7 Mar 1977.

Granade, H. R., 'The Use of International Monetary Fund Facilities by Different Groups of Countries, 1952–1971', *Southern Economic Journal*, Oct 1972.

Hawkins, R. G., and Rangarajan, C., 'On the Distribution of New International Reserves', *Journal of Finance*, Sep 1970.

Helleiner, in *Journal of Development Studies*, 1974.

Horsefield (ed.), *The International Monetary Fund 1945–1965* (1969).

Horsefield, in *Finance and Development* 1969.

Horsefield, J. K., 'What Does it Really Mean? Fund Quotas', *Finance and Development*, Sep 1970.

IMF, *Compensatory Financing of Export Fluctuations: Executive Board Decision* (24 Dec 1975).

Krasner, in *International Organization*, 1968.

Leipziger, D. M., 'Determinants of Use of Special Drawing Rights by Developing Nations', *Journal of Development Studies*, July 1975.

Machlup, *Remaking the International Monetary System* (1968).

Marquez, J., 'Developing Countries and the International Monetary System: the Distribution of Power and its Effects,' in the Colloquium on the Interests of Developing Countries in International Monetary Reform, *Money in a Village World* (1970).

Mookerjee, in *IMF Staff Papers*, 1966.

Morrison, T., and Perez, L., *Export Earnings Fluctuations and Economic Development: An Analysis of Compensatory Financing Schemes*, AID Discussion Paper no. 32 (Washington, DC: US Agency for International Development, 1975).

Payer, *The Debt Trap* (1974).

Perez, L., 'Export Subsidies in Developing Countries', *Journal of World Trade Law*, x (1976).

Reichmann, T., and Stillson, R., 'How Successful are Programmes Supported by Stand-By Arrangements?' *Finance and Development*, Mar 1977.

Santapillai, V. E., 'Assistance for Export Promotion', *Journal of World Trade Law*, iv (1970).

Scott, in *Columbia Essays in International Affairs: The Dean's Papers* (1967).

Thirlwall, A. P., and Barton, C. A., 'Inflation and Growth: the International Evidence', *Banca Nazionale del Lavoro Quarterly Review*, Sep 1971.

Triffin, R., 'The Use of SDR Finance for Collectively Agreed Purposes', *Banca Nazionale del Lavoro Quarterly Review*, Mar 1971.

UNCTAD, *Supplementary Financial Measures: Final Report of the Inter-Governmental Group* (New York: United Nations, Nov 1967).

Williams, D., 'The Fifth General Review of Quotas,' *Finance and Development*, Sep 1970.

Chapter 9

Beek, D. C., 'Commercial Bank Lending to the Developing Countries', *Federal Reserve Bank of New York Quarterly Review*, Summer 1977.

Corea, G., 'The Debt Problem of Developing Countries', *Journal of Development Planning*, no. 9.

Holsen, J. A., and Waelbroeck, J. L., 'The Less Developed Countries and the International Monetary Mechanism', *American Economic Review*, May 1976.

IBRD, *World Debt Tables*, EC 167/76.

IBRD, *Borrowing in International Capital Markets*, EC 181/764.

IMF, *IMF Survey*, various issues.

Kapur, I., 'The Supply of Euro-currency Finance to Developing Countries', *Finance and Development*, Sep 1977.

Michalopoulos, C., *Financing Needs of Developing Countries: Proposals for International Action*, Essays in International Finance no 110 (Princeton, NJ, June 1975).

Mohammed, A. F., and Saccomanni, F., 'Short-Term Banking and Euro-Currency Credits to Developing Countries', *IMF Staff Papers*, Nov 1973.

Pakenham, K., and Gore-Booth, J., 'The Euro-currency Markets as a Source of Finance for the Developing World', *ODI Review*, no. 2, 1974.

Chapter 10

Ady, P., 'Fluctuation in Income of Primary Producers: A Comment', *Economic Journal*, Sep 1953.

Bauer, P. T., and Paish, F. W., 'The Reduction of Fluctuations in the

Incomes of Primary Producers', *Economic Journal*, Dec 1952.

Behrman, J., 'International Commodity Agreements' (mimeo.), prepared as part of the Overseas Development Council New International Economic Order Research Project, Oct 1976.

Bird, G. R., 'Primary Product Price Instability: A Proposal for Financing Stabilization Schemes', *Economic Notes*, IV (1975).

Bird, G. R., 'The Role of SDRs in Financing Commodity Stabilization', *Journal of World Trade Law*, x (1976).

Bird, in *ODI Review*, 1977.

Brook, E. M., and Grilli, E. R., 'Commodity Price Stabilization and the Developing World', *Finance and Development,* Mar 1977.

Colebrook, J., 'The Cost of Storing Primary Commodities', *Journal of World Trade Law,* XI (1977).

Desai, M., 'An Econometric Model of the World Tin Economy', *Econometrica*, Jan 1966.

Fox, W. A., *Tin: The Working of a Commodity Agreement*, (London, 1974).

Friedman, M., 'Commodity Reserve Currency', *Journal of Political Economy* LIX (1951).

Friedman, M., 'The Reduction of Fluctuations in the Incomes of Primary Producers Further Considered', *Economic Journal*, Dec 1954.

Goudriaan, J., *How to Stop Deflation?* (London, 1932).

Graham, B., *World Commodities and World Currency* (New York: McGraw-Hill, 1944).

Grubel, H. G., 'The Case Against an International Commodity Reserve Currency' *Oxford Economic Papers*, Mar 1965.

Hart, A. G., Kaldor, N., and Tinbergen, J., 'The Case For an International Commodity Reserve Currency', in *Proceedings of the UN Conference on Trade and Development*, vol. III (New York: United Nations, 1964).

Hart, A. G., 'The Case For and Against an International Commodity Reserve Currency', *Oxford Economic Papers*, July 1966.

Hart, A. G., 'The Case as of 1976 for International Commodity-Reserve Currency', *Weltwirtschaftliches Archiv*, CXII (1976).

Henderson, P. D., and Lal, D., 'UNCTAD, the Commodities Problem, and International Economic Reform', *ODI Review*, no. 2, 1976.

Hill, M. E., 'Fluctuation in Incomes of Primary Producers', *Economic Journal*, June 1953.

IMF–IBRD, *The Problem of Stabilization of Prices of Primary Products*, Joint Staff Study (1969).

Johnson, H. G., 'World Inflation, the Developing Countries and "an Integrated Programme for Commodities"', *Banca Nazionale del Lavoro Quarterly Review*, Dec 1976.

Kaldor, N., 'Stabilising the Terms of Trade of Underdeveloped Countries', in *Essays on Economic Policy*, ii (London: Duckworth, 1964).

Kaldor, N., 'Inflation and Recession in the World Economy', *Economic Journal*, Dec 1976.

Keynes, J. M., 'The International Control of Raw Materials', Treasury Memorandum 1942, reprinted in *Journal of International Economics*, no. 4, 1974.

Luke, J. C., 'Inflation-Free Pricing Rules for a Generalised Commodity Reserve Currency', *Journal of Political Economy*, LXXXIII (1975).

Massell, B., 'Some Welfare Implications of International Price Stabilisation', *Journal of Political Economy*, LXXVIII (1970).

Michalopoulos, C., and Perez, L. L., 'Commodity Trade Policy Initiatives and Issues' (mimeo.), presented at the Ford Foundation Conference on Stabilising World Commodity Markets, Analysis, Practice and Policy, Mar 1977.

Smith, G. W., and Schink, G. R., 'The International Tin Agreement: A Reassessment', *Economic Journal*, Dec 1976.

Swerling, B. C., 'Buffer Stocks and International Commodity Problems', *Economic Journal*, Dec 1953.

UNCTAD, *The Development of an International Commodity Policy*, TD/8 (New York: United Nations, 1969).

UNCTAD, *Integrated Programme for Commodities*, TD/B/C 1/166 (New York: United Nations, Dec 1974).

UNCTAD, *Consideration of Issues Relating to the Establishment and Operations of a Common Fund*, TD/B/IPC/CFL (New York: United Nations, Dec 1976).

UNCTAD, *UNCTAD Seminar Programme Newsletter* no. 2 (Mar 1977).

Williamson, J., 'International Liquidity', *Economic Journal*, Sep 1973.

Chapter 11

Abbott, G. C., 'How Inflationary is the Link Scheme', *Economia Internationale*, Feb 1975.

Aliber, R. Z. 'The Cost and Benefits of the US Role as a Reserve Currency Country', *Quarterly Journal of Economics*, August 1964.

Aliber, R. Z., 'The Benefits and Cost of Being a World Banker:

Comment', *National Banking Review*, Mar 1965.

Bauer, P., 'Inflation, SDRs and Aid', *Lloyds Bank Review*, July 1973.

Bird, G. R., 'The Liquidity–Aid Link and the Maintenance of Full Employment and Balance of Payments Equilibrium in Developed Countries', *Economic Notes*, III (1974).

Bird, G. R., 'The Informal Link Between SDR Allocation and Aid: A Note', *Journal of Development Studies*, Apr 1976.

Bird, in *Journal of World Trade Law*, x (1976).

Bird, in *ODI Review*, 1977.

Clark, P. B., 'Interest Payments and the Rate of Return on International Fiat Currency', *Weltwirtschaftliches Archiv*, 1972.

Cline, *International Monetary Reform and the Developing Countries* (1976).

Cohen, B. J., *The Future of Sterling as an International Currency*, (London: Macmillan, 1971).

Cohen, B. J., 'The Seigniorage Gains of an International Currency', *Quarterly Journal of Economics*, Aug 1971.

Cooper, *Currency Devaluation in Developing Countries* (1971).

Dell, S., *Report of the Sub-Committee on International Exchange and Payments of Joint Economic Committee, US Congress* (Washington, DC, 1969).

Diaz-Alejandro, in. *A World Divided*, ed., Helleiner (1976).

Goldstein, H. N., 'Does it Necessarily Cost Anything to be World Banker?', *National Banking Review*, Mar 1965.

Group of Countries Participating in the General Arrangements to Borrow, *Report of the Study Group on the Creation of Reserve Assets*, (Rome: Bank of Italy Press, 1965).

Grubel, H. G., 'The Benefits and Costs of Being the World Banker' *National Banking Review*, Dec 1964.

Grubel, H. G. 'The Distribution of Seigniorage from International Liquidity Creation', in *Monetary Problems of the International Economy*, ed. Mundell and Swoboda (1969).

Grubel, H. G., 'Basic Methods for Distributing SDRs and the Problem of International Aid', *Journal of Finance*, Dec 1972.

Grubel, H. G., 'Interest Payments and the Efficiency of the International Monetary System', *Economic Notes*, II (1973).

Haan, R. L., *Special Drawing Rights and Development* (Leiden: Stenfert Kroese, 1971).

Haberler, G., 'The Case Against the Link', *Banca Nazionale del Lavoro Quarterly Review*, Mar 1971.

Hawkins and Rangarajan, in *Journal of Finance*, 1970.

Helleiner, in *Journal of Development Studies*, 1974.

Hirsch, F., *An SDR Standard: Impetus, Elements and Impediments*, Essays in International Finance, no. 99 (Princeton, NJ 1973).

Howe, J., 'SDRs and Development: Let's Spread Them Around', *Foreign Policy*, Fall 1972.

IMF, Committee on Reform of the International Monetary System and Related Issues, *International Monetary Reform: Documents of the Committee of Twenty* (1974).

Inter-American Committee on the Alliance for Progress, *International Monetary Reform and Latin America*, (Washington, DC: Pan American Union, 1966).

Isard, P. and Truman, E. M., 'SDRs, Interest and the Aid Link: Further Analysis', *Banca Nazionale del Lavoro Quarterly Review*, Mar 1974.

Johnson, H. G., *Efficiency in Domestic and International Money Supply* (Guildford: University of Surrey, 1970).

Johnson, H. G., 'A Note on Seigniorage and the Social Saving from Substituting Credit for Commodity Money', in *Monetary Problems of the International Economy*, ed. Mundell and Swoboda (1969).

Johnson, H. G., 'The Link that Chains', *Foreign Policy*, Fall 1972.

Johnson, H. G., 'The Effect of the Monetary Problem on Development Co-operation: Linking Special Drawing Rights and Development', *Malayan Economic Review*, Oct 1972.

Kahn, R., 'SDRs and Aid', *Lloyds Bank Review*, Oct 1973.

Kareken, J. H., 'How Much does Being World Banker Cost?', *National Banking Review*, Sep 1975.

Kessler, G. A., 'Should Development Aid be Linked to SDR Creation?' *De Economist*, cxix (1971).

Keynes, J. M., *Proposals for an International Clearing Union* (London, 1943).

Kirman, A. P., and Schmidt, W. E., 'Key Currency Burden: the UK Case', *National Banking Review*, Sep 1965.

Maynard, G. W., *Special Drawing Rights and Development Aid*, Overseas Development Council Occasional Paper no. 6 (Sep 1972).

Maynard, G. W., 'Special Drawings Rights and Development Aid', *Journal of Development Studies*, July 1973.

Maynard and Bird, in *World Development*, 1975.

Mundell, R. A., *Monetary Theory: Inflation Interest and Growth in the World Economy* (Pacific Palisades, Calif: Goodyear, 1971).

Mundell, R. A., and Swoboda, A. K., *Monetary Problems of the International Economy* (Chicago: University of Chicago Press, 1969).

Park, Y. S., *The Link Between Special Drawing Rights and Development*

Finance, Essays in International Finance no. 100 (Sep 1973).

Patel, I. G., 'The Link Between the Creation of International Liquidity and the Provision of Development Finance', *Report of the Committee on Invisibles and Financing Related to Trade: Further Consideration of the Report of the Expert Group on International Monetary Issues*, (Geneva: UNCTAD, 1967).

Polak, *Some Reflections on the Nature of Special Drawing Rights*, (1971).

Polak, J. J., *Valuation and Rate of Interest of the SDR*, IMF Pamphlet Series no. 18 (Washington, DC, 1974).

Salant, W. A., 'The Reserve Currency Role of the Dollar: Blessing or Burden to the US?', *Review of Economics and Statistics*, May 1964.

Scitovsky, T., 'A New Approach to International Liquidity', *American Economic Review*, Dec 1966.

Scitovsky T., *Requirements of an International Reserve System*, Essays in International Finance no. 49 (Princeton, NJ, 1965).

Stamp, M., 'The Fund and the Future', *Lloyds Bank Review*, Oct 1958.

Streeten, P., 'Killing Two Birds with One Stone', *International Affairs*, Jan 1970.

Triffin, R., *Gold and the Dollar Crisis* (New Haven, Conn.: Random House, 1960).

Triffin, in *Banca Nazionale del Lavoro Quarterly Review*, 1971.

UNCTAD, *International Monetary Issues and the Developing Countries* (1965).

UNCTAD, *International Monetary Reform and Co-operation for Development, Report of the Expert Group on International Monetary Issues* (New York: United Nations, 1969).

US Congress Sub-Committee on International Exchange and Payments of the Joint Economic Committee, *Guidelines for Improving the International Monetary System*, report (Washington, DC, 1965).

Williamson, J., 'SDRs Interest and the Aid Link', *Banca Nazionale del Lavoro Quarterly Review*, June 1972.

Williamson, J., 'The Financial Implications of Reserve Supply Arrangements', *IMF Staff Papers*, Nov 1974.

Williamson, J., 'The Link' (mimeo.), paper presented to the MIT Conference on the New International Economic Order, 17–19 May 1976.

Williamson, in *Economic Journal*, 1973.

Chapter 12

Black, S. W., 'Exchange Policies for Less Developed Countries in a

World of Floating Rates', in *The International Monetary System and the Developing Nations*, ed. Leipziger (1976).

Cline, W. R., *International Monetary Reform and the Developing Countries* (1976).

Connolly and Taylor, in *Journal of Political Economy*, LXXXIV (1976).

Cooper, in *Government and Economic Development*, ed. Ranis (1971).

Cooper, R. N., 'Monetary Theory and Policy in an Open Economy', *Scandinavian Journal of Economics*, LXXXII (1976).

Corden, W. M., *Monetary Integration*, Essays in International Finance no. 93, (Princeton, NJ, 1972).

Crockett, A. D., and Nsouli, S. M., 'Exchange Rate Policies for Developing Countries', *Journal of Development Studies*, Apr – July 1977:

Diaz-Alejandro, in *A World Divided*, ed. Helleiner (1976).

Fleming, J. M., 'On Exchange Rate Unification', *Economic Journal*, Sep 1971.

Giersch, H., 'On the Desirable Degree of Flexibility of Exchange Rates', *Weltwirtschaftliches Archiv*, CIX (1973)

Haberler, G., 'The International Monetary System: Some Recent Developments and Discussions', in *Approaches to Greater Flexibility of Exchange Rates*, George N. Halm (Princeton, NJ: Princeton University Press, 1970).

Helleiner, in *Journal of Development Studies*, 1974.

Heller, H. R., 'The Choice of an Exchange Rate for a Developing Country', paper presented to a Conference on External Financial Policy sponsored by the Organisation of American States and the Central Bank of Chile, 31 Mar – 2 Apr 1977.

Ingram, J. C., *Regional Payments Mechanisms: The Case of Puerto Rico* (Chapel Hill, NC: University of North Carolina Press, 1962).

Ishiyama, Y., 'The Theory of Optimum Currency Areas: A Survey', *IMF Staff Papers*, 22 July 1975.

Kenen, P. B., 'The Theory of Optimum Currency Areas: An Eclectic View', in *Monetary Problems of the International Economy*, ed. Mundell and Swoboda (1969).

Kreinin, M. E., and Heller, H. R., 'Adjustment Costs, Optimal Currency Areas, and International Reserves', ch. 6 of *International Trade and Finance: Essays in Honour of Jan Tinbergen*, ed. W. Sellekaerts (White Plains, NY: International Arts and Sciences Press, 1974).

Leipziger, D. M., 'An Essay on Floating Exchange Rates: Developing

Country Concerns', *United Malaysia Bank, Economic Review*, XIII (1977).

McKinnon, R. I., 'Optimum Currency Areas', *American Economic Review*, Sep 1963.

Miller, R. H., 'Forward Exchange Facilities in Developing Countries', *Finance and Development*, Mar 1975.

Mundell, R. A., 'A Theory of Optimum Currency Areas', *American Economic Review*, Sep 1961.

Osunsade, F. L., 'Generalized Floating and Problems of Policy Response in the Developing Countries', *IMF Survey*, 2 Feb 1976 and 1 Mar 1976.

Tower, E., and Willett, T. D., *The Theory of Optimum Currency Areas and Exchange Rate Flexibility*, Special Papers in International Economics no. 11, International Finance Section, Princeton University (Princeton, NJ, 1976).

Williamson, *The International Monetary System and the Developing Nations*, ed. Leipziger (1976).

Chapter 13

Bird, G., 'The IMF and the Developing Countries: Evolving Relations, Use of Resources and the Debate over Conditionality', *ODI Working Paper* No. 2, Mar 1981(a).

Bird, G., 'Financing Balance of Payments Deficits in Developing Countries: The Roles of Official and Private Sectors and the Scope for Co-operation Between Them', *Third World Quarterly*, July 1981(b).

Bird, G., 'Developing Country Interests in Proposals for International Monetary Reform', paper presented to an Addington Palace seminar on 'The IMF, the Third World and the Global Payments Problem', Oct 1981(c).

Bird, G. and Orme, T., 'An Analysis of Drawings on the International Monetary Fund by Developing Countries', *World Development*, June 1981.

Brandt, W. and others, *North-South: A Programme for Survival*, Pan Books, 1980.

Connors, T. A., 'The Apparent Effects of Recent IMF Stabilization Programs', *Federal Reserve System International Finance Discussion Paper*, no. 135 (Washington: Apr 1979).

Dell, S. and Lawrence, R., *The Balance of Payments Adjustment Process in Developing Countries* (Pergamon, 1980).

Gold, J., *Conditionality*, IMF Pamphlet no. 31, 1979.

Killick, T., 'Eurocurrency Market Recycling of OPEC Surpluses to Developing Countries: Fact or Myth?', *The Banker*, Jan 1981.

Killick, T., Bird, G., Sharpley, J. and Sutton, M., *The IMF and Economic Management in Developing Countries* (forthcoming).

Reichmann, T. M., 'The Fund's Conditional Assistance and the Problems of Adjustment', *Finance and Development* Dec 1978.

Reichmann, T. M. and Stillson, R., 'Experience with Programs of Balance of Payments Adjustment: Stand-by Arrangements in the Higher Credit Tranches', *IMF Staff Papers*, June 1978.

Southard, F. A., 'The Evolution of the International Monetary Fund, *Princeton Essays in International Finance*, no. 135 (Princeton University, 1979).

Williamson, J., 'Economic Theory and IMF Policies', paper presented to Carnegie-Rochester Conference at Pittsburgh, Dec 1979.

Index of Names

Abbott, G. C., 328
Agarwal, J. P., 103
Aghevli, B. B., 139
Aliber, R. Z., 328
Andic, F., 78, 308
Andic, S., 78, 308
Archibald, G. C., 309
Askari, H., 36, 59

Balassa, B. A., 68, 81, 308
Ball, R., 79, 308
Barton, C. A., 318
Bauer, P., 328
Behrman, J., 325
Bhagwat, A., 135
Bird, G. R., 101, 309, 325, 326, 328, 329
Boissonreault, L., 315
Brown, W. M., 100

Castree, J. R., 67, 68, 69
Clark, P. B., 93, 309, 310, 326
Cline, W. R., 272, 328
Clower, R. W., 99, 309
Cohen, B. J., 328
Connolly, M., 134, 135, 136, 138, 139, 314, 329
Connors, T. A., 295
Cooper, R. N., 134, 136, 138, 139, 329
Coppock, J. D., 36, 59, 307
Corden, W. M., 316
Corea, G., 146, 305, 318, 319
Crockett, A. D., 287, 329
Cutler, D. S., 315

Dell, S., 272, 328
De Vries, J., 318, 322
Diaz Alejandro, C., 314, 329
Dosser, D., 78, 308

Erb, G. R., 40, 59, 306

Fitch, J., 49
Flanders, M. J., 94, 310, 317
Fleming, M., 315
Fox, W. A., 324
Francis, J., 78
Frenkel, J. A., 98, 101, 108, 312

Glezakos, G., 38, 49, 59, 307
Gold, J., 146, 294, 304, 315, 329
Goldstein, H. N., 328
Goreux, L. M., 319, 320
Grubel, H. G., 309, 325, 326, 328
Gupta, D., 315

Hambolu, W., 59
Hart, A. G., 234, 237, 238, 320, 323, 325, 326
Hawkins, R. G., 320
Helleiner, G. K., 327
Heller, H. R., 102, 108, 291, 309, 312
Henderson, P. D., 323
Horsefield, J. K., 146, 182, 304, 305, 316
Houthakker, H. S., 79

Iyoha, M. A., 88, 97, 98

Jacobsson, P., 18
Jayarajah, C. A. B. N., 313
Johnson, H. G., 312, 324, 326
Johnson, O. E. G., 100

Kafka, A., 101
Kahn, R., 328
Kaldor, N., 237, 323, 324, 325, 326
Kapur, B. K., 313
Kapur, I., 212
Kareken, J. H., 328
Katrak, H., 306
Kelly, M. G., 94, 309, 310
Kenen, P. B., 17, 49
Kessler, G. A., 328

Keynes, J. M., 237, 257, 304, 325, 326
Khalaf, N. G., 36, 40
Khan, M. S., 79, 134, 139, 314
Killick, T., 297, 330
Kingston, J. L., 36
Kirman, A. P., 328
Knight, J. B., 313
Konig, W., 305, 313
Krasner, S. D., 146, 305, 318
Kreinin, M., 309

Lal, D., 323
Lamfalussy, A., 100
Lawson, C. W., 40, 59, 306, 307
Leipziger, D. M., 204, 309
Lim, D., 49
Lipsey, R. G., 99, 309
Lovasy, G., 146

MacBean, A., 48, 58, 307
Machlup, F., 100, 305, 309, 315
Magee, S. P., 79
Maizels, A., 49
Marquez, J., 181, 316, 318, 319
Marwah, K., 79, 308
Massell, B. F., 36, 37, 49, 59, 306, 307, 323
Maynard, G. W., 309, 326, 327, 328
McKinnon, R. I., 313
Michalopoulos, C., 311, 322, 325, 326
Miller, R. H., 328
Mookerjee, S., 305
Morrison, T., 319
Mundell, R. A., 305, 326

Naya, S., 49, 59
Niehans, J., 310
Nsouli, S. M., 287, 329

Olivera, J. H. G., 99
Onitsuka, Y., 135
Orme, T., 329

Park, Y. S., 326
Payer, C., 185, 305
Pearson, L., 49
Perez, L., 318, 319, 325, 326
Polak, J. J., 315

Porter, R. C., 37
Prebisch, R., 66

Rangarajan, C., 49, 306, 320
Reichmann, T., 187, 295
Rhomberg, R. R., 312, 315
Richmond, J., 309
Rooth, I., 18, 304

Salant, W. S., 100, 328
Santapillai, V. E., 318
Scammell, W. M., 312
Schiavo-Campo, S., 40, 59, 146, 306
Schink, G. R., 234, 324
Schleiminger, G., 305
Schmidt, W. E., 328
Schumacher, B., 78
Scitovsky, T., 100, 257, 258
Scott, A. D., 18, 146, 305, 315, 316, 319
Seers, D., 17
Singer, H., 146
Sinha, R. P., 67, 68, 69
Smith, G. W., 234, 324
Southard, F. A., 296
Stamp, M., 257
Stern, R., 78, 307, 312
Stewart, F., 311
Stewart, M., 311
Stillson, R., 187, 295
Streeten, P., 313
Sundararajan, V., 49, 306

Taylor, D., 134, 135, 136, 138, 139, 314, 329
Tew, B., 315
Thirlwall, A. P., 318
Thornton, J. C., 146
Tinbergen, J., 237, 308, 323, 326
Triffin, R., 257, 258, 320, 328

Voivodas, C. S., 49

Weil, G., 36, 59
White, H. D., 304
Williams, D., 317, 318
Williamson, J., 281, 296, 309, 311, 325, 326, 327
Wilson, T., 67, 68, 69

Yudin, E., 309